A CENTURY OF CHURCH HISTORY

The Legacy of Philip Schaff

Edited by Henry W. Bowden

Foreword by Jaroslav Pelikan

SOUTHERN ILLINOIS UNIVERSITY PRESS
Carbondale and Edwardsville

Library of Congress Cataloging-in-Publication Data

A Century of church history : the legacy of Philip Schaff / edited by
Henry W. Bowden : foreword by Jaroslav Pelikan.
p. cm.
Includes index.
1. Church history—Study and teaching—United States—History.
2. American Society of Church History—History. 3. Schaff, Philip,
1819–1893.   I. Bowden, Henry Warner.
BR138.C36 1988   270'.09—dc19   87-15630
ISBN 0-8093-1439-8   CIP

86.134326

Contents

Contents

Foreword

Jaroslav Pelikan

How our past has understood its past is an important component in our understanding of the past—and therefore in our understanding of ourselves. As this is true of literature, politics, and the arts, so it applies *a fortiori* to the understanding of Christianity, rooted as it is in a special concern with history. Having been a member of the American Society of Church History for just under half of its total history and having had the privilege of serving as its president in 1965, I am honored by the invitation to contribute this Foreword to the distinguished collection of essays by my friends and colleagues, and in the process to lay my own wreath at the monument to the genius of Philip Schaff.

The history of Christianity as an academic discipline is itself relatively short, having come into being not in the Reformation, as is sometimes supposed, but in the Enlightenment; thus the American Society of Church History has been in existence for roughly one-third of that history. For despite the Acts of the Apostles, it is by no means obvious that the imperatives of the Christian faith lead to an interest in the history of the church. Most of us who teach (and defend) that interest have at one time or another quoted the words of Psalm 143:5, "I remember the days of old; I meditate on all thy works; I muse on the works of thy hands," to justify it. Those words have stood, in one language or another, on the pages of everyone's Psalter throughout the centuries, but not everyone has drawn from them the conclusion that the chronological review of the history of the church, with its institutions, practices, and beliefs, is a key to the understanding of the church and the gospel. In fact, the opening words of what is usually identified as "the first church history," the *Ecclesiastical History* of Eusebius of Caesarea, make it clear that his primary apologetic and polemical *Tendenz* was just the opposite: to demonstrate that the history of heresy was a record of "novelty-mongering [*kainotomia*]," while the authentic Christian message was characterized by "continuity [*diadoche*]." Even if one does not go so far as to accept the judgment of Jacob Burckhardt that Eusebius was "the first thoroughly dishonest historian in antiquity," a critical study of the *Ecclesiastical History* does show an almost obsessive attention to "continuity"—of bishops in their succession from the apostles of institutions such as monasticism (to the point of claiming

Philo's description of the Jewish Essenes as evidence for the continuity of Christian monasticism with apostolic times), of saints' lives (especially that of Eusebius' hero, Origen), and of church doctrines (even though, in the event, the version of the doctrine of the Trinity that Eusebius espoused was denounced as heresy). And although Jerome's remembering of "the days of old" did lead him to do historical research, particularly in his book *On Illustrious Men*, such major contemporaries of Jerome's as Gregory Nazianzus and Basil the Great in the East or Ambrose and Augustine in the West did not become historians in the course of becoming theologians.

The thought and work of Philip Schaff, and by extension the history of the American Society of Church History, as both of these are recounted in the chapters of this book, make clear that for our view of the place of church history we are indebted to the convergence of at least four historical influences: (1) the study of the Reformation, broadly defined so as to include not only what George Huntston Williams calls "the magisterial Reformers" like Luther and Calvin, but both the "radical Reformation" about which Williams has written with such erudition and the "Catholic Reformation"; (2) the critical-historical methodology worked out by the scholars who came out of the Enlightenment, such as Johann Lorenz von Mosheim, who, according to *The Oxford Dictionary of the Christian Church*, "may be considered the first of modern ecclesiastical historians"; (3) the special sympathy with history and with the "works of old" characteristic of nineteenth-century Romanticism, above all in the German Protestantism in which Schaff was educated; and (4) the contemporary (and related) discovery by Americans of their own past, for which Francis Parkman— who died in 1893, the same year as Schaff—may stand as the prime exemplar. The second and third of these, the Enlightenment and Romanticism, have provided the methodology and inspiration for a large proportion of the scholarly work that has appeared in the pages of *Church History*.

Yet it is no accident that the first and the fourth, the history of the Reformation and American church history, should have provided so much of the subject matter of that same scholarly work. It is clear that denominational and confessional provenance has played an important part in the "roots trips" of American Reformation scholarship, with Lutherans writing on Luther, Presbyterians on Calvin, Mennonites on Menno Simons, and the like. Perhaps the most far-reaching change in Reformation study during the past generation has been the discovery of the close connection between the Reformation and the later Middle Ages, resulting in the interaction between confessional prejudice and ecumenical or Romantic sensitivity in shaping medieval studies in America. For inevitably, denominational patriotism has been obliged to come to terms with insights and interpretations in Reformation history that transcend narrow local interest, regardless of where the authors of such interpretations may have gone (or not gone) to church. It would, for example, be highly instructive to compile for *Church History* the kind of citation index that is standard with scientific journals, but even in the absence of such an index I am confident that the names of Max Weber and Ernst Troeltsch have figured decisively in many of the Reformation studies that have appeared in its pages.

The prominence of American church history is obvious even to the casual reader of the journal; and, having served on its editorial board, I should add that the proportion between American church history and everything else has usually been even more lopsided in the number of the articles submitted than in the number of those that have eventually been published. Three chapters in this book are needed to do even basic justice to the importance of American studies. It is an easy assignment, and also something of a snobbish "cheap shot," for someone who works in the fields that I do to minimize that importance. I recall coming to Copenhagen in 1956 and seeking out Professor Hal Koch, whose *Pronoia und Paideusis* of 1932 had fundamentally shaped my understanding of Origen and of ante-Nicene Christian thought generally. To my surprise and chagrin, Hal Koch was doing nothing in patristics, but was concentrating on N. F. S. Grundtvig. When I expressed that surprise, he replied that there would always be plenty of scholars elsewhere to work on Origen, but that if he and other Danes did not do research on Grundtvig it would not be done.

A similar sense of special obligation, and hence of mission, has often attended the study of American church history. My chief teacher in this field was William Warren Sweet, who did not even try to be subtle about that sense of mission. Impatient of theological subtlety and liturgical nicety, Sweet applied and then refined the "frontier hypothesis," associated with Frederick Jackson Turner, in his interpretation of the history of the American churches (chiefly the Protestant churches). Both through his own publications and through those of his many students, as presented in a library of books and articles as well as in the programs and publications of the society, Sweet put his mark on the self-definition of American church history, which he often tended to see more as part of American history than as part of Christian history. For several reasons, including that one, attention to Protestantism in America, and to its Anglo-Saxon roots, predominated.

More recently, both the non-Protestant and the non-English components have been receiving a larger part of their proper share of study. I am pleased here to join in acknowledging the pioneering work of my friend and colleague, Monsignor John Tracy Ellis, in making the study of

Roman Catholic church history in the United States an important and exciting scholarly discipline. Although it has continued to be true that scholars from each group have often concentrated on their own tradition, this history of church history—from a basic work on the Mormons by a Roman Catholic scholar to patristic studies by free-church Protestants—discloses what a social scientist would call a "paradigm shift" also in this regard, with consequences that have enriched the perspectives of all of us.

Even more far-reaching a paradigm shift is taking place in the very understanding of what "church history" or "the history of Christianity" is, of the academic context within which it is best studied and taught, and of the other fields of knowledge and methodologies that a scholar needs to learn in order to carry it on. The growth of "religious studies" as an academic field, and then as a department in colleges and universities, has meant that the dominance of the theological seminary as the arena for church history has been effectively challenged and significantly reduced. Perhaps the most constructive result of that shift is one that members of the generation of William Warren Sweet, John T. McNeill, and Wilhelm Pauck, and of course Philip Schaff himself, would have welcomed: the closing, or at least the narrowing, of the gap between church history and "secular (or, as it used to be known, "profane") history. A less gratifying consequence has sometimes been that young scholars have been entering the field of the history of Christianity without adequate preparation in the biblical, ecclesiastical, liturgical, and theological issues with which, after all, much of that history has been preoccupied, and have therefore been compelled to acquire, only after the doctorate (if then), what seminary graduates used to bring as a prerequisite to graduate study and research.

It will not, I hope, appear to be merely an argument *pro domo* (in the literal sense of that metaphor) to observe that the most painful lacuna—shocking, but not surprising, to paraphrase a remark of Dr. Johnson—in the meetings and publications of the American Society of Church History, and therefore also in this volume, is an (almost, but not quite) complete lack of attention to Eastern Christendom, whether Greek or Slavic or Levantine. The liturgical, political, and doctrinal history of Eastern Christendom is an indispensable component of any responsible research in all of those fields, but ignoring the Christian East has long been characteristic both of the churchmanship and of the scholarship of the West, whether Roman Catholic or Protestant. Nevertheless, the study of New Testament and patristic Greek at American divinity schools could have served as a preparation for work in Byzantine church history, but it has not. And as programs in Russian studies have gradually sprung up at American universities and the knowledge of "exotic" languages such as Russian, Church

Slavonic, and Serbo-Croatian has at least begun to spread, there has not been a corresponding growth in research and writing on Eastern Orthodox church history. I find it hard to imagine that such a condition will still be prevailing when a volume like this one is published for the sesquicentennial of the American Society of Church History in 2038.

We who spend our lives on the past are understandably hesitant about projections for the year 2038, and I intend to take no such risks. But I am sure that there will continue to be the kind of fruitful interchange between the historiography of Christianity and other scholarly fields that my colleagues have described here. As the development of fields like biochemistry, astrophysics, and comparative literature suggests, some of the most important intellectual and scholarly innovations of our time have erupted on the borders between traditional academic fields. If that continues to be the case across the scholarly spectrum generally—and it will, I suspect, increase exponentially—the historiography described in that projected sesquicentennial volume will almost certainly reflect the work that is now being done, or is about to be done, throughout much of the humanities and social sciences, perhaps even in the biological and physical sciences. Most of us, for example, know pathetically little about the history of jurisprudence. Yet the names of Sohm, Stutz, and Bohatec in our bibliographies suggest what promising research awaits anyone who can relate the history of the church to the history of legal institutions and ideas.

Even as it interacts with those fields, however, the field of church history will also continue to be what it has been: continuity-*cum*-change will be a quality that it not only describes but manifests. For in the words of Schaff's great contemporary and sometime bête noire, John Henry Newman, speaking both about the church and about his own faith, "it changes . . . in order to remain the same. In a higher world it is otherwise, but here below to live is to change, and to be [mature] is to have changed often."

Introduction

I N 1988 the American Society of Church History marks the centenary of its founding. All of the society's different functions will receive attention through varied centennial observances. As the core of this organization is critical historical scholarship, many members have thought it fitting that this *raison d'être* be emphasized in a special volume. So the essays contained herein survey themes and issues that have been crucial to developments in the historical understanding of religious life over the last hundred years.

History covers an unmanageable number of topics, and in the study of religion focusing on churches does little to simplify matters. Since religion has figured importantly in most facets of human activity, the outer reaches of church history touch upon virtually the whole spectrum of experience. Even within ecclesiastical institutions the array of topics is daunting because it includes questions on theology, polity, leadership, worship, daily behavior, and relationships with secular institutions and power. Deciding which areas to emphasize in a retrospective volume is a delicate task, but a particular circumstance helped ease our difficulty. At its inception the ASCH owed almost everything to one man, Philip Schaff, a scholar of prodigious energy and comprehensive interests. Schaff did not confine himself within narrow chronological or topical definitions. His genius shed light on multiple subjects, and he kept the society open to most of the themes that together comprise historical inquiry into Christianity. The following essays focus on those areas that interested Schaff over a long and fruitful career. They also demarcate familiar categories that are now taken as the best arrangement of the field.

There is perhaps no better way of beginning an overview of historiographical development than by learning how nineteenth- century scholars understood historical awareness. In the first essay David Lotz explains how Schaff perceived church history to be theological science, humanistic artistry, and ecumenical support. As a student of modern German ideas Schaff provided a bridge over which the latest theology and philosophy of history came to this country. In this chapter on the ASCH founder as mediator and critic, Lotz shows how he was fitted as no other man to interpret Teutonic learning to the scholarship of America. He also clarifies dominant theories on ecclesiology and organic development, key features in the complex idea of church history as the continuation of Christ's life and work on earth. Schaff's influential conceptions have become super-annuated, but they are still a crucial starting point for later students when they reflect on the content, structure, style, and explanatory scheme of their own research efforts.

A study of Christianity itself starts logically and chronologically with beginnings. Schaff's work always gave full scope to the patristic period, and that vital area remains strong today. Glenn Chesnut notes the dominant place of German Protestant scholarship in the historiographical period under review, and he explains why emphases on Hellenic philosophy and Greco-Roman culture emerged as salient priorities. He is able to show why Catholic scholars found themselves constrained by Neo-Thomism up to the 1920s and after that time how they began making significant con-tributions to theological interpretations of institutional and sacramental developments. By contrast he points out the way in which Anglicans followed no dogmatic perspective during the past century, preferring a flexiblity that acknowledged a wide range of causal factors at work in early Christianity. He also mentions Eastern Orthodox authors whose unap-preciated works are valuable because they comprehend church beginnings as something other than prolegomena to Augustine, Thomas, or Luther. At present the field is rich and diversified with viewpoints oriented toward psychology, sociology, and literary classics. Cross-fertilization increases the possibility of an even better understanding of this period's historical sig-nificance.

If there is a "poor cousin" in church history today it is probably medieval studies. Bernard McGinn shows that there has, nevertheless, been dynamic change in this area of professional concentration. In spite of uncertainties about when their time period begins, medievalists have cus-tomarily pursued topics related to language, jurisprudence, and the arts. McGinn traces the subsequent influence of anthropology and sociology on historical inquiries, explaining how they added valuable dimensions to the older tradition of classical studies. In more integrated cultural histories of the Middle Ages there is now an emphasis on broad trends as well as on privileged elites, on intellectual and social unrest rather than on hier-archical order. The ASCH, dominated by Protestants in early decades, gave only moderate attention to medieval topics. Catholic strengths were largely unrepresented there before the 1960s, and McGinn rightly decries the fact that confessional differences as well as competing topical prefer-ences led to the foundation of separate scholarly organizations. Medieval studies currently enjoy a rejuvenation, but the ASCH now affords less of an outlet for results than in earlier years. Still, the field shows vigor resulting from new viewpoints and techniques applied to a millennium of European culture.

While medieval topics were slighted over the past hundred years, Reformation categories have loomed large. This seemed natural if not inevitable in German universities that stimulated so much modern scholarship, in North America shaped by Protestant traditions, and with the Society's founder who embodied both of those impulses. Robert Kingdon alludes to the initial focus on Luther as prototypical reformer and to Germanic environs as the epicenter of religious controversy. A subsidiary but complementary focus on Calvin flourished in this hundred-year period too. These characteristics have remained strong in Reformation studies to the present, as have early interests in theology and a general orientation toward intellectual history. But recent historiographical trends have expanded investigations into other Reformation topics, and Kingdon points to secular approaches that highlight areas such as social and economic inquiries into popular culture in addition to clerical elites. He also chronicles the impact of French scholars in this field and shows that studying the Reformation has in our day resulted in increased ecumenical understanding rather than institutional polemics. European initiatives seem to stay slightly ahead of American ones, and Kingdon ends by observing that scholars in this country can utilize several avenues of research as they realize the potential of their topic.

Schaff immigrated to these shores with pronounced attitudes about Americanization and its role in the larger sweep of historical progress. Immigrants have always been a pivotal factor in American life, but until recently historians rarely incorporated this view into their narratives. Jay Dolan explains why this topic was first seen as a sociological problem and only later as a viewpoint to be employed in recounting American history. While the phenomenon of three centuries' duration continued, observers perceived it as a challenge to transform alien multitudes into American citizens. After legislation in the 1920s virtually ended the process, historians turned to it as a key for understanding the composite nature of American character. Dolan charts various studies related to pluralism, nativist hostility, a search for norms in the socialization process, models of Americanization, and the resurgence of ethnic identities. He also points out that, even though such concerns are vitally connected to religion in American life, secular scholars have been most active in the field. Church historians have as yet made little use of immigration, ethnicity, and processes of Americanization. Current work on the place of religion in past immigrant communities is analytically an important factor in historical explanation, but it remains peripheral to most American church history. Future scholarship may benefit from immigration studies, but the latent promise is not yet realized.

Another topic that fascinated Schaff was the unique relationship between church and state in American experience. John Wilson shows how the society's founder understood this departure from European patterns and how he grasped the essential qualities of self-government, voluntary religious action, and freedom for ecclesiastical organizations. Wilson also points out that Schaff recognized the importance of judicial review in a continuous monitoring of religious factors in daily life. Since there is no absolute separation between religious impulses and civil authority, magistrates continue to explore the question of boundaries in such touchy areas as marriage, schools, and Sabbath observance. Wilson expounds on the implications of applying federal constitutional clauses to state policies, on new scholarship about Supreme Court decisions regarding the workings of American tradition, and on post–World War II definitions of freedom. Schaff was prescient in identifying many issues that are significant today, but some of his categories no longer apply. Contemporary developments have moved beyond a situation where cultural observers could assume that Protestant, or even Christian, principles undergird the structure of American life. Wilson opens new vistas with questions about Christianity and present-day cultural accommodation, the conflicting tendencies of religious variety and political centralization, and the issues of coping with persistent pluralism.

Christianity demonstrated missionary impetus during its early formation. That characteristic never entirely died out, and global exploration in the Reformation era gave it additional vigor. Schaff thought of himself as a missionary in coming to these shores, and his interest in the topic concerned historical movements as well as evangelical programs in his own time. Gerald Anderson chronicles the movement in Protestant North America from 1886 to the present time. He notices not only the personnel and organizations that have supported missionary activity but also the changes that have occurred in overseas programs. This period began with tremendous confidence, some called it "imperialism of righteousness," that by the 1960s had shifted to a new appreciation of cultural diversities. Questions about motives, message, methods, and aims have been integral to all missionary work and more especially to understanding it from a historical perspective. Perhaps the most important part of Anderson's essay is his underlying observation that missions have been studied by participant-observers. Thus his survey of missions studies cannot be dissociated from the movement itself. The books, periodicals, library collections, professorships, and agencies he mentions are germane to missions as they have experienced change. They also supply the materials with which we may now study them in times of theological reformulation and new denominational alignments.

A category fundamental to religious expression has always been the faith and experience transacted by communities. Schaff was rather distinctive in his day for appreciating the importance of creeds and liturgies as a means of understanding this core aspect of Christianity. Aidan Kavanagh provides an overview of studies in this area where a professional analysis of historical texts blends with personal concerns about repristinating common worship. He shows how the last quarter century has been especially enriched by new insights into the importance of ritual ceremony, symbolism, poetry, music, and art. Historical scholarship has been crucial in authenticating facts and documents in liturgical development. In addition to explaining how such studies correct pious obscurantism, Kavanagh goes on to discuss the implications for his field of new inquiries into the nature of symbolic discourse and the anthropology of ritual behavior. Those viewpoints make it possible to anticipate cooperation across disciplinary lines, and the historical study of liturgies seems bright with promise. Another by-product of this advance in academics is a greater ecclesiological understanding of what is being studied, a more nuanced grasp of references to the visible and invisible church. This contemporary situation has resulted in (and from) less theological hostility among religious groups today. The discovery of liturgical variety in history has aided greater acceptance of today's pluralities where religious and social concerns intersect in worship.

A leitmotif running through most of the essays in this volume alludes to greater interdenominational acceptance among students of past ecclesiastical life. Hopes for such an eventuality dominated much of Schaff's own professional scholarship and religious consciousness. John Ford concentrates on this theme of ecumenism and traces its development as a category of both scholarly analysis and ecclesiastical activity. He provides a valuable assessment of Schaff's thought and activity in light of how those elements are currently understood. Beyond that, Ford makes important distinctions regarding options in this large field of inquiry: factors instrumental in dividing Christians, search for theological synthesis, and practical strategies leading to union or at least a resolution of denominational differences. He leads readers through this century's central events from early conventions to today's bilateral conversations. This survey of the movement is accompanied by listings of the important documents and the most helpful historical studies. Ford's own contribution culminates in giving readers perspective, discussing not only viewpoints and pertinent scholarship but the value of different factors for both past influence and continuing relevance.

A concluding essay in this collection focuses on the society itself. Institutional growth is rather difficult to perceive in an organization whose members across the continent meet only biannually. Still, something can be gleaned from statistical tabulation and a review of constitutional changes, and this author hopes his minimal findings might stimulate a more capable investigation into the association of professional church historians. It is equally difficult to trace intellectual change in a group so diverse. Without pretending to represent all interests or values in the ASCH at any point, the author depicts broad conceptual revisions by focusing on presidential addresses that grappled specifically with the idea of church history. Those representative expressions illustrate how church history has moved from a subsection of theology to a department of critical, humanistic learning in the past century. Questions about theological orientation remain important in historical research. But theological dominance has been replaced by greater concern for exacting method and interdisciplinary interpretive models. The mixture of ecclesiastical and academic interests in the ASCH makes for fascinating prospects in regard to both institutional growth and intellectual progress.

The essays in this volume concentrate on important fields in church history, and they highlight discrete contributions of limited, though fruitful, applicability. Each one of these authors provides guidelines to vital changes that have occurred in segmented categories of ecclesiastical experience. Though written independently, these essays nevertheless touch upon several constants that are worth mentioning in a summary introduction. One of the most striking of these common emphases is the importance of German scholarship. In the decades leading up to 1888 German historians were much more influential than their French or English counterparts in shaping academic life in North America. This overwhelming dominance continued in all branches of historical study up until World War I. Since then there has been more parity among scholars from different nations, but there is still decidedly more transfer of European initiatives to this country than vice versa. Church historians in various subcategories recognize the value of European innovations and welcome continued exchange of ideas for mutual benefit.

Another common factor discernible in these several essays is recognition that we are heirs to a major change in historical self-understanding. Over the course of a century we have moved from views where history taught lessons of exclusivist rectitude to an appreciation of shared heritage and mutual development. Instead of using history to promote some type of confessional, institutional, or cultural elitism, contemporary students of the past tend rather to perceive common forces that made various forms more similar than separate. This truly ecumenical consciousness of shared development marks a shift in historical awareness that underlies all relevant observations about crossfertilization of compatible methods and about the decline of denominational suspicions among individual historians.

So there is a coming together among investigators of various churches and their different Christian priorities, among students of religion as related to secular societies. At the same time current scholarship is characterized as perhaps never before by increased specialization. This aspect of modern investigations is the third and final common denominator found within this volume's essays. The ideal of integrating special studies into a comprehensive overview may persist, but it recedes in the face of practical realities. Each author shows that truly pioneering researches in each area has produced greater fragmentation within the field. Monographs and treatises concentrate on detailed analysis of regions or narrow topics; they use new methods of inquiry to add further considerations in understanding information already complex. Beyond that, many contemporaries raise different kinds of questions about familiar topics, and their findings augment a cornucopia of data. Historical studies of churches in various settings and times comprise an expanding agenda. The basic challenge to each practitioner is to keep abreast of developments in his field while perhaps attempting to maintain equilibrium by means of some comprehensive overview.

This volume's essayists have tried to bring readers up to date by noting benchmark contributions in each of the special areas surveyed. They hope that these centennial essays help orient historians within various topics and stimulate colleagues as they pursue further investigations into a common past.

A CENTURY OF
CHURCH HISTORY

Philip Schaff and the Idea of Church History

David W. Lotz

O N Friday evening, 23 March 1888, seventeen academics and church-men assembled in New York City with a view to forming a profes-sional society for the study of ecclesiastical history. They had come together at the invitation of the Reverend Dr. Philip Schaff (1819–93), long the most widely known and respected Protestant church historian in North America and, at the time, Washburn Professor of Church History in New York's Union Theological Seminary. Meeting at Schaff's home in midtown Manhattan and joined in spirit by forty colleagues who had communicated "their regret at necessary absence and their desire to become members of the proposed society," the group unanimously resolved to establish such a society, adopted a constitution, and elected its officers, including Schaff as president.[1]

Prior to these actions, having been asked to state the meeting's pur-pose, "Dr. Schaff spoke upon the desirability and prospective usefulness of an American society of Church History on a catholic and irenical basis in the development of a taste and talent for historical theology by special researches, and by bringing into personal contact the workers in this department, and thus indirectly aiding the cause of Christian union." When the new society held its first annual meeting in Washington, DC, 28 Decem-ber 1888, President Schaff began the proceedings with the reminder that the society "was formed for the purpose of cultivating church history as a science, in an unsectarian, catholic spirit, and for facilitating personal intercourse among students of history as a means of mutual encourage-ment."[2]

Philip Schaff's introductory speeches on these two occasions were anything but *pro forma*. Though his exact words were not recorded, the sentiments attributed to him by the secretary were "pure Schaff": they conveyed his lifelong understanding of—and deepest convictions about—the nature, purpose, and value of his craft. Church history, he made plain, is supremely a theological discipline, synonymous with historical theology; yet it is no less a science and must be cultivated as such. In keeping with its dual character, church history should be pursued in an irenic, unsectarian

I

and catholic spirit, which means without partiality, without denominational bias and unedifying polemic, and with universality of vision, with patient attention to and empathy for all the variegated phenomena of both sacred and secular history, so far as this history exhibits what is truly human and (therefore) truly Christian, and so far as this catholic sensibility compromises neither justice nor truth. Carried out in this spirit, within a society that facilitates professional cooperation and coordination of efforts, and that transcends party lines and confessional divisions, church historical scholarship will materially assist the present-day church to carry out its most exigent task, which is nothing other than the divinely ordained goal of church history itself: the reunion of Christendom in the form of an evangelical Catholicism.

Such, *in nuce*, are the leading features of Schaff's remarkable "idea" of church history as a theological science and art. My main purpose in this essay is to examine this idea in the requisite detail and depth, doing so both descriptively and analytically, with due attention to the historical context of Schaff's thought and labors. I thus join in commemorating the centennial of the American Society of Church History by commemorating its estimable founder, who served as its presiding officer and guiding spirit until his death on 20 October 1893.

Schaff's Idea in Retrospect

Let it be said at the outset: Philip Schaff's idea of church history is superannuated. Any repristination of his views—not in every respect, of course, but in their root premises—is out of the question. Some reasons for this "outdating" will be considered in this essay. Nevertheless, Schaff's "philosophy of church history" (the phrase is his own) is of more than antiquarian or casual interest. It possesses intrinsic interest and importance, and is worthy of studious attention. Three retrospective observations may be offered in support of this claim.

1. Schaff's idea of church history, viewed in its totality, is a unique phenomenon in the annals of American church historiography. I say "in its totality" because it was by no means unique in every particular. Certainly the great majority of Schaff's colleagues from the 1850s into the 1890s shared his understanding of church history as "salvation history" and as the "progressive advance" of the kingdom of God through the ages. And many of his more recent successors—once their standing as "ordinary" historians was established—have periodically offered their quasi-philosophical "reflections" on their craft, and some few have even ventured a "reading" of universal history in the light of the Christian gospel. Schaff's

approach to his discipline, however, was far more systematic and speculative. He insisted that history must be grasped as an organic whole, both
in the concatenation of its events and in the historian's reproduction of
these events (so that the "form" of written history mirrors the "matter"
of actual history). Little wonder that he began his career by articulating
a substantive philosophy of history—a comprehensive interpretation of
the whole of historical reality from the creation of the world to its consummation. This philosophy determined the content (selection of the data),
the structure (ordering of the data), the style (rhetorical encoding of the
data), and the explanatory scheme (explicit interpretation of the data) of
Schaff's historical works. His "idea" of church history, in short, amounted
to a full-blown "system," at once self-generating (from its first principles)
and self-contained (ending where it began). In this light Schaff appears
sui generis among America's church historians past and present: he was,
in effect, the "Hegel" of his guild.

2. Schaff's preoccupation with the nature and purpose of church
history led him to write the first history of church historiography originating on American soil, as well as the first American exposition of the
"idea of 'organic' development" in its import for church history. Both feats
were accomplished in 1846 in his little book, *What Is Church History? A
Vindication of the Idea of Historical Development*.[3] Schaff later revised and
expanded this material to form the impressive "General Introduction to
Church History" that prefaced his *History of the Apostolic Church* (1853).[4]
The 1846 book thus antedated what is probably the best-known (and
unquestionably the finest) critical history of church historiography published in the nineteenth century: Ferdinand Christian Baur's *Die Epochen
der kirchlichen Geschichtsschreibung* (1852).[5] Baur had been one of Schaff's
professors at Tübingen in 1837–39, and the young student obviously "appropriated" some of his teacher's most original constructs. Schaff readily
acknowledged that he had gained from Baur his "first idea of historical
development or of a constant and progressive flow of thought in the
successive ages of the church."[6] Hence one cannot attribute high originality
to Schaff's monograph of 1846 and his "General Introduction" of 1853. But
this consideration only underscores their contextual importance: through
them Schaff transmitted to his American readers the most recent and most
seminal German thought about the nature of church history, in particular
the "Baurian" concept of development.

Schaff himself, to be sure, was always intensely critical of his erstwhile
mentor, admiring Baur's "rare genius and scholarship" but lamenting the
"sad havoc [he made] with the literature of the apostolic age."[7] Schaff
reserved his highest praise for his revered teacher at Berlin, August Nean-

der, with whom he had studied in 1840 and to whom he dedicated the original German edition of his *Apostolic Church* (1851). Neander, however, was little given to, and had little aptitude for, "philosophy of history" and "methodology." The fact remains that Schaff, in his earliest and most foundational writings in America, was playing a role comparable to Baur's in Germany. He presented an innovative history of church historiography and, in the process, advanced a speculative idea of church history, which, with its bold theory of progressive development, was immensely challenging to Protestant America in mid-century. Thus this "Hegel" among the nineteenth-century American church historians was no less their "Baur" (notwithstanding that he also stood among them as an " 'awakened' Evangelical" and, in his last years, as a "Neander *redivivus*").

3. Four years before the founding of the ASCH, the American Historical Association had been established as the first national historical society in the United States. Its chief architect was Herbert Baxter Adams (1850–1901), a tireless promoter of professional history who served as the AHA's secretary until 1900. In 1876—the same year he received his Ph.D. degree at Heidelberg under Johann Bluntschli—Adams joined the faculty of the newly opened Johns Hopkins University. There he supervised historical studies during the 1880s and 1890s, becoming director of its celebrated Historical Seminary in 1881 and, in 1882, editor of its influential *Studies in History and Political Science*.

John Higham has said of Adams that he "probably did more than anyone else to Germanize American historical scholarship."[8] Perhaps this claim is true as regards university-based research. If, however, "historical scholarship" includes the study of church history in theological seminaries and divinity schools—as it surely does, then Higham's assertion requires a significant modification: the name of Philip Schaff must be joined to that of Adams, who *together* must be reckoned among the most influential "Germanizers" of history in nineteenth-century America. Schaff's biographer justly said of him: "Any future study of the influence of the theology of Europe upon American thought in this century will not overlook his name. His services in this sphere constitute the unique feature of his career. . . . Dr. Schaff was fitted, as no other man, to interpret Teutonic learning to the scholarship of America."[9]

Schaff's credentials as an expert in "Teutonic learning" were unimpeachable. He delighted in saying of himself: "I am a Swiss by birth, a German by education, an American by choice."[10] Born on 1 January 1819 at Chur, in the canton of Graubünden (Grisons), he spent his most formative years in Germany: first (1834–35) at the academy founded by Swabian Pietists in 1819 at Kornthal, in Württemberg, where he underwent a "conversion"; then (1835–37) at the gymnasium in nearby Stuttgart, where he mastered Latin, Greek, and Hebrew. Thereupon followed his university studies: two years at Tübingen (1837–39) and a semester each at Halle and Berlin (1839–40), culminating in his reception of the licentiate in theology at Berlin in May 1841. During these years Schaff heard lectures by Germany's leading historians (Heinrich Leo at Halle, Ranke and Karl Ritter at Berlin) and historical theologians (Baur and I. A. Dorner at Tübingen, Neander at Berlin). His favorite professors bore an evangelical-Pietist stamp and most of them represented the so-called *Vermittlungstheologie* (the "theology of mediation" between Christian faith and modern culture). Chief among them, besides Neander and Isaac Dorner, were C. F. Schmid at Tübingen, F. A. Tholuck and Julius Müller at Halle, Ernst Hengstenberg and August Twesten at Berlin.[11]

Something that Schaff did not learn directly from his professors, however, was his high doctrine of the church as the divine-human body of Christ, the continuation of the Incarnation, and thus the "necessary organ" for mediating Christ's work of redemption to the world. He owed this all-important teaching, as well as his pivotal concept of evangelical catholicity, to the leading representatives of the so-called Prussian (Lutheran) High Orthodoxy, chief among them the jurist and lay theologian Ludwig von Gerlach, who associated themselves with Hengstenberg and his immensely influential journal, the *Evangelische Kirchenzeitung* (founded 1827).[12] Schaff attached himself to this group during his years in Berlin.

Nevertheless, Schaff was not an uncritical adherent of any single party or school. Throughout his career he remained a theological cosmopolitan. After leaving Germany and Europe in 1844, he kept in regular touch with the foremost theologians of his old homeland, Catholics as well as Protestants, both through copious correspondence and through private conversations during the course of his fourteen return trips to Europe. Herbert B. Adams, by contrast, neither wrote his former professors in Germany nor sent them his publications; he actually maintained "a much more intimate contact with English scholars."[13] It seems, in fact, that Adams' role as a "Germanizer" has been exaggerated. About Schaff's role there can be no doubt.

In late 1842, after his return from a fourteen-month tour of Italy and Sicily, Schaff was licensed as a *Privatdozent* at Berlin and commenced his teaching activity. Prospects for a distinguished career as a full professor at a German or Swiss university lay before him. In October 1843, however, he received a call from the German Reformed Church in the United States to serve as professor of church history and biblical literature in its theological seminary at Mercersburg, Pennsylvania. Resigning himself to God's will, and at the urging of his former professors, Schaff accepted the call. He was ordained to the pastoral ministry in April 1844, spent six weeks visiting England in May-June (conversing with, among many notables, F. D. Maurice and E. B. Pusey), embarked on a transatlantic voyage of five weeks, and in August arrived in Mercersburg, where he joined the redoubtable John W. Nevin as the seminary's second professor. Thus, within less than six months, Schaff had moved from the famed and flourishing university in Prussia's capital city to a struggling, relatively obscure seminary in a remote village in the foothills of the Appalachians. He could scarcely have anticipated that within six years he and Nevin would achieve notoriety as the advocates of a distinctive "Mercersburg theology" and would be caught up in controversies that stirred much of American Protestantism and brought down charges of heresy upon their heads.[14]

Already in 1844, then, six years before Herbert Adams was born, Schaff had come to the United States as, in his own words, "a missionary of science," namely, as a transmitter of the German philosophy and theology of history to a country whose "religious relations and views are pervaded with the spirit of Puritanism, which is unhistorical in its very constitution, and with which, in fact, a low esteem for history and tradition has itself stiffened long since into as tyrannical a tradition as is to be met with in any other quarter."[15] By the time Adams took his Ph.D. degree in Germany, Schaff had been teaching in America for over three decades: from 1844 to 1863 at the Mercersburg seminary, and from 1870 (until his death) at Union Seminary. Throughout these years he remained America's chief mediator of German theology and religious thought, not only to his students and colleagues, but to a wider audience in church and society as well. Conversely, through his many visits to Britain and the Continent, which usually included public lectures, Schaff kept the Europeans abreast of developments in American religious, social, and political life, especially as regards the novel American experiment of separating church and state, about which the Europeans harbored misgivings and misconceptions.[16]

No doubt Schaff's preeminent contribution to American historical scholarship lay in his transformation of the traditional idea of church history by means of the new "German idea of history," with its twin concepts of individuality (uniqueness) and development (progressive change), and its doctrine of *Einfühlung* (penetration of historical data through "empathy").[17] Schaff, in sum, was America's leading theological interpreter and representative of the epoch-making "historicism" that took its rise in Germany in the later eighteenth century under the influence of Justus Möser and, above all, J. G. Herder; that received its classical theoretical formulation in writings by Leopold von Ranke and Wilhelm von Humboldt; that informed—and was equally indebted to—the great post-Kantian systems of German idealism (Fichte, Schelling, Hegel) and the works of the German Romantics (Wackenroder, Tieck, Goethe, Schiller, the Schlegels, Hölderlin, Novalis, Brentano); that renewed and transformed German Protestant theology (Schleiermacher, Neander, Baur) by enabling it to transcend the old, sterile conflicts between rationalism and supernaturalism; that determined the assumptions and methods of the Historical School of law (Savigny, Eichhorn) and the Historical School of economics (Roscher, Knies, Schmoller); and that remained "firmly established in the [German] social and cultural sciences until the late nineteenth century."[18]

Schaff, of course, never claimed to be, nor was he in fact, an interpreter of German historicism in all its forms and mutations over the course of a century and more. Nor was he a "pure" representative of historicist thought. His traditional orthodox supernaturalism materially transformed his legacy from the *moderni*, given their "pantheistic" principle of "identity" between finite spirit and Absolute Spirit. Nonetheless, Schaff's idea of church history was decisively shaped by his training under Baur and Neander and, through them, by the inescapable influence of Friedrich Schleiermacher— the century's premier theologian and progenitor of the New Protestantism, who taught at the University of Berlin from its founding in 1810 until his death in 1834. Schleiermacher, along with his "disciples" Neander and Baur, rendered theology historical and church history "historicist."[19] It was precisely this latter idea of church history, with all due modification, that Schaff introduced to the American scene and thereafter interpreted for his many readers in the "land of the Puritans."

In 1892 Schaff completed fifty years of academic teaching, dated from his appointment as a docent at Berlin. He received congratulatory addresses from friends and institutions throughout America and Europe, but possibly the one he cherished most was sent by the renowned theological faculty of the Friedrich-Wilhelms-Universität (Berlin), bearing the signature of the faculty's dean, Bernhard Weiss, but composed (or so Schaff was informed) by Adolf Harnack. The address focused on Schaff's importance as a mediator of *Wissenschaft* and reads in part:

> Like Martin Bucer, who three hundred years before you had crossed over to England to carry thither the light of German theological science, you went over to the New World to sow there the seeds of the same culture, and thus became, through your tireless and richly blessed work, the Theological Mediator between the East and the West. If today the famous theological seminaries in the United States

have become nurseries of theological science, so that the old world no longer gives to them alone, but receives from them instruction in turn, this is owing chiefly to your activity.[20]

Mindful of Schaff's "lively interest in both the original text of the New Testament and its translation into English," the address also likened him to Jerome, "the great Mediator between the Greek and the Latin Church in the past," save that Schaff, unlike the contentious saint, ever sought "to promote reconciliation, to draw together the various parties in the Church, and everywhere to bring about 'the speaking of the truth in love.' "[21]

Philip Schaff likened to Hegel and Baur, and now—on the weighty authority of the Berlin theologians—to Bucer and St. Jerome! These comparisons may be judged more ingenious than apt, but if understood contextually, in reference to Schaff's actual *Sitz im Leben* in nineteenth-century America, they have the merit of emphasizing three indisputable and ever-memorable facts about his life and thought: his dramatic appearance in antebellum America as a bold historical "theorizer," intent upon elevating church history to the rank of a science; his role, especially during his Mercersburg years, as an outspoken critic of the "historylessness" of American theology and ecclesiastical life, which, in the absence of any profound sense of the church's organic growth over the centuries, could conceive of no other relationship between Protestantism and Catholicism than that of implacable opposition; and his incessant labors as a theological mediator between the old world and the new, aiding both worlds to break through their respective parochialisms and to curb their inclinations to cultural imperialism.

Main Components of Schaff's Theory

Schaff's idea or theory of church history is set forth most fully and winsomely in his first three books: *The Principle of Protestantism* (1845); *What Is Church History?* (1846); and *History of the Apostolic Church* (1853). The first of these is a brilliant work that can fairly be judged the Protestant counterpart to and the equal of another, perhaps better remembered, book of the same year: John Henry Newman's *An Essay on the Development of Christian Doctrine.*[22]

Schaff's mind was not profoundly creative. It was, rather, remarkably assimilative (one of his favorite words!), and he seems to have poured into his earliest works everything he absorbed from the lectures of his university professors, from his wide-ranging reading in theology, history, philosophy, and belles lettres, and from his personal converse with eminent persons on two continents. These writings have a freshness, vigor, tensive strength, and ironic wit that are not often found in his later writings. With age he became less speculative and more practical or, as he would have said, more "Americanized." Yet he never lost the animating vision of his youth, only the visionary gleam.

Any summary attempt to identify and delineate the main components of Schaff's complex idea of church history is a difficult matter and risks caricature. Still, on any attentive reading of his early works, the following components present themselves as central to his perspective: (1) the idea of the church; (2) the idea of development; (3) the "typical" import of the apostolic church; (4) the nature of, and the relationship between, Catholicism and Protestantism; and (5) the goals of history. In explicating these components, I have aimed to display their internal coherence. Once Schaff opted for his particular "idea of the church," he necessarily confronted many thorny problems, which he sought to resolve precisely by elaborating the remaining components of his "system."

1. The Idea of Church

Schaff considered it axiomatic that if one is to study and write the church's history properly, one must know what the church is. Hence "a right conception of the church is indispensable for a living apprehension and satisfactory exhibition of its history." Although one knows a phenomenon by observing what it has become, and thus knows the church in and through its actual development, the right idea of the church remains "the *spiritus rector*, the controlling genius of the church historian." Lacking this guiding idea, the historian confronts only the church's "external forms" devoid of their profound "symbolic meaning."[23]

What, then, is the church rightly understood? The answer to this question, replied Schaff, depends on the answer to a prior question: Who is Jesus Christ? Ecclesiology and Christology are inseparably joined. "The question of the person and work of Christ and the church question are at bottom one."[24]

Who, then, is Jesus Christ? Schaff's answer echoed the language of the Creeds and of Chalcedonian orthodoxy. Christ is God incarnate: the eternal Word of God, the Second Person of the Trinity, become flesh in order to reconcile sinful, estranged humanity to God its maker. He is thus truly God and truly man ("theanthropic"): God's complete being dwells in him and, at the same time, he is the Second Adam, the representative of the entire human race and the head of regenerate humanity. "The specific

9

character of Christianity," accordingly, "consists in this, that it is the full reconciliation and life union of man with God, centering in the person of Jesus Christ," whose divine-human life "flows over by the different means of grace to believers, so that, as far as their new nature reaches, they do not live themselves, but Christ lives in them."[25]

In this light, then, what is the church? Schaff answered: It is, in the most profound and pregnant sense, the body of Christ. It is indeed a *body*, an organic union of different members under a single head, but it is specifically the body *of Christ*, "the dwelling-place of Christ, in which he exerts all the powers of his theanthropic life, and also the organ, through which he acts upon the world as Redeemer, as the soul manifests its activity only through the body, in which it dwells."[26] Christ and his Christians, the soul and his body, are joined in lively union, one that is not merely moral, a harmony of wills, but is "mystical"—a real incorporation of the faithful with Christ in the most intimate albeit ineffable way. Therefore, the church's story, properly told, is the story of the "uninterrupted presence of Christ, the God-man, in and among his people," in keeping with his promise: "Lo, I am with you alway, even unto the end of the world" (Matt. 28:20).[27] The church historian, accordingly, must reckon with the real presence of Christ in *every* age of the church, even those that appear most benighted. No theory of a "general apostasy" during any period is tenable, since the soul has never abandoned his body.

For Schaff, in sum, the church is the *Christus prolongatus*—"the continuation of the life and work of Christ upon earth."[28] Like Christ, and as objectively existing in Christ, the church possesses a divine and a human nature, save that "freedom from sin and error cannot be predicated of [it] in the same sense as of Christ" owing to the imperfections in faith and life that still attend its militant stage this side of the last day.[29] Among baptized Christians there are also hypocrites and unbelievers, whose relationship to the church is merely external and nominal. Thus the "visible" or, as Schaff preferred to call it, the "mixed" church must be distinguished from the "invisible" or "pure" church, the latter being composed of all who truly live in union with Christ. Though the pure church is known to God alone, and will become fully manifest only at the last judgment, it is always present *within* the mixed church and may be recognized by its outward marks (the means of grace). The historian must always keep *both* churches in view, since they "act together and influence each other continually."[30]

The right idea of the church as the body of Christ, therefore, turns on this central supposition: "the presence of the Redeemer in the church—invisible and supernatural of course, but none the less real and effective on this account—in his whole undivided and invincible glorified personality, with all the powers that belong to it, whether human or divine."[31] It may be objected that this real presence is insupportable because Christ has ascended to heaven and is now seated at God's right hand. To this it must be said—"over against a rude contracted exegesis"—that God's "right hand" is not to be taken literally but "denotes his Almighty power as it upholds and fills the whole universe." Furthermore, one must distinguish between Christ's *individual* and his *generic* character. The particular human individual, Jesus of Nazareth, is no longer present on earth, not even in his glorified form. But Christ is not merely one individual among others: "he bears at the same time a universal character." The evangelist (John 1:14) does not say "The Word became 'a man' [*anthrōpos*]," but "The Word became 'flesh' [*sarx*]," in order to make plain that the Logos "assumed humanity, or the general human nature."[32] Christ, therefore, is the Ideal Man, in whom human being has at last fully become what God intends it to be. He is also the Second Adam, the head of regenerate humanity, even as Adam is the head of natural, fallen humanity, though Adam's headship is destined to be abolished by the triumphant advance of Christ's headship.

Now just "as every single individual has his history, so has humanity also as a whole. Its biography is Universal or World History," which runs its appointed course from the world's beginning to its end under the leading of divine providence. The mainspring of this universal history is the endeavor of the world's peoples to realize "the idea of humanity, as formed from God and for God"—inasmuch as human beings attain wholeness only in union with the God who is the source and goal of all being. Each people and each age has its distinctive role to play in this great drama of progressive humanization. Secular history, however, has been decisively transformed by sacred history, i.e., by the appearance of Jesus Christ, the God-man, in whom God and humanity have been joined in vital permanent union through the Word's assumption of the general human nature. Thus the Christian religion, considered in its "objective ideal aspect" as exhibited in Christ himself, does not merely continue the course of previous history or even elevate it to a higher plane. "It must be regarded rather as a new creation by which a new principle, a divine life is communicated to humanity itself." In Christ, in short, the idea of humanity has been fully actualized. Even so, "Christianity forms the turning point of the world's history; and Christ, the true polar star of the whole, is the centre also around which all revolves; the key . . . which alone can unlock the sense of all that has taken place before his advent or since."[33]

What, then, is church history? Schaff's ecclesiology and Christology leave no doubt about the answer: church history is the progressive development within regenerate humanity of God's new creation in Christ on behalf of all humanity. Put otherwise: it is the gradual actualization in Christ's body, the church, of the ideal humanity that exists fully in Christ himself, whereby, through the church's agency, all of Adamic humanity is steadily changed into the likeness of the Second Adam.

2. The Idea of Development

The church is the theanthropic body of Christ. This idea is the *spiritus rector* of the church historian. If that is so, what need is there for a historian at all? Does the church actually possess a *history*? Are not "church" (the mystical body of the changeless God-man) and "history" (the ordinary human realm of constant change) mutually exclusive? How can a supernatural entity be subject to the natural processes of growth? Yet Schaff was ever emphatic that "the church is not to be viewed as a thing at once finished and perfect, but as a historical fact, as a human society, subject to the laws of history, to genesis, growth, development."[34] Patently, then, the *right* idea of development is as indispensable to the church historian as the right idea of the church. Schaff held that this proper understanding of development is itself of modern provenance, a "new thing" in church historiography.

The old orthodox Catholic and Protestant historians, from the fourth through the seventeenth centuries, were at one in rejecting any notion of an inward development in the nature of the church itself (as distinct from outward changes in its fortunes).[35] They regarded the church's doctrine and life as complete from the outset, fixed for all time in the original biblical revelation as the immutable truth. By contrast, the rationalist historians of the eighteenth century considered the whole of church teaching to be in constant motion and flow: "a confused chaos of opinion, changing with every period."[36] These two positions thus stood to one another as thesis to antithesis. Yet, in Schaff's judgment, each involved a correct perception. Orthodoxy rightly insisted on a principle of permanence in church history; rationalism rightly posited a principle of change. These opposing principles now awaited their reconciliation in a higher synthesis, which would preserve the truth of each while abolishing its attendant one-sidedness. Schaff concluded that just such a synthesis had at last been achieved by Herder and the German Romantics and the German idealists, chiefly Schelling and Hegel, as well as by Schleiermacher, Baur, and Neander.

The core concept of this new German idea of history is that of *organic* development, which views historical phenomena "as a fluid mass permeated with spirit."[37] History, in other words, "is no longer viewed as an inorganic mass of names, dates, and facts, but as spirit and life, and therefore process, motion, development, passing through various stages, ever rising to some higher state, yet always identical with itself, so that its end is but the full unfolding of its beginning."[38]

The proper model of historical development, therefore, is that supplied by an organism, a living entity such as a plant or a human being. The proper metaphors of development are thus botanical and biological. The tree grows from the seed, the latter unfolding itself first in root and trunk and then in branches, leaves, blossoms, and fruit. The human being grows from embryo to mature age through the intermediate stages of infancy, childhood, and youth. All organic growth is progress from the lower to the higher and so to the better, namely, to completeness or perfection. Yet each stage is integrally related to the whole, and so each possesses its own integrity as well as its distinctive beauty. The completed entity, moreover, is already potentially present in its "germ," so that the whole is really prior to the parts and the end is the full realization of the beginning.

Organicism thus gives due weight to both stability and mobility in history—a proper synthesis, in Schaff's judgment, of the polar principles that traditional Christian supernaturalism and modern rationalism had so one-sidedly advocated. This perspective fully allows for change in historical phenomena ("a fluid mass"), but such change is never random or accidental. It takes place in keeping with the inmost nature of its living subject and so proceeds by an immanent necessity. Hence all change is seen to be regular, lawlike, teleologically determined, once one knows the essential constitution of the subject under investigation. This perspective also fully allows for permanence. Though a subject undergoes continuous development, it ever remains self-identical in its unfolding precisely because it is an organism, a living entity ("permeated with spirit") whose life principle endures through every stage of growth.

Schaff's application of historical organicism (or "historicism") to church history is evident at every turn. His basic premise is that the church itself is a living entity, an organism—the body of Christ, whose individual members are united in an organic whole by virtue of their union with Christ, the body's guiding head and animating soul. Just so, as an organism subject to the laws of organic development, the church is properly seen to be at once changeless and ever changing, complete and ever growing to completion—depending upon the viewpoint adopted.

Considered under its *ideal, objective* existence in Christ himself—and also in the mind of God, in the divine intention effected in the Incarnation—the church is "from the first complete and unchangeable."[39] In Christ dwells all the fullness of the Godhead and thus he participates in the divine immutability: "the same yesterday, today, and forever." In him the union of God and humanity has finally been accomplished, not merely to the highest degree possible for finite spirit (as Baur contended), but to an absolute degree. Inasmuch, then, as the church—understood as the whole of regenerate humanity intended by God for salvation—already exists "potentially" in the God-man, by virtue of the Word's assumption of a universal human nature, the church must be considered perfect and immutable. Likewise, the revealed word of Christ, his divine teaching exhibited in the New Testament scriptures, "is eternal truth and the absolute rule of faith and practice, which the Christian world can never transcend."[40] The same infallibility and unsurpassability attend the writings of Christ's apostles, whose teaching is no less the supreme norm of Christian faith and life.

Considered under its *actual, subjective* existence, however, the church develops.[41] That is to say, the ideal church existing "intentionally" in God's eternal plan and "potentially" in Christ's theanthropic person undergoes progressive realization on earth. The ideal becomes actual: the fullness of the divine life in Christ gradually imparts itself to, and is possessed by, humanity at large; the union of the divine and the human in Christ (which occurred by nature or "hypostatic union") is progressively repeated in humanity at large (which occurs by grace or "mystical union," i.e., by the inward working of the Spirit of Christ through the church's outward means of grace). Even so, humanity is progressively divinized and, therewith, humanized, since it becomes ever more conformed to the image of Christ, the Ideal Man and Second Adam, until, at the end of time, human life fully becomes what it already is in Christ himself. Likewise the doctrine of Christ and of his apostles is progressively apprehended and appropriated by human consciousness during the church's successive ages.

In sum: if one is rightly to comprehend the church in its stability and mobility, its permanence and change, one must rightly distinguish between the ideal church and the actual church, between the church in potency and in realization, between objective divine revelation and subjective human appropriation. One must also rightly distinguish between random change and regular change. The church's development is always regular, lawlike, because it is organic: the progressive growth, in accord with its inner nature and immanent teleology, of the "germ" of new life implanted by God in humanity, namely, the theanthropic life of Christ himself. The church, as the body of Christ, and like Christ himself in his human nature, passes through its stages of infancy, childhood, youth, and mature age. All these stages form one integrated whole, and each has its intrinsic value and unique charm (which thus requires of the historian a truly catholic spirit, impartiality, freedom from prejudice and party zeal). The end of this development is a return to its beginning. The perfected church of the end time is identical to the perfect church of the primal time, except that what once existed only in potency will have become fully realized. Even so, the church preserves its self-identity from first to last: while the "body" develops and changes, the "soul" remains one and the same unchanging Christ.

The actual development of the church is both external and internal.[42] In keeping with Christ's parable of the mustard seed (Matt. 13:31–32), the church is destined to embrace all nations by illuminating them with the light of the gospel through missionary activity. Concurrently, in keeping with Christ's parable of the leaven (Matt. 13:33), the church's own doctrine, life, worship, and government are progressively transformed by the new principle of life imparted by Christ to humanity, while the teaching of Christ and the apostles is grasped with ever more adequacy. Each age builds on the work of earlier ages and to this degree surpasses them, while penetrating the biblical revelation ever more deeply.

The body of Christ exists in and for the world. Through the church's agency the New Creation is gradually extended to the world at large.[43] The "world," to be sure, in its pejorative biblical sense, is a realm of gross sin and error, of relentless hostility to Christ and his body. It is the theater of Satan and the demonic powers no less than of God and his angels and saints. The church stands in unyielding opposition to the ungodly world, even as church history and profane history are in mutual conflict. Yet wickedness does not belong to human nature as such, which comes from God; hence God's grace aims not to abolish nature but to perfect it by purging it of corruption, just as God's revelation does not destroy human reason but fulfills it by infusing it with divine truth. Fittingly, then, may the Christian say with the pagan poet (Terence): *Homo sum, nihil humani a me alienum puto* ("Human being that I am, I deem nothing human foreign to me"). In due course, as promised in the parable of the leaven, every sphere of human culture will be permeated by the life of the God-man. The family, the state, the sciences, the arts, the moral life of individuals and nations: all are destined to be progressively formed and so transformed by God's new creation in Christ, "till God shall be All in all."

3. The Typological Import of the Apostolic Church

One can readily see why Schaff considered the idea of organic development "the key to the understanding of history."[44] It enabled him to "synthesize" the ideal church and the actual church, namely, the supernatural and the natural, the immutable and the mutable, the metahistorical and the historical. Above all, this idea enabled him to assert, explain, and defend what he regarded as the church's—and church historiography's—sine qua non: the uninterrupted presence of Christ, the church's life principle, throughout the centuries. All change is ordered and progressive, from a lower stage of life to a higher, without any break in the continuity of life. But how, then, account for radical oppositions in church history, for dramatic reversals in the course of development—changes that, to all appearances, amount to a revolutionary rupture with the preceding stage(s)? In particular, how account for the fundamental opposition between Protestantism and Catholicism, which, in Schaff's judgment, is the determining factor in church history since the sixteenth century? Beyond this, how can such opposition be seen as intrinsic to essential Christianity itself and so be consonant with the basic premise of Christ's continuous presence in his body?

Schaff addressed these issues, and resolved them to his satisfaction, through the idea of the typological significance of the apostolic church: the idea, namely, that the apostolic age was "prophetic" or "prefigurative" of the whole subsequent history of the church, including the opposition between Protestantism and Catholicism. He owed this idea largely to lectures by Schelling on "The Philosophy of Mythology and Revelation," delivered at the University of Berlin from 1841 to 1845.[45] Schaff first reported on Schelling's "speculation" in *The Principle of Protestantism*. He later gave this idea extended treatment, making it his own, in *History of the Apostolic Church*.[46]

Schaff viewed the apostolic era (A.D. 30–100) as altogether unique in church history. It was truly a "century of miracles" because it was guided by men who were "filled in an extraordinary degree with the Holy Spirit" and who remain, for all ages, "the infallible vehicles of divine revelation."[47] The apostles' teaching, however, was not uniform but exhibits a striking diversity, albeit a diversity in unity. Indeed, the three leading apostles—Peter, Paul, and John—may be seen as types and representatives of the three main ages of the church: Catholicism, Protestantism, and the ideal church of the future.[48]

Peter, the apostle of Jewish Christianity, represents the "conservative" principles of law, authority, and objectivity, the same principles that characterize Catholic Christianity at its best. Paul, the apostle of Gentile Christianity, represents the "progressive" principles of gospel, freedom, and subjectivity, the same principles that characterize Protestantism at its best. These principles and their correlative types of Christianity stand in polar tension, but they are not irreconcilable. They achieved reconciliation in John, the apostle of unitive Christianity, who represents the principle of consummate love, the same principle that characterizes the coming church, the ideal church of the future, which will be the church of evangelical catholcity. In this light, then, the apostolic church must be considered the "preformative" or "model" church: "In a rapid superhuman course that church virtually went through the entire process, which subsequently unfolds itself in larger cycles in a series of centuries. . . . It contained in embryo all succeeding periods." [49]

Plainly, at this juncture, Schaff had appropriated the leading idea of both Hegel and Baur that historical development is carried forward "dialectically" by means of the opposition and ultimate reconciliation of logical polarities.[50] The original unity of apostolic doctrine is seen to include a diversity of types, and this diversity-in-unity sets in motion the dialectic of church history. A first principle—that of Petrine law and objectivity—becomes creative by generating its own contrary (Pauline freedom and subjectivity), which it then proceeds to reconcile to itself (Johannine "charity"). This forward movement—for which Hegel used the familiar punning verb *aufheben*— simultaneously *annuls* the previously existing forms (since each principle is one-sided taken in isolation), *preserves* their essence (since each principle is intrinsically correct and necessary), and thereby *elevates* them to a higher stage (by eliminating their respective one-sidedness and realizing the unity that all along had bound them together).

One could scarcely overstate the importance for Schaff of this idea of the "typical" apostolic church. It entailed the most weighty conclusions. The church's development is dialectical as well as organic, proceeding by way of the opposition and reconciliation of logical principles ("thesis, antithesis, synthesis") as well as by the gradual unfolding of a new life principle. Also, the apostolic pattern of doctrinal development is no less "germinal" for church history than is the theanthropic life of Christ: both are "preformative," and when both have at last been fully formed in regenerate humanity, that end will be but a return to the beginning. Moreover, change and growth are already evident *within* the circle of ideal Christianity itself—within the body of infallible apostolic teaching, whose perfection thus includes both diversity and progress. Indeed, this very perfection displays and develops itself in *conflict*, which tests but does not break its inner unity—a conceptual unity that is rooted in the apostles' living unity with Christ, and his with them. Hence the great postapostolic contest between "Petrine" and "Pauline" Christianity, between Catholicism and Protestantism, is not alien but integral to ideal Christianity—a necessary stage on the way to the ideal church of the future, which is identical to the ideal church of the apostolic past: the Johannine church of perfect love, uniting Peter and Paul, Catholic and Protestant, authority and freedom, objectivity and subjectivity, the claim of the universal and the claim of the individual, in the grand and glorious synthesis of evangelical Catholicism.

4. Catholicism and Protestantism (the Reformation)

It was incontestable for Schaff, given his interpretation of the apostolic church, that Catholicism and Protestantism alike belong to the essence of the church. He considered it equally incontestable that the Protestant Reformation of the sixteenth century was "an absolute historical necessity."[51] How did Reformation come about? Why was it necessary? Schaff's answers follow directly from his idea of the church's organic growth and dialectical advance. Briefly stated: the Reformation necessarily occurred because the medieval church had become "fixated" in an outdated stage of development and, simultaneously, had fallen into "dialectical imbalance," i.e., into an extreme one-sidedness in its religious life.

Schaff's theory entailed that the Catholic principles of law, authority, and objectivity are both chronologically and logically prior to the Protestant principles of freedom, independence, and subjectivity. Catholicism, therefore, possessed special importance and weight during the church's "childhood," when a strict disciplinary regimen was required for individuals and peoples. During the early Middle Ages, the Roman church provided just such salutary tutelage in faith and morals to the newly converted Germanic tribes. But during the succeeding centuries (from the papacy of Gregory VII), Rome increasingly refused to acknowledge the just claims of many of the faithful (such as the Waldenses, Lollards, and Hussites) for a degree of freedom and independence commensurate with their progress in Christianity. The medieval church thus failed to mature along with its members, seeking instead to keep them in a condition of childish dependence.

The root problem, averred Schaff, was this: the Roman Catholicism of the Middle Ages had gradually devolved into a *Romanism* that was no longer fully Catholic. In the spirit of the emperors of old Rome, the bishops of new Rome labored to erect a universal monarchy. The result was a de facto papal-caesarism and spiritual despotism. Even the medieval papacy's greatest achievement—the magnificent cultural synthesis of the twelfth and thirteenth centuries, which rightly made religion the center of every enterprise of thought and action—was as much a product of worldly coercion (Inquisition and Crusade) as of the leavening influence of Christ's divine-human life. In the event, the Catholic principles of law and authority had degenerated into legalism and authoritarianism, while genuine Catholic universalism had been supplanted by a time- and place-bound particularism.

Likewise, Catholic objectivity was gradually replaced by sheer objectivism. The valid principle that the Christian is always dependent on the church's means of grace was invoked, in a most one-sided way, against the evangelical claim that these ministrations, to be effective, must be personally appropriated in the heart's depths. Religion was thereby turned into something formal and external, losing the passion of inwardness. Yet, in keeping with their dialectical polarity, the nisus of objectivity is ever toward subjectivity: one yearns to possess—to make one's own in feeling, thought, and will—what is merely "given" from without. Schaff discerned this subjective yearning throughout the Middle Ages—from St. Augustine through St. Bernard and Thomas a Kempis to Johann von Staupitz, but chiefly in the German (Rhineland) mystics. The late medieval papacy, however, had come to distrust this *Innerlichkeit*, seeing in it the seeds of an anti-institutional subjectivism, and so it sought to control rather than to cultivate the heart's desires for "immediacy" with God. Thus the papal church failed to make the requisite dialectical advance from an exterior to an interior piety.

To Schaff's mind, therefore, the Reformation was historically inevitable. It was a necessary reaction against serious disease in the church, which, like any organism, is beset by manifold debilities in the course of its growth. The diseased organism must undergo a curative process, i.e., a reformation. "Protestantism" is the name for this perennial process. Sixteenth-century Protestantism, therefore, was not directed against Catholicism as such (its dialectical partner), but only against the disease of Romanism, and so against the intransigent papalism that thwarted the church's divinely ordained growth from childhood to young adulthood.

On the basis of Scripture and a purified church tradition, the Reformers (Luther, Melanchthon, Zwingli, Bucer, Calvin) rooted out this disease by means of the Protestant principle per se—the venerable Pauline principle of evangelical freedom from authoritarianism and legalism, *not* from the church's objective means of grace (word and sacraments) or from its teaching office (ordained ministry). The Reformers' cardinal doctrine of justification by God's grace alone through faith alone made the personal appropriation of Christ's saving work the very center of church teaching. Thus the Reformers—fully Catholic themselves and fully attuned to the profoundest strains of Catholic piety over the centuries—made Protestantism synonymous with progress by bringing the Catholic church at large out of its minority into its majority, and out of a legalistic, exterior piety into the religion of free, christocentric inwardness. Even so, in Schaff's summary judgment, "the Reformation is the greatest act of the Catholic Church itself, the full ripe fruit of all its better tendencies."[52]

With Schaff, therefore, one sees that in the Reformation era medieval Roman Catholicism was *aufgehoben* or "transcended": its Romanism-papalism was annulled, its essential catholicity preserved, and its thought and life elevated to a new and higher plane—that of Christian liberty and a mature independence, that of Catholic objectivity now thoroughly interiorized by Protestant subjectivity.

The Reformers themselves, said Schaff, held the principles of objectivity and subjectivity in delicate balance, but their achievement bore within itself the possibility of a new dialectical imbalance. Given their opposition to Romanism, they perforce gave the strongest emphasis to freedom and subjectivity. The history of modern Protestantism, especially since the beginning of the eighteenth century, is largely the story of the *one-sided* development of these Reformation principles. Whereas medieval Roman Catholicism gave way to a rigid objectivity, post-Reformation Protestantism has succumbed to a loose subjectivity. The latter is exhibited both in rationalism, whose homeland is "scientific" Germany and the Lutheran church, and in sectarianism, whose classic soil is the Reformed Church in "practical" England and America. The older historical-critical rationalists (J. S. Semler and company) resolved the Christian religion into morality; the newer speculative rationalists (D. F. Strauss, Bruno Bauer, Ludwig Feuerbach) have reduced it to myth. The sect system, which flourishes under the American separation of church and state and draws its spiritual capital from the Puritanism of Old and New England, is unhistorical and unchurchly throughout, zealous for the sovereignty of God but not for the body of Christ. Thus Protestant liberty has degenerated into licentiousness, Protestant independence into an arrogant self-sufficiency. Nonetheless, great maladies though they be, rationalism and sectarianism—like all heresies and schisms—have their relative justification: the former in reaction to a fossilized orthodoxy, the latter to manifest evils in the church at large.

Meanwhile, according to Schaff's analysis, post-Tridentine Catholicism has continued as Romanism, still opposing the church's necessary progress to Christian freedom. Yet this communion is far less threatening to modern Protestantism than is the heresy, apostasy, and schism in the latter's own midst. Meanwhile, the secular realms of science, art, government, and social life have increasingly dissociated themselves from the church, largely with the tacit concurrence of orthodox Protestantism, which remains unperturbed by this "secular schism." Indeed, in North America, most of the orthodox Protestant bodies have become preoccupied with subjective piety in the form of revivalism; have played off the Bible against the church's living tradition; have undervalued the sacraments in favor of preaching, while abandoning the Reformation's liturgical treasures; and have shown themselves indifferent to sectarian and denominational divisions in the larger church, on the supposition that their own particular denomination is the pristine bearer of gospel truth. Schaff's diagnosis of the diseases of modern Protestantism led, ineluctably, to this prescription: "the Reformation must be regarded as still incomplete. It needs yet its concluding act to unite what has fallen asunder, to bring the subjective to reconciliation with the objective."[53]

5. The Goals of History

History is progress—the sometimes painfully slow but always sure movement of worldly reality to its God-appointed end: the perfect realization in the church, and in humanity at large, of the New Creation embodied in the Second Adam. For Schaff, accordingly, there is one overarching goal of universal history, that is, of profane history and church history alike: that God-in-Christ be All in all. This "final" end will be reached by the simultaneous realization of two "instrumental" ends: the total transformation of human culture and the entire natural order by the leaven of Christ's theanthropic life, such that Christianity becomes identical with nature; and the total transformation of Christ's own body by the same leaven, such that the actual church becomes the ideal church exhibited in Christ's person and in the Johannine church of the apostolic age. History thus ends with God's "third creation": the union of the first "natural" creation with the second "moral" creation (the Incarnation) in the "absolute glorification of Nature in Spirit, of the world in the kingdom of God."[54]

The church aims to make itself the substance of all cultural forms, that is, to penetrate them ever more deeply with its new life principle and so shape them to the image of Christ. The historical paradigm for this endeavor is the "grand and venerable" *corpus christianum* of the Middle Ages, when religion became "the all-moving, all-ruling force."[55] But this culture shaping must now be genuinely evangelical (Protestant), not legalistic (Romanist), proceeding by way of assimilation, not arrogation, and through persuasion, not coercion. Renouncing monastic and pietistic *Welt-flucht* and confident in the spirit and power of the gospel alone, the church will become ever more at home in the world and thereby effect, from within, its total renovation. This process will be complete when church and state have become identical, not by the church dissolving itself into the state (as Richard Rothe thought), but by the state being transformed into the church, i.e., into a true theocracy; and when all the sciences have been "raised and refined" into theosophy, all art has been spiritualized in worship, and personal and corporate morality, now purged of sin and error, has become identical with holiness.[56]

If Christ is to transform culture, however, then his own body must be healed of its present debilitating ills. Since Protestantism, in Schaff's judgment, is the main religious force in modern civilization, it is imperative that it recover its vitality, for the world's sake as well as its own. It must bring to completion the unfinished Reformation by reuniting what has fallen asunder—Protestant subjectivity and Catholic objectivity. To do so, it must purge out the old leaven of radical religious subjectivism, of rationalism and sectarianism, which are at one in their contempt for history.

How is this purging to be effected? How are the subjective and the objective to be reunited, to the end that Protestantism progresses beyond rationalism, sectarianism, and contentious denominationalism into organic union? Schaff insisted that this "unitive reformation"—recovering classical Protestantism's evangelical catholicity but transcending its overemphasis on subjectivity—could not come about by "reductionism," i.e., by seeking to impose on the church at large some minimalist creed that had been fabricated in a scholar's study. That, Schaff declared, is but a "mechanical" notion of church union based on doctrinal indifferentism and utter disregard for history.[57] Protestantism, rather, must reappropriate its Reformation heritage, its grand basal principles of *sola gratia* and *sola scriptura*. It must do so, however, in the spirit of the more recent and now prevailing German evangelical theology—not the spirit of a narrow, rigid confessionalism but the spirit of evangelical catholicity itself, which has been created and nurtured by the new German idea of history.

Therefore, concluded Schaff, the reunion of subjectivity and objectivity, and Protestant unity itself, can only come about through the right idea of the church and of its development. The proper study of church history is itself the proper way to conquer the maladies of church history. History must overcome history! Evangelical catholicity in the church is a fruit of understanding the church in an evangelical-catholic manner. Organic union is a fruit of understanding the church organically. The church's organic growth and dialectical advance occur not beyond but within the church's own self-understanding. Ideas have consequences! Even so, "the different branches of the church should be brought, by a thorough study of [its] history, to know and respect and love one another more; and thus come more and more clearly to the consciousness that no one of them is perfect, but that they are mutually necessary one to the other, and should severally leave their faults behind, and unite their advantages and virtues into a harmonious whole."[58]

The goal of church history, however, is not Protestant union but *Christian* union. The church is one and universal in idea; it must now become so in fact. Protestantism, therefore, must come to the full realization that "it cannot be consummated without Catholicism," since both belong to the church's essence.[59] To be sure, modern Roman Catholicism is also diseased; it must yet rid itself of papalism and thereby prove itself evangelically catholic. Can this happen? Schaff himself admitted to serious reservations, especially after Vatican I's dogma of papal infallibility (1870). Yet he took heart from the prediction of the eminent Roman Catholic historian, Johann Adam Möhler (d. 1838), that "Catholics and Protestants will in great multitudes meet one day and give each other the hand of mutual friendship" on the basis of an "open confession of mutual guilt," which will usher in "the festival of reconciliation."[60] In 1845, in his first book, Schaff declared that "the Lord still has great things in store" for the Roman church.[61] In 1893, in his last publication, he expressed his belief that "the twentieth century has marvelous surprises in store for the Church and the world" (among which, surely, he would have included Vatican II).[62]

But however ambiguous the signs of the times, Schaff knew the final outcome. The great schism of the sixteenth century will assuredly be healed because the history of the apostolic church is repeating itself in the history of the postapostolic church. Even as the opposing but equally valid principles of Peter and Paul were reconciled by John, the apostle of love, so also the opposing but equally valid principles of historical Catholicism and Protestantism are progressively being reconciled by the spirit of charity that is a sign of Christ's uninterrupted presence in his body. The Johannine church of consummate love is surely coming, may well be at hand. Whatever, in God's good time, modern Protestantism and modern Roman Catholicism will be *aufgehoben*. Their respective errors will be abolished; the substance of their common Christian faith will be preserved; and they will be united and so raised to the higher stage of evangelical Catholicism— higher because it takes up into itself all the positive accomplishments of the church's past, since, in the economy of God, "nothing which has once come to be of true historical weight can be absolutely negated or made to become null."[63]

A Brief Appraisal

The error of Protestantism was in that it broke with tradition, broke with the past, and cut itself off from the body of Christ, and therefore from the channel through which the Christian life is communicated. Protestantism was a schism, a separation from the source and current of the Divine-human life which redeems and saves the world.

These words were written in 1857 in an autobiographical novel by a former Presbyterian, former Unitarian minister, former Transcendentalist, and since 1844, prominent convert to the Roman Catholic church: Orestes Augustus Brownson.[64] His lines from *The Convert* are strikingly reminiscent of lines written a dozen years before by Philip Schaff in *The Principle of Protestantism*:

[Puritanism] has no respect whatever for history. It would restore pure, primitive Christianity, with entire disregard to the many centuries of development that lie between. . . . Tradition is the channel by which [the biblical revelation] is carried forward in history. . . . God's will is that the body of the redeemed should exhibit an organic communion, that may be the image of the union that holds between himself and the only-begotten Son. This conception of the church, however, as the Body of Christ, few here [in Protestant America] seem to have reached, in its depth and glory.[65]

These two judgments, so similar sounding, were diametrically opposed. Whereas Brownson was excoriating what he took to be essential Protestantism, Schaff was lamenting the hegemony in America of a diseased, pseudo Protestantism. And Schaff ever labored to show that Brownson's familiar type of charge touched *only* this false, sectarian Protestantism but was totally invalid in respect of classical, Reformation Protestantism: "The sect system, like rationalism, is a prostitution and caricature of true Protestantism, and nothing else."[65] Still, Schaff would not have denied that Brownson's charge justly implicated much if not most evangelical Protestantism in antebellum America. Any adequate assessment of Schaff's idea of church history, therefore, would require a full account of its significance vis-à-vis that nineteenth-century evangelicalism (Schaff's "Puritanism") that dominated American Protestant thought and life well into the century's second half.

I think it is clear, for example, that Schaff's multifaceted, complex,

subtly nuanced philosophy of church history served as an important coun-
terweight to many of evangelicalism's "indigenous passions":[67] its zeal for
revivalism and Finneyite "new measures," correlative to its idea of the
church as the creation of personal faith and thus as constituted by "reborn"
individuals; its fierce anti-Catholicism, equating the papacy with Antichrist
and identifying Roman Catholics as conspiratorial agents of papal despotism; its unshakable certainty that the Reformation was a revolutionary
break with medieval Catholicism and owed nothing to the hated Church
of Rome; its "great apostasy" model of church historiography, consigning
almost the entire Middle Ages (Dark Ages!) to the realm of the papal
Antichrist and linking the Protestant reformers chiefly to the medieval
Waldenses in southern France, who, in turn, had presumably maintained
unbroken continuity with "apostolic" Christianity in southern Gaul; its
rejection of a normative tradition of biblical interpretation in the name of
sola scriptura, thereby embracing a traditionless *nuda scriptura*; its repristinating biblicism, viewing one's own denomination as the latter-day restoration of the pure New Testament church; and its unrestrained impulse
to schism, to the fragmentation of Protestantism into warring schools and
separated, self-dividing churches.

Little wonder, then, that during the years 1845–46 Philip Schaff was
twice obliged to stand trial in the German Reformed church on charges
of heresy lodged against him by leading clerics and, though twice vindi-
cated, was subjected to scathing criticism for his publications until the
mid-1850s.[68] At the root of these charges and criticisms was the "evangelical"
certainty that Schaff was a "Romanizer." His subtle notion of evangelical
catholicity was far too subtle for many of his coreligionists, who believed
that "true Protestantism" required them to put asunder what Schaff had
so skillfully joined together.

Schaff's idea of church history must also be appraised "from within,"
in respect of its adequacy as a theoretical construct, no less than "from
without," in respect of its contextual importance. I said at the outset of
this essay that his theory is superannuated. This is not to state categorically
that it is untrue, only that it is, in fact, outdated. It fails to elicit assent
from church historians who adhere to the canons of modern critical-
historical scholarship—the same standards that were accepted by many of
Schaff's contemporaries.

Judged by these canons, Schaff's position is seen to be "pre-critical"
in many respects. For example, he regarded the Acts of the Apostles as an
unvarnished history of the primitive church. He accepted the Gospel of
John as a reliable "biography" of Christ and gave it the central place in
his exposition of Christ's person and work. He all but ignored Strauss'

Life of Jesus (1835), dismissing it as the most notorious specimen of modern infidelity. While acknowledging development, diversity, and even conflict in "apostolic" doctrine (and here Schaff notably broke with traditional orthodoxy), he rejected out of hand Baur's thesis of radical opposition and contradiction between Petrine and Pauline Christianity in favor of a harmonizing approach that facilely posited unity in diversity. Given his adherence to the orthodox doctrine of the Bible's plenary inspiration and inerrancy, he dispensed with content criticism of the New Testament literature and so made no effort to probe behind these texts in order to reconstruct the hidden historical development.

Schaff's idea of the organic development of doctrine precluded any fundamental criticism of this process, to which he attributed an immanent necessity. Hence he viewed the Trinitarian and christological dogmas as the inevitable outcome of the early church's progressive apprehension of the biblical revelation.[69] He could draw a straight line of development from the Gospel of John to the Councils of Nicaea and Chalcedon. Later in the nineteenth century, Adolf Harnack (and Albrecht Ritschl) would interpret dogma as the baneful work of the Greek spirit on the soil of the gospel. Schaff, however, was predisposed by his organicism to see in the growth of orthodox dogma always an evolution in Christian consciousness, never a possible devolution from the Christian gospel. The point is not that his conclusion was necessarily wrong, but that he arrived at it by theoretical supposition rather than by historical criticism.

One of Schaff's most striking omissions, from a critical perspective, was his failure to address the so-called hermeneutical problem. The New Creation, he maintained, progressively assimilates to itself every sphere of cultural endeavor. But he never paused to consider that human self-understanding undergoes dramatic changes over time, and that the Christian gospel must adapt itself to these changes if it is effectively to leaven culture and society from within. How can Christ transform culture by persuasion, not coercion, if the church's message is not "intelligible," is not articulated in relation to that culture's own prevailing patterns of thought and language?

One sees why Schaff ignored this complex problem. He held that the church aims to make itself the substance of all cultural forms, but the relationship that obtains here is strictly one of an active, dominant subject to a passive, subservient object. Cultural forms exist only to be shaped; they exercise no shaping influence in return. Hence the Christian message is always addressed *to* culture, but never *by* culture in such a way that the language and thought forms of the culture are taken up into the substance of the message. Schaff thus envisioned only a religion-shaped culture, by no means a culture-shaped religion—one attuned to modernity. Though no "liberal" theologian of the nineteenth century surpassed Schaff as an advocate of *Kulturprotestantismus*, the New Protestant effort to fashion a viable "culture Christianity" was entirely foreign to his perspective. His vision of "Christ transforming culture" culminated in a theocracy, namely, "Christ *ruling* culture." (At this juncture Schaff allied himself with evangelicalism's indigenous passion to create and preserve a Protestant Christian America.)

One also knows why Schaff used to say of himself, "I am an inveterate hoper."[70] He saw history as inevitable progress to the higher and the better because the power of the New Creation is steadily re-creating both church and society. But, granted that the Christian church covered more of the globe in the nineteenth century than ever before, how could Schaff—how could anyone—demonstrate, on strictly empirical grounds, that history involves constant *moral* progress, that the church (not to speak of the world at large) is "always more and more [throwing off] the elements of sin and error still remaining from the state of nature"?[71] What possible evidence would license the conclusion that the nineteenth-century church was more pure, more advanced in the Christian life of sanctification, than, say, the second-century church? The problem here is not simply one of gathering evidence but one of first knowing what would *count* as evidence for the church's steady progress in holiness, as well as what would constitute *proof* of such progress. Church history itself teaches that outward appearances of sanctity are no guarantee of its inward reality.

A related problem has to do with Schaff's view of the end or consummation of history. His position here is shadowed by ambiguity and ambivalence. He can speak of the end as the culmination of an immanent process of development, i.e., it "arrives" when the whole of worldly reality is "at last" completely transformed by the New Creation.[72] But he also envisions the end as God's miraculous intervention in the course of history in order to complete the process that began with God's own incarnation.[73] These two perspectives are incompatible. Yet Schaff was not being inconsistent with his premises; he was simply operating with two competing "logics"—one derived from his Romantic-idealist legacy, the other from his traditional supernaturalism.

The idea of the end as *immanent* to history is required by the model of organic growth, namely, of the gradual unfolding of the seed of new life implanted by God in humanity at large in the person of the God-man. In due *time*, that seed grows to maturity, fulfilling its telic drive to perfection. The idea of the end as *transcendent* to history is required by the supposition that the end is a return to the beginning, since, in this case, the beginning is a miracle, i.e., the Incarnation itself, or the ideal church as it exists *timelessly* in God's eternal plan and in Christ's changeless person. Just as church history was initiated by a miracle—Christ's first advent, so it ends with a miracle—Christ's second advent. Just as the ideal church exists beyond time, so also its full realization transpires beyond time (at the dawn of eternity). This last miracle accomplishes what history itself—even the history of the New Creation—cannot effect: the abolition of sin and error in regenerate humanity, which happens only in the resurrection of the body, when the corruptible shall put on incorruption.

History ends, moreover, with the (re)appearance of the Johannine church of "reconciliation," the evangelical Catholic church. Now *this* church seems to be immanent to history—the final outcome of the church's own dialectical advance; but it has been "prefigured" by the ideal church of the apostolic age, and *that* church was the outcome of the "century of miracles." Thus the unitive church of the end time is no less a miraculous appearance than the unitive church of the primal time. God effects *von oben* what cannot finally come about *von unten*.

For Schaff, then, as also for the German Romantics and idealists, history is not truly linear, but circular: the end is a return to the beginning (*Endzeit ist Urzeit*), symbolized by the snake with its tail in its mouth.[74] Actually, however, Schaff regards history as *both* linear and circular. It is linear "between the times," between the world's creation and its consummation, and, specifically, between Christ's first advent and his second. But the Incarnation exerts such immense pressure on the line of world history that it necessarily bends this line inward and upward. Thus the time line assumes the shape of a circle, of which the God-man is the center around whom the whole of history revolves. Still, the circle can be closed only by another divine intervention: the God-man's return in triumphal glory. The time line is ultimately rendered circular by the combined weight of the Incarnation and the Second Coming.

To be sure, what happens on the "line" of history "between the times" is of lasting significance. The gradual unfolding of Christ's theanthropic life in humanity is not annulled. Hence the end is not simply a return to the beginning. It is also an "enhancement" (*Steigerung* is Goethe's term), since the end sweeps up into itself all that was positive in the intervening development, i.e., it incorporates the redeemed humanity and the renovated culture that Christ's new life principle has called into being. The circle of history, therefore, is actually an *ascending* circle, namely, a *spiral*, which closes where it began, but on a higher plane. The idea of history as a spiral thus fuses the idea of circular return with the idea of linear progress. This construct enabled Schaff to join the supernatural (circular return) and the natural (linear progress) in a "natural supernaturalism."[75] Like the German Romantics and idealists, he could readily speak of the progressive humanization of the divine as well as the progressive divinization of the human. For Schaff, however, such progress is not owing to any underlying principle of identity between finite spirit and Absolute Spirit—to some ontological link between divine being and human being. It is made possible, rather, only by the Incarnation itself—the decisive event "from above" that introduced the divine life into human history in an absolutely unique and unsurpassable union of God and man, the same event that "pressures" universal history into its circular shape and thereby turns this history into the story of humanity's "circuitous journey home" to God its source and goal.[76]

I judge, then, that the "logic of transcendent miracle," rather than the "logic of immanent growth," is the *controlling* logic in Schaff's comprehensive idea of church history. The spiral of history is not self-moving and self-ascending. God has put it in motion through the enfleshment of the Word and God elevates it to its final, highest plane at the Last Day. Moreover, the realm of nature must be grounded on, anchored by, the realm of supernature—lest historical change be only endless mutability, lest development be nothing but devolution, lest progress be not toward but away from God-in-Christ, lest growth be not into Christ's "perfect manhood" but into Christianity's "old age," its senescence, when culture has presumably advanced beyond a superannuated Christ. If history is assuredly to move "from Christ through Christ to Christ," it must be controlled first and last by God's mighty acts. Remove this divine superintendence and history collapses into chaos: "Things fall apart; the centre cannot hold;/ Mere anarchy is loosed upon the world" (Yeats). History becomes the province of directionless change and boundless relativism, while Christianity becomes but one religion among the religions, deprived of its absoluteness. (At century's end, Ernst Troeltsch would struggle mightily with the exigent problem of how to overcome historical relativism by critical-historical inquiry itself, not by metahistory or dogma, i.e., by traditional Christian supernaturalism).

It is, of course, Schaff's controlling supernaturalism that has rendered his idea of church history outdated. Church historians who abide by the "rules" and the "ethos" of critical-historical thinking cannot appeal to "acts of God" for interpretive and explanatory purposes. A miraculous event shatters the continuity of historical events and so passes historical understanding. An absolutely unique, totally nonanalogous event lies beyond the historian's purview, which presupposes the comparability of events. Human history, in brief, "makes sense" precisely because it is made by human beings. F. C. Baur long ago identified the Achilles' heel of super-naturalist historiography: "If Christianity is an absolutely supernatural miracle, shattering the continuity of history, then history has nothing further to do with it, it can only stand before the miracle and see in it the end of its research and understanding. As miracle, the origin of Christianity is an absolutely incomprehensible beginning."[77]

Furthermore, as Schaff's case makes plain, supernaturalism involves the church historian in a highly problematic "rhetoric of commitment." Said Schaff: the church is the continuation of the Incarnation, Christ's own theanthropic body, whose members are joined with him in mystical union and in which he is continuously present; this "pure" church is always present within the "mixed" church, and the historian must tell the story of both churches. Such claims, however, whatever their theological-confessional validity, are not open to historical verification and, indeed, saddle the historian with an impossible task: to write the history of the "invisible" church!

Not surprisingly, then, Schaff's idea of church history had become passé by his life's end. It was steadily being replaced by the "scientific" history that had become the "new orthodoxy" in the guild of professional historians.[78] It is not the case, however, as has often been thought, that Schaff's idea sealed its own fate by being demonstrably "unscientific." Measured by earlier nineteenth-century standards, his perspective was *wissenschaftlich*, employing as it did the acknowledged "laws" of organic growth and dialectical advance. In 1820 Wilhelm von Humboldt declared that "in its final, yet simplest, solution the historian's task is the presentation of the struggle of an idea to realize itself in actuality."[79] Exactly! agreed Schaff, who in 1846 declared that the church historian's highest duty is to trace the progressive realization of the idea of the church. It is a supreme irony that one of Schaff's Berlin professors, the century's greatest idealist historian, Leopold von Ranke, had by century's end come to be imaged as the premier positivist historian—the prototype, as it were, of Mr. Gradgrind in Dickens' *Hard Times*: "Now, what I want is, Facts. . . . Facts alone are wanted in life."

Schaff's idea of church history thus fell into disfavor because it no longer counted as scientific when judged by the newly prevailing norms. One could say summarily, and no doubt too simply, that Schaff's "natural supernaturalism" gave way to "pure naturalism," that his Romantic-idealist organicism was supplanted by a "Rankean" positivism that abhorred theory, venerated documents, proscribed appeals to acts of God in history, and replaced the rhetoric of commitment with one of "dispassionate description." As a result, church historians (most notably, perhaps, Ephraim

Emerton, installed in 1882 as the first Winn Professor of Ecclesiastical History at Harvard)[80] were on their way to becoming phenomenologists of the Christian religion and historians not of the one church catholic but of the many churches in particular.

By 1900, therefore, church history was no longer regarded as a specifically theological discipline but as a strictly historical one, involving the objective ("presuppositionless") study of Christian ideas, institutions, polities, liturgies, missions, etc. *Church* history had metamorphosed into the history of *Christianity*. Underlying this development was the assumption (largely unexamined) that "theology" implies "metahistory," i.e., that *any* theological understanding of the church necessarily lands the historian in the forbidden territory of the supernatural. Whether this assumption is valid is quite another matter and is eminently disputable, though church historians have but infrequently debated it.[81]

Schaff's idea of church history has been superseded but not, I think, surpassed as an admirable attempt to unite theology, philosophy, and historical thinking in a comprehensive vision of the church historian's craft. In the course of preparing this study of Schaff's now outdated viewpoint I often called to mind the closing lines of Wordsworth's sonnet "On the Extinction of the Venetian Republic": "Men are we, and must grieve when even the Shade / Of that which once was great is passed away." In place of the poet's "men" I should wish to put "historians," mindful especially of those who today pursue their high calling in the society that Philip Schaff founded one hundred years ago.

Notes

1. *Papers of the American Society of Church History* 1 (1889) v–viii.

2. Ibid., vi–vii, xv.

3. P. Schaff, *What Is Church History?*, trans. from Schaff's German manuscript by John W. Nevin (Philadelphia, 1846); reprinted, with original pagination, in *Reformed and Catholic: Selected Historical and Theological Writings of Philip Schaff*, ed. Charles Yrigoyen, Jr., and George H. Bricker (Pittsburgh, 1979), 17–144 (original pagination = pp. 1–128). Hereafter cited as *WCH*, followed by original page number(s).

4. P. Schaff, *History of the Apostolic Church, with a General Introduction to Church History* (New York, 1853), trans. Edward D. Yeomans from *Geschichte der Apostolischen Kirche, nebst einer allgemeinen Einleitung in der Kirchengeschichte* (Mercersburg and Philadelphia, 1851; 2d ed., rev. and enl., Leipzig, 1854). The translation was based on the manuscript of the second German edition. Hereafter cited as *HAC*.

5. See *The Epochs of Church Historiography* in *Ferdinand Christian Baur: On the Writing of Church History*, ed. and trans. Peter C. Hodgson (New York, 1968), 41–257.

6. David S. Schaff, *The Life of Philip Schaff, in Part Autobiographical* (New York, 1897), 20. Hereafter cited as *Life*.

7. Ibid.

8. John Higham, with Leonard Krieger and Felix Gilbert, *History: The Development of Historical Studies in the United States* (Englewood Cliffs, NJ, 1965), 11.

9. *Life*, 498.

10. *Life*, 1. The fullest discussion of Schaff's "Teutonic learning" is Klaus Penzel, "Church History and the Ecumenical Quest: A Study of the German Background and Thought of Philip Schaff" (Th.D. diss., Union Theological Seminary, New York, 1962). Also valuable is K. Penzel, "Church History in Context: The Case of Philip Schaff," in *Our Common History as Christians: Essays in Honor of Albert C. Outler*, ed. John Deschner, Leroy T. Howe, and Klaus Penzel (New York, 1975), 217–60.

11. Schaff devoted chapters to each of these theologians, except Schmid, in his *Germany: Its Universities, Theology, and Religion* (Philadelphia and New York, 1857).

12. See Hans Joachim Schoeps, *Das Andere Preussen: Konservative Gestalten und Probleme im Zeitalter Friedrich Wilhelms IV*, 2d rev. and enl. ed. (Honnef/Rhein, 1957), 11–114, 219–45. Besides Gerlach and Hengstenberg, the group

included General Leopold von Gerlach (Ludwig's brother), the historian Heinrich Leo, and (after Schaff had left Berlin) the jurist Friedrich Julius Stahl.

13. W. Stull Holt, *Historical Scholarship in the United States* (Seattle, 1967), 7. One should note that Schaff was no less an Anglophile than Adams.

14. See James Hastings Nichols, *Romanticism in American Theology: Nevin and Schaff at Mercersburg* (Chicago, 1961).

15. *WCH*, 4. The phrase "a missionary of science" is from *The Principle of Protestantism*, 54. (See n. 22 for bibliographical details.)

16. See P. Schaff, *America: A Sketch of Its Political, Social, and Religious Character*, ed. Perry Miller (Cambridge, MA, 1961). A new edition of lectures delivered in Germany in 1854 and originally published in New York, 1855.

17. See Georg G. Iggers, *The German Conception of History* (Middletown, CT, 1968).

18. G. G. Iggers, "Historicism," article in *Dictionary of the History of Ideas*, 4 vols., ed. Philip P. Wiener (New York, 1973), 2:456–64, see 460.

19. Cf. Wilhelm Pauck, "Schleiermacher's Conception of History and Church History," in *From Luther to Tillich: The Reformers and Their Heirs*, ed. Marion Pauck (San Francisco, 1984), 66–79.

20. *The Semi-Centennial of Philip Schaff, 1842–1892* (privately printed, New York, 1893), which contains both the original German text (3–8) and the anonymous translation (9–13) here quoted, 10.

21. Ibid., 11.

22. P. Schaff, *The Principle of Protestantism as Related to the Present State of the Church* (Chambersburg, PA, 1845), trans., with an introduction, by John W. Nevin from *Das Princip des Protestantismus* (Chambersburg, PA, 1845); reprinted as *The Principle of Protestantism* in the Lancaster Series on the Mercersburg Theology, vol. 1, ed. Bard Thompson and George H. Bricker (Philadelphia and Boston, 1964). I use the reprint ed., hereafter cited as *PP*.

23. *WCH*, 37

24. *HAC*, 678

25. *WCH*, 36

26. *HAC*, 8

27. *WCH*, 36

28. *HAC*, 8

29. *PP*, 220

30. *WCH*, 31

31. *WCH*, 32

32. *WCH*, 32–33

33. *WCH*, 38–40

34. *HAC*, 9

35. Cf. *WCH*, 41–60; *HAC*, 51–69.

36. *WCH*, 67. Cf. *WCH*, 60–71; *HAC*, 69–86.

37. *WCH*, 27

38. *HAC*, 90

39. *HAC*, 10. Cf. *WCH*, 80–83; *PP*, 221.

40. *HAC*, 10

41. See *HAC*, 10–11; *WCH*, 81–87.

42. *HAC*, 11; *WCH*, 88–90

43. See *HAC*, 13–15.

44. *WCH*, 80

45. See Klaus Penzel, "A Nineteenth Century Ecumenical Vision: F. W. J. Schelling," *Lutheran Quarterly* 18 (November 1966): 362–78, which includes a translation of Schelling's thirty-sixth and thirty-seventh lectures on "Philosophy of Revelation" that were of seminal importance for Schaff.

46. See *PP*, 216–18; *HAC*, 185–88, 614–18, 674–78.

47. *HAC*, 187

48. See *HAC*, 36–46.

49. *HAC*, 675

50. See *HAC*, 91; *WCH*, 91–94; *PP*, 222.

51. *PP*, 51. Throughout this section I am summarizing and interpreting the main themes of *PP*. Schaff's notion of the "unfinished Reformation" is discussed by Klaus Penzel, "The Reformation Goes West: The Notion of Historical Development in the Thought of Philip Schaff," *Journal of Religion* 62 (July 1982): 219–41.

52. *PP*, 224

53. *PP*, 225–26

54. *HAC*, 437

55. *PP*, 175

56. *PP*, 184, 221; *HAC*, 14–15. Schaff discussed Rothe's views in *Germany: Its Universities*, 371–75. Cf. *HAC*, 119–21.

57. *WCH*, 124. Schaff was here specifically referring to, and reacting against, Samuel S. Schmucker's *Overture for Christian Union* (1846).

58. *WCH*, 127

59. *PP*, 216

60. P. Schaff, "German Theology and the Church Question," in *Reformed and Catholic*, ed. C. Yrigoyen and G. H. Bricker, 340 (trans. from the September 1852 issue of Schaff's journal, *Der deutsche Kirchenfreund*). Schaff was quoting from Möhler's *Symbolik*.

61. *PP*, 215

62. P. Schaff, *The Reunion of Christendom: A Paper* (New York, 1893).

63. *WCH*, 82–83

64. As quoted by R. W. B. Lewis, *The American Adam: Innocence, Tragedy, and Tradition in the Nineteenth Century* (Chicago, 1955), p. 189.

65. *PP*, 146, 147–48

66. *PP*, 153

67. The phrase is Perry Miller's from his "Editor's Introduction" to Schaff's *America*, xx.

68. See George H. Shriver, "Philip Schaff: Heresy at Mercersburg," in *American Religious Heretics*, ed. G. H. Shriver (Nashville, 1966), 18–55.

69. Cf. *HAC*, 22–23.

70. *Life*, 459.

71. *PP*, 221

72. Cf. *PP*, 105; *HAC*, 437.

73. Cf. *HAC*, 14, 18.

74. On the geometrical figures (circle and ellipse) underlying the works of the Romantics, see Marshall Brown, *The Shape of German Romanticism* (Ithaca, NY, 1979). I am especially indebted to the extraordinary book by M. H. Abrams, *Natural Supernaturalism: Tradition and Revolution in Romantic Literature* (New York, 1971). The phrase "natural supernaturalism" is from Carlyle's *Sartor Resartus*.

75. Cf. *HAC*, 13: "Thus the supernatural becomes natural. It becomes more and more at home on earth and in humanity."

76. Cf. *HAC*, 184: "With the cry [of John the Baptist]: 'Repent and believe!' the Iliad of humanity closed, and its Odyssey began." This image is probably derived and adapted from Schelling, who likened the two-part epic of humanity (departure from and return to the Absolute) to the circular voyage of the Homeric hero.

77. Baur, *The Epochs of Church Historiography*, in Hodgson, 213, apropos of Neander's view of Christianity.

78. The fullest and best treatment of this development is by Henry Warner Bowden, *Church History in the Age of Science: Historiographical Patterns in the United States 1876–1918* (Chapel Hill, NC, 1971). See 31–68 on Schaff. On the "new orthodoxy," see Higham, 92–103; and Holt, 15–28.

79. W. von Humboldt, "On the Historian's Task," *History and Theory* 6 (1967): 57–71, 70.

80. See Emerton's inaugural address, "The Study of Church History," *Unitarian Review and Religious Magazine* 19 (January 1883): 1–18. Cf. Bowden, 99–114.

81. Cf. David W. Lotz, "The Crisis in American Church Historiography," *Union Seminary Quarterly Review* 33 (Winter 1978): 67–77.

A Century of Patristic Studies, 1888–1988

Glenn F. Chesnut

AT the time of the founding of the American Society of Church History in 1888, the young Adolf von Harnack was well on his way to becoming the most outstanding patristics scholar of that generation.[1] The first edition of his three-volume *Lehrbuch der Dogmengeschichte* was currently in the process of appearing (1886–89), a work of sweeping range and detail.[2] He had already, in 1882, founded the famous *Texte und Untersuchungen* series of studies of early Christianity.[3] *Das Wesen des Christentums* was to be published in 1900, and its impact was to be felt almost immediately all over the Protestant world.[4]

Only a year after the founding of the American Society of Church History, in 1889, another great scholar, Albrecht Ritschl, died. Any account of how the writing of early church history has changed over the past century must begin with the world of Ritschl and Harnack—and behind the two of them, the figure of Ferdinand Christian Baur. The basic presuppositions with which most Protestants went into the writing of early church history in the late nineteenth and early twentieth centuries were marked to one degree or another by what Baur, Ritschl, and Harnack had said. This is the most general observation, even though there were some, like Philip Schaff, who managed in part to rise above those debates.

Roman Catholic patristics scholarship must be looked at too. Though some elements of their historiography represented a deliberate and conscious attempt to provide a counterposition to Harnack's, there were also internal developments peculiar to Roman Catholicism itself extending from the latter part of the nineteenth century to the latter part of the twentieth. The Anglicans, and the Eastern Orthodox, also deserve their own special sections.

There are also nonreligious approaches to the patristic period, which have become increasingly important in the last half of the twentieth century: psychological analyses of the phenomenology of early Christian religious experience, sociological studies of the social world of early Christianity, and purely secular accounts (by scholars in classical and postclassical studies) of the same figures, the same events, and the same pieces of literature which the more religiously oriented patristics scholars had traditionally written about.

Newly rediscovered documents have also revolutionized patristics studies over the course of the past century, from the large corpus of Gnostic documents discovered in the sands of Egypt at Nag Hammadi in 1945–46, to the identification of one of the ancient manuscripts in the cathedral library in Verona in 1916 as the long-lost *Apostolic Tradition* of Hippolytus. New fields of investigation have been opened up, from the study of women in the early church, to the many new fascinating studies of those whom later orthodoxy had labeled as the great "heretics" of the early church.

It is above all with Adolf von Harnack, however, that an account of this sort must begin. Harnack had a central thesis that he wished to argue, and he laid it out in the first chapter of his famous *Lehrbuch der Dogmengeschichte* (the *History of Dogma*, as the English translation interpreted its title): "Dogma in its conception and development is a work of the Greek spirit on the soil of the Gospel."[5] The dogmas that the church developed during the patristic period, he went on to say, did attempt to express Christian belief in God and the significance of Jesus Christ, but they did this in the form of a philosophical system borrowed from the world of Greek philosophy.[6] Although these dogmas developed originally in the context of theological discussion and attempts to make the gospel intelligible, once they were formed, the process of thought that had led to those dogmas was denied, and they were themselves regarded as "the revealed faith itself."[7]

In his *History of Dogma*, Harnack argued that the basic transition to "the incipient Catholic Church" had already taken place within the first century.[8] In *Das Wesen des Christentums* (the English title was *What Is Christianity?*) he traced out the further consequences of this in Lecture 11 under the heading, "The Christian Religion in Its Development into Catholicism": By the year 200 "it is only by mediation that a man can approach God at all, by the mediation of right doctrine, right ordinance, and a sacred book. The living faith seems to be transformed into a creed to be believed; devotion to Christ, into Christology; . . . the ministers of the Spirit, into clerics; the brothers, into laymen in a state of tutelage."[9]

In the third through the sixth centuries, Harnack believed, in the Greek portions of the Roman Empire there then developed an Eastern Orthodoxy that, except for a doctrine of creation and a belief in the union of the divine and human natures in the incarnate Christ, differed in no essential way from pagan Greek philosophy.[10] It had basically forsaken any idea of the moral implications of Christian teaching about Christ. On later Eastern Orthodox ritual, Harnack said: "There is no sadder spectacle than this transformation of the Christian religion from a worship of God in spirit and truth into a worship of God in signs, formulas, and idols. . . . *It was to destroy this sort of religion that Jesus Christ suffered himself to be nailed to the cross!*[11] One must ask at this point whether one is dealing with real historiography in Harnack or with simply an enormously erudite polemical pamphleteering. The answer is probably some of both.

The Western development into Roman Catholicism fared no better in Harnack's mind. It is "in fundamental contradiction with" the gospel "when every possible measure which serves to maintain the *earthly* empire of the Church—for example, the sovereignty of the Pope—is proclaimed as the divine will."[12] The parts of his lectures dealing with Roman Catholicism are filled with chains of hostile phrases: "the infallible Pope, the 'Apostolico-Roman polytheism,' the veneration of the Saints, blind obedience, and apathetic devotion"; "holy water, . . . the Pope on his throne, . . . and St. Anne."[13]

At first glance, all this seems to be a mixture of the Enlightenment (Voltaire's "humanity shall not be free until the last king is strangled in a noose made from the entrails of the last priest") and the intolerant anti-Catholicism of that formative Reformation-era history, the *Magdeburg Centuries*.[14] There was nevertheless something far more important at stake to Harnack than simply producing a trenchant and learned attack on Roman Catholicism. To see the real context of his work, it is necessary to go back to two earlier figures: Ferdinand Christian Baur and Albrecht Ritschl.

In the case of Ferdinand Christian Baur (1792–1860) one must distinguish between the real Baur and what most subsequent scholars thought Baur had said. For the former, Peter C. Hodgson's work is the best introduction in English.[15] For the latter, Baur was believed to have been a strict Hegelian who interpreted the history of the earliest Christian communities in terms of a rigid Hegelian dialectic: Petrine Jewish Christians formed the *thesis*, Pauline Gentile Christians formed the *antithesis*, and Catholicism was the *synthesis* that ultimately emerged. The idea that early Christianity had to be interpreted in terms of an all-defining battle between a primitive Jewish Christianity at the beginning, and a later Greek attempt to Hellenize Christianity to the core, became a basic operating presupposition of increasingly greater numbers of Protestant New Testament and patristics scholars as the decades passed, and is still very much alive in many quarters today.

In 1845, the young Albrecht Ritschl (1822–89) went to Tübingen expressly to study with Baur, and while still strongly under Baur's influence, did his habilitation dissertation on Marcion and the Gospel of Luke.[16] To understand the ultimate turn that Ritschl's thought was going to take, however, it is necessary to go back to his family background and then to some of his own later professional experiences.

Ritschl came from the Prussian "establishment." In 1827, when he was five years old, his father was made bishop of Stettin and general super-intendent of the churches in Pomerania. Only ten years earlier, in 1817, King Frederick William III had used the tricentennial celebration of the Protestant Reformation to force a union, by royal decree, of all Protestants in Prussia, into a single Prussian Union Church. The more conservative of the Lutherans, forming a "confessional" or "orthodox" opposition, were bitterly hostile to the theological compromises involved in this union. They were very strong in Pomerania, and Ritschl's father, as bishop and representative of the Prussian ruling elite, had the rather unenviable task of trying to force them into cooperating with this dream of a unifying German religious system.[17]

When Ritschl himself began his teaching career at Bonn, the confessionalist Lutherans immediately started to harass him just as they had his father before him, and did not let up for his entire eighteen years there. To them, Ritschl represented both the hated Prussian Union Church and the radical ideas of Baur. In 1854, Ritschl finally decided to move to Göttingen in Hannover to become professor of theology in what would hopefully be a better situation. One attraction there was that the German state of Hannover was still independent of Prussian control at that time and, although completely Lutheran, had no imposed Union Church to bring out an embattled Lutheran counterreaction.[18] Then, unfortunately, two years later, the victory of Prussia over Austria in the short war of 1866 resulted in Bismarck's swift annexation of many of the northern German states, including Hannover, and therefore the city of Göttingen. As Philip Hefner puts it, Ritschl was simply "ostracized" by the rest of the faculty.[19] Ritschl represented all that they hated—not only a supporter of liberalism and the Union Church, but also a Prussian agent (as far as they were concerned) ensconced within their own faculty.

The rise of Protestant liberalism cannot in fact be totally disengaged, in its later stages, from the career of the Prussian Junker, Otto von Bismarck, the effective founder of the modern German state. After becoming prime minister to King William I in 1862, Bismarck used Prussia as a nucleus for gradually assembling most of the German-speaking areas in north-central Europe into what finally became officially an Empire with a Kaiser at its head in 1871. Lutheran confessionalism was seen as a foe of any all-embracing Prussian Protestant church. Anti-Catholicism also helped to determine the map of modern Germany that Bismarck was creating. He at first deliberately excluded all of the Roman Catholic German-speaking areas in the south from consideration for any kind of Prussian takeover and never would attempt to take Austria even at points when that would have been possible. The *Kulturkampf* then propelled Bismarck into an attack on Roman Catholicism within his German Empire itself from 1871 to 1887. In other words, Ritschl, and especially Harnack, were working in a period when anti-Catholicism was rampant in many parts of Germany, and when the state could be counted on to support more liberal modes of thought against strict Lutheran confessionalism.[20]

When he began teaching at Bonn, Ritschl had quickly taken up work on his first major book, *Die Entstehung der altkatholischen Kirche: Eine kirchen- und dogmengeschichtliche Monographie*.[21] The second edition in particular, which appeared in 1857, provided the basis for some of the central theses in the work of Ritschl's later disciple, Adolf von Harnack.[22] Although Ritschl's most famous work was *Die christliche Lehre von der Rechtfertigung und Versöhnung* (3 vols., 1870–74),[23] an even more important one for understanding his approach to the patristic doctrines of God and Christ was his essay on "Theology and Metaphysics" that appeared seven years later.[24] In that work, Ritschl said that there was a Christian cognition of God, but that one knew the Father only through Christ in his role as "God for us."[25] He used a mixture of the philosophies of Kant and Lotze, the latter his fellow colleague at Göttingen, to set up a rigidly *post rem*, anti-Platonic epistemology, emphasizing the concreteness of actual sensory experience.[27] His rejection of any kind of Platonizing theological language meant that to him most patristic thought, at least as it was being read by the Lutheran confessionalists who were his contemporaries, had to be wrong on principle.

The real enemies for Ritschl were the conservative Lutherans of his own German world. The patristic creeds had to be attacked principally because the confessional Lutherans relied so heavily on them, and they had to be attacked in the form in which the confessionalists believed they should be read. He passed this mission on to his disciple Adolf von Harnack, who expressed himself even more vigorously than his teacher had. Harnack played strongly to late-nineteenth-century Protestant antipathy toward Roman Catholicism. But it would be a mistake to think that this was the principal, or at any rate, the only, reason for linking the patristic period as he did to Catholicism in every possible way. Harnack hoped to smear the conservative, confessional Lutherans of his own generation with the idea that they were merely being "Roman Catholic," whether they realized it or not, in their objections to liberal Protestantism. And when Harnack then wrote a history of the early church in which he accused patristic theology in general of subordinating Christian truth to the ideas of Plato and Aristotle, this meant that he could also therefore accuse contemporary conservative, confessional Lutherans of being not only the unwitting purveyors of Catholicism, but of Greco-Roman paganism as well.

In other words, Harnack's *History of Dogma* was a polemical work in a dispute then going on within Continental German Protestantism. But this did not mean that the central thesis of that work could not find approval in other parts of the world as well, albeit on quite different grounds. In the United States, for example, the more evangelical Protestants fought with all their might against the Protestant liberals who so avidly read Harnack's *What Is Christianity?* But insofar as they were aware of Harnack's *History of Dogma*, these same evangelical Protestants found that it simply further confirmed their already deeply held belief that everything past the close of the New Testament was Roman Catholicism, a religion that had sold its soul to the Roman emperor and rejected the simple teachings of the Bible. The United States in the late nineteenth century was in great part "hostile territory" for patristics scholars.[28]

In America, Philip Schaff, the founder of the American Society of Church History, stands out as such an inspiring figure because he managed to rise up above these polemics perhaps more than anyone else in the America of his generation. Protestantism and Roman Catholicism were for Schaff simply branches growing from a single trunk, the common Christian past. All the successive periods in the long history of the church had developed organically from the preceding ones as an expression of necessary and irresistible historical trends, grounded in God's providence and the essential nature of Christianity itself. And to Schaff, the hope of the future lay in his sweeping ecumenical view of an "evangelical catholicism," moving with an irresistible momentum, and composed of the best of Protestantism and Catholicism *aufgehoben* to a higher plane to become the true Bride of Christ.[29] Unfortunately, Schaff was not going to win the day at that point in history; his wise and embracing vision was too far ahead of its time.[30]

In part, what Harnack did was not bad for the development of patristic scholarship over the following hundred years. He had argued that Christian thought from the patristic era could only be understood by seeing the influence on it of "the Greek spirit."[31] But there was no need to portray this in the exceedingly negative way in which Harnack had. Werner Jaeger, for example, in his *Early Christianity and Greek Paideia*, triumphantly turned Harnack's strongest criticism into a virtue and proclaimed Greek patristic theology as the great capstone and triumphant culmination of the thousand-year-long development of Hellenic thought. And there in Jaeger one truly had a great scholar who understood both the classical world and the early Christian world.[32]

Dennis E. Groh wrote an interesting essay in 1978 discussing recent changes in patristics scholarship, and he commented that the most outstanding characteristic of the patristics scholars writing there in the late 1970s was an extremely thorough knowledge of one aspect or another of that world of pagan Greco-Roman thought in which the early Christians had actually lived.[33] There were those who, like G. Christopher Stead,[34] looked at Greek philosophical concepts as Harnack specifically suggested. Aiding in this has been recent work by scholars like John M. Dillon, which enables us to know far more than Harnack could have of the world of late Hellenistic philosophy.[35]

But "the Greek spirit" meant many other influences in addition to purely philosophical ones. Rosemary Radford Ruether, Robert Dick Sider, and Robert C. Gregg were among the scholars who investigated the influence of Greek *rhetoric*, for example, on patristic argument and thought, with numerous fascinating new insights emerging at every turn.[36] *Historiography* was another area: in the late 1970s, the writings of the first Christian historians began to be studied in detail with respect to their relationship to the preexisting tradition of pagan Greco-Roman history writing,[37] building on the earlier work (in the 1960s) of Glanville Downey and Arnaldo Momigliano.[38] Robert L. Wilken, in *The Christians as the Romans Saw Them*, did an excellent general study of nearly all the important Greco-Roman pagan material that we possess in which Christianity was explicit singled out for criticism, giving some marvelous indirect insights into why early Christianity reacted as it did to what Harnack called "the Greek spirit."[39]

The manifold fruits produced by the use of this particular methodology in recent years has been Harnack's vindication. Increasingly, however, these fruits have tended to vindicate Harnack's methodology but not what he thought would be the results. There is perhaps a delightful irony here. Some specific cases will illustrate the point. When Gregory of Nyssa, for example, spoke of generic human "nature," he used this word in a sense totally different from the way in which it would have been used by a Greek philosopher like Plato or Aristotle. Gregory seems to have intended it to refer to a sort of "concrete universal," an interrelating and interreacting whole, in which anything which affected any individual member of that organic unity affected all.[40] The christological term "hypostasis" as used in the fifth century and afterward to refer to the principle of individuation of a particular human being was also not translatable in any simple manner into classical Platonic or Aristotelian terms, as evidenced by the puzzle later medieval theologians faced in trying to define it. Boethius attempted to read it as a special kind of *substantia*; Richard of St.-Victor said instead that it was the very *existentia* itself of an individual human being.[41] The two translations were not only mutually contradictory; neither truly grasped the complete meaning of the term in its full implications.

It is also been observed that the recurrence of fundamentally non-Hellenic modes of thought continued through all the centuries of patristic thought, even down to the fifth and sixth centuries and beyond. Roberta C. Chesnut, for example, in her work on *Three Monophysite Christologies*, showed that one of these three post-Chalcedonian theologians, Severus of Antioch, was quite Platonic in his theological outlook, thus at least partially vindicating Harnack. But Philoxenus of Mabbug, the second member of the group, had a Christology centering on "the paradox of faith" as one might call it today, far more similar to a Martin Luther than to anything conceivably Platonic; and the third theologian, Jacob of Sarug, lived in a mythological thought-world little different at its basis from that of second-century Gnosticism.[42]

It is still clear that a good knowledge of Greek philosophy and Romano-Hellenistic culture is vitally important to a patristics scholar. Harnack gave valuable advice on that point. Sometimes this knowledge helps enormously in understanding what an early Christian was actually saying. Nevertheless, patristics scholars are becoming more cautious about what look at first, in ancient Christian writings, like familiar Greek philosophical terms, but that turn out on closer inspection to have undergone surprising transformations in meaning.

There was another serious problem raised by Harnack's argument that "dogma in its conception and development is a work of the Greek spirit on the soil of the Gospel," particularly when it was combined with the popular misunderstanding of Ferdinand Christian Baur's hypothesis about Jewish Christians and Gentile Christians in the early church. It too easily produced the impression that Greek (and particularly philosophically oriented) interpretations of Christianity quickly came to absolute dominance in patristic theology and suppressed "the simple biblical faith" and the "Jewish thought-forms" of the first disciples.

The influential French patristics scholar Jean Daniélou deliberately took on Harnack in the 1950s in his work on *The Theology of Jewish Christianity*: Because "Harnack . . . regarded Theology as born from the union of the Gospel message and Greek philosophy" the unfortunate result was that "in his *History of Dogma* a Jewish Christian theology finds no place, simply because he never suspected its existence." There were in fact three different cultural worlds continuously involved in the making of early Christian thought, Daniélou argued—Jewish, Hellenistic, and Latin. None of the early patristic authors belonged totally to one of these worlds alone, so that some overlapping of two or more of these cultures was always involved.[43] By "Jewish Christian" elements Daniélou meant in particular a group of ideas and motifs that Harnack had consistently discounted or ignored: apocalyptic eschatology, Late Jewish angelology and demonology, and elements of a more "mythological" worldview.[44] They were precisely those thought forms that (in the popular misunderstanding of the Baur hypothesis) were supposedly rapidly supplanted and totally replaced by "Hellenistic Christian" ideas.

There is in fact an increasing appreciation in modern patristics scholarship for the degree to which apocalyptic thought of one kind or another continued throughout the entire patristics period. Even a radical and rationalistic Origenist like Eusebius of Caesarea in the early fourth century, still believed, like first-century Jews and Christians, that the Roman Empire was the last of the great kingdoms in Daniel's vision, and that when Rome eventually fell a few generations hence, its collapse would be followed by the total destruction of this entire present physical universe.[45] The importance of the figure of Tyconius, the late fourth-century theologian whose commentary on the Book of Revelation was so influential during the sixth, seventh, and eighth centuries, has been known for some time.[46] Scholars involved in the study of the medieval period have also long been fascinated with the radical apocalyptic movements of the later middle ages,[47] and Bernard McGinn has now been producing excellent studies of the process of transmission by which the Middle Ages obtained these ideas from the patristic period.[48]

Apocalyptic was not the only area in which Jewish influence continued to be felt in early Christianity. It has become more and more apparent over the last few decades that early Christian biblical exegetes and their Jewish contemporaries remained in vital and living contact with one another for centuries after the time of the first apostles. Sometimes it was quite explicit—a Justin Martyr in the second century, an Origen in the third, or a John Chrysostom in the late fourth and early fifth centuries, will explicitly cite a Jewish interpretation or position in order to refute it. But what is also slowly becoming clear is that there was what one might call an "exegetical overlap" as well, where the same new way of interpreting a given Old Testament passage often seems to have appeared, without announcement as to its source, almost simultaneously in both Christian and Jewish writings during the very same century. Other interesting phenomena also occur: Willis A. Shotwell, for example, in his study of *The*

Biblical Exegesis of Justin Martyr (1965), discusses a series of scriptural passages on which Justin and the Hellenistic Jewish philosopher Philo both commented, and shows that it was the Christian patristic theologian Justin, not Philo, who kept closest to the standard rabbinic interpretations.[49] This is not the picture of things that Harnack wished to give!

The whole topic of patristic biblical exegesis has had more and more good scholars working on it over the past several decades. Rowan Greer's *Captain of Our Salvation: A Study in the Patristic Exegesis of Hebrews* and Maurice Wiles' *Divine Apostle: The Interpretation of St. Paul's Epistles in the Early Church* are two excellent examples.[50] It is becoming clear that one could write an entire history of the development of early Christian doctrine simply by presenting a careful account of their changing exegesis of certain important biblical passages.[51] But this means that Harnack's thesis was fundamentally misleading in suggesting that the disputes of the patristic period were grounded at root in what were only philosophical issues, when they so often arose in fact from problems in interpreting particular crucial biblical texts.

The incorporation of new scriptural concepts could have other profound effects. One of the major watersheds in Augustine's thought, for example, came around A.D. 395 when he first began to read Paul's Epistle to the Romans thoughtfully, as displayed particularly in his *Ad Simplicianum* written in the following year. J. Patout Burns, in *The Development of Augustine's Doctrine of Operative Grace*, skillfully traces out all that came before that point, and all that came afterward.[52] In his comments on that profound transition point, Peter Brown, writing in 1967, points out things that Harnack could never have seen:

In Milan, Augustine and Simplicianus had met as metaphysicians: they had found common ground between the Platonists and S. John in their description of the structure of the spiritual universe. Now Simplicianus will pose a totally different kind of question: why was it that God had said "I have hated Esau"? It is a long journey from the contemplation of a Logos, whose existence can be "hinted at by innumerable rational proofs," to this acute posing of the unfathomable nature of individual destinies.[53]

The best patristics scholars of the last two or three decades have not been insensitive to the influence of Greek philosophical ideas on early Christian theology, but scholarship has moved far beyond Harnack, over the past hundred years, in sensitivity to issues of other sorts as well, and what has emerged has been better *historiography* as well, telling it more truly *wie es eigentlich gewesen ist*.[54]

Perhaps, however, the most important change of all those that have taken place during the hundred years that separate us from Harnack, is the new ecumenism. In the festschrift that Patrick Henry edited for Jaroslav Pelikan in 1984, Albert C. Outler wrote an essay[55] comparing the five-volume work on the history of Christian doctrine that Pelikan was then in the process of completing,[56] with Harnack's similar project a century before. As Outler notes, both of these two historical studies are alike in being monumental creations of enormous scholarly erudition and scope. But he then goes on to point out that they nevertheless reflect basically different outlooks—poles apart in fact—so much so that Pelikan's work could be regarded "as a landmark in a major paradigm shift in historical self-understanding over the course of a century." In place of the old Enlightenment-oriented perspective of Harnack, there had built up instead a new "ecumenical consciousness," based on a quite different understanding of the idea of development. The old nineteenth-century Protestant-Roman Catholic-Eastern Orthodox hatreds, animosities, and polemics are missing from Pelikan's work. Yet Pelikan's history is an exceptionally honest piece of scholarship, that never tries to gloss over real differences in an effort to produce an illusion of ecumenical agreement, which is as it ought to be. As Outler puts it, "cheap unity ('letting bygones be bygones'), like cheap grace, is self-deceiving."[57]

In reading the best articles and books written in the area of patristics studies over the past two decades or so, one would usually be hard-pressed—that is, without looking at the author's name, or the publisher, or biographical material incidentally included in a preface—to tell whether the author was Protestant, Anglican, Roman Catholic, or Eastern Orthodox. F. L. Cross, Lady Margaret Professor of Divinity at Oxford University, convened the First International Conference on Patristic Studies in 1951, which has continued at four-year intervals ever since, and which has always stressed the ecumenical nature of patristic scholarship. Even the first drew around two hundred scholars from every continent, and a variety of Christian traditions, although a last-minute fiat issued to the members of one particular Roman Catholic order forbade any of them from attending, precisely on the grounds of its ecumenical character. In contrast, by 1967 the fifth in this series of conferences was opened by Cardinal Pellegrino, a mark of the success of this ecumenical approach to patristics.[58] The major national and international patristics conferences are all completely ecumenical now, and it is by this point being done with such a total absence of self-consciousness on the part of the participants, that one can say that, among trained patristics scholars, a context for the study of Christian ideas that is truly *katholikos* in the original sense of that word, has come into being for the first time in many centuries.

One cannot assume that this new spirit will continue to flourish without conscious effort. A truly ecumenical patristics scholarship is something that the present generation of scholars may have to fight to maintain. Yet it is part of the most significant change in Christian perspectives in 450 years—actually in 900 years, for the Eastern Orthodox involvement is vitally significant as well—and if there were ever to be anything worth fighting for, the re-creation of greater unity in Christendom is one. On historiographical grounds alone, the polemical spirit of the late nineteenth century produced exceptionally bad and distorted histories of early Christianity whenever its prejudices came into play.

Roman Catholic patristics scholars also had their problems in the late nineteenth and early twentieth centuries. The French Revolution had been frightening enough—the memory still remained of such things as Robespierre's grotesque attempt in 1793–94 to make the openly atheistic "Cult of Reason" the national religion of France. It was Italian unification, however, that now made Roman Catholics fear for the very survival of their church. The Papal States were a peculiar and anomalous institution— an essentially secular state stretching across all of central Italy, with the city of Rome at its center and the pope as its secular head of state. But the Papal States had for centuries given the papacy a modicum of military and political buffering against those who would attempt to bring the Roman church under their control. Italian unification meant the creation of a central government for all of Italy, which in turn required that the Papal States be dismantled and absorbed into the new nation-state.

In 1860, Garibaldi and the Thousand invaded and took, first Sicily, then the Neapolitan mainland. In that same year, Piedmont annexed Tuscany and the papal territory of Romagna in the month of March, then in September sent troops to occupy the papal territories of Umbria and the Marches. Pope Pius IX was now pinned up in Lazio, the small area around the city of Rome itself, surrounded by Italian unificationists on all three sides.

The new Kingdom of Italy proclaimed in March 1861 did not attack the church immediately. But then in 1866, in July and afterward, laws were passed suppressing most monastic orders, seizing their property, and also taking over all other church property not used specifically for religious purposes—a total of 1.7 billion lire worth of ecclesiastical property in all was dispossessed.

It was in this context that Pope Pius IX called the First Vatican Council into session. On 18 July 1870 the council approved the constitution *Pastor Aeternus*, which for the first time made it mandatory on all the Catholic faithful that they believe in the infallibility of the pope. The very next day, July 19, war broke out between France and Prussia; the French troops who had been guarding Rome had to be withdrawn. On September 20 the city surrendered to the invading Italian army. Pope Pius IX responded on 1 November 1870 by excommunicating all Italians who had approved or participated in the invasion and occupation of Rome.

His successor, Pope Leo XIII (1878–1903), issued the bull *Aeterni Patris* on 4 August 1879 in which the study of Thomas Aquinas was enjoined on all theological students. Leo's motives are not totally clear. There was a great Neo-Thomist revival in the sixteenth and seventeenth centuries, but in the eighteenth century and most of the nineteenth, this had shrunk to a handful of theologians, largely Italian, of limited influence.[59] Neverthless, in spite of the ease with which a papal bull could be ignored or quickly forgotten, Leo's public espousal of a return to Thomism in *Aeterni Patris* received rapid and widespread support not only among clergy but also among Roman Catholic intellectuals. He did argue in the encyclical that Catholic thought was, and always had been, unitary. Intellectual pluralism began only in the sixteenth century, Leo believed, and this had led inevitably to the theological and social chaos of his own time.[60]

The immediate question was what problems this mandatory Neo-Thomism might create for Roman Catholic scholars writing about the early church. The patristic period had been pluralistic and (obviously) non-Thomistic, yet publishing research on it could possibly be regarded as disloyalty to a severely threatened institutional system.

Louis Duchesne and Joseph Tixeront show what was and was not considered acceptable Roman Catholic historiography by the first decades of the twentieth century: Tixeront's *Histoire des dogmes* (1905–12) received the *Nihil obstat* and *Imprimatur*; Duchesne's *Histoire ancienne de l'église* was put on the Index in 1912, only a few years after it came out. Both are marvelously well done studies, extremely useful to scholars even today.

Duchesne was closely associated with the rise of the modernist movement in late nineteenth-century Roman Catholicism, although he distanced himself from some of its later developments. Modernism rejected Harnack's attempt to find the essence of Christianity by going behind the dogmatic accretions of later centuries to some primitive historical kernel (located of course for Harnack principally in the teaching, as he interpreted it, of the historical Jesus). Modernism instead took a teleological approach to history: the essence of Christianity was to be found in the fully developed church as it had grown under the guidance of the Spirit over the centuries following the coming of Christ.[61] Even if it could be argued that Jesus himself did not truly found a church or institute sacraments, these were in fact valid expressions of the developed Christian faith. The modernists however also tended to reject what they regarded as the sterile overintellectualism of scholastic philosophy, so they had no sympathy for the late nineteenth-century attempt to revive Thomism as the vehicle for the expression of Catholic faith.

To give an example of the way Duchesne worked, he did accept the Lutheran interpretation of the Apostle Paul's teaching as a more historically accurate reading of the text than the usual Roman Catholic accounts, but he rejected any notion that this conception of faith and law was binding on himself or any other Catholic Christian. The later Catholic tradition had accepted some of what Paul had said, but it had wisely modified other parts by almost universal consensus.[62] Duchesne likewise dealt with the apocalyptic elements in early Christian thought with healthy Gallic nonchalance: "St. Paul," he quippped, was at least "occasionally free from this obsession."[63] But he was also far more aware than Harnack that belief in the imminent end of the world extended deep into the second and third centuries. Duchesne's apparently rather free method in fact enabled him to describe accurately what was going on in early Christianity without having to fit it into a Procrustean system.[64]

Duchesne's spirit was basically antithetical to the nineteenth-century revival within Roman Catholicism of a rigid, scholastic, philosophical Thomism. He did not speak kindly in his history of the importation of Platonic philosophy into Christian teaching. One sees this negative influence, he comments, as early as Philo, "threatening to dissipate in philosophic dreams the old religion of the people of God."[65] Clement of Alexandria and Origen "attached too much importance to knowledge." They seemed to have believed that a person's knowledge of Platonic philosophy "increased his moral worth."[66]

Yet Duchesne was no Protestant, liberal or otherwise. The central importance of Rome was a de facto reality in early Christianity, Duchesne argued, leaving all theology aside. Figure after figure made the pilgrimage to Rome—Polycarp, Marcion, Valentinus, Justin, Tatian, Irenaeus.[67] "As soon as attention was directed to apostolic traditions, and the privileges connected with them, the Church of Rome is known to the whole of Christendom as the Church of St. Peter."[68]

On the other hand, Duchesne stated firmly that the church was governed in late apostolic times by councils of elders, not a monarchical episcopacy.[69] Only gradually, in the second century, did one member of this ruling council clearly become the presiding officer.[70] Although he believed that the evolution to a single governing bishop was to some degree a necessary process,[71] Duchesne made a strong plea for greater collegiality and less authoritarianism in the Roman Catholic church of his own time. He held out as a model instead the earliest Roman popes of the first and second centuries, who, he stated,

> must clearly be regarded as assisted, in the government of the Church, by a college of priests who shared the rule of the Christian community. . . . In the expressions of the time, the bishop does not always stand out very prominently from his college of assessors, nor were the clergy always differentiated from the rest of the congregation. . . . all that was done or said was the affair of the whole body, rather than of the leaders.[72]

Even less did Duchesne approve of a church totally controlled by the Vatican. He quoted the famous words of Cyprian, the third-century bishop of Carthage, reprimanding Pope Stephen for attempting to dictate to the Catholic bishops of North Africa:

> We judge no one, nor do we propose to put out of communion those who think otherwise. None of us wishes to pose as a Bishop of bishops, or to force the agreement of his fellows by a tyrannous terror. Every bishop, in the fulness of his liberty and authority, retains the right to think for himself; he is no more amenable to the judgment of another, than he is at liberty to judge others.[73]

At the time Duchesne was writing, however, Pope Pius X was surveying a series of further catastrophes for the Roman church. In 1905, the French government had begun to take possession of the remaining church property. In the Portuguese revolution of 1910, the teaching of religion in the schools was forbidden, the religious orders were expelled from the country and their properties confiscated. In Mexico the revolutionary 1906 manifesto of the Regeneration group had proclaimed that the hold of the Catholic church on their country had to be broken, and the Mexican constitution of 1917 would ultimately declare that the church could own no property in its own name. Pope Pius X put some of the modernist Loisy's books on the Index in 1903, formally condemned modernism in the decree *Lamentabili* and the encyclical *Pascendi* in 1907, excommunicated

Loisy after he continued to publish in 1908, and put Duchesne's *Histoire ancienne de l'église* on the Index in 1912.

It should be pointed out parenthetically that Roman Catholics had no monopoly during that period on attacking scholars who threatened the status quo. Protestants had their own way of doing this. Harnack's student Arthur Cushman McGiffert was driven out of the Presbyterian church here in the United States at around the same time, for example, by a series of church trials.[74]

But to return to the Catholic experience, Joseph Tixeront's *Histoire des dogmes* had, unlike Duchesne's history, ecclesiastical approval and success. It was an excellent piece of scholarly work, still very much worth studying today, for his careful treatment of a number of patristic figures. He cited a surprising amount of the same patristic data that Duchesne had, but handled it quite differently.[75]

Tixeront supported his church and the decisions that had been made several decades earlier and set up his general theological framework in line with the spirit of Pius IX and Leo XIII. He attacked Harnack by name, and appealed instead to the *Essay on the Development of Christian Doctrine* of John Henry Newman.[76] Against Harnack's concept of development, Tixeront in particular proclaimed the doctrine of "the substantial immutability of dogma."[77] The object of his history of dogmas was "to set before our eyes the intimate working of Christian thought on the primitive data of Revelation; a working by means of which it grasps them more and more fully; illustrates them and makes them fruitful, develops them; and finally marshals them into a harmonious and scholarly system without however—so Catholics hold—altering their substance."[78]

A dogma is a revealed truth, "which the faith of the Christian is obliged to accept." Dogmas are "but Revelation reduced to formulas."[79] Tixeront assumed (like Harnack) that dogmas were cast in Greek philosophical form from the time of the late second century, but he strongly defended this: "Christianity would never have conquered the world nor become a universal religion, had she not cast herself into the only form of thought that could then *and can still claim to be universal*:—the Hellenic form."[80] The italics are mine, but one must not miss the point that Tixeront was not only defending the assumption that patristic theologians cast the most important parts of their thought in Greek philosophic form but also defending the Thomistic revival initiated by Pope Leo XIII in 1879 as the Roman Catholic church's best defense against the forces of the Enlightenment.

Tixeront, like the majority of his fellow Roman Catholics, supported the call for a united Catholic front against the perils then threatening the church. He fully accepted the role of a strong papacy. One reads, for example, in a passage from the preface to the second volume of his *Histoire des dogmes*, dated October 1911, from Lyons, a strong declaration of total loyalty both to papal authority and the traditional dogmatic teaching of the church:

> Most of this work had been written before the Encyclical *Pascendi* appeared. After reading the Pontifical document and comparing it with my work, I found in the latter nothing that had to be changed or suppressed. Thank God, I needed not the doctrinal decision of Pius X to be reminded of the regard due to the Fathers of the Church, and I have always made my own the words of Newman: ". . . . Sooner may my right hand forget her cunning, and wither outright, . . . ere I should do aught but fall at their feet in love and in worship, . . . whose musical words were ever in my ears and on my tongue!"[81]

The special importance of Tixeront for this period is that he showed that patristics scholarship could be carried out successfully within Roman Catholicism if it was used to help rather than threaten the church.

In the next two generations patristics was the area where some of the brightest and best Roman Catholic theologians and historians chose to work. The work of the Jean Daniélous, Johannes Quastens, Polycarp Sherwoods, and scores of others, produced a real efflorescence of Roman Catholic patristics studies. Some of them worked primarily as Tixeront had to help support the idea of the development over the centuries of what eventually became the genius of Thomism. Others possibly went into patristics simply because one could be freer and more creative there—Neo-Thomism was such a well-articulated system that very little room for truly ground-breaking research was left.

As a result of the large quantity of excellent patristics scholarship pouring out between 1920 and 1960, without anyone even being fully aware of it there was an enormous underground shift in the real center of balance of Roman Catholic theology—a shift from the thirteenth century to something more like the third or perhaps the fourth century. When the Second Vatican Council met from 1962 to 1965 and produced so many massive changes in the Roman Catholic church, Marcia Colish has insightfully observed the way in which "so many of the council's documents were framed in biblical and patristic, rather than scholastic, language."[82] Significantly, when the Roman mass was totally revised as a result of the

Second Vatican Council, it was to fit patristic rather than medieval models. The underground shift going on between 1920 and 1960 had surfaced in an entirely new, more patristics-oriented Catholicism, and the effects are still being felt today.

A third major group who have contributed greatly to patristics scholarship over the past one hundred years have been the Anglicans. As a result of the Oxford movement many nineteenth-century Anglicans had come to see many aspects of both the patristic and medieval church as a norm for Christian belief and practice.

One can see the spirit of the Anglican approach clearly in J. F. Bethune-Baker's *Introduction to the Early History of Christian Doctrine* (1903), an important example of turn-of-the-century English patristics scholarship.[83] Bethune-Baker believed that true Catholicism in no way meant that one had to adhere to some rigid, monolithic, universally mandatory system of dogmatic interpretations. One should be able to hold "different opinions without loss of the rights of communion—opposite points of view without disloyalty to the Catholic Creeds and the Church."[84] He was well aware of the impact of the current historical-critical methodology on biblical studies and knew that one had to leave room for interpretation there as well. One could "no longer make the portentous assumption that the Gospels are a photographic representation in writing of the actual facts of our Lord's life and the very words of His teaching."[85] But patristic theology could help the biblical theologian maintain his balance. It gave advance warning of some of the dangers inherent in the more radical German New Testament scholarship of that time: "the semi-conscious Ebionism and the semi-conscious Docetism . . . of much professedly Christian thought today" had been tried before, he said, back in the early church, and the ultimate consensus of early Christianity itself had been that such approaches were inadequate to a proper profession of the Christian faith.[86] In many ways in fact, patristic theology seemed firmer ground to many Anglicans of that time than biblical studies, where so much had recently been turned upside down.

There was in Bethune-Baker a commitment to what the English call "common sense." This was a more complicated concept than might appear at first glance. It meant to be sure a profound scepticism about basing life upon the furthermost flights of abstract academic theory. But as historiographical principle, it also meant a commitment to the proposition that the range of ordinary human motivation and everyday human concern did not vary that much over the course of human history—only the outward forms changed.

The English commitment to tradition was also there in Bethune-Baker as well. Although, he said, we may not be bound to the strict letter of every single pronouncement that patristic theology made, in another sense,

> The work of the great leaders of Christian thought in the interpretation of the Gospel during the earlier ages can never be superseded. They were called upon, in turn, to meet and to consider in relation to the Gospel and to Jesus Christ nearly all the theories of the world and God which human speculation and experience have framed in the mystery of human life; and the conclusions which they reached must still be at least the starting-point for any further advance towards more complete solution of the problems with which they had to deal.[87]

Anglican scholars were willing to treat patristic issues critically, but they were deeply committed to taking them seriously.

The contributions of Anglican patristic scholarship continued over the many decades that followed. When I was a student at Oxford in the 1960s, for example, one could see such scholars as J. N. D. Kelly, wearing a pair of half glasses perched on his nose, poring over volumes in the Bodleian Library as he worked on the next edition of his *Early Christian Doctrines*. That (still standard) survey had been originally intended, in spite of the difference in format, as an up-dated version of Bethune-Baker's now half-century-old *Introduction to the Early History of Christian Doctrine*, invoking the memory and scholarship of Harnack and Tixeront as well.[88]

Henry Chadwick was also there at Oxford, as Regius Professor of Divinity. He had recently published (in 1953) his edition of Origen's *Contra Celsum*, displaying his enormous knowledge of the Greek classics in hundreds of explanatory footnotes, and was just finishing his contributions on Philo, Justin Martyr, Clement of Alexandria, and Origen for *The Cambridge History of Later Greek and Early Medieval Philosophy*.[89] Harnack's insistence that one had to know the Greco-Hellenistic world in order to understand the early Christian world was quite true, and Chadwick showed what could be done by a scholar who knew both worlds so well. Yet when I, as a brash young graduate student, blithely stated the Baur-Harnack assumption about the decay of first-century Christian presuppositions in the second century (referring to apocalyptic beliefs and the like), Chadwick calmly told me not to take that theory quite so seriously and to go to the library and read some patristic commentaries on Daniel, from *any* period of early Christian history.

During that same era, S. L. Greenslade, the Regius Professor of Ecclesiastical History at Oxford, had just finished (in 1964) the second edition of his *Schism in the Early Church*, where the English "common sense" approach was used so beautifully to display the delicate nuances within the various causal factors operating in any particular rupture. Some of the causes, in his analysis, were in fact genuinely theological or ecclesiastical: diversity in worship, for example, and problems of Christian discipline and standards of moral purity. But other causes were better described as secular, social, or psychological: nationalistic movements and socioeconomic tensions disguised under theological language, political rivalry between leading churches, and sometimes, unfortunately, a simple personal rivalry between two strongheaded individuals that eventually triggered a major, long-lasting ecclesiastical schism.[90]

The American scholar, Robert M. Grant, who for many years held the key patristics chair at the University of Chicago, should also be listed among the Anglicans. He first made his reputation as one of the pioneers of the revolution in Gnostic studies that took place in the 1950s and 1960s. Two of his most important works still appear on almost every bibliography of scholarly works on the Gnostic movement.[91] His work on *Eusebius as Church Historian* is one of the basic studies that has helped produce a coherent dating of Eusebius' writings, which in turn has helped produce such a startling reevaluation of Eusebius over the past decade or so.[92] Grant's slightly earlier book on *Early Christianity and Society* showed other facets of his thought, including his detailed knowledge not just of classical literary texts but also of the concrete structure of Greco-Roman society.[93]

In that work, Grant's very Anglican notion of "common sense" set him squarely against some of the other patristics scholars writing on the social history of early Christianity. He argued that early Christian communities were not predominately made up of the marginal poor, caught in a powerless fringe area of Greco-Roman society, who then sublimated their anxieties in apocalyptic dreams. Instead one saw, again and again, solid members of the artisan and middle class, worrying about taxes, compulsively committed to the work ethic and not squandering money on fancy luxuries (which presupposed they had money that could have been spent on such things), concerned with "looking respectable" in the eyes of their pagan neighbors, rarely criticizing slavery or any other prevalent institution, and simply assuming authoritarian Roman models of government for both secular and religious institutions.

Another major religious group that has contributed to patristics scholarship is Eastern Orthodoxy. In terms of works in widely read modern Western languages, their output has been comparatively small, but it is vitally important that these works be more generally studied. Vladimir Lossky's writings, for example, are easily accessible to the Western Christian reader. Forced to leave Russia in 1922, he had to learn to express Orthodox theological ideas to French and American audiences who knew little of that part of the Christian world. His superb little book, *The Vision of God*, begins with Irenaeus in the second century and concludes with Gregory Palamas in the fourteenth, showing a trajectory of thought totally unfamiliar to too many Western-oriented patristics scholars.[94]

The Orthodox force us to see that all patristic literature is not simply a prolegomenon to Augustine, Thomas Aquinas, and Luther. There is an entire independent and coherent world of thought there in the Greek theologians of the patristic period, where one speaks of the vision of God and the image of God, of free will and human solidarity, of participation in the cosmic liturgy and re-creation in the hypostasis of God the Word, and of a human fallenness that (just as in the old Greek tragedies) is produced by some terrible blinding of the understanding rather than by a defect in the will. Eastern Orthodox theologians can help all of us in the field to see better how to "cut with the grain" of what was really going on in early Greek patristic thought. The new availability, beginning in the mid-twentieth century, of increasing numbers of Eastern Orthodox studies of patristic figures, is one of the most significant, still largely unassimilated, developments in modern patristics scholarship.

What can be said about the more evangelical or "low church" wing of Protestant Christianity? My own teacher Albert C. Outler, who is well known for his work as a theologian, a Wesley scholar, and an important figure in the ecumenical movement as well, did a good deal of work during the middle of the twentieth century to get Methodists to take patristics studies more seriously, with some significant success. There are some quite good patristics scholars scattered here and there among the Southern Baptists, Disciples of Christ, and other evangelical denominations. But one wishes that there were a good many more, with at least some of them asking a totally different set of questions than those that traditionally have been asked by more Catholic-oriented scholars. Why should the history of the patristic period be only a history of dogma, liturgical rituals, and monasticism? E. Glenn Hinson's *Evangelization of the Roman Empire*, for example, asks us to study what is also a totally appropriate question, and a quite consequential one indeed—what was the role of evangelism and preaching in patristic Christianity?[95]

An ancient bishop like Paul of Samosata or John Chrysostom often got his real power from the simple fact that he could preach a rousing good sermon. In this regard, Timothy E. Gregory's *Vox Populi* also begins to raise some of the same questions about the way the fourth- and fifth-century church really functioned.[96] No emperor, Gregory observes, could depose with impunity a popular bishop who had won the loyalty of his flock, and no emperor in the century he studied ever managed to destroy a well-developed popular movement among the general Christian population, no matter how much persecution or how many imperial troops he used. Patristics scholarship must start asking more questions of this sort about evangelism, preaching, missions, popular Christian resistance to imperial attempts to control their purely theological beliefs, and the like. Our knowledge of the patristics period will be the richer for it.

The preceding scholars were all looking at the patristic period from within a theological framework. But as early as the eighteenth century, Edward Gibbon had shown that one could write an account of that period from a totally nonreligious standpoint. Chapters 15 and 16 in volume 1 of his *Decline and Fall of the Roman Empire* created a scandal when they first appeared in 1776. He accounted for the spread and eventual success of the Christian movement totally on what would now be called sociological and psychological grounds. In this survey of the development of patristics scholarship over the last hundred years, it will therefore be necessary to speak as well of three different nonreligious traditions of writing on early Christianity. Let us call them loosely the psychological, the sociological, and the classical/postclassical studies traditions.

The psychological tradition as it has developed over the last hundred years has been deeply indebted to William James' *Varieties of Religious Experience* in terms of basic approach.[97] James' method throughout the bulk of the book was simply to give a purely phenomenological account of how people of various types and categories actually described their religious experiences, putting this in their own words whenever possible, without making any judgments as to the truth or falsity of those beliefs. The most important task of the investigator was to develop appropriate categories and to show the internal psychological dynamic of each basic type.

In 1933 Arthur Darby Nock, in his book *Conversion*, showed the power of this technique in dealing with the patristic period.[98] Essential to the methodology was the refusal to discriminate per se between "Christian" religious experience and "pagan" religious experience, as though they were totally different phenomena. E. R. Dodds, a master of the classical and late antique philosophical world, expanded Nock's analysis further in 1951 in his *Pagan and Christian in an Age of Anxiety*.[99] There he acknowledged, as had Nock, that Augustine gave us perhaps the fullest personal account from the early period of a Christian's experience of religious conversion.

It is in this context, I believe, that Peter Brown's *Augustine of Hippo: A Biography* should properly be placed.[100] When this book first appeared in 1967, it created instant fame for the young Brown, who showed himself, by his erudition and insight, to be one of the most knowledgeable people in the field. There is the possibility that he may come to be regarded, a hundred years from now, as having been in many ways as archetypal a representative of the present period as Harnack was of his. Brown has also been greatly admired by the sociologists of religion (about which more later), but his Augustine biography belongs basically more in the psychological tradition.

Brown had the advantage of having had a practicing psychiatrist for his first wife. He knew how good psychological counselors actually did their everyday work, which is very different from the oversimplified popular approach seen in Erik Erikson's published analysis of Martin Luther. Brown listened as a good clinical psychologist does, with the "third ear." Augustine originally came from the North African hinterland, he noted, and he never totally escaped that point of view—even in later years, although bishop by that time of an important port city, Augustine "almost never mentioned the sea in his sermons." Or Brown will comment on the deep psychological need apparent in the fact that Augustine was "never alone"— even his conversion experience was in a garden filled with his friends.

Brown's *Augustine of Hippo* was not only good psychology and psychiatry, it was also one of the most highly acclaimed works of Late Roman historical scholarship produced within our own generation. But perhaps the most important thing about his work, and his unique personality, was that he showed the patristic period filled with real people rather than just mere names who created abstract dogmas.

Another way of analyzing the patristic period—the sociological approach—has risen to special prominence in the last two decades or so. In the basic sense, there is nothing new here—Gibbon did it, and the Marxist historians, and Arnold Toynbee with his theory of early Christianity as the religion of an internally seceded proletariat. But in the last couple of decades or so, a large number of quite fascinating sociological studies have appeared, principally in the United States, building on earlier analyses by those sociologists of religion who worked on nineteenth- and twentieth- century sectarian movements like the Seventh-day Adventists and Jamaican eschatological cults. The investigation of socially conditioned attitudes toward property and wealth has also been important in this new approach. There is not room in this brief survey even to begin to mention all the excellent monographs that have appeared, in the 1970s and 1980s in particular. Two good examples however would be John G. Gager's *Kingdom and Community: The Social World of Early Christianity,* and L.

William Countryman, *The Rich Christian in the Church of the Early Empire: Contradictions and Accommodations.*[101]

From this point of view, earliest Christianity often appears as a typical sectarian, millenarian movement, obviously similar in its basic structure to many nineteenth- and twentieth-century movements that we can study in more detail. One sees it mutate into typical second- and third-generation forms. At all times, one sees early Christians immersed in a real human society, where kinship ties, social status, power, earning a livelihood, and dealing with surplus wealth form real human issues. This is a methodology that has shed light already on many interesting phenomena of early Christianity and will of necessity form part of the overall scholarly perspective on early Christianity in years to come.

Some of Peter Brown's work in the 1970s and 1980s illustrates a slightly different way of approaching Christianity from a sociological perspective, one more indebted to that variety of social anthropology that studies primitive tribal structures and so-called primitive religious practices, and influenced as well by the studies that have recently been appearing (done by a long list of good secular historians) of popular culture in the early modern period. In the early 1970s, his seminal article on "The Rise and Function of the Holy Man in Late Antiquity" laid out one major theme he was to continue to pursue. Earlier work by social anthropologists like Rudolf Otto and Mircea Eliade on the primitive concept of the holy lay in the background here. Brown's article in 1970 on "Sorcery, Demons and the Rise of Christianity: From Late Antiquity into the Middle Ages" showed other themes, including his constant pursuit of linkages between religious belief and shifts in the power structures of human societies.[102] His books and his influence have been, and continue to be, as important in the social anthropological study of early Christianity and in the study of the connection between early Christianity and popular culture, as his earlier work on Augustine had been.[103]

Another important part of the social and cultural world of early Christianity, which was (until the 1970s and 1980s) strangely and unconscionably left out of the account of early Christianity, is the topic of women in the early church. Fortunately, a whole host of studies are now beginning to emerge into print: Elizabeth Schüssler-Fiorenza's *In Memory of Her*, Elizabeth Clark's *Jerome, Chrysostom, and Friends*, Roger Gryson's *Ministry of Women in the Early Church*, and Jean Laporte's *Role of Women in Early Christianity* are excellent examples of recent work.[104] The socioeconomic system of the ancient world tended to push women out of view, no matter how brilliant and articulate, and no matter how much influence they in fact had in the establishing of key monasteries, the furthering of theological scholarship, and the creating of doctrinal positions. Recovering some knowledge of what they accomplished takes patient digging and an attention to detail, but it is vital that the real and important role of women in the early church be given its rightful place in all future studies of the period.

To move to an entirely different area, scholars within the fields of classical and postclassical studies who have traditionally been concerned with the purely secular study of Graeco-Roman literature, politics, and institutions have been writing far more on early Christianity during the past several decades, and far more of that work has been of the highest quality. If one goes back to the latter nineteenth century, one can see how different things used to be. At that time, histories of Rome and its empire were written for the most part as though Christianity was only a peripheral and totally negligible part of the Roman world, even though the Romans themselves very clearly found it a deeply disturbing and disconcerting phenomenon.

The one place however where secular historiography had to deal with Christianity even in the late nineteenth century was in the figure of Constantine. In that era, one interpretation often encountered was the attempt to regard him as a manipulative politician who feigned conversion to Christianity with the shrewd knowledge that he could use it as an ideology to bind his fragmented empire together. There was also a tendency at the end of the nineteenth century for many secular historians to assume out of hand that any documents purporting to show that Constantine was a Christian (such as the many letters from his hand) were "obviously" later forgeries.[105] And studies by purely secular historians and classicists on Christian figures prior to the Constantinian era were rare.

Starting in the 1930s and 1940s, more and better studies began to appear however, for example, Charles Norris Cochrane's excellent *Christianity and Classical Culture*.[106] With each succeeding decade, more works written from a predominantly secular standpoint appeared, including many truly excellent and sensitive studies. Some were basically secular studies of Christian topics, while others were works by classicists and Byzantinists in which Christianity was treated as a serious part of the overall account: for example, W. H. C. Frend's *Donatist Church: A Movement of Protest in Roman North Africa* in 1952, the volume Arnaldo Momigliano edited on *The Conflict between Paganism and Christianity in the Fourth Century* in 1963, Francis Dvornik's *Early Christian and Byzantine Political Philosophy* in 1966, F. E. Peters' *Harvest of Hellenism: A History of the Near East from Alexander the Great to the Triumph of Christianity* in 1970, and A. E. Cameron's *Circus Factions: Blues and Greens at Rome and Byzantium* in 1976.

After doing his impressive studies of *The Art of Persuasion in Greece* and *The Art of Rhetoric in the Roman World, 300 B.C.–A.D. 300*, the eminent classicist George Kennedy then produced two further volumes, *Greek Rhetoric under Christian Emperors* in 1983 and *New Testament Interpretation through Rhetorical Criticism* in 1984. The beautifully done work by Robin Lane Fox, *Pagans and Christians*, which just came out in 1987, should perhaps be included in this category also, though it has links to the methodology of Nock and Dodds as well. Fox's book seems likely to become one of the classics in this area.[107]

On the figure of Constantine, the hypercritical approach of the late nineteenth century began to turn into a more balanced treatment. A. H. M. Jones' article in 1954, "Notes on the Genuineness of the Constantinian Documents in Eusebius' Life of Constantine,"[108] can be contrasted with Henri Grégoire's article, only sixteen years earlier, which he entitled "Eusèbe n'est pas l'auteur de la 'Vita Constantini' dans sa forme actuelle et Constantin ne s'est pas 'converti' en 312."[109] By 1976, a classicist like H. A. Drake was publishing *In Praise of Constantine: A Historical Study and New Translation of Eusebius' Tricennial Orations* in which he observed that the Christians, even after their triumph, were still trying to extend an olive branch of peace to one wing of the neo-pagan party.[110] Timothy Barnes' *Constantine and Eusebius* and *The New Empire of Diocletian and Constantine* were masterpieces of secular historiography, showing the truly excellent work going on by the 1980s.[111]

It is extremely important that the gap is now being bridged between theologically oriented patristics studies on the one side and the work of scholars trained in psychology of religion, sociology of religion, and general classical and postclassical studies on the other side. The mandatory divisions and cleavages of Harnack's day are almost totally absent now, a hundred years later, and this is entirely for the best. Obviously, a scholar who holds a strong religious position will not always agree with one who attempts to maintain a totally secular viewpoint. Some of those using psychology of religion or sociology of religion as a tool are in fact attempting to "explain away" much of early Christian belief, where the content of religious faith is interpreted as only a symbolic expression of totally this-worldly social forces or of internal human psychological states. One cannot invoke the name of both God and Durkheim simultaneously (or God and Freud either) to explain the same aspect of the same religious phenomenon. But there are so many areas of overlap, where different levels of the same phenomenon can be seen to be arising from different kinds of forces, and so many opportunities as well for cross-fertilization of ideas, that the present blurring of the boundaries is still far better than the old impenetrable walls. What has come about in the 1980s is producing better historiography in all camps.

No survey of this sort could be complete without looking at some of the new discoveries and new topics for investigation that have appeared in the past century. The most major was of course the revolution in Gnostic studies produced by the discovery of a large collection of Gnostic treatises at Nag Hammadi in Egypt in 1945–46. For the first time, the scholarly world had a sizable body of material from within this controversial movement itself, instead of having to rely almost exclusively on hostile accounts of Gnostic belief from orthodox Christian writers.

Harnack's conception of the Gnostics, expressed over half a century before the discovery of the Nag Hammadi corpus so changed our perception of these theologians, is well known: "the Gnostic systems represent the acute secularising or hellenising of Christianity, with the rejection of the Old Testament; while the Catholic system, on the other hand, represents a gradual process of the same kind, with the conservation of the Old Testament."[112] To Harnack, any elements of ancient Near Eastern myth in Gnosticism were merely surface phenomena. Down at its core, Gnosticism represented a total triumph of the Hellenic spirit: "with regard to the most important Gnostic systems the words hold true, 'The hands are the hands of Esau, but the voice is the voice of Jacob.' "[113]

A reaction back the other way soon sprang up, seen clearly in such works as Hans Jonas' *Gnosis und spätantiker Geist*.[114] Jonas regarded Gnosticism as a resurfacing of ancient Near Eastern ideas and attitudes that had somehow continued to survive for several centuries at some subliterate level after the triumph of Hellenism in the fourth century B.C. had forced these ideas out of the literature of the educated elite. The discovery of the Nag Hammadi corpus in 1945–46 pushed this reaction even further, so that it soon became the fashion to preface books on Gnosticism with trenchant attacks on Harnack's assessment of the movement.[115] The Greek elements in Gnosticism were played down, and the principal question was regarded to be whether Gnosticism had its roots in some pre-Christian, non-Jewish gnosis (as many German scholars argued) or in heterodox Judaism (as most English scholarship argued).

The pendulum may now be swinging back again, at least part of the way. Compared to the school textbook versions of Plato and Aristotle, Gnosticism looks very strange indeed. But to a scholar who knows the world of Pythagorean pseudepigrapha, Porphyry's *On the Cave of the Nymphs*, and ancient commentaries on Plato's *Timaeus* and Cicero's *Dream of Scipio*, the Gnostics begin to look less strange. Significantly, the best current book on the strange world of first- and second-century Hellenistic philosophy, by John Dillon, places the Gnostics under the category of "the Platonic underworld."[116]

Elaine Pagels' *Gnostic Paul: Gnostic Exegesis of the Pauline Letters* has recently shown other fruitful avenues of research.[117] Part of the debate between the Gnostics and the more orthodox Christian theologians was over the exegesis of large numbers of specific scriptural passages. Pagels shows the detailed knowledge that can be gained of Gnostic exegesis by analyzing the anti-Gnostic arguments in orthodox Christian scriptural commentaries of the period. One could argue that this produces yet a different view of Gnosticism, as basically a biblical hermeneutic *manqué*.

Other major new texts have been discovered also. In 1916, R. H. Connolly showed that the supposed *Egyptian Church Order* contained in a Latin codex in the cathedral library at Verona was in fact the *Apostolic Tradition* of Hippolytus, which meant that one now had a detailed description of the actual rites of the Church of Rome at the beginning of the third century, together with a sample of the actual kind of wording used in the all-important eucharistic prayer.[118] All of the massive changes made later in the twentieth century in the Roman Catholic mass and the Anglican communion liturgy derive from that discovery, with profound effects on the liturgies of many other Christian communions as well.

The actual ideas of Nestorius, another extremely important figure, suddenly became accessible for the first time in other than fragmentary and misleading form, around 1895, with the discovery of the the so-called *Bazaar of Heracleides*, which was in reality a collection of some of Nestorius' own writings, preserved by some ancient sympathizer who deliberately put a new title on the manuscript to save it from the bookburners. J. F. Bethune- Baker brought this new find to the general notice of the scholarly world in 1908 in his *Nestorius and His Teaching*.[119] This has had a profound effect on the modern understanding of the fifth-century christological controversy. Nestorius now appears more as the victim of rivalries between powerful patriarchal sees than he does as a "heretic," which he was not in any real sense at all.

At the end of the seventeenth century, Gottfried Arnold had declared in his *Unparteiische Kirchen- und Ketzer-Historie* (1699–1700) that church history should not be restricted to the history of the "orthodox" alone. It took many generations for his plea to be seriously heard. Although some nineteenth-century Lutheran church historians had a fondness for Marcion, it has not been until the twentieth century that truly large numbers of careful and sympathetic studies of nonorthodox and repudiated teachers like Nestorius and the Gnostics have begun to appear, where these theologians are looked at from within, and where they are not constantly subjected to evaluation from the external perspective of later orthodox belief. Robert Evans' work on Pelagius, Robert Gregg and Dennis Groh's study of Arius, Thomas Kopecek's book on Aetius and Eunomius, and Henry Chadwick's biography of Priscillian would be additional excellent examples of highly revealing work of this sort done during the last three decades.[120]

Patristics studies is a vital and lively field here at the end of the twentieth century. Over the past hundred years it has enormously expanded its scope and its understanding of the different ways in which its materials can be interpreted. Our understanding of early Christianity has become enormously much clearer, richer, and less bound by old walls of prejudice and preconception. If one supposed that, by the craft of someone like the great Odysseus, the ghost of Harnack could be brought back to life today, it would take some time for a person even of his considerable energy and ability to read through even the major works that have appeared since his death.[121] But in spite of having used him repeatedly as a point of contrast in the preceding pages, he was also an enormously competent and honest reader of an ancient text, and one who preached above all a spirit of tolerance and freedom of inquiry and thought. One imagines that Harnack's ghost would be greatly surprised, by the more recent scholarship in particular. But I still cannot think that he would not be, secretly, deeply pleased at where we, his successors, have arrived today.

Notes

1. Part of the research for this article was carried out at Boston University during my year there as visiting professor of history and theology in 1984–85. I wish to thank Howard Clark Kee, chairman of the Graduate Division of Religious and Theological Studies; Richard D. Nesmith, dean of the School of Theology; and Thomas F. Glick, chairman of the Department of History, for helping make my year there so pleasant.

2. Adolf von Harnack, *Lehrbuch der Dogmengeschichte* (Freiburg i.B.: Mohr, 1886–89). English translation, *History of Dogma*, from the 3d ed. by N. Buchanan et al., 7 vols., 1894–99; rpt. in 4 vols. (New York: Dover Publications, 1961). Agnes von Zahn-Harnack, *Adolf von Harnack*, 2d ed. (Berlin: W. de Gruyter, 1951), is the standard biography, written by his daughter. See also G. Wayne Glick, *The Reality of Christianity: A Study of Adolf von Harnack as Historian and Theologian* (New York: Harper and Row, 1967), and Wilhelm Pauck, *Harnack and Troeltsch: Two Historical Theologians* (New York: Oxford University Press, 1968).

3. Originally co-edited with Oscar von Gebhardt, *Texte und Untersuchungen zur Geschichte der altchristlichen Literatur* (Leipzig: J. C. Hinrichs, 1882–).

4. Adolf von Harnack, *Das Wesen des Christentums* (Leipzig: J. C. Hinrichs, 1900). English translation, *What Is Christianity?* by T. B. Saunders (London: Williams and Norgate, 1901).

5. Harnack, *History of Dogma* 1:17.

6. Ibid., 21–22, cf. 46–47. In *What Is Christianity?* 201–3, one can see that for Harnack "Greek philosophy" meant Platonism, and above all the concept of the Logos.

7. *History of Dogma* 1:9, 15, 18, 53; cf. *What Is Christianity?* 211.

8. *History of Dogma* 1:71.

9. *What Is Christianity?* 193. Cf. Kant's famous essay "What Is Enlightenment?" for the reference to tutelage.

10. *What Is Christianity?* 229.

11. Ibid., 238.

12. Ibid., 264.

13. Ibid., 267, 269.

14. The official title of what came to be called the *Magdeburg Centuries* was *Ecclesiastica Historia, integram Ecclesiae Christi ideam, . . . secundum singulas centurias . . . per aliquot studiosos et pios viros in urbe Magdeburgica*, written and published under the supervision of the radically intolerant Serbo-Croa-

tian Lutheran Matthias Flacius (Matija Vlacic, 1520–75). See Ferdinand Christian Baur, *The Epochs of Church Historiography*, in *Ferdinand Christian Baur on the Writing of Church History*, ed. and trans. Peter C. Hodgson (New York: Oxford University Press, 1968), chap. 2, sec. 1, 79–105 (including 82–83n); Robert L. Wilken, *The Myth of Christian Beginnings: History's Impact on Belief* (Garden City, NY: Doubleday, 1971), chap. 5; and Albert C. Outler, "The Idea of 'Development' in the History of Christian Doctrine: A Comment," in *Schools of Thought in the Christian Tradition*, ed. Patrick Henry (Philadelphia: Fortress Press, 1984), 7–14.

15. Peter C. Hodgson, *The Formation of Historical Theology: A Study of Ferdinand Christian Baur* (New York: Harper and Row, 1966), esp. 22–24, 204, 207–10; also Hodgson's introduction and notes to *Ferdinand Christian Baur on the Writing of Church History*, esp. 11, 33. See also Robert William Mackay, *The Tübingen School and Its Antecedents: A Review of the History and Present Condition of Modern Theology* (Edinburgh: Williams and Norgate, 1863).

16. Philip Hefner, introduction (1–50) to Albrecht Ritschl, *Three Essays*, trans. Philip Hefner (Philadelphia: Fortress Press, 1972), 7–8.

17. Ibid., 4.

18. Ibid., 12–13.

19. Ibid., 13.

20. Karl Barth, *Protestant Theology in the Nineteenth Century: Its Background and History*, trans. B. Cozens and J. Bowden (London: SCM Press, 1972), was more than a little unfair however in describing Ritschl (656) as "the very epitome of the national-liberal German bourgeois of the age of Bismarck."

21. Bonn: Adolph Marcus, 1850; 2d rev. ed., 1857.

22. Hefner, introduction to Ritschl, *Three Essays* 9 and 25. Cf. Barth, *Protestant Theology in the Nineteenth Century*, 654.

23. Bonn: A. Marcus, 1870-74. English translation of vol. 1 appeared as *A Critical History of the Christian Doctrine of Justification and Reconciliation*, trans. J. S. Black (Edinburgh: Edmonston and Douglas, 1872). Vol. 3 appeared as *The Christian Doctrine of Justification and Reconciliation: The Positive Development of the Doctrine*, ed. H. R. Mackintosh and A. B. Macaulay (Edinburgh: T. and T. Clark, 1900).

24. The 1st ed. appeared in the same vol. as the 2d ed. of Ritschl's *Unterricht in der christlichen Religion* (Bonn: Adolph Marcus, 1881). English translation as "Theology and Metaphysics," in Albrecht Ritschl, *Three Essays*, trans. Philip Hefner, 149–217 (Philadelphia: Fortress Press, 1972). See also Hugh Ross Mackintosh, *Types of Modern Theology: Schleiermacher to Barth* (London: Nisbet, 1937), 5, "The Theology of Moral Values: Albrecht Ritschl," 138–80, esp. 142–49.

25. Ritschl, "Theology and Metaphysics," 152, 184.

26. Rudolf Hermann Lotze (1817–81), author of *Metaphysik*, 2d ed. (Leipzig: S.

Hirzel, 1884); English translation, *Metaphysic*, by B. Bosanquet (Oxford: Clarendon Press, 1884). See Hefner's introduction to Ritschl's *Three Essays* 27 and 31.

27. Ritschl, "Theology and Metaphysics," 179–87.

28. The entire reaction to the study of church history during this period is investigated in Henry Warner Bowden, *Church History in the Age of Science: Historiographical Patterns in the United States, 1876–1918* (Chapel Hill: University of North Carolina Press, 1971).

29. Bowden, 35, 43, 45, 60, 62–63, 66–67. It was Ferdinand C. Baur and, above all, August Neander from whom Schaff had learned (42, 53).

30. Significantly, the next great American church historian to deal with the patristic period, Arthur Cushman McGiffert, had earned his doctorate at Marburg under Adolf von Harnack (Bowden, 137).

31. Harnack, *History of Dogma* 1:17.

32. Werner Jaeger, *Early Christianity and Greek Paideia* (Cambridge, MA: Harvard University Press, 1962).

33. Dennis E. Groh, "Changing Points of View in Patristic Scholarship," *Anglican Theological Review* 60 (1978): 447–65.

34. G. Christopher Stead, *Divine Substance* (Oxford: Clarendon Press, 1977), on the concept of *ousia* from Plato to Athanasius.

35. John M. Dillon, *The Middle Platonists, 80 B.C. to A.D. 220* (Ithaca: Cornell University Press, 1977). Harnack was acutely aware of his own lack of knowledge of those Hellenistic philosophers who were actually contemporary to the patristic theologians he studied (*History of Dogma* 1: x), but he does not seem to have acknowledged the potentially fatal aspect of the general methodological flaw inherent in his usual assumption that a philosophical term in, say, Athanasius in the fourth century A.D., meant the same thing it had meant to Plato seven centuries earlier.

36. Rosemary Radford Ruether, *Gregory of Nazianzus: Rhetor and Philosopher* (Oxford: Clarendon Press, 1969); Robert Dick Sider, *Ancient Rhetoric and the Art of Tertullian* (Oxford: Oxford University Press, 1971); Robert C. Gregg, *Consolation Philosophy: Greek and Christian Paideia in Basil and the Two Gregories* (Philadelphia: Philadelphia Patristic Foundation, 1975).

37. Groh, "Changing Points of View in Patristic Scholarship," 455, 458. Glenn F. Chesnut, *The First Christian Histories: Eusebius, Socrates, Sozomen, Theodoret and Evagrius* (Paris: Editions Beauchesne, 1977); 2d rev. ed. (Macon, GA: Mercer University Press, 1986).

38. Glanville Downey, "The Perspective of the Early Church Historians," *Greek, Roman, and Byzantine Studies* 6 (1965): 57–70; Arnaldo Momigliano, "Pagan and Christian Historiography in the Fourth Century A.D.," in *The Conflict between Paganism and Christianity in the Fourth Century*, ed. Arnaldo Momigliano, 79–99 (Oxford: Clarendon Press, 1963).

39. New Haven: Yale University Press, 1984.

40. J. N. D. Kelly, *Early Christian Doctrines*, 3d ed. (London: Adam and Charles Black, 1965), 381, still gives the older interpretation, reading Gregory's idea of human nature as an example of "Platonic realism." But a Platonic idea could not turn all the disparate individuals that participated in that idea into "a single living being," as Gregory put it. See Glenn F. Chesnut, *Images of Christ: An Introduction to Christology* (San Francisco: Harper and Row/Seabury, 1984) 113–15.

41. Chesnut, *Images of Christ*, 153. The christological sense was originally borrowed from an analogy used in the preceding century by Gregory of Nyssa in his trinitarian treatise *Ad Ablabium quod non sint tres dii*, PG 45:125.

42. Roberta C. Chesnut, *Three Monophysite Christologies: Severus of Antioch, Philoxenus of Mabbug, and Jacob of Sarug* (Oxford: Oxford University Press, 1976).

43. Jean Daniélou, *The Development of Christian Doctrine before the Council of Nicaea*, vol. 1, *The Theology of Jewish Christianity*, trans. and ed. J. A. Baker (London: Darton, Longman and Todd, 1964), 1–3; original French ed., 1958.

44. Ibid., 4.

45. Glenn F. Chesnut, *The First Christian Histories*, chap. 6 (1st ed.), chap. 7 (2d ed.), "Eusebius: Hellenistic Kingship and the Eschatological Constantine."

46. See, e.g., E. Dinkler, "Ticonius," in Pauly-Wissowa, *Real- Encyclopädie*, Zweite Reihe 6.1 (1936): 849–56. The serious study of Tyconius had already started during the late nineteenth century.

47. One of the best-known studies is by Norman Cohn, *The Pursuit of the Millennium*, 2d ed. (New York: Harper, 1961).

48. Bernard McGinn, *Visions of the End: Apocalyptic Traditions in the Middle Ages* (New York: Columbia University Press, 1979); *Apocalyptic Spirituality: Treatises and Letters of Lactantius, Adso of Montier-en-Der, Joachim of Fiore, the Franciscan Spirituals, Savonarola* (New York: Paulist Press, 1979).

49. Willis A. Shotwell, *The Biblical Exegesis of Justin Martyr* (London: SPCK, 1965), 94–99.

50. Rowan A. Greer, *The Captain of Our Salvation: A Study in the Patristic Exegesis of Hebrews* (Tübingen: Mohr, 1973). Maurice F. Wiles, *The Divine Apostle: The Interpretation of St. Paul's Epistles in the Early Church* (Cambridge: Cambridge University Press, 1967).

51. The genuine exegetical dimension in this sense was also recognized clearly in Robert C. Gregg and Dennis E. Groh, *Early Arianism—A View of Salvation* (Philadelphia: Fortress, 1981). The older approach still intrudes into Ralph E. Person, *The Mode of Theological Decision Making at the Early Ecumenical Councils: An Inquiry into the Function of Scripture and Tradition at the Councils of Nicaea and Ephesus*, Theologischen Dissertationen 14 (Basel: Friedrich Reinhardt Kommissionsverlag, 1978), which fails to grasp the sense of the continuous exegetical struggle with the living biblical text.

52. J. Patout Burns, *The Development of Augustine's Doctrine of Operative Grace* (Paris: Etudes Augustiniennes, 1980). See also Paula Fredriksen Landes, ed. and trans., *Augustine on Romans: Propositions from the Epistle to the Romans, Unfinished Commentary on the Epistle to the Romans*, Society of Biblical Literature Texts and Translations 23 (Chico, CA: Scholars Press, 1982).

53. Peter Brown, *Augustine of Hippo: A Biography* (Berkeley: University of California Press, 1967), 153.

54. The famous tag line associated with the name of Leopold von Ranke (1795–1886), the "father of modern historiography," whose emphasis on the systematic use of *all* possible documents from the historical period being studied has actually been far more formative on the development of contemporary patristics and New Testament studies than almost any other factor. See Herbert Butterfield, *Man on His Past: The Study of the History of Historical Scholarship* (Cambridge: Cambridge University Press, 1955) and Glenn F. Chesnut, "From Alexander the Great to Constantine: Supplying the Context," *Second Century: A Journal of Early Christian Studies* 1 (1981): 43–49.

55. Albert C. Outler, "The Idea of 'Development' in the History of Christian Doctrine: A Comment," in *Schools of Thought in the Christian Tradition*, ed. Patrick Henry, (Philadelphia: Fortress Press, 1984), 7–14.

56. Jaroslav Pelikan, *The Christian Tradition: A History of the Development of Doctrine*, 5 vols. (University of Chicago Press, 1971–).

57. Albert C. Outler, "The Idea of 'Development' in the History of Christian Doctrine: A Comment," 13. See also Outler's interesting article on "Doctrine and Dogma" in the *Encyclopaedia Britannica*, 15th ed., 5:927–29.

58. There is a fine short biography of Frank Leslie Cross (1900–1968) in the front matter (xxvii–xxxi) of *The Oxford Dictionary of the Christian Church*, 2d ed., ed. F. L. Cross and E. A. Livingstone (London: Oxford University Press, 1974), see esp. xxix.

59. Marcia L. Colish, "St. Thomas Aquinas in Historical Perspective: The Modern Period," *Church History* 44 (1975): 433–49, see esp. 440, 445.

60. Ibid., 446, 435.

61. Compare Alfred Loisy, *L'Évangile et l'Église* (Paris: A. Picard et fils, 1902), who had been closely associated with Duchesne at the Institut Catholique in Paris.

62. Louis Duchesne, *Histoire ancienne de l'église*, 2d ed., 2 vols. (Paris: A. Fontemoing, 1906–7). The quotations and references in the text are from the English translation, *Early History of the Christian Church*, 3 vols., trans. from the 4th ed. (New York: Longmans, Green, 1909–24) 1:28–29.

63. *Early History of the Christian Church* 1:31.

64. Ibid., 197.

65. Ibid., 239–40.

66. Ibid., 247.

67. Ibid., 175, 184, 187.

68. Ibid., 45, cf. 164.

69. Ibid., 13, 18.

70. Ibid., 62–70.

71. Ibid., 69.

72. Ibid., 173.

73. Ibid., 309.

74. See Henry Warner Bowden, *Church History in the Age of Science*, 139–42.

75. Joseph Tixeront, *Histoire des dogmes*, 3 vols. (Paris: V. Lecoffre, 1905–12). English translation, *History of Dogmas*, 3 vols., 2d ed., trans. from the 5th French ed. by H. L. B. (St. Louis, MO: B. Herder, 1910–16); 1:84, 109, 118, and 127 on the development of the monoepiscopacy, are examples of his quite different technique.

76. *History of Dogmas* 1:7n, 16. Lytton Strachey's biography of Newman in his *Eminent Victorians* (London: Chatto and Windus, 1918) makes a tendentious selection of the data in places, but Newman had in fact been no real friend to the new Catholicism during his life. The fact that he could now be cited in this fashion by Tixeront showed a profound change in Rome's evaluation of Newman.

77. Tixeront, *History of Dogmas* 1:7n.

78. Ibid., 2–3.

79. Ibid., 1–2, 5.

80. Ibid., 55, my emphasis.

81. Ibid., 2:ii.

82. Colish, "St. Thomas Aquinas in Historical Perspective," 448.

83. Repeatedly reprinted after its initial publication in 1903. My own copy is the twelfth printing (London: Methuen, 1962). Biographical data on Bethune-Baker can be found in *Who Was Who, 1951–1960*, 98.

84. Ibid., xi.

85. Bethune-Baker, xiii.

86. Ibid., vii, cf. 6–7.

87. Ibid., vii–viii.

88. J. N. D. Kelly, *Early Christian Doctrines*, preface to the 1st (1958) ed.

89. Origen, *Contra Celsum*, trans. Henry Chadwick (Cambridge: Cambridge University Press, 1953; rpt. with corrections 1965). Henry Chadwick, "Philo and the Beginnings of Christian Thought," p. 2 of *The Cambridge History of Later Greek and Early Medieval Philosophy* (Cambridge: Cambridge University Press, 1967), 133–92.

90. S. L. Greenslade, *Schism in the Early Church*, 2d ed. (London: SCM Press, 1964), viii–ix.

91. Robert M. Grant, *Gnosticism: An Anthology* (London: Collins, 1961) and *Gnosticism and Early Christianity* (New York: Columbia University Press, 1959, 2d ed. 1966).

92. Robert M. Grant, *Eusebius as Church Historian* (Oxford: Clarendon Press, 1980). See also Timothy D. Barnes, *Constantine and Eusebius* (Cambridge, MA: Harvard University Press, 1981), and for a fuller description of the importance of Grant's work, Glenn F. Chesnut, *The First Christian Histories: Eusebius, Socrates, Sozomen, Theodoret and Evagrius*, 2d. rev. ed. (Macon, GA: Mercer University Press, 1986), chap. 6, "Eusebius: From Youthful Defender of Religious Liberty to Spokesman for the Constantinian Imperial Church."

93. Robert M. Grant, *Early Christianity and Society* (San Francisco: Harper and Row, 1977).

94. Vladimir Lossky, *The Vision of God*, trans. A. Moorhouse (London: Faith Press, 1963). See also his *Orthodox Theology: An Introduction*, trans. I. and I. Kesarcodi-Watson (Crestwood, NY: St. Vladimir's Seminary Press, 1978), and *In the Image and Likeness of God*, ed. J. H. Erickson and T. E. Bird (Crestwood, NY: St. Vladimir's Seminary Press, 1974).

95. E. Glenn Hinson, *The Evangelization of the Roman Empire: Identity and Adaptability* (Macon, GA: Mercer University Press, 1981). Hinson, who is at Southern Baptist Theological Seminary, has continued this interest, as shown in his paper for example on "Spiritual Gifts in the Evangelization of the Roman Empire" at the meeting of the American Society of Church History at Fort Worth, Texas, in April 1986.

96. Timothy E. Gregory, *Vox Populi: Popular Opinion and Violence in the Religious Controversies of the Fifth Century A.D.* (Columbus: Ohio State University Press, 1979).

97. William James, *The Varieties of Religious Experience: A Study in Human Nature* (New York: Longmans, Green, 1902).

98. Arthur Darby Nock, *Conversion* (Oxford: Clarendon Press, 1933).

99. E. R. Dodds, *Pagan and Christian in an Age of Anxiety* (Cambridge: Cambridge University Press, 1951).

100. Peter Brown, *Augustine of Hippo: A Biography* (London: Faber and Faber, 1967).

101. John G. Gager, *Kingdom and Community: The Social World of Early Christianity* (Englewood Cliffs, NJ: Prentice-Hall, 1975). L. William Countryman, *The Rich Christian in the Church of the Early Empire: Contradictions and Accommodations* (Lewiston, NY: E. Mellen, 1980).

102. Peter Brown, "The Rise and Function of the Holy Man in Late Antiquity," *Journal of Roman Studies* 61 (1971): 80–101, and "Sorcery, Demons and the Rise of Christianity: From Late Antiquity into the Middle Ages," *Witchcraft Confessions and Accusations*, Association of Social Anthropologists Monographs 9 (1970): 17–45. See also Rudolf Otto, *The Idea of the Holy*, trans. J. W. Harvey (London: Oxford University Press, 1923), and Mircea Eliade,

The Sacred and the Profane: The Nature of Religion, trans. W. R. Trask (New York: Harcourt, Brace, Jovanovich, 1959).

103. For example, Peter Brown, *Religion and Society in the Age of Saint Augustine* (New York: Harper and Row, 1972), which deals with a good deal more than just Augustine; *Society and the Holy in Late Antiquity* (Berkeley: University of California Press, 1982); and *The Cult of the Saints: Its Rise and Function in Latin Christianity* (University of Chicago Press, 1982). In part, Brown is bringing to bear (on the patristic period) a methodology already being employed by historians of the early modern period in such works as Peter Burke, *Popular Culture in Early Modern Europe* (London: Temple Smith, 1978) and Robert Mandrou, *Magistrats et sorciers en France au XVIIe siècle: Une analyse de psychologie historique* (Paris: Plon, 1968).

104. Elizabeth Schüssler-Fiorenza, *In Memory of Her: A Feminist Theological Reconstruction of Christian Origins* (New York: Crossroad, 1984); Elizabeth A. Clark, *Jerome, Chrysostom, and Friends,* Studies in Women and Religion 1 (New York: Edwin Mellen Press, 1979); Roger Gryson, *The Ministry of Women in the Early Church*, trans. Jean Laporte and Mary Louise Hall (Collegetown, MN: Liturgical Press, 1976); Jean Laporte, *The Role of Women in Early Christianity*, Studies in Women and Religion 7 (Lewiston, NY: Edwin Mellen Press, 1982).

105. J. Burckhardt, *Die Zeit Konstantins des Grossen* (1853) had begun the modern critical study of Constantine in the mid-nineteenth century. H. Grégoire, "Eusèbe n'est pas l'auteur de la 'Vita Constantini' dans sa forme actuelle et Constantin n'est pas 'converti' en 312," *Byzantion* 13 (1938): 561–83, carried the late nineteenth-century critical approach of earlier scholarship to its extreme limit, but the difficulties in this position were already being seen by the point in the 1930s when Grégoire was writing.

106. Charles Norris Cochrane, *Christianity and Classical Culture: A Study of Thought and Action from Augustus to Augustine* (Oxford: Clarendon Press, 1940).

107. W. H. C. Frend, *The Donatist Church: A Movement of Protest in Roman North Africa* (Oxford: Clarendon Press, 1952). Arnaldo Momigliano, ed., *The Conflict between Paganism and Christianity in the Fourth Century* (Oxford: Clarendon Press, 1963). Francis Dvornik, *Early Christian and Byzantine Political Philosophy: Origins and Background*, 2 vols. (Washington, DC: Dumbarton Oaks, 1966). F. E. Peters, *The Harvest of Hellenism: A History of the Near East from Alexander the Great to the Triumph of Christianity* (New York: Simon and Schuster, 1970). A. E. Cameron, *Circus Factions: Blues and Greens at Rome and Byzantium* (Oxford: Clarendon Press, 1976). George A. Kennedy, *The Art of Persuasion in Greece* (Princeton University Press, 1963); *The Art of Rhetoric in the Roman World, 300 B.C.-A.D. 300* (Princeton University Press, 1972); *Greek Rhetoric under Christian Emperors* (Princeton University Press, 1983); *New Testament Interpretation through Rhetorical Criticism* (Chapel Hill: University of North Carolina Press, 1984). Robin Lane Fox, *Pagans and Christians* (New York: Alfred A. Knopf, 1987).

108. *Journal of Ecclesiastical History* 5 (1954): 196–200.

109. *Byzantion* 13 (1938): 561–83.

110. H. A. Drake, *In Praise of Constantine: A Historical Study and New Translation of Eusebius' Tricennial Orations* (Berkeley: University of California Press, 1976).

111. Timothy D. Barnes, *Constantine and Eusebius* (Cambridge, MA: Harvard University Press, 1981) and *The New Empire of Diocletian and Constantine* (Cambridge, MA: Harvard University Press, 1982).

112. Adolf von Harnack, *History of Dogma* 1.227-28.

113. Ibid., 229–30.

114. Hans Jonas, *Gnosis und spätantiker Geist* (Göttingen: Vandenhoeck and Ruprecht, 1923); see also his *Gnostic Religion*, 2d ed. (Boston: Beacon Press, 1963).

115. See for example, R. McL. Wilson, *Gnosis and the New Testament* (Oxford: Basil Blackwell, 1968), 5.

116. John M. Dillon, *The Middle Platonists, 80 B.C. to A.D. 220* (Ithaca: Cornell University Press, 1977).

117. Elaine Hiesey Pagels, *The Gnostic Paul: Gnostic Exegesis of the Pauline Letters* (Philadelphia: Fortress Press, 1975).

118. Richard Hugh Connolly, *The So-Called Egyptian Church Order and Derived Documents* (Cambridge: Cambridge University Press, 1916).

119. J. F. Bethune-Baker, *Nestorius and His Teaching* (Cambridge: Cambridge University Press, 1908). The best recent treatment of the dispute over the actual composition of the *Bazaar* and Nestorius' Christology is Roberta C. Chesnut, "The Two Prosopa in Nestorius' *Bazaar of Heracleides*," *Journal of Theological Studies* (Oxford), n.s. 29 (1978): 392–409.

120. Robert F. Evans, *Pelagius: Inquiries and Reappraisals* (London: Adam and Charles Black, 1968), Robert C. Gregg and Dennis E. Groh, *Early Arianism—A View of Salvation* (Philadelphia: Fortress Press, 1981), Thomas A. Kopecek, *A History of Neo-Arianism* (Cambridge, MA: Philadelphia Patristic Foundation, 1979), and Henry Chadwick, *Priscillian of Avila: The Occult and the Charismatic in the Early Church* (Oxford: Oxford University Press, 1976).

121. *Odyssey*, Bk. 11. Harnack died in 1930.

" The Gold of Catholicity "

Reflections on a Century of American Study of Medieval Church History

Bernard McGinn

I N 1846 Philip Schaff (1819–93), future founder of the American Society of Church History, in his provocative monograph *What Is Church History?* argued a case for the importance of church history that not only was advanced for its time but is still not realized today. As a theological disciple of Friedrich Schleiermacher, a historical pupil of Leopold von Ranke, a church historian much influenced by Johann August Wilhelm Neander and an admirer of Ferdinand Christian Baur's learning if not his conclusions, Schaff brought the full weight of German erudition to American shores a generation before it was to become popular in other circles.

Philip Schaff's organic and dialectical view of church history doubtless seems dated today,[1] but the power of his vision remains remarkably fresh in a more ecumenical age. In an era and country frequently marked by polemics and adversary positions, it enabled him not only to insist that the study of the totality of church history was necessary for theological education but also to claim that the Catholic Middle Ages and the Protestant Reformation were dialectically related as expressions of the objective (Petrine) and subjective (Pauline) elements of the church. Schaff saw these elements as tending toward a coming higher synthesis of evangelical Catholicism, a perfect Johannine (almost Joachimist) stage of Christianity to be realized on American soil.[2] His ideal was that of the "truly catholic historian," who has "too exalted a view of truth, to think of confining it to the narrow horizon of an individual or a party,"[3] and hence it is not surprising that he was willing to speak of the "gold of catholicity" still contained in the Church of Rome at a time when this was an unusual, and indeed a dangerous, thing for a Protestant divine to say.[4]

Schaff's views on the nature of church history and its place in theological education are not the subject of this essay, but they are important for what will follow. Whether we agree or disagree with Philip Schaff's eloquent call for church history as a discipline that would be both theologically indispensable and ecumenically inclusive, his vision and tireless energy deserve thoughtful consideration on the centenary of the organization he hoped would help realize these aims. Medievalists are perhaps more bound than others to such considerations, not only because Schaff was so ahead of his time in appreciating the importance of medieval Christianity, especially among Protestant Christians,[5] but also because the founding of the American Society of Church History corresponds so closely in time to the beginnings of academic study of the Middle Ages in the United States.

There are a number of useful discussions of the development of medieval studies in the United States, though no definitive treatment.[6] There is no study I know of that treats of medieval church history as a distinct topic. This essay does not pretend to fill this gap but is rather intended as a preliminary and partial consideration of the relation between the larger arena of the growth of medieval studies in North America and the more restricted one of medieval church history as it has been been reflected in the work of the American Society of Church History. In the absence of any history of the society, my evidence is drawn almost exclusively from its surviving publications.

According to any definition, the Middle Ages covers a large (perhaps too large) territory. While there is traditional consensus about its closure at the onset of the Reformation,[7] there is little agreement about its start. Whether we see the Middle Ages as beginning with Constantine in the fourth century, with the barbarian invasions in the fifth and sixth centuries, or as late as the eighth century with Charlemagne, no other conventional division of European history has as much ground to cover. Doing justice to this millennium or more has proven increasingly difficult in recent years. David Knowles, the premier English medievalist of his time, in surveying a century of the development of English medieval studies between 1868 and 1968 claimed that "the greatest single revolution in medieval historiography" was the recognition that "thought and institutions were never wholly static" during the period.[8] The emphasis on movement, change and variety in medieval history, not least of all in the history of the medieval church, has grown appreciably in recent years.

Though the polemics of the sixteenth century had much to do with the creation of the first large-scale church histories, that of the Centuriators of Magdeburg on the Protestant side (1559–74) and the *Annales ecclesiastici* (1588–1607) of Cardinal Baronius on the Catholic, the scientific study of the medieval church, and of medieval history in general, really begins with the labors of the Bollandists and the Maurists in the seventeenth and eighteenth centuries.[9] The vast materials gathered and edited by these devoted scholars and their creation of the necessary auxiliary disciplines of paleography and diplomatics formed the foundation upon which modern "scientific" history was erected in the nineteenth century. The appointment of Leopold von Ranke to the position of professor of history at Berlin in 1825 and the influence of the seminar he conducted there from 1833 down to his death in 1886 have rightly been seen as decisive aspects in the triumph of the new German understanding of history; but they were, of course, only part of a broader movement. From the viewpoint of medieval history, the foundation of the *Monumenta Germaniae historica* by Baron Karl von Stein in the 1820s and the rigorous methods of editing and scholarship worked out by the early Monumentists, such as Georg Heinrich Pertz and Georg Waitz, was the most decisive contribution.[10] On the church historical side, the work of Johann Neander in Berlin (whose lectures the young Philip Schaff attended) and especially the critical efforts of the Tübingen School under the leadership of F. C. Baur marked a new stage. According to Norman Cantor, "For a hundred years the German school was consistently the greatest school of medieval scholarship. Especially in medieval intellectual history, the pre-eminence of the Germans remained unchallenged until the 1930s."[11]

The growth of medieval studies in the nineteenth century was not just a movement of academic appropriation but was decisively influenced by broad cultural trends that turned against Enlightenment prejudices regarding the Middle Ages. However much it may disturb professional medievalists, it is imposssible to separate the history of medieval studies from the history of "medievalism," the nostalgia for the Middle Ages that has affected Western society in various ways over the past two centuries. In its German Romantic forms, it antedates the rise of the new history and contributed much (at least indirectly) to its popularity. In France it was well represented by historians like Charles René Montalembert, whose *Moines d'Occident* (1860–67) was almost as popular in its English translation as it was in French. In England, medievalism rose to prominence through the historical romances of Sir Walter Scott and the aesthetic propaganda of the Gothic Revival.

The young United States was not immune to the spread of medievalism.[12] Walter Scott was widely read, especially in the South; Gothic Revival had a powerful effect in America; and such popular authors as Washington Irving, W. H. Prescott, and Henry Wadsworth Longfellow were touched by Romantic medievalism in various ways.[13] In the period following the Civil War the leading proponents of medievalism were two

New England aristocrats who taught at Harvard. Charles Eliot Norton as professor of art and Henry Adams who briefly served as assistant professor of medieval history (1870–77) both used their romantic visions of medieval culture to criticize the increasingly drab industrial society they saw triumphing in their country. Henry Adams' famous *Mont-Saint-Michel and Chartres* (1904) remains the most powerful statement of American medievalism.[14]

Henry Adams, however, played a dual role in the development of medieval studies in America. Though *Mont-Saint-Michel and Chartres* is pure medievalism, the seminar that he ran at Harvard was based upon the new German models of historical research and resulted in the publication of his *Essays in Anglo-Saxon Law* in 1876, a volume that shows his interest in the constitutional and legal questions so common to nineteenth-century medieval scholarship and his admiration (though not uncritical) of German scholarship.[15]

Henry Adams' historical seminar created on the German model was the first example of the new history's appearance on the American scene, but not the last. Ephraim Emerton, a student of Adams who had gone on to take a degree at Leipzig, returned to Harvard to teach a medieval seminar from 1876 to 1918. Charles Gross took a degree at Göttingen in 1883 and taught at Harvard from 1888 to 1909. His *Guild Merchant* published in 1890 was a classic contribution to the municipal history of the Middle Ages.[16] The young prodigy Charles Homer Haskins, rejected by Harvard College as underage, received his doctorate from Johns Hopkins in 1890 and taught at Harvard from 1902 until 1932. The dominant American medieval historian of his generation, Haskins' effect on medieval studies came not only through his writings but also through the eminent line of historians he trained.[17]

Harvard was not the only school in the last quarter of the nineteenth century to initiate formal medieval studies. At Johns Hopkins, Herbert Baxter Adams, whose degree came from Heidelberg, was an influential teacher of medieval history from 1876 until 1901. Yet another Adams, George Burton Adams, took a doctorate at Leipzig in 1886 and began teaching English constitutional history at Yale. George Lincoln Burr at Cornell, James Harvey Robinson at Columbia, Dana C. Munro at Wisconsin, and James Westfall Thompson at the new University of Chicago are other important names that can be added to the list. The scholars who introduced the study of medieval Latin and paleography to the American universities in the early years of the present century, men like Edward K. Rand, Charles A. Beeson, E. A. Lowe, and B. L. Ullman, were also products of German training, specifically that of the great Munich Latinist, Ludwig Traube.

The first generation of American medieval historians was not noted for any special interest in the history of the medieval church save as it impinged upon the legal, constitutional and political concerns that they had absorbed from their German teachers and that were also dominant in contemporary English medieval history through the influence first of Bishop William Stubbs and subsequently of the great F. W. Maitland.[18] Philip Schaff had brought German church historical concerns and methods to the United States in the 1840s; little more than a decade later, the only great native born church historian of the nineteenth century, Henry Charles Lea (1825–1909), had begun his writing career. Lea was the great outsider of American medieval church history and arguably still its most distinguished practitioner.[19] (Maitland praised Lea for looking at the legal documents of continental Europe "with the naked eye instead of seeing them—a much easier task—through German spectacles.")[20] A self-educated Philadelphia businessman, Lea's reputation rests upon eighteen volumes devoted to the history of the Latin church, especially to the institutional and legal means by which the church gained and maintained its control over minds and consciences. According to Lea, "The Latin Church is the great fact which dominates the history of modern civilization";[21] but the historical impact of this fact he took to be deleterious, at least in its political implications. Writing to Solomon Reinach in 1901 he said: "I commenced my medieval studies without any preconception adverse to Catholicism, but I found the Church as a political system adverse to the interests of humanity. Against it as a religion I have nothing to say."[22]

Lea's most noted studies, such as his *History of Sacerdotal Celibacy in the Christian Church* (1867), *A History of the Inquisition of the Middle Ages* (1887), *A History of Auricular Confession and Indulgences in the Latin Church* (1896), and *A History of the Inquisition of Spain* (1906–7), maintain their importance to this day. Lord Acton's well-known remark that Leas' *History of the Inquisition* was "the most important contribution of the new world to the religious history of the old" can still be defended.

It may seem surprising that American Catholics played such a relatively small role in first-generation medieval studies in the United States, but it must be remembered that in the nineteenth century American Catholicism was an immigrant church without a highly developed system of higher education and that its intellectual leaders were formed by a Catholicism largely untouched by Romantic medievalism.[23] The foremost Catholic contribution to medievalism was James J. Walsh's book, *The Thirteenth, Greatest of Centuries* (1907), a far less evocative work than the almost-contemporary *Mont-Saint-Michel and Chartres*. The great initiative that gave the study of medieval history and thought a central place in modern Catholicism was the Thomist revival promoted by Leo XIII's 1879 Encyclical *Aeterni Patris*.[24] The intellectual, social, and political implications of the program envisaged by the pope did have their effects in American Catholic medievalism and in Catholic study of the Middle Ages, but not until well into the twentieth century. American Catholicism produced no contemporary medievalist or church historian of the stature of Schaff or Lea, and it is significant that it was not until 1919 that the American Catholic Historical Association was founded.

The First World War did much to dampen the enthusiasm for things German, not only in American society at large, but also in the scholarly world. French influence, and to a lesser extent English, came to the fore in the second and third decades of the present century.[25] The influence of the great Belgian medieval economic historian, Henri Pirenne, and subsequently the arrival of French neo-Scholasticism on these shores through Maurice de Wulf's teaching at Harvard and the foundation of the Pontifical Institute of Mediaeval Studies by Etienne Gilson at Toronto in 1929 are evidences of this shift. If the earliest great strengths of American medieval history had largely been in institutional, economic, and legal issues, the twentieth century began to reveal considerable achievement in aspects of medieval intellectual history. While general works like Henry Osborn Taylor's *Medieval Mind* (1911) were soon outdated, great and lasting contributions were made to the history of medieval science by Lynn Thorndike, George Sarton, and Charles Homer Haskins.[26] The same decades saw medieval art history established on a secure and impressive foundation through the work of scholars like A. Kingsley Porter at Harvard and C. R. Morey at Princeton whose name will always be associated with the notable Princeton Index of Christian Art.

The 1920s saw the native American penchant for organizing spread to the ranks of medieval scholars. The first impetus came not from the historians of the American Historical Association (founded 1884) but from the students of medieval literature of the Modern Language Association (1883). At the 1920 meeting of that society its president, the noted Chicago Chaucer scholar John M. Manley, called for better ways to promote cooperation among specialized scholars working in related areas. At the 1921 annual meeting a special session was devoted to "The Influence of Latin Culture on Medieval Culture," and in 1922 this led to the formation of a special committee of the MLA with E. K. Rand as chairman and G. R. Coffman as secretary. Its scope soon proved too small, so a new Committee on Mediaeval Latin Studies was organized under the sponsorship of the recently founded American Council of Learned Societies. Interest rapidly grew both among academicians and interested outsiders, especially Ralph

Adams Cram, a noted architect and proponet of medievalism,[27] and John Nicholas Brown, a New England philanthropist. The committee was aided in its investigation of the spread of medieval studies in the United States by the appearance in 1924 of the first *Bulletin of Progress of Medieval Studies in the United States of America* by James F. Willard, which listed sixty scholars in the field (by 1932 Willard's *Bulletin* was to list five hundred). Thus, on 23 December 1925, the Mediaeval Academy of America was incorporated in Boston as an independent endowed body "to conduct, encourage, promote and support research, publication, and instruction in Mediaeval records."[28] In January of 1926, the first issue of *Speculum*, the society's journal, appeared under the editorship of E. K. Rand.[29]

The Mediaeval Academy has been central to the pursuit of medieval studies in North America since its formation, though its history has in some ways not lived up to the high hopes of its founders. Although the impetus for the formation of the new society had been nationwide, the accidents of development led to the academy having a definite East Coast and Harvard tinge. In its early days the academy did distribute funds for research on occasion, and it has taken sporadic interest over the years in the teaching of medieval studies; but its central concern has been publication not only of *Speculum* but also of a monograph series that now numbers over ninety volumes. *Speculum*'s lengthy and excellent book reviews are justly famed, but the tendency toward increasingly specialized articles has been viewed with concern.[30]

The academy grew from 761 members in 1926 to 1,062 members in 1931, attracting many nonacademics who doubtless were much enamored of the Middle Ages. Membership declined during the Great Depression and remained erratic until 1945 when a period of growth ensued that reached a high in 1978 with 3,901 members. Since that time membership once again declined to reach a total of 3,590 in April of 1983. In reviewing the demographic history of the academy in 1983, then President David Herlihy noted: "The concentration of the Academy members in New England and the eastern seaboard is in itself not surprising, but the degree of this concentration, which our figures emphasize, is nonetheless disconcerting."[31] Herlihy's statistics also show that the academy continues to have a higher representation of academics from linguistic disciplines than from history. Given the extraordinary growth in American higher education over the sixty years of the academy's life, it is also not surprising that its membership now reflects less than half of those who teach medieval studies in some capacity.[32]

The growth of medieval studies in North America has always been strongly influenced by events and new trends in scholarship in Europe.

The deepening clouds of the 1930s and the onset of Nazi persecution of the Jews displaced many premier scholars to American shores, not least of all important medievalists who were to affect the history of the discipline in significant ways. This wave of learned immigrants continued until at least 1950 and included such names as Paul Oskar Kristeller in the history of thought, historians of the stature of Ernst Kantorowicz, Gerhart Ladner, Robert Lopez, and Hans Baron, and especially a gathering of brilliant art historians (e.g., Erwin Panofsky, Ernst Kitzinger, Richard Krautheimer, Adolf Katzenellenbogen). It was also in the 1930s that a group of relative outsiders in the French historical profession teaching together at the University of Strasbourg effected a revolution in historical studies that was symptomatic of important shifts in medieval studies in the second half of this century.

Henri Berr (1862–1955) was the intellectual father of the new school; but its two foremost proponents were Lucien Febvre (1878–1956), who worked primarily in early modern history, though his essays and books have been much read by medievalists, and Marc Bloch (1886–1943), a medievalist whose best-known book, *Feudal Society* (1940), capped a series of highly original works that called for historians to move out beyond the traditional confines of political, institutional, and economic history taken all too often in isolation in order to produce a more integrated picture of an entire social system. Bloch's achievement owed much to his ability to make use of the methods of social sciences such as anthropology and sociology, as well as his rejection of the old humanism of the elite classical tradition in favor of what Karl Morrison has called "a wider humanism that would include the entire range of human endeavor, society's inarticulate as well as its educated components."[33] In the face of the increasing dangers of fragmentation and overspecialization this new method, as well as Bloch's advocacy of comparative history, offered a hope of integration and cooperation that made it exceptionally powerful. The fact that in the hands of one of Bloch's followers, Fernand Braudel (1902–85) it led to the production of an even more impressive reconstruction of an era in his *Mediterranean in the Age of Philip II* (1946) guaranteed that the influence of Bloch and his followers (frequently called the Annales school from the journal they founded in 1929 now called *Annales: Economies, Sociétés, Civilisations*) was to be profound both in Europe and North America.[34]

The standard of a "new history" raised by the Annales school was only the most visible part of a geological shift taking place in the practice of medieval studies in the decades after 1930.[35] Obviously, there was no question of a common program; but rather something like a series of partially overlapping circles of interest created centers of intersection that moved historians away from concern with events, ideas, and institutions, taken by themselves, toward attempts to study their social functions and cultural implications. This accounted for a renewed interest in "cultural history," the most diffuse of all the supposed types of historical construction, the grab bag into which historiographers are tempted to put impressive works that cannot be easily categorized.[36] The Dutch historian Johan Huizinga's *Waning of the Middle Ages* was first published in 1919, but its popularity as a mesmerizing evocation of forms of life, thought, and art in northern Europe in the fifteenth century owes much to the change in attitudes that had to wait several decades to really take hold. At the same time, topics that narrow political and intellectual history had rarely examined, particularly those relating the wider life of a society and to its rooting in geography, climate, and culture as well as its imaginative life, came to the fore.

In France the work of Gabriel Le Bras, an associate of the Annales group, in its concern for the importance of religious sociology fundamentally changed the way in which the history of medieval ecclesiastical institutions were understood,[37] while Etienne Delaruelle pursued the much-neglected piety of the medieval laity. Marie-Dominique Chenu broadened the narrow model of the history of thought found in most neo-Scholastics to embrace a broader social history of theology in his epochal *La théologie au douzième siècle* (1957). Another break with the traditions of neo-Scholasticism established by *Aeterni Patris* took place in the early 1940s when Etienne Gilson, the premier historian of Scholastic thought, advised his Benedictine student Jean Leclercq to concentrate on the long tradition of monastic thought and culture rather than the much-plowed scholastic field. The result was not only a new edition of the works of St. Bernard but a vast outpouring of books and articles of which the best known is *The Love of Learning and the Desire for God* (1957). Similar changes were underway in Germany, especially in the work of Herbert Grundmann, who put the study of medieval heresy on a new footing, and who investigated the social setting and dynamics of the new religious movements of the twelfth and thirteenth centuries in his *Religiöse Bewegungen im Mittelalter* (1935). Carl Erdmann, Heinrich Fichtenau, and more recently Karl Bosl also represent a shift away from older German models of intellectual and political history. In Italy the influence of Raffaello Morghen and Raoul Manselli tended in the same direction.

The major English medievalists of the middle period of the century, David Knowles, Beryl Smalley, and Richard Southern, also show a break with older traditions of legal, constitutional, and administrative history, though in a less theoretical way. David Knowles' four volumes dealing with the development of the monastic and religious orders in medieval England (published between 1940 and 1959) at first glance might be taken as largely institutional history, but read in their entirety they present a very different and wider picture of the lived experience of religious life in the Middle Ages. Beryl Smalley's concerns with the history of exegesis and, subsequently, with the role intellectuals played in politics seemed marginal or bizarre to her teachers. Richard Southern's influential work on the cultural and religious transformations of the High Middle Ages combines an opening to the social-functional thrust of much recent Continental work with a typically English appreciation of the role of personality, a dimension of history that has become less and less evident in the Annales historians, at least since the death of Lucien Febvre. As displayed in his *Making of the Middle Ages* (1953), this combination has had a profound effect on the past generation of American medievalists. An important representative of the new history in the English language has been Peter Brown, whose work, beginning with his biography *Augustine of Hippo* (1967), is more directly related to the social sciences but no less engagingly humanistic than that of his predecessors. Brown's work concentrates on the late antique period, the uneasy transition between the ancient and medieval worlds. Given the fact that he has taught in the United States for over a decade, it is perhaps permissable to see him as another of the important émigrés.

The Continental medieval historians who established solid reputations since the 1960s have largely followed in the wake of the great shift that took place in the 1930s. This is evident in France where the most influential of the "Annalesists" and their successors, men like George Duby, Jacques Le Goff, and Emmanuel LeRoy Ladurie, have been deeply affected both by anthropology and by folkloric studies and have come to emphasize what is now frequently referred to as the history of *mentalité* (which bears a relation to the classic term *Zeitgeist*, similar to that of Morrison's "wider humanism" to traditional humanism). Though the dream of integral history remains, the reality seems ever more distant. The pursuit of increasingly specialized topics of research, the stress upon localization and particularization, the questionable thesis of the split between clerical and popular culture,[38] as well as the debate over how far medieval Europe may be said to have been Christianized at all, has rendered the picture of the unified Catholic Europe of the Middle Ages defended with enthusiasm less than a generation ago by historians like Christopher Dawson, seriously anachronistic. Perhaps the fissiparous tendencies have gone too far, and one notes with alarm how often illuminating case studies become the basis for dubious generalizations; but there can be no question that the new history has destroyed many of the myths not only of medievalism but also of older views of the Middle Ages.[39]

The development of medieval studies in North America over the past fifty years is difficult to characterize, not only because of the greater variety in comparison with the first fifty years, but also because of the difficulty of evaluating just how profound the influence from Europe has been. (Rightly or wrongly one must admit that influence has not generally worked in the other direction.) As in Europe, the story is one of greater diversification and the gradual (though slower) emergence of new styles of history that break with the narrow political, legal, and institutional concerns of the past. In North America this diversification was facilitated by the increase in higher education after the Second World War and the consequent proliferation of medievalists.

One way of charting the growth of American medieval studies is to sample the pattern of Ph.D. candidates enrolled and degrees granted. The number of Ph.D. candidates doubled between 1927 when 120 were counted, mostly at Harvard, Columbia, and Chicago, and 1941, when there were 250 at a much larger number of institutions.[40] Karl Morrison has surveyed the figures for doctorates in medieval history granted in the United States between 1960–61 and 1977–78.[41] According to published accounts, seventy-seven institutions granted 549 degrees during these years with a peak of 54 doctorates awarded by thirty institutions in 1972–73. The division by topics seems to suggest that the new history had not yet made a substantial impact. For example, the largest number (73) dealt with English history and 31 of these were studies of law and institutions. Somewhat surprising for church historians is the fact that the study of ecclesiastical history ranked a close fourth on the list with 40 dissertations.

As far as the institutions granting the degrees are concerned, Wisconsin was out in front with 40, followed by Columbia with 28, Berkeley and UCLA each with 25, and Chicago with 24. Princeton and Yale each gave 23, and Harvard was somewhat surprisingly further down the list with 14. This list fails to take account of the Centre for Medieval Studies at Toronto (now combined with the Pontifical Mediaeval Institute) that granted no less than 73 doctorates in all areas in the years 1968–78.[42] One thing clear from even these partial figures, however, is how medieval history, let alone the broader field of medieval studies, had diversified geographically while maintaining its center in the northeastern part of the country.

Of course, sheer numbers of any kind are not always the best guide to detecting both weight of influence and important new trends. One could argue, for instance, that although Princeton produced fewer medieval historians in the years surveyed than some other institutions, the influence there of Joseph R. Strayer was second to none in the years after 1950 through the numerous distinguished medievalists he trained. Similarly Giles Constable of Harvard would have to be counted among the most important medieval historians of the period, however many the dissertations he supervised. The career of David Herlihy first at Wisconsin and subsequently at Harvard, with his concerns for social history, especially the history of the family, and the large number of dissertations he has directed point to the impact of newer modes of investigation pioneered abroad. Long-standing American interest in the history of medieval science also continued during these decades and even took new turns in the way in which the UCLA medievalist, Lynn White, Jr., sought to relate medieval technology and social change. Over the past fifty years interest in medieval church history has tended to shift away from broad surveys to more detailed regional and institutional issues frequently stressing the social role of ecclesiastics and their policies and practices. Within the past decade or so there has also been a marked emergence of studies relating to the whole range of medieval piety and religious life, not just that reflected in the spiritual elites of clerics, monks, and mendicants. Books on the cult of the saints, relics, pilgrimages, penance, preaching, sexual morality, marriage, death and dying, and especially on heresy, have abounded.

It might be argued, however, that it has been in the realm of intellectual history, specifically the history of medieval philosophy and theology, that North American medieval studies made their greatest contribution. Though Etienne Gilson (1884– 1978), the dominant figure of the neo-Scholastic movement, was quintessentially French, the fact that he spent half his teaching time for several decades at the Pontifical Institute that he helped found in Toronto gave him a lasting impact on medieval studies in America. His students and colleagues, such as A. C. Pegis, F. Maurer, N. Häring, made Toronto the major center for American neo-Scholasticism, though a number of other Catholic institutions, notably Catholic University in Washington, Notre Dame, and Fordham, also contributed to the dissemination of neo-Scholasticism. Two Protestant historians of theology have made signal contributions to medieval studies in the past decades. Jaroslav Pelikan, first at Chicago and later at Yale, wrote extensively on many aspects of church history. The first four volumes of his *Christian Tradition: A History of the Development of Doctrine* (1971–84) deal with aspects of the history of medieval theology. The Dutch scholar, Heiko A. Oberman, who taught for a number of years at Harvard Divinity School, helped reopen interest in the history of late medieval theology and its relation to the Reformation. A score of students trained by Oberman have continued to make contributions in this area over the past two decades. A number of major medievalists of diverse background and approach, such as Gerhard Ladner, Ernst Kantorowicz, and Karl Morrison, have also made important contributions to the history of medieval thought.

Another phenomenon of weight in the past fifty years has been the growth of new areas of investigation. Byzantine studies were largely absent in early decades of the present century. Their slow growth was considerably aided by the establishment of the Dumbarton Oaks Center for Byzantine Studies by the Trustees of Harvard University in 1940. It is significant that during the years covered by Morrison's survey seventeen institutions awarded 31 degrees in what was once an unknown field of scholarship in North America, and that a number of renowned Byzantinists, such as John Meyendorff and Deno Geanakopolos, can now be found on these shores.

Another area that came to flourish in North America and that has deeply affected medieval studies here has been that of the history of canon law. Catholic University of America for many years had a School of Canon Law, but it was not until the establishment of the Institute of Medieval Canon Law there in 1955 by the Austrian scholar Stephan Kuttner that the history of canon law became an important part of its concerns. Kuttner's Institute, subsequently moved to Yale and then to Berkeley, has done much to make American scholars aware of the central role of canon law in medieval civilization. Brian Tierney, also first at Catholic University and later at Cornell, is another historian who made considerable use of canon law in his groundbreaking studies on conciliarism and papal history.

The past two decades have witnessed important attempts to unify the increasingly diverse and fragmented world of medieval scholarship in a variety of ways, especially through the creation of new organizations, the spread of programs of medieval studies, and the proliferation of conferences and meetings, usually of a interdisciplinary nature.

Medievalists, like most academics, have always been much given to conferences and meetings; but the activity in recent years has been unusual, even taking into account the multiplication of numbers of those engaged in teaching aspects of medieval civilization. Sometimes it seems as if the desire to meet together has become the only way to affirm the underlying unity of a field of studies too large and divided to be bound together in any intellectually meaningful way. (The reason for the spread of such meetings doubtless also has much to do with the needs of younger scholars to find a forum in which to present their research.) The most important of these new conferences are those that have been held every year since

1962 at Western Michigan University in Kalamazoo. In recent years these international conferences on medieval studies have featured the presentation of hundreds of papers and have been attended by thousands of medievalists—numbers that would surely have amazed the handful of pioneers of medieval studies of a century ago.

In the United States the Medieval Institute at Notre Dame, founded in 1946, appears to be the oldest program to give advanced degrees in medieval studies. It was not until the 1960s that the rage for both graduate and undergraduate degrees in medieval studies took hold (Mount Holyoke College in 1965 appears to have been the earliest of the B.A. programs).[43] Today these programs are widespread throughout the country. While they all agree on some form of interdisciplinary approach, they are too varied in conception and execution to lend themselves to easy summary. Medieval studies degrees require medieval studies programs and committees to oversee them, and hence the past two decades have seen scores of universities and colleges create such bodies, though in most cases these were formed by adding more chores to existing faculty already serving in traditional departments, rather than hiring personnel for a new venture.

The desire for more organization spread beyond the boundaries of individual schools to embrace regional associations, both small and large, all with their own acronyms and many with annual meetings. The Midwest Medieval Conference was founded in 1962; subsequent groups of interdisciplinary character include the Medieval Association of the Pacific (1966), the Rocky Mountain Medieval and Renaissance Association (1968), the New England Medieval Conference (1974), the Southeast Medieval Association (1975), the Mid-America Medieval Association (1976), and the Medieval Association of the Midwest (1979). A number of smaller regional groupings also were founded during these years.[44] In 1969 the Medieval Academy recognized the importance of this new wave of organization by establishing CARA, a Subcommittee on Centers and Regional Associations that has tried to be a central clearing house for information on the increasingly complex infrastructure of the eight thousand people who are actively engaged in the pursuit of medieval studies in contemporary America.

It would take a bold scholar to give any summary of the state of medieval studies in North America in 1986. Not surprisingly perhaps, the academic world of the scholars has come to look more and more like the world it studies—not a civilization where a few elite figures can tell us the story, but one in which large masses of the relatively anonymous need to be polled in order to present the broad trends; not a unified culture in any practical sense, but one that appears to be unable to live without dreams of unity; and finally, not the ideal hierarchical vision of some medieval scholars and all proponents of medievalism, but a world of intel-lectual and social turmoil frequently in doubt of its very survival.

The relation of Philip Schaff's American Society of Church History to the wider evolution of medieval studies in America so briefly delineated above, cannot be described as other than tangential. Despite the "catho-licity" of Schaff's program, the interests of American church historians, at least as reflected in the publications of the society, have given only moderate attention to the millennium or more embraced by the Middle Ages. This is in part explained not only by the natural preference given to the study of the history of American Christianity by those who actually call this continent their home but also by the fact that few American Protestants shared Schaff's ecumenical tendencies a century ago. Fur-thermore, Catholic scholars, as they became more interested in the history of the medieval church, tended to see their investigations primarily from an apologetic perspective, at least during the period up to 1960. While it might be anachronistic to think that it could have been otherwise, one can only lament that the divisions of Western Christianity led to the creation of two major associations devoted to the study of church history in North America rather than one.

A deeper reason for the tangential relation between the broad evo-lution of medieval studies in America and the role of medieval church history in the American Society of Church History probably lies in the training and interests of the members of the society. While I can point to no detailed studies to back up my suspicions, I think that church historians in this country have tended to define themselves horizontally, that is, in terms of their interests and teaching obligations concerning the whole of the history of the Christian church, and not vertically, in terms of one particular chronological period, even though for the most part they may have made their major contributions in one such period. Chronological extensivity, reinforced by thematic and confessional predispositions, may have contributed to a less than intensive awareness on the part of church historians of new trends and dimensions in the study of medieval history on the broad scale. If one had to write a history of medieval studies based on the 153 articles on the medieval church published by the society during the past century it would have only marginal relation to the large-scale history of medieval studies in North America given above.

It is interesting to note that there was no time in the society's history when more attention was given to medieval topics, or by more distin-guished scholars, than in its early years. In the eight volumes comprising the first series of the *Papers of the American Society of Church History* (1888–

96) no less than 14 of the 59 papers given at the meetings of the society dealt with the history of medieval Christianity (23.72 percent). These included three papers by Schaff himself,[45] two papers by Henry Charles Lea,[46] a paper by Dana C. Munro, one of the leading early figures in the academic study of the Middle Ages, and a talk delivered in 1893 by a Roman Catholic scholar, Rev. Thomas O'Gorman, on "The Life and Work of Thomas Aquinas," an early witness to the influence of neo-Scholasticism in America.

A similar interest in the history of the medieval church appears to have characterized the second stage of the history of the society when it was revived in the first decade of the present century. The nine volumes of the second series of the *Papers of the American Society of Church History* (1909–34) show a total of 14 out of 64 papers devoted to medieval topics (21.87 percent). This high percentage may well have been due to the influence of historians in the ecumenical mold of Philip Schaff, such as Joseph Cullen Ayer, Jr., an Episcopal priest who served as president of the society in 1913,[47] and Philip Schaff's son, David Schley Schaff, who completed the medieval sections of his father's imposing *A History of the Christian Church* and also served as president in 1917.[48]

The reorganization of the society that resulted in the establishment of *Church History* whose first number appeared in 1932 was accompanied by an unfortunate regression from the opening to medieval studies found earlier. This is particularly puzzling in light of the fact that the Medieval Academy and many aspects of medievalism and medieval studies were flourishing at the time. It is disconcerting to note that the first ten numbers of the new journal (1932–41) had only 10 articles of 147 devoted to the medieval church (6.8 percent). In the absence of any history of the society one is left to speculate about the reasons for this remarkable schism between the medievalists and the church historians. It is only fair to note, however, that some of these 10 articles were of considerable weight. John T. McNeill, perhaps the only twentieth-century American church historian whose command of the field rivaled that of Philip Schaff, contributed an insightful article on "Asceticism versus Militarism in the Middle Ages" in 1936; and Paul Oskar Kristeller, one of the major early refugees from Nazi persecution, wrote on "Florentine Platonism and its Relations with Humanism and Platonism" in 1939. Also during these years, Matthew Spinka and Ray C. Petry, two historians who were to make notable contributions to the history of the medieval church and the pages of *Church History* over the years, published their earliest entries in the new journal.[49]

The second decade of *Church History* could not but do better in the attention it paid to the Middle Ages, though the change was marginal.

Volumes 11 through 20 featured only 10 medieval articles of 117 (8.54 percent) and 4 of these were published in one year. It is difficult not to think that Philip Schaff would have been upset by the obvious parochialism of his foundation, as well as by the general absence of distinguished medieval contributers to the journal.

Again for reasons upon which we can only speculate, the situation changed rather dramatically in the third decade of the journal's life. Volumes 21 through 30 (1952–61) contained no less than 37 articles out of 183 (20.2 percent) devoted to the Middle Ages, and a good number of these were by distinguished scholars who were also influential on the larger scene of developing medieval studies in North America. Perhaps during no other decade of its existence did the activities of the society, at least as reflected in its journal, have a closer relation to what was going on in medieval studies at large in America. Byzantine studies were given prominence in an issue (vol. 24, no. 4, in 1955) devoted to the Council of Florence (articles by Ivhor Shevchenko, Deno Geanakopolos and Michael Cherniavsky), and a number of distinguished Western medievalists made their first (and frequently only) appearances in the journal's pages (e.g., Richard Sullivan, Ernest McDonnell, Mary McLaughlin, Howard Kaminsky, Donald Weinstein, Francis Oakley, and Heiko A. Oberman). Other important medieval articles by historians of wide reputation graced the journal during these years.[50] Figures for the number of articles relating to medieval studies in the *Publications for the Modern Language Association* (*PMLA*) and the *American Historical Review* (*AHR*) for the period 1950–59 (12 and 6 percent respectively) show how much of a contribution medievalists were making to church historical studies at the time, at least as reflected in the society's official journal.[51]

During the period from 1962 to 1971 *Church History* increased the number of articles published to 250 but managed to have only 30 devoted to medieval topics for a rather dismal 12 percent average.[52] It is only fair to note that the bi-annual reports of the journal over the past twenty years at least have frequently issued calls for more papers devoted to the early and the medieval church. Obviously, many factors were at work in blunting the effectiveness of these invitations. For one thing, these were the very years that witnessed an optimistic expansion of journals devoted to medieval topics, and these may well have siphoned off articles from *Church History*.

This was also the time when the Second Vatican Council made both Protestants and Catholics aware of how much they had in common and how necessary it was to engage in mutual discussion, especially about their common history. Such great changes in the ecumenical dimensions of church history, however, can be detected only with difficulty in the pages of *Church History*. Still, it is important to note that this decade's publications included more than a few articles by distinguished medieval historians, both here and abroad,[53] as well as the welcome innovation of a special issue devoted to the trendy theme of the "counter culture" (vol. 40, no. 1, for 1971) in which three articles concerned the Middle Ages.

The years from 1972 through 1985 still seem ambivalent in terms of the role of medieval studies in American church history. On the basis of our perhaps misleading statistical surveys, the past fourteen years of *Church History* represent no substantial change over the previous decade. Of the 323 articles published only 38 have involved the history of the medieval church for a percentage of 11.76. Medieval church historians can perhaps take comfort in the knowledge that for the period 1970–79 the *PMLA* percentages for medieval pieces fell to 7.5, and the *AHR* figures climbed only to 10.5. But do any of these figures reflect the significance of this period for the disciplines involved? One thing that is evident from a survey of these 38 articles is that the new history, initiated in various ways in Europe over fifty years ago, has definitely begun to penetrate the ways in which American medieval church historians approach their discipline.

Statistical surveys are notoriously misleading indicators of everything from presidential elections to academic trends. Still, they provide one kind of evidence that cannot be rejected, however partial it may be. These figures regarding the numbers of articles devoted to the history of the medieval church in the official publications of the American Society of Church History over the years are not encouraging, at least in terms of the vision of the founder of the society. This is especially evident in light of the great change in the ecumenical atmosphere of the past quarter century—one that would have seemed miraculous, but welcome, to Philip Schaff and his generation.

This is not the place to try to determine why Schaff's totalistic and ecumenical views never really caught on, and why they have not even been evident in the new ecumenical environment of the past quarter century. The much greater complexity, and the present fragmentation of medieval studies in America, make any naive programs of immediately greater utilization of medieval materials, especially with the hope of achieving some unifying consensus, utopian in the extreme. Nevertheless, it is difficult to think that Philip Schaff would have been daunted by a situation that, though outwardly pessimistic, contained such a variety of possibilities. The centennial of the American Society of Church History invites us to reflect on what we can do to further the always unfinished task it set itself, that of "cultivating church history as a science, in an unsectarian, catholic spirit, and for facilitating personal intercourse among students of history as a means of mutual encouragement."[54]

Notes

1. See *Reformed and Catholic: Selected Historical and Theological Writings of Philip Schaff*, ed. Charles Yrigoyen, Jr., and George M. Bricker (Pittsburgh: Pickwick Press, 1979), for a useful collection. On Schaff's thought, see James H. Nichols, *Romanticism in American Theology: Nevin and Schaff at Mercersburg* (University of Chicago Press, 1961), 64–72; and Klaus Penzel, "The Reformation Goes West: The Notion of Historical Development in the Thought of Philip Schaff," *Journal of Religion* 62 (1982): 219–41.

2. *What Is Church History?* in *Reformed and Catholic*, 114, 139–44; and *History of the Apostolic Church*, ibid., 206–11.

3. *What Is Church History?* 42.

4. *What Is Church History?* 137.

5. Philip Gleason in his "Mass and Maypole Revisited: American Catholics and the Middle Ages," *American Catholic Historical Review* 57 (1971): 249–74, has shown how little nineteenth-century American Catholics were interested in the study of medieval church history. On the general slow development of academic study of the Middle Ages, see George H. Callcott, *History in the United States, 1800–1860* (Baltimore: Johns Hopkins Press, 1970), 94–96 (my thanks to Martin Marty for this reference).

6. For the period to 1930 the most complete treatment is that of Hans Rudolf Guggisberg, *Das europäische Mittelalter im amerikanischen Geschichtsdenken des 19. und des frühen 20. Jahrhunderts* (Basel-Stuttgart: Helbing and Lichtenhahn, 1964). Also useful are C. W. David, "American Historiography of the Middle Ages 1884–1934," *Speculum* 10 (1935): 125–37; and esp. William J. Courtenay, "The Virgin and the Dynamo: The Growth of Medieval Studies in America (1870–1930)," in *Medieval Studies in North America: Past, Present and Future*, ed. Francis G. Gentry and Christopher Kleinhans (Kalamazoo: Medieval Institute Publications, 1982), 5–22. For subsequent developments, see S. Harrison Thomson's "The Growth of a Discipline: Medieval Studies in America," in *Perspectives in Medieval History*, ed. Katherine Fisher Drew and Seyward Lear (University of Chicago Press, 1963), 1–18, which deals in broad terms with the period down to 1960; and Karl Morrison's insightful "Fragmentation and Unity in 'American Medievalism,'" in *The Past Before Us: Contemporary Historical Writing in the United States*, ed. Michael Kammen (Ithaca: Cornell University Press, 1980), 49–77, which although it deals explicitly with the decade of the 1970s has valuable broader comments. For remarks on recent work in medieval church history, Bernard McGinn, "Medieval Christianity: An Introduction to Research, 1957–1977," *Anglican Theological Review* 60 (1978): 278–305.

7. This despite Ernst Troeltsch's insistence, now accepted by many historians, that the "classic" Reformation was the last chapter in the medieval struggle for reform. See *Protestantism and Progress* (Boston: Beacon Press, 1958). A more recent attempt to redefine the boundaries of the medieval and modern periods can be found in Heiko A. Oberman, "The Shape of Late Medieval Thought: The Birthpangs of the Modern Era," *Archiv für Reformationsgeschichte* 64 (1973): 13–33.

8. M. D. Knowles, "Some Trends in Scholarship, 1868–1968, in the Field of Medieval History," *Transactions of the Royal Historical Society*, 5th ser., 19 (1969): 149.

9. On these two groups, see the essays of David Knowles in *Great Historical Enterprises and Problems in Monastic History* (London: Thomas Nelson, 1962), chaps. 1, 2.

10. See David Knowles' account of the history of the *Monumenta* in *Great Historical Enterprises*, chap. 3.

11. Norman F. Cantor, *The Meaning of the Middle Ages. A Sociological and Cultural History* (Boston: Allyn and Bacon, 1973), 6.

12. For an overview, see Peter W. Williams, "The Varieties of American Medievalism," *Studies in Medievalism* 1 (1982): 7–20.

13. See Guggisberg, *Das europäisiche*, chaps. 1 and 2 on these figures.

14. See Joseph Byrnes, *The Virgin of Chartres: An Intellectual and Psychological History of the Work of Henry Adams* (Rutherford, NJ: Fairleigh Dickinson University Press, 1981).

15. See Guggisberg, *Das europäische*, 65–76.

16. On Gross, see Charles Homer Haskins, *Studies in Medieval Culture* (Oxford: Clarendon Press, 1929), 262–68.

17. For a brief account and a list of some students, see Courtenay, "Virgin," 14.

18. David Knowles, "Some Trends in Scholarship," 142–46, and Norman Cantor, *Meaning*, 15–17, 24, contain appreciations of the two.

19. On Lea, see Guggisberg, *Das europäische*, 85–101; and Haskins, *Studies*, 256–62. Leas' shifting religious allegiance, a factor of significance given some Roman Catholic attacks on his works, has been studied by E. A. Ryan, S.J., "The Religion of Henry Charles Lea," in *Mélanges Joseph de Ghéllinck, S.J.* (Gembloux: J. Duculot, 1951), 1043–51.

20. *English Historical Review* 8 (1893): 755.

21. *The History of Sacerdotal Celibacy*, 1.

22. Cited in Guggisberg, *Das europäische*, 99.

23. See Gleason, "Mass and Maypole."

24. An insightful evaluation can be found in James Hennesey, S.J., "Leo XIII's Thomistic Revival: A Political and Philosophical Event," in *Celebrating the Medieval Heritage: A Colloquy on the Thought of Aquinas and Bonaventure*, ed. David Tracy, *Journal of Religion* 58 (1978), Supplement, s185–97.

25. See Courtenay, "Virgin," 14–15; and Thomson, "Growth," 6–7.

26. Lynn Thorndike, *A History of Magic and Experimental Science*, 8 vols. (New York: Macmillan, 1923–58); George Sarton, *An Introduction to the History of Science*, 3 vols. (Baltimore: Williams and Wilkins Company, 1927–48); C. H. Haskins, *Studies in the History of Mediaeval Science* (Cambridge, MA: Harvard University Press, 1924).

27. On Cram, see Robert Muccigrosso, "Ralph Adams Cram and the Modernity of Medievalism," *Studies in Medievalism* 1 (1982): 21–42.

28. Quoted in Courtenay, "Virgin," 17.

29. On the history of the formation of the Mediaeval Academy, see George R. Coffman, "The Mediaeval Academy of America: Historical Background and Prospect," *Speculum* 1 (1926): 5–18; George R. Coffman, "The Mediaeval Academy: Evaluation and Revaluation," *Speculum* 22 (1947): 446–57; and Luke Wenger, "The Medieval Academy and Medieval Studies in North America," in *Medieval Studies in North America*, 21–40.

30. See Wenger, "Medieval Academy," 32–34.

31. David Herlihy, "The American Medievalist: A Social and Professional Profile," *Speculum* 58 (1983): 883. The figures given in this paragraph are based on this article.

32. The register of North American medievalists compiled by the Medieval Institute of Western Michigan University at Kalamazoo contains almost eight thousand names.

33. Karl Morrison, "Fragmentation," 54.

34. Much has been written about the Annales School, but I have found nothing so illuminating as Braudel's own "Personal Testimony," in *Journal of Modern History* 44 (1972): 448–67.

35. I am adopting the phrase from a book of Lucien Febvre's essays, *A New Kind of History*, ed. Peter Burke, trans. K. Folca (New York: Harper and Row, 1973).

36. On the issue of cultural history and its problems, see Karl J. Weintraub, *Visions of Culture* (University of Chicago Press, 1966), and E. H. Gombrich, *In Search of Cultural History* (Oxford: Clarendon Press, 1969).

37. On the contribution of Le Bras, see E. Poulat, "La storia sociale e religiosa dopo Gabriel Le Bras," *Ricerche di Storia Sociale e Religiosa*, n.s., 10 (1976): 7–17.

38. The case is presented in several of the essays in Jacques Le Goff, *Time, Work, and Culture in the Middle Ages* (University of Chicago Press, 1980). For another series of essays illustrative of the concerns of the recent "Annalesists," see Emmanuel Le Roy Ladurie, *The Territory of the Historian* (University of Chicago Press, 1979).

39. On the changing views of medieval religion in recent historical scholarship, see John Van Engen, "The Christian Middle Ages as an Historiographical Problem," *American Historical Review* 91 (1986): 519–52.

40. Wenger, "Medieval Academy," 25.

41. Morrison, "Fragmentation," 56–63 with helpful charts.

42. Wenger, "Medieval Academy," 26.

43. These programs are surveyed by George Hardin Brown and Phyllis Rugg Brown in "Medieval Studies Programs in North America," in *Medieval Studies in North America*, 57–80.

44. On these groups, see Paul E. Szarmach, "Medieval Associations in North America," in *Medieval Studies in North America*, 81–96.

45. The topics were "Dante's Theology" in vol. 2 (1889); "The Renaissance, the Revival of Learning and Art in the Fourteenth and Fifteenth Centuries" in vol. 3 (1891); and "St. Thomas of Canterbury" in vol. 5 (1893). In addition, Schaff's inaugural address as first president in 1888 was a characteristically broad piece on "The Progress of Religious Freedom as Shown in the History of Religious Toleration Acts," which included a look at the Middle Ages.

46. Lea wrote on "Indulgences in Spain" for the first volume of 1888, and on "The Absolution Formula of the Templars" in vol. 5.

47. Ayer contributed four papers on medieval topics: "The Development of the Appellate Jurisdiction of the Roman See" (1st ser., 1897); "The Letters of Einhard," trans. Henry Preble and annotated by Ayer (2d ser., vol. 1); "On the Medieval National Church" (presidential address for 1913, published in vol. 4 of the 2d ser.); and "Church Councils of the Anglo-Saxons" (2d ser., vol. 7).

48. David Schaff's presidential address "The Council of Constance: Its Fame and Its Failure" appeared in vol. 6 of the 2d ser. He also delivered a paper on "John Huss's Treatise on the Church" in vol. 4 of the 2d ser.

49. Spinka's "The Latin Church of the Early Crusades" appeared in vol. 8 (1939), while Petry's "Medieval Eschatology and St. Francis of Assisi" appeared in vol. 9 (1940). Petry has other articles in vols. 16, 21, 31, 34.

50. Esp., George Tavard, "Holy Church or Holy Writ: A Dilemma of the Fourteenth Century" in vol. 23 (1954); George H. Williams, "The Sacramental Presupposition of Anselm's *Cur Deus Homo*," in vol 26 (1957); and Hayden White, "Pontius of Cluny, the Curia Romana and End of Gregorianism in Rome," in vol. 27 (1958).

51. Christopher Kleinhenz, "Medieval Journals and Publications Series in North America," in *Medieval Studies in North America*, 122, provides the figures for the *PMLA* and *AHR* cited here and below.

52. This figure is close to the *PMLA* average of 11 percent for the period 1960–69 and well ahead of the dismal 6 percent for medieval articles in the *AHR* for the same period.

53. E.g., R. I. Burns, "The Organization of a Medieval Cathedral Community: The Chapter of Valencia (1238–1280)," in vol. 31 (1962); Claus-Peter Clasen, "Medieval Heresies in the Reformation," in vol. 32 (1963); Jeffrey Russell,

"Saint Boniface and the Eccentrics," in vol. 33 (1964); and R. A. Markus, "The Imperial Administration and the Church in Byzantine Africa," in vol. 36 (1967).

54. Quoted from the "Report of the Secretary" in the *Papers of the American Society of Church History*, ser. 1, 1 (1888): xv.

Reformation Studies

Robert M. Kingdon

EFORMATION studies have always held an important place in the research program of the American Society of Church History. Indeed from the perspective of some, perhaps of medievalists or specialists in modern Europe, they may have held too large a place, a place greater than they deserve for a balanced understanding of the total span of church history. This has been true, however, from the society's beginning, from the days of its foundation by Philip Schaff.

For Schaff can be said to have founded not only the American Society of Church History but also the specialty of Reformation studies within it. Scholarly study of the Reformation remained one of his abiding interests throughout his life. He helped impose upon the early ASCH, furthermore, not only an interest in the Reformation but also a distinctive approach to it. That approach was marked by three qualities:

(1). The geographic focus of Schaff's interest was Germanic, in keeping with his own upbringing in German Switzerland, his education in Germany, and his years of service to the German Reformed community in the United States. Thus his massive multivolume *History of the Christian Church*, one of the many fundamental reference works he wrote, comes to a climax in two concluding volumes, one on the Reformation in Germany, with particular attention to the role of Luther, the other on the Reformation in Switzerland, with particular attention to its development in Zurich and Geneva (first published New York: Scribner's, 1888 and 1892). Only in the latter half of the second volume did he explore in any depth the spread of the Reformation in any area beyond its Germanic homeland. In this work he never did get to its spread to English-speaking countries.

(2). The topical focus of Schaff's interest was intellectual and theological, with some secondary attention to the political context in which the Reformation developed. He devoted relatively little attention to the impact of the Reformation upon the common people or to the social context in which the movement developed. In this he reflected the tendency of his generation in Germany to emphasize the formative power of ideas in history, to some degree no doubt, under the influence of the philosophy of Hegel, and also to consider the formal history of politics. His interest in the theological defining of religious movements is illustrated with particular clarity in yet another fundamental work of reference, his three-volume *Creeds of Christendom* (first published New York: Harper, 1877), which devotes considerable attention to Germanic creeds of the Reformation period but also ranges far more widely than his *History* to include many Anglo-Saxon Protestant creeds and a number of Roman Catholic doctrinal definitions.

(3). For Schaff church history was a handmaiden to theology, and much of its justification was to be found in the contributions it could make to a theology of contemporary value to the society in which he lived. He may have been best known in his own time for his contribution to the Mercersburg theology; in any case his historical studies were designed in part to undergird that theology. He was also known for an ecumenical openness to historical study of other traditions than his own, suggested by the range of his *Creeds of Christendom*, although this openness occasionally got him into trouble with the narrow-minded.

To some degree the approach of Schaff as delineated by these three qualities has continued to characterize Reformation studies within the American Society of Church History in the decades since his death. There is a central current of Reformation studies that continues to draw its inspiration from Germany and to focus its attention upon that country, that continues to inspect the formal theology developed within the Reformation, and that continues to seek to make history relevant by connecting theology then and now. That this has been so is in some degree due to the influence of German education upon a number of the native Americans who succeeded Schaff as specialists on Reformation studies within the leadership of the ASCH. Thus both Williston Walker and William W. Rockwell who were active as leaders of the society in the generation after Schaff's death earned Ph.D. degrees at German universities and published their dissertations in Germany. Walker was trained at the University of Leipzig, taught at Hartford and Yale, and served the society as its president in 1907, the year of its reestablishment as an entity separate from the American Historical Association. Rockwell was trained at the University of Göttingen, taught at the Union Theological Seminary in New York, and served the society in several capacities, as its secretary and editor from 1912 to 1917, then as its president in 1926.[1]

This tendency to follow in the Schaff tradition of emphasizing the Germanic and the theological in Reformation studies has continued to be true in the later twentieth century, in good part due to fresh infusions into the United States of distinguished scholarly immigrants from Europe with interests of this type. Many could be mentioned but two stand out for the charismatic power of their teaching and the range of their influence on their students and contemporaries. They are Wilhelm Pauck, who immigrated to the United States from Germany in 1925, soon after the First World War, and Heiko Oberman, who immigrated to the United States from the Netherlands in 1958.

Pauck had been trained primarily in Berlin during and after the war by the generation of great intellectuals who provided such glory to German scholarship in that period. They included Harnack, for whom history was a crucial tool in the development of a liberal theology; Troeltsch, who blended sociology and history in such masterful and suggestive ways; and Holl, who launched a renaissance in Luther studies. Pauck spent much of his career, first at the Chicago Theological Seminary and the Divinity School of the University of Chicago, then at the Union Theological Seminary in New York, relaying to generations of Americans the teachings of these giants. He had begun his own scholarly career with a dissertation on the ethics of Martin Bucer as they were worked out in England toward the end of Bucer's career, but he did not support in any really major way the further development of studies on Bucer and on the Reformation in England. He rather focused the attention of his students primarily upon the thought of Luther and its massive contributions to the entire Reformation movement. And he guided his students to consider the continuation of the great Lutheran tradition in the hands of his more liberal successors, primarily Schleiermacher in the early nineteenth century and his own colleague Paul Tillich in the mid-twentieth century. For Pauck, thus, as for Schaff, Reformation studies were above all Germanic, theological, and connected to the modern theological enterprise. He continued to look for ways in which the theological insights of Luther could prove useful in modern and secular American circles. And Pauck looked to the American Society of Church History as a primary vehicle for the encouragement of this type of scholarship. He served as its president, in 1936, as one of the editors of its journal, 1943–53, and in many other capacities in his long career. The society in return honored him with a special session devoted to recalling his interests in 1980, shortly before he died.[2]

Pauck's influence has in turn been carried on to yet another generation by his students. Preeminent among them are Jaroslav Pelikan, now at Yale University, and Brian Gerrish, now at the Chicago Divinity School. Both made their most important initial mark as interpreters of Luther, and both have ranged widely beyond the Reformation period in the manner of their mentor. Pelikan helped supervise a team of scholars who prepared the best modern translation into English of all of Luther's works. He then became deeply involved in the dialogue between Lutherans and Catholics sparked by the ecumenical movement issuing from the Second Vatican Council. He turned more recently to a massive multivolume history of Christian doctrine over the centuries on a scale that surely rivals Harnack. That history has now reached the period of the Reformation in its fourth volume, setting the movement more firmly than before within the Catholic context from which it first developed.[3] Gerrish wrote a particularly fine study of the relations between reason and grace in Luther's theology. Then he became much interested in Calvin's theology and in the parallels between Lutheran and Calvinist doctrine in the Reformation period. He also became interested in the development within Lutheranism toward a more liberal position through theologians like Schleiermacher.[4] And he prepared for twentieth-century students an update of Schaff's *Creeds*, in a short but useful source book titled *The Faith of Christendom* (Cleveland: World, 1963). Both Pelikan and Gerrish have written and encouraged the writing of histories of Reformation thought that are highly sophisticated theologically and sensitive to the theological needs of modern society. Both have served the American Society of Church History as presidents, Pelikan in 1965, Gerrish in 1979, and in many other ways. Both have trained students who are now making important contributions to Reformation studies both within the churches and within institutions of higher learning.

Oberman had been raised in the Netherlands during the Nazi occupation, so had been made deeply aware as a boy of the brutality and bigotry of which German culture was capable. But his early training by Dutch experts in the history of theology had introduced him to an intellectual approach that was essentially Germanic, and this he relayed to Americans when he arrived as a junior professor at the Harvard Divinity School in 1958. He encouraged his students to plunge into intensive research upon a theme he felt to be of particular importance, the medieval sources of Reformation thought, and he quickly formed a distinctive school of brilliant young scholars dedicated to exploring this theme. He laid out himself a programmatic statement of his approach to this research problem in his *Harvest of Medieval Theology* (Cambridge, MA: Harvard University Press, 1963). And his students explored facets of this problem in a series of monographs characterized by an erudition and rigor previously uncommon on the American scene. Unlike Pauck, Oberman did not stay in the United States. He moved to Germany in 1966, to become director of the world's largest institute for research in Reformation studies at the University of Tübingen. But he continued to assist and encourage young American scholars from that vantage point. And in 1984 to returned to America, to the University of Arizona from which he will surely continue to exercise an important influence.

Oberman's students include William Courtenay, whose editions of the eucharistic writings of Gabriel Biel clarified one important source of Luther's thought; Steven Ozment, whose studies of the mystical theology of Eckhardt and Tauler clarified another medieval complex of ideas against which Luther reacted; and David Steinmetz, whose studies of the relations between Luther and his own Catholic spiritual adviser, Staupitz, clarified yet another facet of Luther's intellectual background.⁵ The focus of all these studies was Germanic and was upon intellectual history. They served to deepen understanding in important ways of Luther, the most seminal theologian of the Reformation. They were not as carefully connected to the contemporary theological enterprise as the work of Pauck's school, however. And this may help to explain why many of Oberman's students have pursued careers in more secular settings and turned to more secular interests. Not all of them, furthermore, have become active in the American Society of Church History. Courtenay, for example, has become an eminent specialist in medieval intellectual history, with a growing interest in the history of education, who became president of the ASCH in 1988, but whose main professional energies are channeled through societies of medieval specialists. Ozment has become an unusually productive and provocative secular historian of the Reformation, without much interest in the ASCH. Of these three, only Steinmetz has been active continuously in the society, serving as its president in 1985. This pattern of diverging interests points to the fact that Reformation studies in America are no longer being contained within the American Society of Church History but are moving into many other channels, only some of which overlap with the ASCH.

This tendency of Reformation studies in America to diversify has been opposed by some members of the ASCH, most notably by Wilhelm Pauck. Shortly after the end of the Second World War, two eminent American specialists on the Reformation, Harold Grimm of Ohio State, and Roland Bainton of the Yale Divinity School, proposed the creation of a new society devoted solely to Reformation studies, the American Society of Reformation Research. They were both in close touch with leading German specialists on the Reformation and were concerned with attempts to rebuild the German *Verein für Reformationsgeschichte* and its important publication series. They proposed the creation of a sister society in the United States that could provide financial and moral assistance to the Germans in rebuilding their research enterprise from the ravages of war. At an organizational meeting of this new American Society of Reformation Research held under the chairmanship of Grimm at the American Historical Association's annual convention in 1950, Pauck appeared. He made an impassioned plea to Grimm and the other organizers to give up their project, on grounds that it would undercut the work on Reformation studies within the American Society of Church History and dilute American effort in this field. His plea was politely ignored, and the American Society of Reformation Research (recently renamed Society of Reformation Research) was created.

The worst of Pauck's fears proved to be unfounded. Many of the leaders and members of the ASRR also remained or became active in the ASCH. Bainton and Grimm, indeed, both served as presidents of the ASCH, Bainton back in 1940, Grimm in 1961. But there were and are a certain number of historians whose interests are primarily secular who joined the ASRR but not the ASCH. And there also remain a certain number of historians specializing on the Reformation period whose interests are primarily theological who joined the ASCH but not the ASRR. This new society by its very organizational structure, of course, was linked to the Germanic research enterprise, and thus maintained the geographic focus of the central ASCH tradition. But its members began branching out into explorations of new kinds of problems, and thus diversified the topical focus of the ASCH. And this new diversity in turn had distinct effects upon some of the Reformation studies sponsored by the ASCH.

That diversity is illustrated by the interests of the founders of the ASRR. Roland Bainton was born in England but educated within the United States, ending at the Yale Divinity School where he subsequently spent his entire career as a faculty member. He is perhaps most widely known as the most successful single popularizer of Reformation studies, the man who most effectively explained the Reformation tradition to the general public in the twentieth century. He won this reputation primarily with two popular histories, both of which sold at least a million copies and were translated into many languages. They are *The Church of Our Fathers* (New York: Scribner's, 1941), an elementary survey of all church history, of special use in Sunday School classes, and *Here I Stand* (Nashville: Abingdon, 1950), a dramatic popular biography of Martin Luther. Bainton's research interests, however, lay in the struggle between bigotry and toleration in the Reformation period, and his most solid contributions lay in this field. His hero was Sebastien Castellion, that sixteenth-century precursor of liberalism in theology and biblical studies, whose attacks against Calvin for the burning of Servetus were a landmark in the development of the idea of toleration, and whose career suffered as a result. Bainton also wrote erudite monographs on other sixteenth-century victims of religious intolerance, notably Servetus, Ochino, and Joris. When he turned to the theological giants of the Reformation, to Luther and Calvin, his intensive research was directed primarily to their reactions against religious deviance.[6] Like Pauck and Oberman, Bainton was interested in intellectual history, but essentially of a certain kind, a kind he felt to be of supreme relevance to the twentieth century. For Bainton was by conviction a pacifist, with ideas clearly shaped by the two traumatic world wars of the twentieth century. He was firmly opposed to any kind of war, and he wanted to use historical argument to support a continuing Christian campaign against not only war but also all types of human violence. He was too good a scholar to let this passion distort the historical record, but it clearly guided the lines of his research. It also influenced the work of a number of his many students. Thus Franklin Littell, to name one of the more prominent, has devoted much of his career to reminding mainline Christians of their responsibilities for the persecution of minority sects and of Jews and to encouraging reconciliation among Protestants of every type and between Christians and Jews. Many Bainton students became active in the American Society for Reformation Research. Perhaps the most active has been Miriam Usher Chrisman, whose studies of the Reformation in Strasbourg, particularly of the contributions of its publishing industry to sixteenth-century culture, have attracted international respect.[7] She has served as its president and now helps edit its journal. Most Bainton students, however, have also been active in the American Society of Church History. One of them, indeed, Clyde Manschreck, the Melanchthon specialist, served as its president, in 1974.

Harold Grimm was born in the United States, but in a thoroughly Germanic and Lutheran setting. He had been trained in theology while young but soon turned to history of a more secular type. His main contribution to Reformation studies lies probably in his encouragement of work on the social dimensions of the Reformation. He became particularly interested in the history of the city of Nuremberg, in population and in wealth one of the most important of all cities in sixteenth-century Germany, and a leader among the many that adopted Lutheranism. He spent much of the later years of his career in writing a biography of the lay civil servant who guided Nuremberg into the Lutheran camp, *Lazarus Spengler: A Lay Leader of the Reformation* (Columbus: Ohio State University Press, 1978). He was a charismatic teacher and supervisor of theses at the Ohio State University, who guided dozens of students into historical research, often but not always on aspects of the history of Nuremberg. Thus Carl Christensen, to cite one example, has done important work on how the Reformation affected the patronage of art in Nuremberg.[8] While James Estes, to cite another example, has worked on the role of the early Lutheran

Johannes Brenz in organizing the Protestant churches of the duchy of Württemberg.[9] Many of Grimm's students remain active teachers of Reformation studies in colleges and universities all over north America. Most of them, however, have gone in a more secular direction than the students of Bainton and Oberman, and fewer of them are active in the American Society of Church History.

Just as the ASCH proved too confining to provide an outlet for all American work in Reformation studies during the 1950s, so did the ASRR prove too confining to provide an outlet for the growing numbers of scholars entering the field in the 1970s. The result was the creation of the Sixteenth-Century Studies Conference. Its real founder was Carl S. Meyer of the Concordia Seminary of the Lutheran Church-Missouri Synod in St. Louis. This church, of course, was the creation of German immigrants to the United States who were resolutely conservative in their theology, many of whom had wanted to escape the liberalizing tendencies at work in nineteenth-century Germany. They wanted to maintain in the purest possible form the confessional Lutheranism of the late sixteenth and early seventeenth centuries. They were not interested in the modernizing tendencies in theology that attracted scholars like Pauck in universities like Chicago and Harvard. They looked to the study of church history as a way of conserving their tradition, not updating it. And they had tended to stay to themselves and avoid contamination from the wider world both in this country and in Europe in the first decades of their existence.

Meyer, however, was a prime representative of a group within the Missouri Synod who wanted to widen their perspectives, who wanted to find a common ground with representatives of other traditions in a purely scholarly study of the Reformation, and who was prepared to muster the material resources to make that possible. One result was the creation of a Foundation for Reformation Research, now the Center for Reformation Research, in St. Louis, as a library and study center for experts on the Reformation. A further result was the creation of the Sixteenth-Century Studies Conference, which has developed an ambitious publishing program in the field and sponsors an annual conference. These new entities drew together in a curious way scholars who were religious conservatives and who were purely secular. Few of them try any longer to connect Reformation research to the theological needs of modern Christianity. Many of them broke away from the emphasis on Germanic and intellectual topics that had traditionally characterized the field. Many of them, indeed, are not primarily interested in the Reformation at all. Large numbers of specialists in English literature and in other allied disciplines, interested in the period of the Reformation but not always its subject matter, have joined the Sixteenth-Century Studies Conference. Its 1984–85 president, Raymond Waddington, for example, is a specialist in Elizabethan literature.

A considerable number of scholars active in the Sixteenth-Century Studies Conference are students of Lewis Spitz and Robert M. Kingdon. Again there is overlap with the American Society of Church History, since both Spitz and Kingdon have served as its president, in 1977 and 1980 respectively, and a number of their students have been active in it. But there is probably even less overlap between the SCSC and the ASCH than between the ASRR and the ASCH. And there is an even greater, if not universal, tendency for SCSC members to move in secular directions. Spitz is himself a product of the Lutheran Church-Missouri Synod, with theological training. But he completed his training in history departments at Chicago and Harvard and has taught primarily in history departments of secular universities, first at the University of Missouri-Columbia, then at Stanford. He has been a particularly successful undergraduate teacher and has also created a strong school of graduate students. His published research has been focused less on the Reformation than on the Renaissance in Germany, on such crucial figures in the more secular side of the world of thought from which Luther emerged as Conrad Celtis.[10] Spitz's students tend to work more on aspects of Renaissance thought, in Italy and France as well as in Germany. Connections to the Reformation, to be sure, remain obvious in much of their work. Thus James Kittelson has worked on Capito, the German humanist who helped bring Protestantism to Strasbourg,[11] and then upon his successors in the establishment of a firmly Lutheran church in that city. And Anne Schutte has worked on Vergerio, an Italian humanist who converted to Protestantism,[12] and other Italian intellectuals of Protestant tendency. Other Spitz students have branched off in yet other but parallel directions. By concentrating on the generation in which the Reformation began, most of these scholars have made important contributions, both direct and indirect, to a full understanding of the intellectual context in which the Reformation developed. Just as Oberman and his students have helped us understand more fully the ideas in which Luther was trained and against which he reacted, so have Spitz and his students helped us understand more fully the ideas that Luther and his associates assimilated from their immediate environment or with which they had to compete.

It may be indelicate for Kingdon to comment on Kingdon, but for the sake of completeness it seems advisable. He was trained in diplomatic history, moved into ecclesiastical diplomacy and then into other aspects of ecclesiastical history, primarily in Geneva and other French-speaking parts of Protestant Europe.[13] He has taught almost exclusively in secular universities, supervising graduate work at the University of Iowa and then the University of Wisconsin-Madison. A good many graduate students whose work he supervised, however, also had formal training in theology. They would include John P. Donnelly, a Jesuit priest who worked on the development of a scholastic theology in such Reformed thinkers as Peter Martyr Vermigli and is now turning to the history of the Jesuits; Robert A. Kolb, an ordained minister in the Lutheran Church-Missouri Synod, who works on Amsdorf and a variety of other Lutheran theologians of the confessional period in late sixteenth-century Germany; Robert V. Schnucker, an ordained Presbyterian minister, who has become the presiding genius arranging the publication programs of the Sixteenth-Century Studies Conference; Jerome Friedman, who received much of his undergraduate training at the Hebrew University in Jerusalem and has now become an active student of Christian Hebraica of the Reformation period.[14] Some but not all of these scholars have become active in the American Society of Church History, but all of them are even more active in the Sixteenth-Century Studies Conference.

If the central tradition of Reformation studies within the American Society of Church History as established by Schaff was focused upon Germany and upon theology, however, this did not mean that it was focused exclusively upon German theologians. We have already noted that Schaff allowed ample space within his own survey of Reformation history for analysis of Calvin's Reformation as it first developed in French-speaking Geneva, and inspection of some of his other work reveals a considerable interest in Calvin's theology. This is understandable, given Schaff's own background within the Swiss Reformed Church, and it is consonant, indeed, with an important strand of Reformation studies in Germany. While there are French scholars who have made more important contributions to knowledge of Calvin's biography and career, most of the best critical editions of Calvin's writings and most of the really sophisticated analyses of Calvin's thought have come from German scholars. And American specialists on Calvin have tended to follow the lead of this Germanic school of Calvin studies.

Williston Walker was one of several historians who made important contributions to Calvinist studies early in the twentieth century, in good part with his biography, *John Calvin: The Organizer of Reformed Protestantism, 1509–1564* (New York: Putnam, 1906). But the most important and the most influential single American scholar of the century specializing in study of Calvin and early Calvinism was surely John T. McNeill. He was actually a Canadian by birth and a medievalist by training, but his Presbyterian denominational affiliation quickly led him to an interest in Calvin studies, and it is for his work in this field that he is best known. In a long career beginning at the Chicago Divinity School and continuing at the Union Theological Seminary, he pursued and sponsored much useful research on Calvin. One of his earlier interests was in Calvin's attempts to keep early Protestants together in a unified church, revealing a distinctly ecumenical interest, in the Schaff tradition. McNeill also investigated the political and social implications of some of Calvin's writings.[15] But his most influential contributions were probably his synthetic ones, summing up all of Calvin research, notably in his own survey text, *The History and Character of Calvinism* (New York: Oxford University Press, 1954), and in the English translation he sponsored of Calvin's *Institutes of the Christian Religion* (Philadelphia: Westminster Press, 1960). In that translation project, McNeill enlisted the help of an able classicist, Ford Lewis Battles, and Battles went on to make other contributions of importance in the analysis and appreciation of Calvin's Latin writings. Many of McNeill's students and protégés, furthermore, made valuable contributions to our understanding of Calvin's theology. Preeminent among them were Quirinus Breen, who began as an expert on Calvin's debt to Renaissance humanism and went on to more general studies of the debt of early Protestantism to humanist rhetoric,[16] and Edward Dowey, Jr., who prepared a highly sophisticated Zurich dissertation on Calvin's epistemology[17] and who became an excellent trainer of the next generation of experts on the thought of Calvin and his associates. Most of Dowey's teaching career has been spent at the Princeton Theological Seminary, which, because of its Presbyterian affiliation, has particularly encouraged the study of Calvinism. In guiding the intensive study of Calvin at Princeton, Dowey was maintaining a tradition established well before the arrival of Schaff in this country. It is a tradition that promises to continue into the future as well, in good part because of the recent appointment to the Princeton faculty of Jane Dempsey Douglass, the 1983 president of the ASCH, who was originally trained in the medieval background to the Reformation by Oberman, but who has recently turned to Calvin studies. Her most recent work on Calvin's attitude toward the role of women in the church adds a fresh and timely new dimension to this field of studies.[18] McNeill himself was a devoted member of the American Society of Church History, serving as its president in 1935. He actively recruited younger scholars into membership, including this author. It comes as no surprise, therefore, that many of his students have followed him in positions of leadership within the ASCH, with Breen, for example, serving as president in 1956.

Just as scholars affiliated with the Lutheran Church-Missouri Synod have made important contributions to the study of the Lutheran Reformation, because of their own tradition and theological perspective, so have scholars affiliated with the Christian Reformed Church made similar contributions to the study of Calvinist Reformation, because of a very similar tradition and perspective. Most of the early members of this church were emigrants from the Netherlands, who came to this country in part to keep Calvinism pure, to avoid the contamination they saw creeping into the established Reformed Church of the Netherlands from liberal theology. They have accordingly sponsored scholarly study of Calvin's theology, primarily at Calvin College and Calvin Theological Seminary in Grand Rapids, Michigan. And they have recently created the H. H. Meeter Center there for the continuing study of the Calvinist tradition. When plans were being made for this center, Ford Lewis Battles was invited to Grand Rapids and spent the last years of his life there. Its research focus, therefore, predictably follows the interests of Battles, concentrating on Calvin's theology, particularly as expressed in his Latin works. But the Center has also enlisted the interest and assistance of several other scholars, including some of quite secular background. Like the St. Louis complex of Reformation historians, therefore, it combines scholars of conservative theological commitment and of relatively secular interest in a program of pure historical scholarship that does not attempt to link that scholarship very closely with the contemporary theological enterprise.

Some of the most interesting research to issue from this Christian Reformed community, however, is the work of scholars who have broken away from formal affiliation with its church. In an earlier generation, the most eminent of these was Quirinus Breen, who left the Christian Reformed Church to become a Presbyterian and who studied with McNeill. In the present generation, the most eminent is William Bouwsma, a historian whose training at Harvard and career at the University of Illinois at Champaign-Urbana and then the University of California-Berkeley have been resolutely secular, but who retains a strong interest in Calvin. A massive intellectual biography of Calvin that Bouwsma recently completed, seeking to place the Reformer's thought firmly within its sixteenth-century intellectual context, is very likely to prove the next really major contribution to Calvin studies. A number of Bouwsma's students, furthermore, have made important contributions to Reformation studies, primarily in intellectual history. One of the more prominent is Charles Nauert, now of the University of Missouri-Columbia, who published a model study of the sixteenth-century magus and skeptic Agrippa von Nettesheim,[19] and who now directs the monograph series sponsored by the Sixteenth-Century Studies Conference.

A number of these American specialists on Calvin have created a new Calvin Studies Society, with its headquarters in Grand Rapids and its records and publications entrusted to Peter De Klerk of the Calvin College and Seminary Library. But most of them also remain active in the American Society of Church History. Their work thus forms another part of the program of Reformation studies associated with the ASCH.

If many Reformation experts within the American Society of Church History have remained faithful to the tradition of Schaff by their attention to the thought of Luther and Calvin, others have departed from that tradition in one important respect. This is in their attention to the religious radicals of the Reformation period. Luther and Calvin and their associates feared and despised these figures as intemperate fanatics, bent on reviving ancient heresies and destroying existing society and likely to bring destruction to the entire movement for religious reform by provoking to extreme violence the forces of established order. Many of the followers of Luther and Calvin have shared this opinion of these radicals. Only in the twentieth century has the thought of these radicals at last been subjected to close and impartial analysis.

The American scholar who has done the most to shape this fresh line of research is George Huntston Williams of the Harvard Divinity School, the 1958 president of the American Society of Church History. Harvard's own tradition of religious radicalism, beginning with its initial commitment to Congregationalism when that was the most radical form of Puritan protest against the Church of England and continuing with its shift to Unitarianism when the Congregational commitment to a version of Calvinism proved stifling to many in nineteenth-century America, provided a particularly apt milieu for this line of inquiry. Williams' monumental book, *The Radical Reformation* (Philadelphia: Westminster Press, 1962), provides a typology for analysis of the entire movement, fleshed out with information and bibliography on scores of local groups and individual leaders. His translations of sample works by some of the more significant radicals in the volume edited with Angel M. Mergal, *Spiritual and Anabaptist Writers: Documents Illustrative of the Radical Reformation and Evangelical Catholicism* (Philadelphia: Westminster Press, 1957), furthermore, make these texts more widely available to interested students. He continues to work in this field in his retirement, preparing fresh studies of the religious radicals who found refuge in sixteenth-century Poland. And many of his students have pursued parallel studies of religious radicals elsewhere. John Tedeschi, for example, has reinvigorated the whole field of study of the Italian Reformation. He began with studies of such highly intellectual Italian religious deviants as the Sozzinis, then helped organize edition projects, most importantly the *Corpus Reformatorum Italicorum*, in collaboration with scholars in Italy. He is now engaged in studies of the ways in which the Roman Inquisition managed to suppress the development of this type of religious deviation in Italy, and in projects to edit its records.

Another series of studies of these radicals has issued from the Yale Divinity School, from Roland Bainton and his students. For Bainton's interest in problems of religious persecution and toleration inevitably led him to a closer examination of these radicals who were prime sixteenth-century targets of persecution. Recent emigrants from Germany have contributed in important ways to some of this research. Preeminent among them is Hans Hillerbrand, who produced a number of important studies and a very useful series of bibliographies focused particularly on those radicals known as Anabaptists.[20] This was while he was still an active teacher and research scholar at the Duke University Divinity School, before he was lost to academic administration in other universities.

Here again the descendants of a denominational tradition made important contributions to general scholarly understanding of their own peculiar heritage. The most productive and developed of those contributions came from the Mennonite community, and owed a great deal to the formidable energy of Harold S. Bender. He took the lead in making Mennonite schools like Goshen College important centers for Reformation research, in establishing a scholarly periodical, the *Mennonite Quarterly Review* (1926–), and in creating a scholarly work of reference, the *Mennonite Encyclopedia* (1955–). And he published himself important contributions to this line of research, most notably his biography of Conrad Grebel, a leader of the first group of Swiss Brethren in Zurich.[21] It can be argued that Bender and his associates made greater contributions to the study of Mennonite history than any similar group in Europe, one of the few branches of Reformation study for which this claim can be made.

Bender was particularly insistent on separating the peaceful religious radicals who followed the lead of Grebel and Menno Simons from the violent religious revolutionaries who went into battle inspired by Thomas Müntzer during the peasants' wars or who seized the city of Münster in 1536. For him there were two entirely separate strands within the early history of Anabaptism. It was unfair to confound them, to tar the memory of the peaceful brethren from whom the Mennonites had descended with the brush of association with Müntzer and the revolutionaries of Münster. It has been the task of many of his successors, including some within the Mennonite community, to point out that there was a tendency toward hagiography in Bender's work, that the two types of religious radicals were not always that distinct, that peaceful religious radicals could become violent revolutionaries, and that violent revolutionaries, for that matter, could become peaceful religious radicals. It has also been the task of other historians, most notably Claus-Peter Clasen, to point out that most of these communities of religious radicals were small and ephemeral, and that few had much influence in the period of the Reformation itself.[22]

Bender nevertheless reinforced a strong interest in religious radicalism of the Reformation period within the American Society of Church History, serving in 1943 as its president. Particularly during and right after the Second World War the history of these persecuted radicals proved powerfully attractive to many Americans. These radicals were seen as pioneers and precursors, who worked out patterns of church organization and social criticism that provide useful models for later Christian communities, models that are still of value. For these sixteenth-century religious radicals created churches that were truly free, apart from the social contamination that so often goes with established churches, connected as they are with governments and other institutions of social control. The form of church organization these radicals developed, in fact, is the very form that came to dominate the American religious scene after our revolutionary war. It provides a model that Europeans, mindful of the frightful perversions of Christianity that infected so many of the established churches in Nazi Germany, might do well to consider carefully. Franklin Littell made that case with particular cogency in his *Anabaptist View of the Church: An Introduction to Sectarian Protestantism* (Chicago: American Society of Church History, 1952), an ASCH Brewer Prize essay.

Not only that variety of Reformation scholarship found within the American Society of Church History, but really all modern historical scholarship, was the creation of Germans. It was they who worked out the methods, the approaches, and the emphases that came to characterize professional research on all types of history throughout the world. This dependence on German models held true for most types of church history and it certainly held true for research on the Reformation. Reformation specialists within the American Society of Church History were thus patterning their work after the very best models available in the early decades of the society's existence. The overwhelming dominance of Germans in all branches of historical study, including study of the Reformation, however, really continued only up through the First World War. Historical scholarship in Germany suffered massive damage during the Nazi period and during the Second World War. It lost at least one generation of its most promising leaders and it lost the respect of much of the rest of the world. Since that time, accordingly, leadership has been shifting. For most historians, the intellectual leadership of their profession has moved pretty firmly during the last several decades to France. French historians, particularly of the Annales school, have for almost fifty years now generated the kind of excitement and exercised the kind of authority that formerly flowed from German scholarship. This French influence has become increasingly marked in the United States. It logically should have a significant impact on Reformation studies, for the greatest of this new school of French historians, such scholars as Lucien Febvre, Fernand Braudel, Emmanuel Leroy Ladurie, and Jean Delumeau, have been specialists upon the very early modern period of European history in which the Reformation developed. To historians of this school, long-term trends are more important and interesting than daily events, the geographic and economic and social contexts in which history developed are more important and interesting than the chronology of political acts, the mentality of the inarticulate lower classes deserves more research than the formal ideas of the intellectual elite. They thus share with Marxists a tendency to emphasize economic and social history, to focus attention on the lower orders of society, although many of them find the Marxist categories of analysis too schematic.[23]

Reformation study from this perspective has reached the United States of America. Perhaps its foremost exponent is Natalie Z. Davis, formerly of Toronto and the University of California-Berkeley, now of Princeton. In a series of brilliant essays, many of which have won prizes, she has sketched the impact of the religious choices forced by the Reformation upon apprentice and journeymen laborers in the printing industry, upon women, upon peasants.[24] She has drawn upon such allied disciplines as anthropology to explain how religious competition and religious change affected the texture of daily life in sixteenth-century Europe and provoked spasms of savage popular violence. She has helped bring to a wide public a richer sense of what it was like to live during the Reformation, by serving as a consultant to the company that produced the film, *The Return of Martin Guerre*, then writing a short book on the story providing the basis for that film (Cambridge, MA: Harvard University Press, 1983). Her evidence has been drawn largely from the history of France, most commonly from that of the city of Lyons, but much of what she has said has proved suggestive to students of other geographic areas. She has been enormously generous and stimulating to a generation of younger students.

Contributions from a similar point of view have been made by other scholars in America. Thus Gerald Strauss of Indiana University in his *Luther's House of Learning* (Baltimore: Johns Hopkins University Press, 1978) has provoked fruitful controversy by using data drawn from a wide-ranging study of German Protestant visitation reports to suggest that the educational enterprise to which the earliest Lutherans were so deeply committed did not succeed, that the Reformation did not in fact affect popular belief and behavior in any profound or meaningful way. Similarly thought-provoking conclusions have emerged from intensive work by American scholars of a technically demanding type in municipal archives. The study by Thomas Brady of the ruling elites in Strasbourg in the period that city turned Protestant has demonstrated how stimulating a semi-Marxist type of class analysis can be in explaining social change.[25] The studies of E.William Monter of the crucial role of the laity in Calvin's Geneva and of the institutions they created to channel a society that was radically different have demonstrated how many of the changes associated with the Reformation were really not the work of clergymen at all.[26]

Much of this new social history of the Reformation has been undertaken by scholars affiliated with the American Society of Church History. Davis, for example, was a member for a term of the society's executive council (1972–74), and several of these social historians have read papers in ASCH programs. But I think it fair to say that this approach does not represent the main focus of interest among ASCH members.

There are entire types of church history, furthermore, that have been largely ignored by members of the ASCH. From 1923 until his death in 1971, the great French expert on the canon law of the Roman Catholic church, Gabriel Le Bras, and his many students developed highly innovative ways of studying the history of ecclesiastical institutions that used not only traditional methods of legal analysis but also newer methods drawn from geography and sociology. The result was a tremendous outpouring of publications, ranging from magistral surveys to intensive archivally based analyses of local French dioceses. The scholars of the Le Bras school applied these methods primarily in studies of the medieval period, and for this reason are best known in the United States by medievalists. But they also applied these methods on occasion to the period of the Reformation and even later. Le Bras himself wrote important studies on the impact within France of seventeenth-century Jansenism and some of his students wrote comparisons of Protestant and Catholic institutions in areas where they coexisted.[27] These same methods have been used with illuminating results by historians in other countries, notably Poland,[28] but also Italy and even England. The methods of this school could be applied more generally to the study of Protestant ecclesiastical institutions and any such application should be particularly revealing when applied to the period of the Reformation in which those institutions were first created. But this possibility has escaped the notice of American historians of the Reformation. It has barely touched the work of American historians of other periods. One notable exception to this rule is Timothy Tackett's seminal studies of French Catholicism on the eve of the Revolution.[29]

This survey of Reformation studies within the American Society of Church History since the death of Philip Schaff has no doubt proved untidy. But it is untidy because the field is untidy. The Reformation remains one of the most important objects of research attracting members of the society. But their approaches to it differ, and the ongoing work within this country on the Reformation spills over into all sorts of channels outside of the ASCH. So there is no easy way to focus clearly and without distraction upon the state of this branch of church history within the society.

As the American Society of Church History enters its second century, in fact, its Reformation specialists face a choice of some magnitude. Do they wish above all to maintain their great tradition? Do they want to pour most of their energies into the channels first opened by Philip Schaff, to continue to map the terrain he so masterfully surveyed? Do they want to keep doing what they have done so well over the last hundred years? Or are they now prepared to broaden their horizons? Are they willing to dredge out new channels for historical research, channels that could lead in fresh directions that can scarcely be imagined? Are they prepared to risk the disappointments of blind alleys in the hope of gaining fresh new insights? Those are choices the next generation of Reformation specialists within the ASCH must make.

Notes

1. For general information on the role of Reformation studies in the early days of the American Society of Church History, see Henry Warner Bowden, *Church History in the Age of Science: Historiographical Patterns in the United States, 1876–1918* (Chapel Hill: University of North Carolina Press, 1971), especially the appendix on the ASCH, 239–45. See also the relevant volumes of *Church History* and the biographical articles in *The New Schaff-Herzog Encyclopedia of Religious Knowledge* on Philip Schaff, Walker, and Rockwell.

2. See Wilhelm Pauck, *From Luther to Tillich: The Reformers and Their Heirs*, ed. Marion Pauck (San Francisco: Harper and Row, 1984), for information on his career including a chronology, 210–15, and samples of his work.

3. Jaroslav Pelikan and Helmut T. Lehmann, eds., *Luther's Works: American Edition*, 54 vols., (St. Louis: Concordia, 1955–76); *The Riddle of Roman Catholicism* (New York and Nashville: Abingdon, 1959); *The Christian Tradition: a history of the development of doctrine*, vol. 4, *Reformation of Church and Dogma (1300–1700)* (University of Chicago Press, 1984).

4. B.A. Gerrish, *Grace and Reason: A Study in the Theology of Luther* (Oxford: Clarendon, 1962); *The Old Protestantism and the New: Essays on the Reformation Heritage* (University of Chicago Press, 1982).

5. *Gabrielis Biel Canonis Misse Expositio*, ed. Heiko A. Oberman and William J. Courtenay, 4 vols. (Wiesbaden: Steiner, 1963–67); Steven Ozment, *Homo Spiritualis: A Comparative Study of the Anthropology of Tauler, Gerson, and Martin Luther, 1509–1516* (Leiden: Brill, 1968); David Curtis Steinmetz, *Luther and Staupitz: An Essay in the Intellectual Origins of the Protestant Reformation* (Durham: Duke University Press, 1980).

6. Roland H. Bainton, *The Travail of Religious Liberty* (New York: Harper, 1951), provides his own useful general summary of this intensive monographic research, with appropriate references.

7. Miriam Usher Chrisman, *Lay Culture, Learned Culture: Books and Social Change in Strasbourg, 1480–1599* (New Haven: Yale University Press, 1982).

8. Carl C. Christensen, *Art and the Reformation in Germany* (Columbus: Ohio State University Press, 1979).

9. James Martin Estes, *Christian Magistrate and State Church: The Reforming Career of Johannes Brenz* (University of Toronto Press, 1982).

10. Lewis W. Spitz, *Conrad Celtis, the German Arch-Humanist* (Cambridge, MA: Harvard University Press, 1957); *The Religious Renaissance of the German Humanists* (Cambridge, MA: Harvard University Press, 1963).

11. James M. Kittelson, *Wolfgang Capito: From Humanist to Reformer* (Leiden: Brill, 1975).

12. Anne Jacobson Schutte, *Pier Paolo Vergerio: The Making of an Italian Reformer* (Geneva: Droz, 1977), an ASCH Brewer Prize essay.

13. For an introduction to his work, see Robert M. Kingdon, *Church and Society in Reformation Europe* (London: Variorum Reprints, 1985), a collection of previously published articles.

14. For samples of their work, see John Patrick Donnelly, *Calvinism and Scholasticism in Vermigli's Doctrine of Man and Grace* (Leiden: Brill, 1976); Robert Kolb, *Nikolaus von Amsdorf (1483–1565)* (Nieuwkoop: De Graaf, 1970); Jerome Friedman, *The Most Ancient Testimony: Sixteenth-Century Christian-Hebraica in the Age of Renaissance Nostalgia* (Athens: Ohio University Press, 1983).

15. John T. McNeill, *Unitive Protestantism* (New York: Abingdon, 1930); ed., *John Calvin on God and Political Duty* (New York: Liberal Arts, 1950).

16. Quirinus Breen, *John Calvin: A Study in French Humanism* (Grand Rapids, MI: Eerdmans, 1931), and *Christianity and Humanism: Studies in the History of Ideas* (Grand Rapids, MI: Eerdmans, 1968), a collection of articles.

17. Edward A. Dowey, Jr., *The Knowledge of God in Calvin's Theology* (New York: Columbia University Press, 1952).

18. Jane Dempsey Douglass, *Women, Freedom, and Calvin* (Philadelphia: Westminster Press, 1985). Cf. her first book, *Justification in Late Medieval Preaching: A Study of John Geiler of Keisersberg* (Leiden: E. J. Brill, 1966).

19. Charles G. Nauert, Jr., *Agrippa and the Crisis of Renaissance Thought* (Champaign: University of Illinois Press, 1965).

20. Hans J. Hillerbrand, *A Bibliography of Anabaptism* (Elkhart, IN: Institute of Mennonite Studies, 1962); *A Bibliography of Anabaptism, 1520–1630: A Sequel, 1962–1974* (St. Louis: Center for Reformation Research, 1975); *A Bibliography of Menno Simons* (Elkhart, IN: Institute of Mennonite Studies, 1962).

21. Harold S. Bender, *Conrad Grebel, ca. 1498–1526: The Founder of the Swiss Brethren, Sometimes Called the Anabaptists* (Goshen, IN: Mennonite Historical Society, 1950).

22. Claus-Peter Clasen, *Anabaptism, a Social History, 1525–1618* (Ithaca: Cornell University Press, 1972).

23. Perhaps the most seminal single work of the *Annales* school is Fernand Braudel, *La Méditerranée et le monde méditerranéen à l'époque de Philippe II* (Paris: Colin, 1949, 1966—substantially revised), which concentrates upon the period of the Catholic Counter-Reformation but devotes relatively little consideration to religious developments. Probably more suggestive to experts on the Reformation itself are such more specialized books as Lucien Febvre, *Le problème de l'incroyance au XVIe siècle: la religion de Rabelais* (Paris: A. Michel, 1942); Emmanuel Leroy Ladurie, *Le carnaval de Romans . . . 1579–1580* (Paris: Gallimard, 1979); Jean Delumeau, *Le catholicisme entre Luther et Voltaire* (Paris: Presses universitaires de France, 1971). All four have been translated into English.

24. Natalie Z. Davis, *Society and Culture in Early Modern France* (Stanford University Press, 1975), a collection of essays, provides the best introduction to her work.

25. Thomas A. Brady, Jr., *Ruling Class, Regime, and Reformation at Strasbourg, 1520–1555* (Leiden: Brill, 1978).

26. E. William Monter, *Studies in Genevan Government (1536–1605)* (Geneva: Droz, 1964); *Calvin's Geneva* (New York: Wiley, 1967).

27. For basic biographical and bibliographical information on Le Bras, including a list of analyses by others of his approach, see *Etudes d'histoire du droit canonique dédiées à Gabriel Le Bras*, 2 vols. (Paris: Sirey, 1965), I: v–xxxiii; for an example of one of the many local studies he sponsored, this one including some Protestant-Catholic comparisons, see André Schaer, *Le clergé paroissial catholique en haute Alsace sous l'ancien régime, 1648–1789* (Paris: Sirey, 1966).

28. See the publications of Jerzy Kloczowski and his colleagues at the Catholic University of Lublin. Kloczowski also chairs the Parish Studies Group of the International Commission for the Comparative Study of Ecclesiastical History that seeks to apply these methods in comparative studies across national boundaries.

29. Timothy Tackett, *Priest and Parish in Eighteenth-Century France: A Social and Political Study of the Curés in a Diocese of Dauphiné, 1750–1791* (Princeton University Press, 1977).

Immigration and American Christianity
A History of Their Histories

Jay P. Dolan

THE celebration of the centennial of the Statue of Liberty in 1986 excited millions of Americans. Lady Liberty has long been a symbol of freedom with which all Americans could identify, most especially immigrants and their descendants. Countless stories are told of how grown men and women wept with joy as they sailed into New York harbor and caught sight of the nation's landmark. Seeing the Statue of Liberty for the first time was for these newcomers an event as moving and momentous as stepping on the moon. The prominence of the Statue of Liberty in the nation's memory and its landmark status as a symbol of freedom and the gateway to the New World underscore the importance of immigration in American history. When Oscar Handlin sat down to write a history of immigration he came to the conclusion that the "immigrants were American history." The English historian, Maldwyn Jones, was equally emphatic when he wrote that immigration is "America's historic *raison d'être* . . . the most persistent and the most pervasive influence in her development."[1]

This essay will examine how historians of American Christianity have incorporated immigration into their historical writing. It will focus on books published since the middle of the nineteenth century, landmark studies if you wish, rather than articles and will concentrate on the history of American Christianity rather than American religion in general.

When the first federal census was taken in 1790 immigration had been going on for almost two hundred years and already the United States was a "mosaic of peoples." English-stock Americans accounted for about half of the population with Blacks, Germans, Irish, Scots, Dutch, French, and Swedes making up the other half. In the next one hundred years the nation underwent tremendous changes—cities mushroomed in population, the nation's boundaries moved West eventually stretching from the Atlantic to the Pacific, and the United States became the leading industrial nation in the world. The steam engine, the factory, the light bulb, the elevator, the sewing machine and countless other technological innovations changed the way people lived and worked. Between 1790 and 1890 more than fifteen million immigrants had come to the United States and they too changed the course of the nation's history.[2]

People from every part of the world immigrated to the United States during the nineteenth century. Most immigrants came from Germany and the British Isles with Ireland numbering more than England, Scotland, and Wales combined. The arrival of so many foreigners scared Americans out of their wits, and for two decades and more, from the 1830s to the 1850s, a nativist crusade captured the nation's imagination and turned Americans against the foreigners. It was obvious that the newcomers were perceived as a threat to the nation's future. A major reason for this was religion. Large numbers of these immigrants were Roman Catholic and at this time Roman Catholicism was not welcomed in the American religious pantheon.

Americans could tolerate ethnic diversity. This was an accepted feature of the American identity. They could also tolerate religious diversity, as long as it was among Protestants. But the arrival of millions of Roman Catholic immigrants posed a serious problem to the level of toleration among Americans. The religious reformation of the sixteenth century and decades of religious wars had left deep scars among both Protestants and Catholics. They really did not like one another; in fact, it would be accurate to say that they hated each other. In Europe they solved the problem by not living in the same geographical and political area. In colonial America a similar pattern prevailed with Catholics choosing to live in the remote tidewater counties of southern Maryland. But large-scale immigration redesigned the religious map of the United States. Not only did Catholics live in every state of the land but they had also become the single largest denomination in the United States. After a generation of religious hostility in the antebellum period Catholics and Protestants began to learn how to get along with each other. Though religious bigotry never totally disappeared in the nineteenth century, the relationships between Catholics and Protestants were much better in 1890 than they were in the 1840s and 1850s.

A reading of immigration texts gives the impression that most nineteenth-century immigrants were Roman Catholic and for that reason immigration must have had a much larger impact on the Catholic church than on Protestant churches. This is only partially correct, however. Close to 70 percent of nineteenth-century German immigrants were Protestant; the percentage is much higher with immigrants from the Scandinavian countries, and the same was true with immigrants from England, Scotland, and Wales. The 1890 religious census pointed this out quite clearly. In discussing the Lutheran churches in the United States the census noted that six different foreign languages were used among the Lutherans—Norwegian, Danish, German, Swedish, Finnish, and Icelandic. Methodists had a similarly diverse immigrant quality and were represented among Germans, Spaniards, Swedish, Danish, and Norwegians.[3] Indeed, immigration was central to the nineteenth-century American Catholic experience, but it was also an important part of the American Protestant experience, especially among Lutherans and Methodists.

Throughout the nineteenth century a great deal had been written on the theme of immigration. Most of those who wrote on immigration were economists or sociologists who sought to measure the impact of immigration on American society. As Arthur M. Schlesinger noted, "they regarded immigration as a social problem rather than a social process, and they often wrote for the purpose of influencing governmental policy."[4] Very few professional historians were attracted to the study of immigration and those who were did not probe the meaning of immigration very deeply. It is fair to say that they viewed the immigrants as a problem and hoped that they would conform or assimilate to the Anglo-Saxon norm allegedly prevalent in the United States. As regards the writing of American church history I could not locate any specific study of immigration and the churches in the nineteenth century.[5] Some historians did touch on the issue of immigration as part of a larger work, and an examination of these nineteenth-century church historians and their works reveals a diversity of emphases and viewpoints.

In his study, *Religion in the United States of America*, Robert Baird briefly touched on immigration and like most Americans at the time he viewed it as a problem that religion had to encounter. As he put it,

> while the emigration from Europe into the United States brings us no inconsiderable number of worthy people, it introduces also a large amount of ignorance, poverty and vice. Besides this, it is difficult to supply with religious institutions, and it takes long to Americanise, if I may use the expression, in feeling, conduct, and language, those multitudes from the continent of Europe who cannot understand or speak English.[6]

Philip Schaff, himself an immigrant, incorporated immigration into his optimistic interpretation about America. He believed that immigration was an essential element in developing the national character. "The United States present," he wrote, "a wonderful mixture of all nations under heaven." Out of this diversity emerges "a higher unity, and . . . in this chaos of peoples the traces of a specifically American national character may be discerned."[7] Invoking his famous metaphor he went on to say that

> a similar process of national amalgamation is now also going on before our eyes in America; but peacefully, under more favorable conditions, and on a far grander scale than ever before in the history of the world America is *the grave of all European nationalities*; but a *Phenix* [sic] *grave* from which they shall rise to new life and new activity in a new and essentially Anglo-Germanic form.[8]

Schaff, however, did not limit the influence of immigration to the national character. He also believed that it would have a transforming influence on religion in America.

> America seems destined to be the Phenix [*sic*] grave not only of all European nationalities, as we have said above, but also of all European churches and sects, of Protestantism and Romanism. I cannot think, that any one of the present confessions and sects, the Roman, or the Episcopal, or the Congregational, or the Presbyterian, or the Lutheran, or the German or Dutch Reformed, or the Methodist, or the Baptist Communion, will ever become exclusively dominant there; but rather, that out of the mutual conflict of all something wholly new will gradually arise.[9]

Schaff's optimism about the future of America and its churches enabled him to view immigration in a positive and indeed creative manner. In this regard he was quite different from his contemporaries. Rather than dwell on the dark side of immigration, he stressed its positive role in the social process taking place in the United States that would, in his opinion, result in a new race and a new religion. Though he did not use the metaphor of the melting pot, that is what he meant when he described the process of amalgamation taking place among the immigrants. But Schaff went one step further and believed that a similar transformation would take place among the various religious traditions.

Daniel Dorchester wrote a comprehensive history of Christianity in the United States and devoted serious attention to the theme of immigration. Like most of his contemporaries he viewed immigration as a problem for both the nation and the churches. In Dorchester's opinion the Old World immigrant cultures could contribute very little, if indeed anything at all, to either church or nation. The sooner the immigrant could become American and acquire the virtues of evangelical Christianity the better the nation would be. But Dorchester was uncertain if "old world subjects can be transformed into new world citizens."[10]

Leonard Woolsey Bacon wrote *A History of American Christianity* for the American church history series and devoted an entire chapter to immigration. He discussed the impact of immigration on Roman Catholicism by noting that it had made the church more Irish and more urban; and then touching on a theme that was becoming increasingly common, he stated that because of the large number of immigrants and the "inadequate body" of Catholic clergy the church had experienced the loss of "enormously great" numbers of immigrants. While speaking about German Protestant immigrants Bacon hoped that the "older American churches" would learn something from the "equable, systematic, and methodical ways" of the German Lutheran immigrants. This was clearly a different twist for a nineteenth-century church historian. Rather than totally endorsing the assimilationist model, Bacon believed that American Protestant churches could profit by adopting some of the traits of the Germans.[11]

The uniqueness of Bacon and Dorchester can be appreciated when they are compared to nineteenth-century denominational historians. John Gilmary Shea was the best-known and most prolific historian of Roman Catholicism. In his mammoth (2,817 pages in four volumes) history of Roman Catholicism in the United States Shea did not devote any attention at all to immigration either as a problem or an asset for the church. Given his style of writing about the institutional growth of the church and the achievements of its bishops, such an omission is not surprising. In his essays, however, Shea did deal with the question of immigration. A nineteenth-century assimilationist, he celebrated the gathering of "men of every race and tongue" in the United States where they can be molded "into one homogeneous Christian body" through the agency of the Roman Catholic church. When he spoke about the new immigrants—Italians, Polish, Portuguese, and Spanish or Mexicans—Shea was less sanguine because he feared that they and their children might lose their faith. Thus, he believed, steps will have to be taken "to save them and their children."[12] Thomas O'Gorman wrote *A History of the Roman Catholic Church in the United States* for the American church history series and like Shea he did not consider the theme of immigration. Though he did discuss immigration in his concluding remarks, he did so only in relation to the larger question, widely debated among Roman Catholics, of how many Catholic immigrants had lost the faith in the United States.[13]

Henry Eyster Jacobs authored a *History of the Evangelical Lutheran Church in the United States* for the American church history series. As was true with Roman Catholicism, immigration had a decisive influence on the development of the American Lutheran church. Unlike his Catholic counterpart Jacobs incorporated the theme of immigration and related issues into his history. Jacobs acknowledged the importance of the Old World roots of Lutheranism and perceived the dilemma the American environment posed for the church. He discussed the debate caused by the use of English in prayerbooks and hymnals and also the problems caused by intermarriage with English or Scotch-Irish Protestants. Even more serious, according to Jacobs, was the danger of Lutheran churches adapting certain American evangelical tendencies such as the revival style of preaching.[14]

For nineteenth-century church historians immigration was not a major concern. That is ironic given the large waves of immigration to the United States throughout the century. For these historians immigration was a fact of life and not a theme for analysis. It was a problem for the nation and for the churches and only when it ceased to be a problem would historians be able to study it with any success. Of all the few church historians who touched on the theme of immigration Philip Schaff clearly evidenced the most positive and creative analysis though he never explained how out of all the different religious traditions "something wholly new" would emerge. Like other Americans he envisioned the foreign-born immigrants becoming Americans; for Schaff and his contemporaries this seemed to be not only desirable but inevitable. Yet, in endorsing assimilation or what was called Americanization, nineteenth-century church historians were not as ideologically or politically motivated as their counterparts in the twentieth century would be. For this reason it never became a major theme in their histories.

In the late nineteenth and early twentieth centuries the number of immigrants skyrocketed and in a thirty-year period, 1890–1920, more than 18 million newcomers settled in the United States. In addition, these immigrants came from quite different parts of Europe than their nineteenth-century predecessors. Large numbers of Italians immigrated during these years; scores of people fled from poverty and persecution in Eastern Europe and settled in the United States. Polish, Hungarian, Czech, Slovak, Ruthenians, Slovenians, and numbers of people from other exotic cultural backgrounds streamed into the United States. Americans had never seen such a mosaic of peoples from regions so culturally remote from the Anglo-Saxon heritage that for so long had comprised the bedrock of the American population.

The most unique aspect of this period of immigration was not its volume but its diversity. Australia, Brazil, and other nations benefited from the international migration of these decades, but no nation acquired so many people from so many different parts of the world. By the early twentieth century it was not unusual to find a dozen or more ethnic groups living in the same general urban neighborhood. No other country in the world had gathered its people from so many different places.

Such unusual diversity changed the religious landscape. Foreign-language churches became much more prominent and missionary efforts among immigrant communities became commonplace. The 1916 census of religious bodies included a lengthy section on the use of foreign languages in the churches, and it not only revealed how ethnic the American religious pantheon had become but also the great cultural diversity of peoples gathered in the nation's churches. Of the 200 denominations studied in 1916, 132 reported a part or all of their congregations using a foreign language. That was a remarkably high percentage. Obviously not all immigrants were Roman Catholic. Even more striking was the revelation that 42 languages were in use in the nation's churches. Among Roman Catholics alone 28 foreign languages were spoken; Methodists reported 22 different languages in use.[15]

The diversity of the new immigrants and more especially their cultural and economic backgrounds alarmed many Americans. In the middle of the nineteenth century the religion of Roman Catholic newcomers so alienated the American-born population that a Protestant crusade ensued. In the 1890–1930 period the cultural background of Italian and Eastern European newcomers was the major cause of another crusade of bigotry, but this time it was racial rather than religious. In time a scientific theory of racism developed that exalted the Anglo-Saxon race over against people from Eastern and Southern Europe. Promoted by intellectuals and legitimized by social scientists this racialism gripped the popular imagination. It fueled an anti-immigrant mentality and it was not long before Congress was debating how best to restrict immigration. Despite a presidential veto, immigration laws were eventually passed in 1921 and 1924 that restricted immigration to the United States on the basis of a person's country of origin. Clearly based on racialism this legislation discriminated against those people most culturally removed from the Anglo-Saxon race, namely immigrants from Southern and Eastern Europe. The restrictive legislation of the 1920s effectively reduced the flow of immigration to a trickle—a mere 150,000 newcomers were allowed in each year. In effect, it brought an end to three centuries of immigration from Europe. As far as religion was concerned the European immigrants no longer set the agenda for the churches. The closing of immigration also had a decisive effect on the development of the historical study of immigration.

During the first quarter of the twentieth century, historians had continued to ignore the history of immigration. Those who did include it in their work generally did so in a perfunctory manner. Social scientists continued to dominate the field of immigration studies and they had a particular ax to grind. Their goal was to seek a solution to what by then had become the "immigrant problem." Motivated by a racist ideology that persuaded them to view immigrant newcomers as members of an inferior race, they sought to restrict the flow of immigrants to the United States. Because of the polemical nature of their work and their racial bias they contributed little to the scholarly study of immigration.

In the late 1920s certain changes took place that had a decisive influence on the historical study of immigration. First of all, the climate of opinion began to change and racism as a scientific and scholarly doctrine declined in popularity. The immigration restriction laws that went into effect in 1929 also altered the climate. Henceforth, immigration was no longer a problem nor was it any longer an issue of public debate. For all practical purposes the flow of immigration had ceased in the late 1920s, or so it seemed at that time, and thus it became a topic ripe for historical study. Finally, changes were taking place in the study of history. A new history was emerging at this time and it sought to move beyond the political and institutional focus of nineteenth-century historians and include the study of social, intellectual, and economic developments. This meant that immigration would soon become the concern of a new breed of American historians.

The person most responsible for the initial development of immigration history was Frederick Jackson Turner. Famous for his frontier thesis stating that the key to understanding the American experience could be found in "the crucible of the frontier" where "the immigrants were Americanized, liberated, and fused into a mixed race," Turner's thesis offered the grand synthesis that would influence a generation of historians.[16] In developing the frontier thesis in the 1890s, Turner provided an answer to the question of how the United States had developed. In expounding this thesis Turner stressed the need for a history of immigration because, as he observed, "we (Americans) do not understand ourselves."[17] By emphasizing both the importance of immigration in the development of the American nation and the need for a history of immigration, Turner sought to focus attention on immigration as an area for serious historical study. Very few accepted Turner's call, however, and only in the 1920s when the climate in the United States was more suitable for the scholarly study of immigration did historians take up the challenge raised by Turner thirty years earlier.

The first major historian of immigration was Marcus Lee Hansen. A student of Turner's at Harvard in the 1920s, he devoted his historical career to the study of immigration. His major work, one volume of a projected three volume history, was published posthumously in 1940 as *The Atlantic Migration, 1607–1860*.[18] A path-breaking study, it won the Pulitzer Prize in history. Focusing on the European aspect of immigration, Hansen was "the first historian to treat immigration not in terms of national groups nor in terms of the United States alone but as one aspect of the expansion of Europe. Applying what he had learned from Turner to the entire Western world, Hansen viewed this expansive process as a vast westward movement in which Europeans migrated to a transatlantic frontier and pushed the native Americans onward to a still-farther frontier."[19]

The American-born son of a Danish preacher, Hansen recognized the importance of religion in the process of emigration from Europe. In an important essay published in the *American Historical Review* in 1927 he again underscored the role of religion in the study of immigration and the need for the study of "the great mass of literature connected with the religious condition of the immigrants." In another famous essay, "Immigration and Puritanism," Hansen demonstrated how religious history could illumine immigration history.[20]

The significance of Hansen's work for the history of American Christianity was that he not only recognized the important role religion played in the process of immigration but also sought to integrate church history with the history of immigration. In the European phase of immigration Hansen believed that religion was an important push factor in that process. In the United States, according to Hansen, the American environment had an inherent centrifugal tendency that led to conflict and schism in Old World denominations. With colonial New England as his model he went on to claim that nineteenth-century immigrants, like the Puritans, adopted a strict moral code once they settled in the United States. In Hansen's opinion the immigrant experience of Puritan New England was the norm for any "ecclesiastical establishment planted in the New World."[21]

Carl Wittke was another graduate of Harvard who made an important contribution to the history of immigration. In 1939 he published *We Who Built America*, a long anticipated work that was recognized as "the best history of American immigration yet to appear." A general history of immigration from colonial times to the restriction of immigration in the post–World War I period, Wittke incorporated a great deal of information about the role of the churches in the process of emigration from Europe to settlement in the United States. In some of his many other books he also gave considerable attention to the immigrant church.[22]

Two years after Wittke's general history appeared a twenty-six-year-old Harvard graduate, Oscar Handlin, published his doctoral dissertation, *Boston's Immigrants: A Study in Acculturation*. Unlike Wittke's general history this was a book that would make a difference. In effect *Boston's Immigrants* redirected the course of immigration history studies. Writing some thirty years later one of Handlin's severest critics acknowledged the importance of the study.

> Informed by the insights of anthropology and sociology, the book expertly delineated the impact of immigration upon the culture, economy, ecology, and social structure of Boston. With the exception of the Irish, the newcomers assimilated readily. But the group consciousness and cohesion of the Irish were intensified by the bitter conflicts between them and the "others." From contacts of dissimilar cultures emerged an ethnic pluralism which left Boston a divided city.[23]

Boston's Immigrants demonstrated how revealing an in-depth study of one urban immigrant community could be. Handlin devoted a lot of space to the religion of Boston's Irish Catholic immigrants. Though his assessment of the religion of the Irish was marred by a strong bias against what he judged to be their conservative pessimism, Handlin did seek to understand how religion shaped the minds of the immigrants. In doing so he went beyond the usual litany of topics followed by immigration and church historians up to that time, i.e., the number of churches built, the conflict over what language to use in church, and the organization of fraternal societies. In adopting this approach he underscored the important relation between religion and culture or what today might be called ethnicity. Handlin realized that you could not understand the Irish without trying to understand their religious beliefs.

Other important studies on immigration and the churches appeared in the post–World War I period. For nineteenth-century Catholic historians a major issue had been the loss of faith among the immigrants. In 1925 Gerald Shaugnessy wrote a detailed study of the issue, *Has the Immigrant Kept the Faith?* His answer was yes in that "no great loss has occurred to Catholicity in the United States in the last hundred years."[24] For Shaugnessy the key words were *no great loss*. Another important study written in the 1920s was the work by H. Richard Niebuhr, *The Social Sources of Denominationalism*. Published in 1929 it examined "the social character of the Christian churches" in order to discover the roots of denominational differences in the United States.[25] In this study Niebuhr devoted a good deal of attention to the importance of immigration and religious nation-alism in the development of denominationalism.

The rise of anti-Catholic nativism in the antebellum period was a major episode in immigration history. With the resurgence of nativism in the 1920s historians again turned their attention to the study of nineteenth-century nativism. Ray Allen Billington's book towered above the rest. Published in 1938 Billington's *The Protestant Crusade, 1800–1860: A Study of the Origins of American Nativism* became a landmark study of anti-Cathol-icism.

Like Billington and so many other historians interested in immigration George M. Stephenson received his doctoral degree at Harvard University. In 1926 he published a general history of immigration, *A History of American Immigration, 1820–1924.* His focus was on immigration as a factor in Amer-ican political development and for this reason religion was not a major theme of the study. Stephenson made up for this a few years later when he published *The Religious Aspects of Swedish Immigration: A Study of Immi-grant Churches.*[26] Remarkably thorough, it was an institutional history of the Swedish Lutheran churches in the United States. In his review of this work Marcus Lee Hansen made a very telling remark, echoed by Ste-phenson as well in his preface. Hansen wrote that

> the historian sees lived over again episodes which are usually consid-ered peculiar to the religious life of the colonial period. When a dozen similar investigations have been made, some general principles will be revealed and, then, what was happening in seventeenth century New England will be viewed in a more historical perspective, as the *normal* experience of an ecclesiastical establishment planted in a New World.[27]

For Hansen, Stephenson, and others the immigration experience of the Puritans was looked upon as normative for the entire history of immi-gration. This was Puritan hegemony with a vengeance, a point of view that failed to recognize the differences between so many diverse immigrant groups. Also influencing this point of view was Turner's frontier thesis that looked upon immigration as but one stage in the development of the American nation.

One of Stephenson's colleagues at the University of Minnesota was Theodore C. Blegen. He was to the Norwegians what Stephenson was to the Swedish; he published a two-volume history of *Norwegian Migration to America.* In Blegen's history the immigrant church occupied an impor-tant, though marginal, position.[28]

The 1920s and 1930s were very important years for the development of the history of immigration. Through the influence first of Frederick Jackson Turner and later of Arthur M. Schlesinger, Harvard University became the key center for this development. In this pioneer period religion and the church were consistently incorporated into immigration history studies. A key reason for this was because the New England colonial experience was viewed as normative for immigration in general; since religion was such a central feature in the development of colonial New England, it followed that it would have to be considered in subsequent periods of immigration. In these years historians also believed strongly in the thesis of Americanization, which had been the prevailing interpretation for some time. This neatly blended with Turner's frontier thesis that stressed the importance of immigration as one further stage in the development of the American nation.

The major figure throughout these years was Marcus Lee Hansen. Though his work was cut short by death in 1938 at the age of forty-five, Hansen still managed to dominate this era. Rather than limit himself to studying a specific group or a particular topic, Hansen focused on the big picture and sought to synthesize the history of immigration in his book, *The Atlantic Migration*. Moses Rischin has called him "America's first transethnic historian." According to Rischin Hansen found in the inspiring myth of immigration both a common denominator and a strategy to unite an ethnically fragmented and divided nation in need of an epic that would celebrate the pan European . . . origins of the American people."[29] In his essays Hansen formulated interpretive theses that were both insightful and provocative. But a major problem, recognized by Hansen, was the absence of the monographs necessary to build a plausible interpretive synthesis for the history of immigration. Historians like Billington, Stephenson, Wittke, and Blegen were satisfying this need to a degree as were other less notable historians.

Historians were not the only scholars beginning to focus attention on the immigrants. Sociologists were also conducting research in immigrant communities and were producing some very valuable studies. The most notable work at the time was that of William I. Thomas. Thomas' most significant work was the five-volume study he authored with Florian Znaniecki, *The Polish Peasant in Europe and America*. The study evidences the use of such terms as *culture, attitudes*, and *values*, concepts that were quite innovative at the time. It also offered a very detailed, close-up look at life in the immigrant community through the use of many autobiographical accounts. Moreover, Thomas affirmed the richness and the value of the immigrant culture. No doubt the most lasting impact of his work was at the University of Chicago where his sociological analysis influenced a generation of sociologists; eventually historians of immigration, like Oscar Handlin, would begin to turn to sociological concepts and theory in order to understand more fully the immigrant experience.[30]

The writing of church history began to follow a new direction in the early twentieth century. In the nineteenth century the writing of church history, for the most part, was confined to the province of the seminary professor and often was written to illustrate the providential activity of a very busy deity. In the early twentieth century, church history became much more scientific and methodologically more in tune with secular history. "A pivotal figure in this change" was William Warren Sweet who in 1927 came to "the Divinity School of the University of Chicago as professor of the history of American Christianity, the first such position in any university."[31] At Chicago, Sweet "crusaded persistently for the emancipation of religious scholarship from ecclesiastical triumphalism and for the integration of such scholarship with kindred disciplines in the modern university."[32] Without question he was the most influential historian of American Christianity in the first half of the twentieth century. In 1930 he wrote *The Story of Religion in America,* a general history that remained the definitive work for over thirty years.[33]

For Sweet, Protestantism was the religion of America and as a child of the frontier thesis generation of historians he believed that the frontier was the crucible in which American religion was shaped. For Sweet the critical period of this development was in the antebellum period. Given these basic principles, Sweet did not believe that immigration was an important influence in the development of American religion. When he does mention it in his general history, it is most often as a problem to be overcome and in this regard Sweet's attitude toward immigration is not much different from his nineteenth-century predecessors. "Like many Protestants of his day, Sweet viewed Catholicism as an aristocratic vestige of medieval Europe inimical to America. He claimed that the Lutherans were the least important of all the European churches."[34] It was these two groups, however, that immigration influenced the most and to slight them meant to undervalue the importance of immigration in the history of American religion.

As for the writing of denominational history the theme of immigration did not exert much influence. The most prominent historian of American Catholicism was Peter Guilday. He focused his work on the writing of episcopal biographies, since he believed that given "the scattered and unorganized condition of our archival sources this was the most prudent way to write the history of American Catholicism."[35] In his description of the doctoral program in American church history at Catholic University, Guilday did include the study of immigration, but in studying the 1815–52 period he saw it as one of the chief problems of the Catholic church administration along with trusteeism and anti-Catholic movements.[36] One issue that did attract historians of American Catholicism was anti-Catholicism, with the result that a number of dissertations and some published studies appeared in the 1930s and 1940s. None of them, however, matched the comprehensiveness of Billington's study, *The Protestant Crusade*.

Symptomatic of the age was a history of Lutheranism by Abdel Ross Wentz that first appeared in 1923 and remained the standard history for the next forty years. The uniqueness of Wentz was his insistence on showing how American the Lutheran church in the United States was. Thus, assimilation and Americanization were major themes throughout the book. To his credit Wentz did include a good amount of material on immigration, but the overriding thesis was always "to transform this alien multitude into American citizenship."[37]

In the first half of the twentieth century the study of American church history or what was slowly becoming known as the history of American Christianity was undergoing very positive developments. Church historians were becoming more professional in their work and more in tune with the methodology of their colleagues in the historical academy. As an academic discipline the study of church history was becoming more respected. Given the temper of the times, however, with its strong anti-immigrant and pro-Americanization attitudes and considering the lingering influence of Turner's frontier thesis on American historiography, it is not surprising to find little attention given to the role of immigration in the development of American Christianity. Add to this the bias of the era that the history of American Christianity was the history of Protestantism, most especially of evangelical Protestantism, and the lack of importance attributed to immigration becomes even more comprehensible. The result was that in the first half of the twentieth century, historians of immigration, namely secular historians who brought a strong dose of scientific and scholarly detachment as regards the study of religion, were the scholars most engaged in studying the relationship between religion and immigration. It is fair to say that Marcus Lee Hansen and not William Warren Sweet made a greater contribution to the study of the role of religion in the process of immigration. It is also accurate to claim that nineteenth-century church historians were more aware of the importance of immigration than their counterparts in the early twentieth century.

The decade of the 1940s and most especially World War II had a decisive influence on the way people thought about the American nation.

"Indeed it would be difficult to exaggerate the importance of the war," wrote Philip Gleason, "as the central event in shaping America's understanding of their national identity for the next generation."[38] The war effort brought together people from diverse backgrounds and emphasized the unity of the nation both politically and culturally. Social scientists began to reflect on the meaning of the American character and to stress the uniqueness of the American experience. In this period the Americanization model was riding a wave of popularity.

In 1951, in the midst of this climate of opinion, Oscar Handlin published his history of immigration, *The Uprooted*. Winner of the Pulitzer Prize in history, it soon became the most popular and influential book ever written on immigration history. Highly personal in style and written in an "elegiac tone," it read more like a novel than a history text.[39] It revealed Handlin to be as much a literary artist as an immigrant historian. The thesis of *The Uprooted* was clear—in coming to the United States the immigrants were uprooted from their Old World environment. Because of this they experienced alienation in the New World, but in breaking the ties with Old World traditions they were able to achieve freedom as citizens of a new world, as Americans. As in *Boston's Immigrants*, religion occupied an important spot in *The Uprooted*. Handlin viewed the religion of the old country in a very simplistic, idealized manner. As a central ingredient in the lives of the people, religion was part of a mythical past rooted in the Old World village. Immigration forced the immigrants "to transplant a way of religious life to a new environment." But this proved to be most difficult. Many people resisted any adjustment at all and according to Handlin, became fiercely conservative as they sought to preserve the traditions of the past. Because others wanted to change and adapt religion to the new environment conflicts erupted and schisms occurred. Throughout it all there was always alienation, a "frustrating sense of loss" because "a possession of infinite value had disappeared in the course of the migration—the inner meaning of their own existence in the universe."[40]

The influence of Marcus Lee Hansen on *The Uprooted* is quite clear, most especially in Handlin's insistence on the inevitable religious conflict resulting from immigration. The social theory of William I. Thomas with his emphasis on disorganization and disruption is also evident. What distinguishes the book is the clarity with which the main thesis is stated, right from the title page through to the final chapter. Nonetheless, Handlin could not escape a persistent ambiguity because of his desire to end the immigrant saga on the upbeat note of liberty and freedom. John Higham pointed this out very emphatically. "Oscar Handlin has shaped each of his major books as a story of disintegration and mobility," observed Higham.

"Handlin's history begins, characteristically, with a stable, orderly community . . . which makes life meaningful and whole. Then the shock of migration disrupts the community, breeding strife and freedom; and uprooted men pursue their separate, clashing purposes." As a result Handlin's history is "an anguished story, heavy with a sense of loss and alienation. It is also highly ambivalent, for the author admires the growth of freedom while lamenting the decline of order."[41]

This ambiguity is evident in Handlin's treatment of religion. He described the immigrant's desire to conserve the old order of religion in the new American environment where a person could "change his religion as freely as his hat."[42] He also acknowledged the strong desire of others to adjust and change. Thus, Handlin acknowledged both the persistence of traditional religion as well as the phenomenon of religious adaptation. But with the finality and comprehensiveness of a nuclear fallout alienation somehow overcomes everything. This serves to de-emphasize the importance of persistence and change in the area of religion and never allows Handlin to analyze the religious experience of the immigrants for its own sake. The study of religion is only useful insofar as it illustrates Handlin's larger thesis about the immigrant saga.

Even though historians today have many quarrels with *The Uprooted*, Handlin's interpretation was very influential. He soon became the leading historian of immigration as well as a scholar of national renown. Moreover, he helped to elevate "the study of the immigrant to a central place in the study of American history and society."[43] It was clear that by the 1950s immigration had become a key to unlocking the meaning of the American experience. As Handlin put it so poignantly in the first lines of *The Uprooted*— "once I thought to write a history of the immigrants in America. Then I discovered that the immigrants *were* American history."[44] Nonetheless, immigration history still remained peripheral "to the concerns of most American historians."[45]

Another key book written in the 1950s was *Protestant, Catholic, Jew* by Will Herberg. Though Herberg did not have a degree in sociology, or even a college degree for that matter, he subtitled his book *An Essay in American Religious Sociology*. Well-written and comprehensive in scope it became a best seller. The novelty of the book was Herberg's thesis that religion, not ethnicity or nationality, was the identification tag for Americans. Rather than a single melting pot theory he offered a triple melting pot whereby the three major religious traditions, Protestantism, Catholicism, and Judaism, became the means for social identity. Herberg believed that not only had the immigrants become Americanized, but the religion of the immigrants had also become Americanized. Thus, when people asked the question who am I? they answered by stating that they were either Protestant, Catholic, or Jewish rather than Italian-American, German-American, and so forth. According to Herberg the importance of religion as an identification tag explained the religious revival of the 1950s. Of course this made his thesis and the book all the more attractive. His thesis became very popular and thrust the issue of immigration into the center of discussion on the meaning of the American religious experience. The uniqueness of Herberg was that like H. Richard Niebuhr before him, he theorized about the relationship between religion and immigration.[46]

Like so many other scholars who wrote on the topic of religion, immigration, and Americanization, Will Herberg was Jewish. Though the focus of this essay has been on the historical writing of American Christianity, it would be negligent not to mention the contribution of Jewish scholars to the study of immigration. Horace Kallen introduced the term "cultural pluralism" in his book *Culture and Democracy in the United States* (1924) "to designate his radically anti-assimilationist viewpoint."[47] Kallen's insights substantially revised the analysis of immigration and Americanization. The Jewish playwright, Israel Zangwill, coined the phrase "the melting pot"; Franz Boas "who did more than any other individual to refute racialism as a scientific doctrine" was also Jewish and so too was Oscar Handlin.[48] In recent years such Jewish scholars as Nathan Glazer, Milton Gordon, and Moses Rischin have made significant contributions to the study of immigration history.

While Jewish scholars like Herberg grappled with the relationship between religion and ethnicity, historians of American Christianity continued to keep immigration on the periphery of their studies. John Tracy Ellis was an exception. In a series of lectures given at the University of Chicago and published in book form in 1955 under the title *American Catholicism*, Ellis offered a brief history of Roman Catholicism in the United States. One of his lectures was on immigration, and for Ellis immigration was clearly an important force in the development of nineteenth-century American Catholicism. Endorsing the prevailing thesis of Americanization he believed that through its ministry to the immigrants the Catholic church was an effective agency of Americanization.[49] In addition, he explained other ways in which immigration shaped the development of American Catholicism. Nonetheless, Ellis had to acknowledge that "one of the weakest areas in the literature of American Catholicism is immigration history." Though there were some studies done by students of Ellis on immigration related topics, the climate of the 1950s was more conducive to studies focusing on topics related to Americanization and the American character.[50] The 1960s changed all that.

As was true for much of American society, the 1960s ushered in a new era in historical studies. The social awakening of this decade made many people more conscious of their ethnic heritage and their identity as both immigrant and American. In the academy historians were becoming more interested in social history, the history of the people and their culture, rather than just the history of presidents and generals. These two developments sparked a renaissance in immigration history; coupled with this was the large increase in college graduates as a result of the G.I. Bill and the subsequent increase in doctoral students in history. Immigration history suddenly was in and dissertations began to multiply like rabbits. The following statistic dramatically illustrates this development; of all the dissertations written on immigration between 1899 and 1972, 50 percent were done in one decade, 1962–72.[51] Reflecting this new development a group of American historians founded the Immigration History Society in 1965; shortly thereafter a newsletter began to be published to serve as a means of communication among immigration historians. On college campuses courses in immigration history became more commonplace. Centers for ethnic studies began to multiply and the publication of books related to immigration studies increased substantially. This new research changed the understanding of the American past and put the immigrants on the center stage of American history. In the 1960s and 1970s people discovered what Oscar Handlin had realized in 1951—the immigrants were American history.[52]

One major intellectual development in recent immigration studies has been the reevaluation of the Americanization thesis. For much of the twentieth century, historians accepted the theory that over the course of time, generally by the third generation, immigrants became Americanized. The metaphor most commonly used was that of the melting pot; though it could have a variety of meanings the melting pot generally conjured up the image of the immigrants being melted down so that they could become American. This thesis celebrated the unity of American culture and the assimilation of the immigrants to the American way of life.

The social awakening of the 1960s posed a mighty challenge to the Americanization thesis. There was a resurgence of ethnic or group consciousness both in America and abroad. The civil rights movement awakened Black Americans to a new and heightened self-consciousness; Hispanic Americans underwent a similar transformation. An ethnic revival took place among European immigrants and their descendants; buttons and bumper stickers, parades and festivals celebrated the virtues of being ethnic. The scholarly implications of this were substantial. Not only did it foster an increased interest in immigration studies, but this ethnic renaissance led to a reexamination of the nation's past, most especially the Americanization thesis. As a result scholars began to champion the cultural pluralism of the nation, its diversity rather than its unity. Rather than stress the assimilation of immigrants to the American way of life, historians now emphasized how immigrant groups retained their Old World cultures. They stressed the retention of ethnic identity and the maintenance of cultural pluralism as important features of the American landscape. As a result of this historians began to redirect their "research toward collecting evidence about the transmission of immigrant and ethnic identities from the Old World and about the retention or adaptation of cultural traits and social institutions in the New."[53] The popularity of social history reinforced this tendency by encouraging historians to do community studies of immigrant groups. What was previously looked upon as parochial, ethnocentric history became the vogue and more than one college professor was promoted to tenure because he or she had written a book on the Germans in Milwaukee or the Irish in New York.

Several books appeared in the 1960s that helped to change the way people thought about immigration. The most significant was Milton M. Gordon's study, *Assimilation in American Life: The Role of Race, Religion, and National Origins*.[54] Gordon evaluated the main theories of assimilation and then presented his own. By distinguishing between cultural pluralism and structural pluralism he underscored the point that ethnicity not only persisted among the American people but it also was transformed over the generations. Rather than a simple one-way street whereby all Americans, regardless of nationality, became part of an homogeneous group through the mythical melting pot phenomenon, Gordon stessed the integrity and persistence of ethnicity. Daniel Patrick Moynihan and Nathan Glazer wrote an acclaimed study, *Beyond the Melting Pot: The Negroes, Puerto Ricans, Jews, Italians, and Irish of New York City*.[55] The authors gave considerable attention to the relationship between religion and ethnicity and put forth the thesis that "the ethnic group in American society became not a survival from the age of mass immigration but a new social form." For them, as for Gordon, ethnicity persisted, "but it was transformed in the process."[56]

Another significant development that occurred with the questioning of the Americanization thesis was the increased interest in Eastern and Southern European immigrants or those people historians called the new immigrants. Prior to the 1960s much of the historical study of immigrant groups focused on the old immigrants, the Irish and Germans. The ethnic renaissance of the 1960s changed this. Though they hardly neglected the old immigrants, historians now focused more attention on immigrants from Eastern and Southern Europe. This obviously filled a need and scholars welcomed this development. But there was another aspect to this. By studying the new immigrants, Italians, Polish, Slovaks, Ukrainians, and other Eastern European groups, historians were studying the most recently arrived European immigrants and quite naturally they found evidence of the retention of Old World cultures rather than evidence of pronounced assimilation and Americanization. For this reason, the extensive research done in immigration studies in the last twenty years has tended to demonstrate that cultural pluralism rather than Americanization, diversity rather than unity, is the key to understanding the immigrant experience in the United States.[57]

The increased attention given to immigration history has certainly influenced the writing of American church history. Three general histories of American Christianity have appeared in the last twenty years and each of them incorporated the theme of immigration into the historical narrative.[58] These works by Sydney Ahlstrom, Robert Handy, and Winthrop Hudson differed from earlier general histories in that the theme of immigration was more integrated into their work and thus became more central to the mainstream of American church history. Analytically, however, they really do not make much of an advance in terms of using immigration or ethnicity as a category for historical analysis.

In addition to these general histories of American Christianity numerous other studies have appeared that sought to examine the interrelationship between immigration and religion or immigration and the churches. Though more limited in scope, these studies have made a valuable contribution by unlocking the past of specific immigrant communities. The surge in ethnic studies encouraged this development as did the celebration of the nation's bicentennial in 1976 that had the effect of persuading many people and institutions, churches included, to investigate their historical roots.[59] Nonetheless, the number of historical studies that specifically focused on both immigration and the churches or immigration and religion was quite small. A search of books reviewed in the four major historical journals over the course of twenty years, 1965–85, revealed a total of fifty-eight books that studied both immigration and religion or immigration and the church in the United States. That is a very meager number; in fact, in one year alone the *Journal of American History* reviews about four hundred books. The bulk of those books that studied both immigration and religion were published in the 1965–75 period; in the last decade a noticeable falling off has occurred in the popularity of the history of immigration and religion. Another statistic that further illustrates the meager attention given to studies of religion and immigration is that of the 3,534 dissertations written on immigration history between 1885 and 1983 only 128 or 3.6 percent dealt with the topic of religion.[60]

In much of the new historical literature on immigration, religion and the churches were generally touched on but only in a peripheral manner because most historians at the time either did not understand or did not appreciate the importance of religion in immigration studies. Though this was not as true of Hansen's generation, it was evident in the 1960s and 1970s. A notable exception to this was what was called ethnocultural political analysis of immigrant groups. These studies, done by such historians as Robert P. Swierenga, Richard Jensen, and Paul Kleppner, have analyzed the political behavior of immigrant groups in the nineteenth century and have demonstrated how influential religion was in shaping politics in the immigrant community.[61]

Some of the most significant work on the interrelation of immigration, religion, and ethnicity has been done in essays written by Timothy L. Smith and Philip Gleason. For a number of years Philip Gleason has studied the phenomenon of Americanization, assimilation, and cultural pluralism. As an intellectual historian he has given serious attention to the role of religion in the development of the American identity. For Gleason religion, in this case Roman Catholicism, was a key element in the definition of American identity in the nativist, antebellum period of the nineteenth century. Judaism exercised an important influence around the turn of the century and in the 1940s and 1950s Roman Catholicism, in Gleason's opinion, once again surfaced as a major factor in the debate over the American character. In all of his essays Gleason has argued that an understanding of the development of the American identity cannot be achieved without attention given to the role of religion in helping to define this concept.[62]

Timothy L. Smith's contribution has been quite different from that of Gleason. In a 1966 essay in the *American Historical Review* Smith offered a new agenda for immigrant historians. A major aspect of this new approach was his heavy focus on religion. Smith argued for a study of the "dynamics of congregational life," the study of lay leaders in immigrant communities, and the impact of schooling on the children of the immigrants.[63] In later essays he explored some of these issues in detail and persuaded several of his graduate students to probe even more deeply the history of various immigrant communities. In all of this work religion became a key analytical category.[64]

In 1978 Smith published an interpretive essay on "Religion and Ethnicity in America" in the *American Historical Review*. This was clearly a most ambitious endeavor. In this essay Smith set out to analyze the relationship between religion and ethnicity. Though people have since quarreled with his interpretation, he boldly put forth an analytical framework by which historians could better understand the relationship between ethnicity and religion. He stated that immigration

> produced three important alterations in the relationship of faith to ethnic identity: (1) a redefinition, usually in religious terms, of the boundaries of peoplehood, bringing folk memories to bear upon new aspirations; (2) an intensification of the psychic bases of theological reflection and ethnoreligious commitment, due to the emotional consequences of uprooting and repeated resettlement; and (3) a revitalization of the conviction, whether from Jewish messianism or from Christian millennialism, that the goal of history is the creation of a common humanity, a brotherhood of faith and faithfulness.[65]

The notes to this article read like a bibliography of the most recent literature on the topic and one cannot help but admire Smith's effort to bring together such a vast amount of material and synthesize it into a meaningful, interpretive theory.

A persistent problem with immigration studies has been the tendency toward ethnic parochialism. A similar problem has existed in American religious history, namely the tendency toward parochial denominationalism. In his 1978 essay Smith sought to rise above such limitations and offer an interpretive theory that would help both immigrant and religious historians to make sense of a vital past. The testing of his theory in future research will determine how valuable his interpretation is.

In the early 1980s two new histories of immigration appeared. Indicative of the diversity of opinion present among immigrant historians they took two entirely different approaches and offered two opposing interpretations. *Becoming American* by Thomas Archdeacon, as is evident from the title, supported the assimilationist, Americanizing position. The other book, *The Transplanted*, written by John Bodnar, took the position, prominent in the 1960s and 1970s, of cultural pluralism and argued for the maintenance of Old World cultures in America. Even more telling was the treatment of religion and the church in each of these histories. Though the immigrant church was not as important an analytical category for Bodnar as such concepts as class or work, he gave the institutional immigrant church serious attention in one chapter of his study. Archdeacon, on the other hand, integrated the category of religion more thoroughly into his study; Roman Catholicism had an especially prominent position in his study. It is fair to say that of all the general histories of immigration

Becoming American does the best job of analyzing the role of religion in the immigrant community.[66]

In the last fifty years, since the pioneer work of Marcus Hansen, immigration history has slowly but decisively carved its own niche in American historical studies. It is now commonplace for historians to use immigration as an analytical category in their efforts to understand the meaning of the American experience. Because the Americanization thesis was all-consuming, historians emphasized the New World aspect of immigration in the process whereby the immigrants became American. As a result of the social and intellectual changes of the 1960s historians have turned their attention to the persistence of cultural traditions among the immigrants. Americanization and assimilation no longer explain the immigrant experience in its totality; the persistence of cultural tradition has also become a key analytical category in immigration studies.

For historians the implications of this shift are significant. It means that to understand the immigrant experience completely it is necessary to understand the history and culture of the immigrants prior to their arrival in the United States. To study the American dimension of immigration without studying the native culture of the immigrants not only is inadequate but can also be misleading. Marcus Hansen realized this and began his study of immigration in the archives of Europe. Few followed the lead of Hansen, but with the increased emphasis on the cultural richness of various immigrant traditions historians have begun to incorporate the native history and culture of the immigrants into their work. For historians of religion this is especially important because it will allow them to compare the American experience with the Old World tradition and discover not only how much of this Old World religious culture actually was transplanted to the United States, but also how American culture influenced the changing of religion in the New World.

Since the changes in immigration laws in the 1960s, thousands of new immigrants have come to the United States. Mostly Spanish-speaking or Asians, these new immigrants must also be incorporated into any history of immigration in the churches that is written in the closing years of the twentieth century. No history of twentieth-century American Christianity will be complete if it neglects to study the rich cultural and religious traditions of these new immigrants.

In the last twenty years the writing of the history of American Christianity has moved beyond the era of sectarianism. This was a major advance from the era of William Warren Sweet and was clearly in the tradition of Philip Schaff whose ecumenical instincts were well known by his contemporaries. The absence of sectarianism is not enough, however. The history of American Christianity must also probe the meaning of religion in the lives of the people and to achieve this a key category of analysis must be immigration. For if immigration is "America's historic *raison d'être* . . . the most persistent and the most pervasive influence in her development," then surely it must be central to the development of American religious culture.[67]

Notes

1. Quoted in John Higham, *Send These to Me* (New York: Athenaeum, 1975), 4.

2. Thomas J. Archdeacon, *Becoming American: An Ethnic History* (New York: Free Press, 1983), 24 and 27.

3. *Report on Statistics of Churches in the United States at the Eleventh Census: 1890* (Washington, DC, 1894), 435 and 505.

4. Marcus Lee Hansen, *The Atlantic Migration, 1607–1860* (Cambridge, MA: Harvard University Press, 1940), xiv; see Appleton Prentiss Clark Griffin, *A List of Books on Immigration* (Washington, DC, 1907).

5. This search included Griffin's bibliography and the *Bibliography of American Church History* by Samuel MacCauley Jackson (New York: Christian Literature, 1894).

6. Robert Baird, *Religion in the United States of America* (Glasgow and Edinburgh: Blackie and Son, 1844), 83.

7. Philip Schaff, *America: A Sketch of Its Political, Social, and Religious Character*, ed. Perry Miller (Cambridge, MA: Harvard University Press, 1961), 45–46.

8. Ibid., 51.

9. Ibid., 80–81.

10. Daniel Dorchester, *Christianity in the United States* (New York: Phillips and Hunt, 1888), 756–65.

11. Leonard Woolsey Bacon, *A History of American Christianity* (New York: Christian Literature, 1897), 319, 321.

12. John Gilmary Shea, "The Progress of the Church in the United States," *American Catholic Quarterly Review* 9, no. 35 (1884): 481, 496.

13. Thomas O'Gorman, *A History of the Roman Catholic Church in the United States* (New York: Christian Literature, 1895).

14. Henry Eyster Jacobs, *A History of the Evangelical Lutheran Church in the United States* (New York: Christian Literature, 1893), 327–31, 354, 370–71.

15. *Religious Bodies 1916* (Washington, DC: 1919), pt. 1, 76 and 85, and pt. 2, 457.

16. Quoted in Rudolph J. Vecoli, "Ethnicity: A Neglected Dimension of American History," in *The State of American History*, ed. Herbert J. Bass (Chicago: Quadrangle Books, 1970), 75.

17. Quoted in Lee Benson, *Turner and Beard* (Glencoe IL: Free Press, 1960), 82.

18. Hansen, *The Atlantic Migration, 1607–1860*.

19. Allan H. Spear, "Marcus Lee Hansen and the Historiography of Immigration," *Wisconsin Magazine of History* 44, no. 4 (Summer 1961): 268.

20. Marcus Lee Hansen, "Immigration as a Field for Historical Research," and "Immigration and Puritanism," in *The Immigrant and American History*, ed. Arthur M. Schlesinger (Cambridge, MA: Harvard University Press, 1948), 216.

21. Marcus Lee Hansen, "Review of *The Religious Aspects of Swedish Immigration: A Study of Immigrant Churches*, by George M. Stephenson," *American Historical Review* 38, no. 2 (January 1933): 386.

22. Ray Allen Billington, "Review of *We Who Built America* by Carl Wittke," *American Historical Review* 46 (October 1940): 154; See Wittke's *The Irish in America* (Baton Rouge: Louisiana State University Press, 1956) and *William Nast: Patriarch of German Methodism* (Cleveland: Wayne State University Press, 1959).

23. Vecoli, "Ethnicity," 79; Oscar Handlin, *Boston'sImmigrants: A Study in Acculturation* (Cambridge, MA: Harvard University Press, 1941).

24. Gerald Shaughnessy, *Has the Immigrant Kept the Faith?* (New York: Macmillan, 1925), 246.

25. H. Richard Niebuhr, *The Social Sources of Denominationalism* (New York: Holt, 1929), vii.

26. Ray Allen Billington, *The Protestant Crusade, 1800–1860: A Study of the Origins of American Nativism* (New York: Macmillan, 1938); George M. Stephenson, *A History of American Immigration, 1820–1924* (New York: Ginn, 1926), and *Religious Aspects of Swedish Immigration: A Study of Immigrant Churches* (Minneapolis: University of Minnesota Press, 1932).

27. Hansen, "Review of *The Religious Aspects of Swedish Immigration*," 386; my emphasis.

28. Theodore C. Blegen, *Norwegian Migration to America*, 2 vols. (Northfield, MN: Norwegian American Historical Association, 1931–40).

29. Moses Rischin, "Marcus Lee Hansen: America's First Transethnic Historian," in *Uprooted Americans: Essays to Honor Oscar Handlin*, ed. Richard L. Bushman et al. (Boston: Little, Brown, 1979), 322.

30. William I. Thomas and Florian Znaniecki, *A Polish Peasant in Europe and America*, 5 vols. (Boston: Richard D. Badger, 1918–20); see Morris Janowitz, ed., *W. I. Thomas: On Social Organization and Social Personality* (University of Chicago Press, 1966).

31. James L. Ash, Jr., "American Religion and the Academy in the Early Twentieth Century: The Chicago Years of William Warren Sweet," *Church History* 50, no. 4 (December 1981): 450.

32. Ibid.

33. William W. Sweet, *The Story of Religion in America* (New York: Harper and Row, 1930).

34. Ash, "American Religion and the Academy," 461.

35. Peter Guilday, *The Life and Times of John England* (New York: American Press, 1927), 2:555.

36. Peter Guilday, *Graduate Studies in American Church History* (Washington, DC: 1922), 17.

37. Abdel Ross Wentz, *A Basic History of Lutheranism in America* (Philadelphia: Muhlenberg Press, 1955), 114.

38. Philip Gleason, "American Identity and Americanization," *Harvard Encyclopedia of American Ethnic Groups*, ed. Stephan Thernstrom (Cambridge, MA: Harvard University Press, 1980), 47.

39. Ibid., 50; Oscar Handlin, *The Uprooted* (Boston: Little, Brown, 1951).

40. Ibid., III, 127.

41. John Higham, with Leonard Krieger and Felix Gilbert, *History* (Englewood Cliffs, NJ: Prentice-Hall, 1965), 225.

42. Handlin, *The Uprooted*, 113.

43. Michael M. Passi, "Mandarins and Immigrants: The Irony of Ethnic Studies in America Since Turner" (Ph.D. diss., University of Minnesota, 1972), 209.

44. Handlin, *The Uprooted*, 3.

45. Vecoli, "Ethnicity," 73.

46. Will Herberg, *Protestant, Catholic, Jew: An Essay in American Sociology* (New York: Doubleday, 1955); see analysis of Herberg in Gleason, "American Identity," 50–51.

47. Gleason, "American Identity and Americanization," in *Harvard Encyclopedia of American Ethnic Groups*, 43.

48. Ibid., 47.

49. John Tracy Ellis, *American Catholicism* (Chicago: University of Chicago Press, 1956), 103.

50. Ibid., 195.

51. Edward Kasinec, "Resources in Research Centers," in *Harvard Encyclopedia of American Ethnic Groups*, 876.

52. See Rudolph J. Vecoli, "The Resurgence of American Immigration History," *American Studies International* 17, no. 2 (Winter 1979): 49–66.

53. Thomas J. Archdeacon, "Problems and Possibilities in the Study of American Immigration and Ethnic History," *International Migration Review* 19, no. 1 (Spring 1985): 122.

54. Milton M. Gordon, *Assimilation in American Life: The Role of Race, Religion, and National Origins* (New York: Oxford University Press, 1964).

55. Daniel Patrick Moynihan and Nathan Glazer, *Beyond the Melting Pot: The Negroes, Puerto Ricans, Jews, Italians, and Irish of New York City* (Cambridge, MA: Harvard University Press, 1963).

56. See Gleason, "American Identity," 53, 54.

57. See Archdeacon, "Problems and Possibilities in the Study of American Immigration and Ethnic History."

58. Sydney E. Ahlstrom, *A Religious History of the American People* (New Haven: Yale University Press, 1972); Robert T. Handy, *A History of the Churches in the United States and Canada* (New York: Oxford University Press, 1976); and Winthrop S. Hudson, *Religion in America* (New York: Charles Scribner's Sons, 1964).

59. See Rudolph J. Vecoli, "European Americans: From Immigrants to Ethnics," in *Reinterpretation of American History and Culture*, ed. William H. Cartwright and Richard L. Watson, Jr. (Washington, DC: National Council for Social Studies, 1973), 81–112, for an extensive bibliography of recent publications in immigration and ethnic history; see also Joseph M. White, "Historiography of Catholic Immigrants and Religion," *Immigration History Newsletter* 14, no. 2 (November 1982): 5–11, for a review of recent literature in American Catholic history; the *Immigration History Newsletter* has published many bibliographical articles on various ethnic groups.

60. My thanks to Susan White for searching the following journals—*American Historical Review, Journal of American History, Church History,* and *Catholic Historical Review*; my thanks to William Hoglund for the information on the doctoral dissertations on immigration history. In surveying the journal reviews I counted only those books that studied *both* immigration and religion or churches.

61. See Robert P. Swierenga, "Ethnocultural Political Analysis: A New Approach to American Ethnic Studies," *Journal of American Studies* 5, no. 1 (April 1971): 59–79, for an informative survey of this literature; Paul Kleppner, *The Cross of Culture: A Social Analysis of Midwestern Politics: 1850–1900* (New York: Free Press, 1970), 402; Richard Jensen, *The Winning of the Midwest: 1888–1896* (University of Chicago Press, 1971), 357.

62. Gleason's major statement on this topic was "The American Identity and Americanization," in the *Harvard Encyclopedia of American Ethnic Groups*; other pertinent essays by Gleason on this topic include "Immigration and American Catholic Intellectual Life," *Review of Politics* 26 (April 1964): 147–73; "The Crisis of Americanization," in P. Gleason, ed., *Contemporary Catholicism in the United States* (University of Notre Dame Press, 1969), 3–31; "Confusion Compounded: The Melting Pot in the 1960s and 70s," *Ethnicity* 6 (1979): 10–20; "Americans All: World War II and the Shaping of American Identity," *Review of Politics* 43 (October 1981): 483–518. Revised from "Americans All: Ethnicity, Ideology, and the American Identity in the Era of World War II," in *The American Identity: Fusion and Fragmentation*, ed. Rob Kroes (Universiteit van Amsterdam, 1980), 235–64; "Pluralism and Assimilation: A Conceptual History," in *Linguistic Minorities, Policies and Pluralism*, ed. John Edwards (London: Academic Press, 1984), 221–57.

63. Timothy L. Smith, "New Approaches to the History of Immigration in Twentieth Century America," *American Historical Review* 71 (July 1966): 1269.

64. See for example "Religious Denominations as Ethnic Communities: A Regional Case Study," *Church History* 35 (June 1966): 1–20; "Immigrant Social Aspirations and American Education, 1800–1930," *American Quarterly* 21 (Fall 1969): 523–43; "Lay Initiative in the Religious Life of American Immigrants, 1880–1930," in Tamara Hareven, ed., *Anonymous Americans* (Englewood Cliffs, NJ: Prentice-Hall, 1971).

65. Timothy L. Smith, "Religion and Ethnicity in America," *American Historical Review* 83 (December 1978): 1161. See James D. Bratt, "Religion and Ethnicity in America: A Critique of Timothy L. Smith," *Fides et Historia* 12, no. 2 (Spring 1980).

66. Archdeacon, *Becoming American* and John Bodnar, *The Transplanted: A History of Immigrants in Urban America* (Bloomington: Indiana University Press, 1985).

67. Quoted in Higham, *Send These to Me*, 4.

Civil Authority and Religious Freedom in America

Philip Schaff on the United States as a Christian Nation

John F. Wilson

I N the decade of the 1880s, the modern guild of historians proper, many of whom looked to Herbert Baxter Adams and Johns Hopkins University for leadership, was beginning to develop. As the most eminent church historian in the United States, it was appropriate that Philip Schaff treat some aspect of religion in the comprehensive series of studies then being produced. In November 1887 he completed a monograph he titled *Church and State in the United States*, presenting it as "a contribution to American Church History, and to the Centennial Celebration of our National Constitution."[1] Since he had been an active participant in the early years of the American Historical Association, it was natural that Schaff should publish this extended essay in the second volume of papers to appear under its sponsorship. However he was at the time also a leading organizer of the American Society of Church History, now about to celebrate its centennial year (1988).

Schaff was, of course, a European by birth (Switzerland) and training (Germany), so it was especially noteworthy that his subject was, in the phrase of his subtitle, "The American Idea of Religious Liberty and Its Practical Effects." Numerous concerns in Schaff's life and thought come together in this comparatively slight publication, many of them enduring and significant beyond his lifetime. Accordingly, it is fitting that the commemorative volume of which this chapter is a part should pay attention to Schaff's comprehensive interest in the church-state question in American society as it is so cogently displayed in this particular essay.

Throughout his experience with America, beginning in 1843, Schaff was intrigued with its departures from patterns characterizing the European society and culture from which it had chiefly sprung. Schaff's magisterial volumes, such as the seven-volume *History of the Christian Church* or the several editions of writings by the church fathers or even the collection he titled "The Creeds of Christendom," are evidence of his interest in and commitment to Christianity understood in inclusive terms. Yet these universal perspectives did not diminish his appreciation for the unique qualities of his new land. Without doubt Schaff saw the social experiment taking place in the United States as a distinctively new development in human history. He attributed this distinctiveness to such factors as the special cast of American society, due to the dominance of Anglo-Germanic migration in its early and formative years, and the consequent Protestant foundation for its cultural life. But in spite of his recognition of these and other such factors, for Schaff the central element in the achievement that was America was condensed in the Constitution. For him its twofold religious provision "protects us against the despotism of a state church, and guarantees to us the free exercise and enjoyment of religion, as an inherent, inviolable, and inalienable right of every man."[2]

Schaff had first systematically enunciated and explored elements of this theme in lectures he developed to give at Berlin in 1854 on his first return to Europe from the New World. Published there as *Amerika*, these lectures were soon translated and augmented by an address given at Frankfurt during the same visit. Scribner's brought them out in 1855 with the title *America: A Sketch of Its Political, Social, and Religious Character*. This volume was in turn reissued by the Harvard University Press in 1961 with a notable introduction by Perry Miller. Schaff used the broad framework of interpretation of American society developed for these lectures again when he came to write on the church-state question at the end of his career.

The first of Schaff's two lectures concerns the "importance, political system, national character, culture, and religion of the United States." Insisting upon the significance of immigration, Schaff delineated America as a "Middle Kingdom." "The people of the United States . . . have control of a whole continent and of two oceans, one arm outstretched towards Europe, the other towards Asia."[3] Thus he characterized North America as without the "last traces of medieval feudalism" save for the "slavery of the southern states."[4] He thought that "the American constitution rests on a groundwork wholly different from all European systems, and thus forms an entirely new phenomenon in the history of the world." In his view the American Revolution shared little with those that came later in Europe. Indeed, in contrast to the revolution of 1789 and its successors, the American struggle was for him the "emancipation . . . of colonies which had arrived at the age of self-government from the guardianship of the mother country, which had become unnecessary and oppressive."[5] Thus the essence of the American political system was freedom as a "rational, moral, self-determination, hand in hand with law, order, and authority."[6] Joined to "the moral earnestness and Christian character of the nation" freedom so understood formed "the basis of the North American republic."[7] For Schaff, America was "*the grave of all European nationalities* but a *Phenix* [sic] *grave*, from which they shall rise to new life and new activity in a new and essentially Anglo-Germanic form."[8]

From this point of departure, Schaff sought to instruct his German audience in some of the finer points of life in the United States. The predominance of the English language and the character traits associated with it were primary factors for him. He also emphasized the strength of what we would call "middle-class culture" and, even at that time, the wide "diffusion of education and the multiplication of institutions."[9] Among these he counted not only schools and colleges but also the beginnings of differentiated professional faculties, such institutions as the new Smithsonian, the founding of notable libraries, and also the growth of publishing.

All this was prelude to Schaff's view of "religion and the church." He based his discussion on two signal characteristics of American life as he understood it. One was the role of Protestantism in providing the ethos, or forming the culture, for American institutions in contrast to the Catholic heritage that manifestly stood behind even Protestantism in Europe. In sum, America was a society in which Protestant presuppositions stood independent of a prior Catholic tradition. The other was the separation of church and state. It is worth quoting several sentences to establish the particular version of this condition observed by Schaff, a construction less rigorous, for example, than that suggested in Thomas Jefferson's metaphor of the "wall of separation."

> State officers have no other rights in the church, than their personal rights as members of particular denominations. The church, indeed, everywhere enjoys the protection of the laws for its property, and the exercise of its functions; but it manages its own affairs independently, and has also to depend for its resources entirely on voluntary contributions. As the state commits itself to no particular form of Christianity, there is of course also no civil requisition of baptism, confirmation, and communion. Religion is left to the free will of each individual, and the church has none but moral means of influencing the world.[10]

Schaff, and we must remember that he was addressing a distinguished Berlin audience, drew back from asserting that the United States had achieved "the perfect and final relation" between church and state.[11] He was too committed to a theory of development in history not to look for continuing penetration and transformation of the state by Christianity. He also acknowledged that in practice separation was not fully and relentlessly carried out. But finally he thought such "blemishes," which he did not seek to deny, were a small price to pay for the remarkable achievement that was—in his experience—the cultural reality of American society.[12]

Schaff's second lecture, part 2 of the book, concerned "the churches and sects." His scheme was to give a "general ecclesiastical view of North America, and then a sketch of each of the most prominent confessions and sects."[13] This section of his argument concerns us less with respect to its details, since it is more of a report upon the religious complexion of America in the mid-nineteenth century than it is an analysis of the principles that he thought undergirded it. Several initial comments, however, are important to expand upon the points made in the first lecture that in turn connect so directly to the later essay that is of primary concern to us. One point is Schaff's insistence that "the principle of religious freedom" is not abstract only or in substance identical to "sheer religious indifference or unbelief." This is his way of characterizing "some modern theories of toleration." Rather, Schaff thought that in America there was "a religious basis" to the principle of religious freedom, namely the "many sufferings and persecutions for the sake of faith and conscience" that Americans had endured to establish the principle.[14]

Joined to this point was Schaff's insistence upon the profound importance of the voluntary principle and some of its implications for the American polity. One implication was that in the absence of an established church a sect system in the continental European sense disappears—all churches are sects, all sects churches.[15] Similarly, when no church is established, none can be dissenting. Here the American situation reflects the pattern that became so pronounced in the English experience: acknowledgment of the right to dissent against an establishment. Of course Schaff's most significant point is that in the American pattern individuals and groups take sustained and vigorous roles in religious activities—displaying, in his felicitous phrase, "regenerate subjectivity." This distinctive outflowing from religious into social activity characterized for Schaff the Protestant form of Christianity.[16] In the larger scheme of Christian development, to be sure, Schaff thought that this impulse needed to be harmonized with its fellow, the objective Catholic construction of Christianity. But in his judgment as a historian, European cultures had manifested no counterpart to the American pattern of the systematic extension of vital religious life to social practice.

In numerous pages Schaff deftly characterizes the families of denominations and the peculiar contributions they had made to this new American culture. He writes as a participant in, and observer of, the antebellum complexion of religious life in the United States. In these terms he has no peer for concise characterization and judicious assessment of his subject matter. But however worthwhile the balance of this lecture, it does not touch on the subject at the center of this essay, Schaff's view of civil authority and its relationship to religious freedom in American society.

Schaff's 1853 lectures at Berlin are a remarkable analysis of American society and culture at mid-century. They are marked by his youth, his relatively recent transposition to the New World—he had been at Mercersburg for exactly a decade—and his immersion in the dynamic life of the new nation. A cloud hung over his discussion, of course. This was caused by slavery and the threat of sectional strife within the United States. To turn from these lectures to his later essay on church and state in the United States is to enter a world at least superficially different. By the mid-1880s, Schaff had repeatedly returned to Europe and achieved a deserved international reputation as a distinguished scholar and representative of Christianity. He had moved to New York City, far from the rural and ethnic context of his initial American period. But what stands out, for all the passage of time and expansion of his experience of the New World, is the continuity of his essential views on questions central to our concerns here. Never one to offer a reduced or simplified explication of his subject, Schaff had insisted that his German audience of 1853 come to terms with aspects of American society they had not imagined. In this very different effort, at the end of his life, he required his American readers almost half a century later to recognize how unique was their solution to the church-state issue—whether or not they recognized it.

At the outset of the 1887 monograph, Schaff posed a question that served to organize his subsequent inquiry: "What is the distinctive character of American Christianity in its organized social aspect and its relation to the national life, as compared with the Christianity of Europe?" His answer was direct and pointed: "It is a FREE CHURCH IN A FREE STATE, or a SELF-SUPPORTING AND SELF-GOVERNING CHRISTIANITY IN INDEPENDENT BUT FRIENDLY RELATION TO THE CIVIL GOVERNMENT."[17] Yet, he opined, for all its significance it had been little studied or reflected upon. This defect Schaff proposed to remedy.

While he thought that little attention had been given to the uniquely American pattern of relations between religion and government, Schaff believed that a theory lay at its base: "The relationship of church and state in the United States secures full liberty of religious thought, speech, and action, within the limits of the public peace and order. It makes persecution impossible."[18] Schaff thought that the theory might be extrapolated from the genesis of this pattern. In his view both church and state were divine institutions, derived from the family as the fundamental government among humankind. Both being necessary, they were "as inseparable as soul and body, and yet as distinct as soul and body."[19] In this formulation, the two agencies of church and state were seen as complementary, respectively concerned with eternal and temporal welfare, religious and secular interests, the reign of love as opposed to that of justice. Yet finally, according to Schaff, both "meet on questions of public morals, and both together constitute civilized human society and ensure its prosperity."[20]

Schaff recognized that this position had evolved over time from the days of early Christianity when there had been no connection between the church and the state. He also insisted that the relationship between these two institutions had taken other forms. Through contrasts, Schaff distinguished the American system from the ante-Nicene (in which the pre-Constantinian church was persecuted by the state), the hierarchical (in which the medieval church controlled the state), the Erastian (in which the state controlled the church for its own purposes), and the system of liberation in modern Europe (in which one church was preferred by the state but sectarian religious behavior was permitted). Finally he thought another option existed that might be termed an infidel pattern, also called the "red-republican system." This latter position was characterized by indifference toward religion and state suppression of the church. Thus Schaff marked out the logical alternatives to the American system and finally emphasized:

> Christianity is the most powerful factor in our society and the pillar of our institutions. It regulates the family; it enjoins private and public virtue; it builds up moral character; it teaches us to love God supremely, and our neighbor as ourselves; it makes good men and useful citizens; it denounces every vice; it encourages every virtue; it promotes and serves the public welfare; it upholds peace and order. Christianity is the only possible religion for the American people, and with Christianity are bound up all our hopes for the future.[21]

With this ringing endorsement of the American pattern of church-state relations Schaff turned to the legal basis for the system. Schaff called attention, correctly, to the significance of the often overlooked but in fact central provision for relating religion to government within the Constitution proper.[22] Article 6, paragraph 3, excludes religious tests for office.

Schaff emphasizes that such tests had been important in English law. There they had functioned, even in the colonial period of American life, effectively to establish churches and to control political appointments. But Schaff went on to analyze the significance of the First Amendment as it moved beyond this provision, which was located in the Constitution proper. It chartered what was for him the positive side, answering to the negative prohibition in the Constitution proper. Thus, through the First Amendment, religious liberty became a central tenet of the new nation.

> The United States furnishes the first example in history of a government deliberately depriving itself of all legislative control over religion, which was justly regarded by all older governments as the chief support of public morality, order, peace, and prosperity. But it was an act of wisdom and justice rather than self-denial. Congress was shut up to this course by the previous history of the American colonies and the actual condition of things at the time of the formation of the national government. The Constitution did not create a nation, nor its religion and institutions. It found them already existing, and was framed for the purpose of protecting them under a republican form of government, in a rule of the people, by the people, and for the people.[23]

A part of the value of Schaff's essay is the attention he gave to the controversy vented in the state conventions that reviewed the proposed Constitution. He emphasized that differences of opinion existed and were strongly expressed on just the points he had enumerated. Further, he recognized that these discussions concerning ratification of the Constitution proper were the source of pressure for the amendments known as the Bill of Rights. So that while the provisions concerning religion were separately located in the original Constitution and the Bill of Rights respectively, Schaff makes much of the important point that the latter evolved directly from the perceived inadequacies of the former.

Beyond directing attention to the circumstances surrounding adoption of the clauses relating to religion, Schaff went on to argue that in practice judicial review was crucial to establishing the boundaries of religious liberty. More than freedom for opinions, the guarantee of free exercise must reach to include "public worship, acts of discipline, and every legitimate manifestation of religion." But, having asserted this principle, he went on to add, "there must be some boundary to religious, as to all other liberty, when it assumes an organized shape or manifests itself in public acts."[24] The critical determination came for Schaff in the Mormon polygamy decision. He apparently thought that the finding in *Reynolds* v. *U.S.* represented the proper limitation through public opinion which ultimately "frames and interprets the laws in a free country."[25]

Part of the strength of Schaff's monograph is the attention he gave to the largely political moves to change or revise the basic terms of the American system. So he took note of the attempts during and following the Civil War to put references to God and Christ in the Constitution.[26] Schaff expressed impatience with the essential superficiality of this point of view. Indeed, he opined that the Constitution was "Christian in substance, though not in form."[27] His argument was that only the ethos of Christianity could have produced a government designed both to support general religious practice and yet to protect true religion from governmental meddling and interference. As another example of political testing of the American position, albeit on the other side of the issue, he reviewed the program of the "Liberal League" to separate radically religion from the state.[28] Such an absolute separation of religion and government Schaff saw as a logical non sequitur: "An absolute separation is an impossibility."[29]

Schaff's comprehensive review also considered several secondary consequences of the federal pattern: for instance, the stances of the separate states and their respective provisions relating to religion. He touched upon the various ways in which the question of establishment was treated and codified in the first state constitutions, and then moved on to review in passing the provisions characteristic of the newer state charters. Another aspect of his essay concerns how various versions of Christianity (i.e., denominations) had amended their creeds to take account of their residence in America. He concluded that "the independence of the church from the state is universally adopted, and religious persecution is universally condemned, even by the most orthodox and bigoted of the American churches."[30]

One of the more significant points made by Schaff is that the American nation had a link to a religion (Christianity, in his judgment) in spite of the elements in the separation of the church from the state that he had enumerated. For him, "state-churchism" most certainly did not exist but in terms of "prevailing religious sentiment and profession" the case looked rather different. Beyond this, there is no question in his mind that at the level of practice, "the American nation is as religious and as Christian as any nation on earth."[31] Here he explicitly cites and agrees with Tocqueville's estimate of the influence of the Christian religion within the American polity.

To support this position, Schaff directs attention to the voluntary religious activities that energize American society. He also points to the explicit recognition given to Christianity by state courts, as well as the

Supreme Court. Such institutional patterns, with official proclamations and messages, are further kinds of evidence for the Christian cast of the culture, a cast that is even more obvious to outsiders, perhaps, than to those within. The use of chaplains by Congress and in the military is also a case in point for Schaff. Finally the place accorded to the Bible within American practices, social and political, suggests its unique status, that of legitimating Christianity.[32]

Beyond these official governmental patterns of action or practice, Schaff calls attention to certain areas of life that do not permit rigid separation between religious and secular concerns. In particular he cites marriage, regulation of the workweek and, of course, public schooling. In the first area, the support for monogamy in America is utterly unequivocal, and is in Schaff's view an indirect if not wholly explicit acceptance of the Christian construction of that social institution. The prominence given to the Sabbath is another clear signal that a broadly Christian construction of the day as one of "rest and worship" prevails. Finally the strong support of minimal religious observances—Bible reading and prayer in particular—indicates the Christian basis of the culture. So Schaff concludes that Christianity has provided the substance that defines the forms of the cultural life of America.[33]

In a more analytical vein, Schaff details the effects of the separation of church and state. And its central outcome in the religious realm has been, in his judgment, to emphasize "the voluntary principle of self-support and self-government."[34] In this sense the American system has returned Christianity to a pattern of independence from the state, which means dependence on its own resources, that is in the larger view, pre-Constantinian.[35] Schaff makes much of the fruits of voluntarism as applied both to support for church activities strictly speaking and to ancillary activities as well. While he is nearly rhapsodic in his estimate of the effectiveness of this experiment in America, Schaff does recognize that in a larger framework of divine purposes this American theory may not be absolute or final.[36]

Characteristically, having begun by placing the American system in reference to Christian history, Schaff concludes his essay by reviewing the influences of the American system on "foreign countries and churches." In this section he offers comparisons and contrasts with the status of religious liberty in the nations of modern Europe, including Greece and Turkey. Finally, Schaff appends to his monograph some illustrative documents that made easily accessible to his readers the variety of materials on which he had drawn to synthesize this ambitious essay.

This summary analysis has been called for to make more widely known

Schaff's remarkable delineation of a badly neglected topic. His views were primarily codified in the essay on church and state in the United States that he wrote late in his life, which was an elaboration of his earlier lectures on American culture. Schaff's claim was correct that the topic had "never received the treatment it deserves, either from the historical or the philosophical point of view. . . . It seems to be regarded as a self-evident fact and truth which needs no explanation and defense."[37] Developments relevant to the broad topic Schaff delineated, and a growing and diversified literature on its various aspects, have been marked characteristics of American society in the last century. In this connection, the remainder of this essay has several objectives. One is to suggest some of the major developments in American society that Schaff did not, indeed could not, fully anticipate. Another is to draw attention to more recent scholarly work on many of the particular issues Schaff grouped together under the church-state rubric. In spite of this work, we must conclude that no comprehensive analysis subsequent to Schaff's monograph can rival it in range and depth.

In his discussion Schaff had correctly stressed that as a narrow point of federal law there had been virtually no testing through interpretation of the First Amendment religion clauses. He made much of the *Reynolds* case, which is the chief exception to this pattern. In Schaff's presentation, this case was evidence that the separation of church and state in America did not mean that a Christian construction of marriage and the family was on the defensive. Rather it was among the operative norms of the society. *Reynolds* was the solitary exception for several reasons. Since Utah was a territory (not yet a state), federal law had direct application to civil life within that jurisdiction. While there was a broad parallel between state and federal provisions to protect rights, it had not yet been determined whether the Bill of Rights of the First Amendment of the federal Constitution was applicable to the states. Therefore at that time only in a territory could the First Amendment freedoms be directly applied to civil cases. Indeed, only after an additional half century was this pattern changed.

Another and broader point is more sociological. In the latter decades of the nineteenth century, patterns in the economy and in business, not to speak of politics and culture, were distinctly regional and decentralized. This meant that practices widely accepted in one region, for instance, having to do with Bible reading in the public schools or appointment of chaplains to state legislatures, could vary from state to state without questions of national standardization seeming appropriate. The pronounced regional structure of the society in combination with its federal government, then, permitted variations that accommodated a significant variety of patterns.

For roughly half a century these conditions continued. But by the 1930s federal rights were explicitly extended to the states and there began a series of tests of the First Amendment religion clauses that has continued with increasing frequency throughout the subsequent decades. First, the "religious liberty" clause was explored in cases largely relating to military service or national loyalties. After World War II the "establishment clause" began to receive attention, especially in cases relating to schools and their practices. The history of this judicial interpretation is well known and does not need to be recounted here except to help elucidate another point. The ensuing attention to these clauses has been so marked as to call into question the degree of consensus on Christianity as the effective, though not formally acknowledged, religion of the American polity. Interpretation of the Constitution has tended toward enlarging the space for religious liberty. In so doing it has at least questioned the kind of entanglement between religious institutions and governments that to Schaff seemed evidence for the deeply Christian character of American social life. This issue leads to the question of religious pluralism, which will require explicit attention later in this essay. But meanwhile it is clear that in the century since Schaff wrote, the federal Constitution has increasingly been interpreted with respect to religion in ways that run counter to the assumptions he made.

Scholarship bearing on these constitutional and legal issues has increased from a trickle early in the century to a torrent in recent decades. It has also taken several different paths. One of these is more strictly historical and has involved numerous case studies of particular episodes or issues as well as broader interpretations of, for example, the development of religious liberty or the significance of dissent in the culture. An early example is M. Louise Greene's careful case study of the development of religious liberty in Connecticut.[38] Another, published shortly after Greene's, is H. J. Eckenrode's meticulous tracing of the stages in the struggle to separate the Anglican church from the colonial government in Virginia in the Revolutionary epoch.[39] Focused on particular colonies and states, these studies illustrate how Schaff's comprehensive problematic of church and state fell out into more discrete topics of scholarly inquiry in the ensuing years. In a more comprehensive historical interpretation—his still useful *Nationalism and Religion in America, 1774–1789*—E. F. Humphrey analyzed how religion had contributed to the emergence of the new nation.[40]

More recently, these kinds of historical interests have been pursued at a new and comprehensive level in such volumes as W. G. McLoughlin's work on New England dissent, which focuses on the role of the Baptists in colonial New England.[41] A very recently published major study by Thomas John Curry titled *The First Freedoms* concerns, in the words of his subtitle, *Church and State in America from the Founding of the Colonies to the Passage of the First Amendment.*[42]

These kinds of studies merge into others that are concerned less with understanding origins than with tracing the development of a specifically American tradition with respect to church-state questions. An example of this genre is William H. Marnell's *First Amendment: The History of Religious Freedom in America.*[43] In some respects the single most important publication concerned with church and state is the three-volume collection of documents with commentary and introduction by Anson Phelps Stokes, *Church and State in the United States.*[44] Stokes subscribes to a broadly separationist interpretation of the uniquely American pattern. Other historical interpretations arguing to specific conclusions are exemplified by the studies of Joseph M. Dawson and Loren P. Beth.[45] Final examples would be Robert L. Cord's monograph, focused narrowly on the First Amendment, which lays claim to it as source and sanction for a particular view of the American church-state tradition,[46] and Michael J. Malbin's *Religion and Politics: The Intentions of the Authors of the First Amendment.*[47]

Increased attention to more strictly constitutional issues followed the Second World War as the Supreme Court, after its decision in *Everson*, began explicitly to interpret the First Amendment. Philip Kurland, for instance, argued in a striking monograph that the two clauses of the First Amendment were to be seen as dynamically interrelated rather than as separate.[48] Wilbur G. Katz and Paul G. Kauper also provided helpful comprehensive discussions of religion in a more strictly legal framework.[49] Articles and books have proliferated in the last few decades, occasioned by the many cases in the lower courts, some of which have made their way to the Supreme Court.

In this regard one comment may be worth making about Schaff's interpretation. As the Supreme Court has explicated church-state law in recent decades, the two clauses of the First Amendment have conventionally been treated as if they respectively addressed the issue of establishment of religion on the one hand and religious liberty on the other. For Schaff, as was indicated above, the line between these respective concerns was drawn at a different point. In the Court's construction, little if any attention has been given to the clause in Article 6 that excludes any religious test for office. But in Schaff's view, this was the clause that prohibited a national establishment of religion, while the two clauses of the First Amendment were, taken together, the positive assurance of religious liberty. Schaff's delineation reflects an understanding of the relationship between these provisions that was prevalent in his day. With the explicit application of the First Amendment to the states in the twentieth century, these clauses shifted to their modern, indeed largely post-Second World War, function. The contrast between Schaff's formulation and the modern definition illuminates the profound cultural changes in the framing of the church-state issue that have taken place within the last century.

If Schaff's essay failed to anticipate certain kinds of development in the church-state question narrowly construed, it is wrong to think it was strictly focused only on governmental regulation and religious activity in the society. In characteristic fashion, Schaff's discussion reached out to encompass far wider cultural, and specifically religious, assumptions. Indeed, this may be the most noteworthy aspect of his later essay. And to properly appreciate and engage with Philip Schaff we must assess his work in these broader terms. To do so, however, evokes seeming contradictions. The essay appears at once obviously dated, because thoroughly determined by theories derived from Schaff's own era, while also remarkably prescient in terms of identifying issues that have become fully recognized only more recently. Far from being paradoxical, this dichotomous appraisal is proposed for a special reason. It is exactly because Schaff's operating assumptions were derived from his own era and drew on the wealth of his experience that they both colored his interpretation and also produced some insights whose acuity has become clear only at some remove.

Among the most obvious of Schaff's assumptions was that of cultural progress or historical linearity. He was deeply imbued with the developmental orientation of his early historical training. This emphasis powerfully forces the contemporary reader to recognize in his work what in modern scholarship would be labeled as a distinctive set of cultural presuppositions—the systematic interrelationship of ideas, values, and actions so as to form a collective reality out of which the future is created. For Schaff, the history of Christianity was, broadly speaking, one of succeeding epochs in which different constructions of the Christian religion had been as the successive souls to different bodies. The developmental cultural scheme at once freed Schaff to recognize in the American nation a synthesis of Christianity with society that was different from any that had preceded it—and to believe that this too might in turn be superseded. So Schaff was profoundly sensitive to the special nuances of American Christianity as a cultural reality, prepared to present and defend it against detractors and challengers, but also prepared to suppose that development might in due course carry Christianity on beyond this stage to an as yet uncodified synthesis of Protestantism and Catholicism perhaps more fully representing the divine origins and end of the religion.

In our time, a century later, after two world wars and impending universal destruction, such a progressive scheme, however nuanced at

Schaff's hands, seems marked by an optimism that is unwarranted. In the Catholic and Protestant theological climates of the last half century, the relatively easy accommodation between Christianity and culture that Schaff took for granted seems fraught with hazards. Among many kinds of evidence we might name complicity in the destruction of European Jewry during World War II, and general insensitivity to the enormous potential for evil of modern political tyrannies and their bloated war machines. In this perspective, late twentieth-century attitudes toward the church-state issue, perhaps especially on the part of self-conscious Christians, are more mixed, inclined to recognize contradictions and tendencies for good and ill rather than to presuppose the relatively uncomplicated linear schemes of development that Schaff took for granted.

Consequently it is not surprising that reflection on the church-state issue has developed within the several American religious communities. In the course of the 1920s a distinctively Roman Catholic perspective began to emerge in a notable study by John A. Ryan and Moorhouse F. X. Millar titled *The State and the Church*.[50] Theirs was the first systematic inquiry into how the Roman Catholic church might come to terms with democracy as a form of government and with modernity as a condition of society and culture. The influential work of John Courtney Murray, best consulted in *We Hold These Truths*, may be seen as climax to this effort.[51] The results of this inquiry also became a broader gift from American experience to the international Roman Catholic church as it wrestled with its commitment to religious liberty in the 1960s.

On the Protestant side, William Adams Brown's programmatic study, *Church and State in Contemporary America*, must be seen as an attempt on the part of liberal Protestant churchmen to explore and think through how the church-state construct applied to the interwar epoch.[52] Among numerous relevant publications that represent continuing Protestant preoccupation with these issues are John Coleman Bennett's *Christians and the State* and a study by Thomas G. Sanders on *Protestant Concepts of Church and State*.[53]

Among other reasons, Schaff's essay had been notable because he seemed to recognize, yet not fully accept, that in some respects church and state were interdependent. At one level he emphasized a correspondence between the plurality of religious denominations on the one side (church) and the multiplicity of governing bodies on the other (state). But he did not ask whether it was the reduction of the European state structure in the New World that finally permitted the variety of religious life to flower. Nor did he ask, in turn, if a centralized government were to develop in the United States whether the same tendencies to centralization in religion could be resisted. Now, a century later, the American national experience has proved to be one of vastly increased central governmental authority and power, although without a state ideology. And corresponding to this, there has been a net centralization of religious bodies. Schaff had looked to a Catholicizing of Protestant Christianity and a Protestantizing of Catholic Christianity in America. Some developments toward common types of Christianity in the United States have certainly occurred, especially dramatically in the last quarter century. But this has been produced more by vastly extended religious bureaucracies and initiatives by extraecclesiastical entrepreneurs as well as by Pentecostal and charismatic influences than by the reconciliation between the Protestant and Roman Catholic branches of Christendom that Schaff anticipated in the New World context.

A further extension of this point concerns his quite extraordinary sensitivity to the cultural relationship between nationalism and religion. While Schaff does not expand upon this perception, he comes close in substance to identifying what has more recently been denominated civil religion—the religious construction of nationalism and its relative independence, perhaps even explicit institutionalization, within the society. In Schaff's view this religion of the nation was in the American case ineradicably Christian, and Christian in a distinctively American guise. In some respects, Sidney Mead's remarkable series of essays, first collected in *The Lively Experiment*, represent explorations of this general topic.[54] Mead has emphasized, far more than did Schaff, the significance of the Enlightenment in transforming Protestant Christianity in America.[55]

Will Herberg, with his insistence that the American way of life constituted the spiritual culture of the nation, in many ways laid the groundwork for the more specific discussion of civil religion that began with Robert Bellah's noteworthy essay in 1967.[56] Numerous articles and books have been produced with respect to this discussion, which has focused upon general religious elements in the culture, elements not necessarily tied to Christianity.[57] The understanding of civil religion that has emerged recently is not so narrowly defined as Schaff's. It would be too much to claim that Schaff emphasizes a civil-religion component of the church-state question in the United States. But it is not too much to suggest that he identified something like civil religious phenomena before it was common to emphasize the religious dimensions of nationalism, let alone discrete national religions.

Schaff's prescience also extended to awareness that the church-state issue was embodied in social and cultural activities. He placed great emphasis on patterns of religious activities—Bible reading and prayer are the most obvious—in the schools. Since Schaff wrote, a remarkably rich literature has developed on the place of religion in the schools, which served as the initial focal point for modern legal determination of practices permissible under the Constitution. Among many studies, Robert Michaelsen's *Piety in the Public School* and the work of Donald E. Boles should be noted.[58]

Schaff's comprehensive treatment of the church-state problematic also identified issues such as chaplaincies, both to legislatures and the military forces, and religious sponsorship of social service agencies. These issues have indeed occasioned recent discussion, but the status of religious institutions with respect to taxation, which Schaff did not address, has possibly been more significant, as Dean M. Kelley's recently edited volume would suggest.[59] The larger point, however, is that Schaff recognized that the location of church-state tensions had been decentralized in modern societies, a relocation that has become dramatically evident in the course of the twentieth century. Schaff identified the beginnings of this process and in that sense in principle laid the groundwork for modern scholarly, as well as partisan, approaches to the issue.

In all of his marvelous openness to the new religious configurations within American society, however, Schaff appears to have ruled out one option explored explicitly by a younger American contemporary, William James. This is the possibility that a radical religious pluralism would come to characterize the culture of the United States. William James worked through his convictions with respect to radical pluralism in an essentially philosophical framework. In his pragmatism he was driven to respect the hypothesis that finally the entire universe might be radically plural, constituted of independent variables, or agents in modern jargon.[60] James himself was not disturbed at the thought of understanding religious phenomena in this light. Indeed, his Gifford Lectures on "The Varieties of Religious Experience" may be taken at one level as acknowledgment that social reality must finally be experienced as plural. Such a step was far removed indeed from Philip Schaff's world. There cultural wholes had internal consistency and it is clear that for him Christianity provided that cultural consistency for America. As we reflect at the end of the twentieth century on American society and the place of religion in it, James' radically pluralistic model seems less implausible than it might have seemed a century ago. In that sense James' musings may put a kind of final question mark to the assumptions Schaff made that church and state were categories under which American social and intellectual reality could be comprehended in the future as well as the past. James might well have charged Philip Schaff with a category mistake in framing his remarkable essay.

But there is a sense in which that is our problem and not Schaff's. What Schaff did in his essay was to identify a question central to American society and culture. This was the question of civil authority in relationship to religious freedom in America. He interpreted that question in terms that connected it to European civilization, indeed that made of America an important new chapter in Western Christianity. And he did this without diminishing either the innovativeness of the American resolution of the issue or the power of earlier paradigms. That was a remarkable contribution to make in the centennial year of the Constitution. Now, a century later, we properly acknowledge and pay tribute to Schaff's many achievements and particularly to this, so noteworthy among them.

Notes

1. *Church and State in the United States or The American Idea of Religious Liberty and Its Practical Effects,* Papers of the American Historical Association, vol. 2, no. 4 (New York: G. P. Putnam's Sons, 1888), preface [p. 5].

2. Ibid.

3. *America: A Sketch of Its Political, Social and Religious Character*, ed. Perry Miller (Cambridge, MA: Harvard University Press, Belknap Press, 1961), 30.

4. Ibid., 31.

5. Ibid., 33.

6. Ibid., 37.

7. Ibid., 38.

8. Ibid., 51.

9. Ibid., 57.

10. Ibid., 73–74.

11. Ibid., 75.

12. Ibid., 75–79.

13. Ibid., 87.

14. Ibid., 91.

15. Ibid., 96ff. This formulation is reminiscent of the kind of observation that later intrigued H. Richard Niebuhr and led to his elaboration with respect to America of Ernst Troeltsch's work upon the relationship between churches and sects. Niebuhr himself argued that the peculiarity of the American pattern was that both churches and sects became denominations. See his *The Social Sources of Denominationalism* (New York: Holt, 1929).

16. Schaff, *America*, 101.

17. Schaff, *Church and State*, 9.

18. Ibid.

19. Ibid., 10.

20. Ibid.

21. Ibid., 16.

22. Ibid., 20–22.

23. Ibid., 23.

24. Ibid., 35.

25. Ibid., 37.

26. Ibid., 38–39.

27. Ibid., 40.

28. Ibid., 43–45.

29. Ibid., 44.

30. Ibid., 53.

31. Ibid., 55.

32. Ibid., 57–68.

33. Ibid., 69–78.

34. Ibid, 78.

35. Ibid., 78–79.

36. Ibid., 83. See first paragraph.

37. Ibid., 9.

38. M. Louise Greene, *The Development of Religious Liberty in Connecticut* (Boston: Houghton, Mifflin, 1905). This followed shortly upon Sanford H. Cobb's *The Rise of Religious Liberty in America* (New York: Macmillan, 1902). For a more recent discussion of this theme, see Elwyn A. Smith, *Religious Liberty in the United States* (Philadelphia: Fortress Press, 1972).

39. H. J. Eckenrode, *Separation of Church and State in Virginia: A Study in the Development of the Revolution* (1910, reprint, New York: Da Capo Press, 1971). A more modern treatment is Thomas E. Buckley, S.J., *Church and State in Revolutionary Virginia, 1776–1787* (Charlottesville: University Press of Virginia, 1977). For a recent discussion of Madison's role see William Lee Miller, *The First Liberty* (New York: Knopf, 1986).

40. Boston: Chipman Law Publishing Co., 1924.

41. *New England Dissent, 1630–1833: The Baptists and the Separation of Church and State*, 2 vols. (Cambridge, MA: Harvard University Press, 1971).

42. New York: Oxford University Press, 1986.

43. Garden City, NY: Doubleday, 1964.

44. New York: Harper and Brothers, 1950. Rev. ed. in 1 vol., with Leo Pfeffer (New York: Harper and Row, 1964). Among several contributions by Pfeffer, see *Church, State and Freedom* (Boston: Beacon Press, 1953).

45. Joseph M. Dawson, *America's Way in Church, State, and Society* (New York: Macmillan, 1953); Loren P. Beth, *The American Theory of Church and State* (Gainesville: University of Florida Press, 1958).

46. *Separation of Church and State: Historical Fact and Current Fiction* (Cambridge, MA: Lambeth Press, 1982).

47. Washington, DC: American Enterprise Institute for Public Policy Research, 1978.

48. *Religion and the Law of Church and State and the Supreme Court* (Chicago: Aldine, 1962).

49. Wilbur G. Katz, *Religion and American Constitutions* (Evanston, IL: North-

western University Press, 1964); Paul G. Kauper, *Religion and the Constitution* (Baton Rouge: Louisiana State University Press, 1964).

50. New York: Macmillan, 1922.

51. Subtitled *Catholic Reflections on the American Proposition* (New York: Sheed and Ward, 1960).

52. New York: Charles Scribner's Sons, 1936.

53. New York: Charles Scribner's Sons, 1958; and New York: Holt, Rinehart and Winston, 1964, respectively.

54. See Mead's *The Lively Experiment: The Shaping of Christianity in America* (New York: Harper and Row, 1963); *The Nation With the Soul of a Church* (New York: Harper and Row, 1975); and *The Old Religion in the Brave New World: Reflections on the Relation Between Christendom and the Republic* (Berkeley: University of California Press, 1977).

55. Another author whose contribution to understanding the interaction of religion and government in America must not be passed over is Mark DeWolfe Howe. See esp. his *Garden and the Wilderness: Religion and Government in American Constitutional History* (Chicago: University of Chicago Press, 1965).

56. Will Herberg, *Protestant-Catholic-Jew: An Essay in American Religious Sociology* (Garden City, NY: Doubleday, 1955). The Bellah essay and related discussions of civil religion are readily available in Russell E. Richey and Donald G. Jones, eds., *American Civil Religion* (New York: Harper and Row, 1974). See also Bellah's subsequent book, *The Broken Covenant: American Civil Religion in Time of Trial* (New York: Seabury, 1975).

57. See John F. Wilson, *Public Religion in American Culture* (Philadelphia: Temple University Press, 1979).

58. Robert Michaelsen, *Piety in the Public School* (New York: Macmillan, 1970); Donald E. Boles, *The Bible, Religion, and the Public Schools*, 3d ed. (Ames: Iowa State University Press, 1965).

59. *Government Intervention in Religious Affairs* (New York: Pilgrim Press, 1982).

60. See *A Pluralistic Universe* (London: Longmans, Green, 1909).

To the Ends of the Earth

American Protestants in Pursuit of Mission

Gerald H. Anderson

N 1886, two years before Philip Schaff founded the American Society of Church History, Dwight L. Moody convened the first Mount Hermon summer conference for college students at Northfield, Massachusetts, that led to the formation of the Student Volunteer Movement for Foreign Missions (SVM) in 1888, with John R. Mott as chairman. Also in 1886, Arthur Tappan Pierson, who addressed the Mount Hermon conference, published the major missionary promotional book of the era, *The Crisis of Missions*, Josiah Strong published *Our Country: Its Possible Future and Its Present Crises*, and Strong became general secretary of the Evangelical Alliance for the United States for which Schaff also served as honorary corresponding secretary. The missionary enterprise in the United States was entering a period of enormous vitality with a crusading spirit that was fueled by duty, compassion, confidence, optimism, evangelical revivalism, and premillennialist urgency.[1]

Manifest Destiny in Missions

The overarching motive for missions at this time was love of Christ and obedience to the Great Commission for the salvation of souls.[2] Underneath, however, was the compelling idea, developing since the 1840s, of America's Manifest Destiny—of a national mission assigned by Providence for extending the blessings of America to other peoples. Herman Melville had written in 1850, "We Americans are peculiar, chosen people, the Israel of our times; we bear the ark of the liberties of the world."[3] Until the 1890s Manifest Destiny was thought of primarily in terms of continental expansion, of "winning the West," with the absorption of settlers into citizenship and statehood. In the 1890s, however, when the United States had reached the limits of prospective continental expansion, there developed agitation for expansion beyond North America. There was a conviction that the United States was a nation divinely chosen or predestined

168

to be the "primary agent of God's meaningful activity in history."[4] The doctrine of Manifest Destiny had its roots in the concepts of Anglo-Saxon racial superiority, of America as the center of civilization in the westward course of empires, the primacy of American political institutions, the purity of American Protestant Christianity, and the desirability for English to be the language of humanity.[5]

Until late in the nineteenth century, the American churches concentrated their missionary efforts in "home missions," to evangelize the pioneers on the frontier, Indians, Hispanic Americans, blacks, and new immigrants in the cities. "In 1874, for example, the Missionary Society of the Methodist Episcopal Church (Northern) supported in whole or in part more than 3,000 missionaries in the United States. In the same year . . . that same church had 145 missionaries overseas."[6]

Of special significance in shaping the mind and mood of American Protestant churches regarding the new frontiers of Manifest Destiny were the published writings of the Reverend Josiah Strong (1847–1916), who came out of a background of work with the Congregational Home Missionary Society. His books, especially *Our Country* (1886), and *The New Era; or, The Coming Kingdom* (1893) "did much to develop the idea of the part America should play in fulfilling Anglo-Saxon destiny as a civilizing and Christianizing power."[7] Austin Phelps, professor emeritus at Andover Seminary, wrote the introduction to *Our Country* in which he said that Americans should "look on these United States as first and foremost the chosen seat of enterprise for the world's conversion. Forecasting the future of Christianity, as statesmen forecast the destiny of nations, we must believe that it will be what the future of this country is to be. As goes America, so goes the world, in all that is vital to its mortal welfare."[8]

This small volume—which sold 175,000 copies over a period of thirty years—emphasized the superiority of the Anglo-Saxon race in general and of Americans in particular as God's chosen people. The Anglo-Saxon, Strong asserted, was "divinely commissioned to be, in a peculiar sense, his brothers keeper."[9] In the closing pages of *The New Era*, Strong summarized his "enthusiasm for humanity" in these words: "Surely, to be a Christian and an Anglo-Saxon and an American in this generation is to stand on the very mountain-top of privilege."

Leaders in the Forward Movement of Missions

While Strong probably did more than anyone else at that time to get Americans interested in the application of Christianity to the problems of the nation, A. T. Pierson, a Presbyterian, is judged to have been "the foremost spokesperson for foreign missions in the late nineteenth century."[10] Of particular importance was Pierson's leadership at the 1886 Mount Hermon summer conference attended by 251 students from nearly ninety colleges, including John R. Mott, Luther D. Wishard, Robert P. Wilder, and Charles K. Ober. Speaking on "God's Providence in Modern Missions," Pierson urged that "All should go, and go to all." By the last day of the conference, 100 young men—"The Mount Hermon Hundred"— dedicated themselves to foreign missionary service.[11] Two students—Robert Wilder and John N. Forman—were delegated to visit American colleges during 1886–87 to enlist further student support for foreign missions. By the time 450 students assembled at Northfield in June 1887 for the second student conference the number of volunteers had increased to more than 2,100—1,600 men and 500 women. During the second year (1887–88), even with no organized deputation to campuses, the number of volunteers who had signed a declaration, "I am willing and desirous, God permitting, to become a foreign missionary," swelled to nearly 3,000. The story of the student missionary uprising generated a revival of missionary interest in the churches. President James McCosh of the College of New Jersey at Princeton, commenting on the new student offering of life for missionary service, asked, "Has any such offering of living young men and women been presented in our age, in our country, in any age, or in any country, since the day of Pentecost?"[12]

In 1887, Pierson became editor of the *Missionary Review of the World*, and he is credited with formulating the watchword, "The Evangelization of the World in This Generation," adopted by the SVM in 1889.[13] Pierson initiated a call in 1885 for a world missions conference and council that was realized initially with the London Centenary Missions Conference in 1888, attended by 1,579 delegates from 139 missionary societies, including Philip Schaff of the Evangelical Alliance, who addressed the conference. Pierson also helped to begin the Kansas-Sudan movement in 1889 and the Africa Inland Mission in 1895 as faith missions.

Along with Pierson, Adoniram Judson Gordon—prominent pastor of Clarendon Street Baptist Church in Boston and author of *The Holy Spirit in Missions* (1893)—was "a father of faith missions" in America.[14] Gordon founded the Boston Missionary Training Institute in 1889 (later evolved into Gordon College and Gordon-Conwell Theological Seminary), where the emphasis was on training in Bible and mission methods for lay persons, especially women, to provide laborers for the mission fields that were viewed as ripe unto harvest. While Pierson and Gordon were premillennialists, the main motives for founding faith missions in the late nineteenth century were not theological or sectarian but practical—to decentralize missionary responsibility for greater efficiency, to overcome denominational separatism, and to supplement the work of denominational agencies. It was not until the fundamentalist-modernist controversy intensified after World War I that theological issues became more pronounced and the American Protestant missionary consensus disintegrated.

Two other late nineteenth-century premillennialists are important for their contributions to American missions: Albert Benjamin Simpson and Cyrus Ingerson Scofield.[15] Simpson was a Presbyterian minister who in 1887 founded two affiliated organizations: The Christian Alliance as a nondenominational fellowship, and the Evangelical (later International) Missionary Alliance for foreign mission work. They merged in 1897 as the Christian and Missionary Alliance, and their workers were trained at the Missionary Training Institute and later at the Jaffray School of Missions (now Nyack College and Alliance Theological Seminary, Nyack, New York). What Simpson established was a missionary agency that became a missionary denomination. Missions in the alliance are the reason for which congregations exist; thus today the CMA has far more members overseas than in the United States.[16]

Scofield was a Congregationalist who founded the Central American Mission as a faith agency in 1890. He is best remembered, says Dana L. Robert, "as the editor of the *Scofield Reference Bible*, an annotated King James Bible that encapsulated the hermeneutical system called premillennial dispensationalism. What is almost never mentioned about the *Scofield Reference Bible* is that its purpose was not to codify a theological system. It was intended to be a one-volume reference work for missionaries who had no access to theological libraries."[17]

Mott—who graduated from Cornell University in 1888 and was now intercollegiate secretary for the North American Student YMCA—was invited to speak at commencement exercises at the University (later College) of Wooster, Ohio, in 1890 by a graduating senior, John Campbell White. "Cam" White became Mott's assistant, later served a term in India, and was subsequently general secretary of the Laymen's Missionary Movement and president of Wooster. His brother, W. W. White, was the founder and lifetime president of the Biblical Seminary in New York. Mott married their sister, Leila, in 1891.[18]

In 1892 Mott could report that already "several thousands of students" had been inspired by the Volunteer Movement to declare their purpose to become foreign missionaries; that "over five hundred volunteers have already gone to the foreign field under the various missionary agencies, and fully one hundred more are under appointment. . . . Moreover, a large majority of the volunteers are still in various stages of preparation." He reported also that "missionary intelligence" had been taken into three hundred colleges and there were now nearly six times as many students in these colleges who expect to become missionaries as there were before the movement. Furthermore, he said, missionary studies and interest had been intensified in forty-five seminaries, and "carefully selected missionary libraries have been introduced into fully seventy-five institutions. . . . It would be difficult now to find an institution where there are not now two or more missionary periodicals on file."[19]

Documentation for reference and research was enhanced with the publication in 1891 of the two-volume *Encyclopaedia of Missions*, edited by Edwin M. Bliss, who had worked in the Middle East for the American Bible Society. This was followed by the publication in 1897–99 of the two-volume work *Christian Missions and Social Progress: A Sociological Study of Foreign Missions* by James S. Dennis, a former missionary in Syria. Dennis sought to show "the larger scope of missions" with "the dawn of a sociological era in missions." He examined the ability of Christianity "to uplift society and introduce the higher forces of permanent social regeneration and progress." His thesis was that non-Christian society, "left to its own tendencies, uniformly and persistently goes the way of moral deterioration and sinks into decadence, with no hope of self-reformation," whereas Christianity "has been invariably the motive force in all noble and worthy moral development" in any "attempt to civilize barbarous races" (2:3).

In a statistical supplement, published in 1902 as *Centennial Survey of Foreign Missions*, Dennis provided massive documentation on the status at the turn of the century of Protestant foreign missions, which he defined as "any more or less organized effort to lead the natives of unevangelized lands to the acceptance of a pure and saving form of Christian truth, and to lift their daily living into conformity with it."[20] His work has been judged "a landmark in the history of American foreign missions as a dividing point between the old stress on snatching the heathen from the jaws of Hell and the new view of missions as a humanitarian agency"— where "conversion of the heathen was gradually becoming a means to an end, namely an improved society."[21]

In May 1893 Mott declined an invitation from Moody to head up his recently established Bible Institute in Chicago. Later that summer at the Chicago World's Fair (Columbian Exposition), Moody held an evangelistic campaign and Mott delivered his first speech to an international audience at the World's Parliament of Religions (where many evangelicals refused to participate); then they were on the Northfield platform together for another summer student conference.[22]

Providence, Politics, and the Philippines

The potent blend of Providence, piety, politics, and patriotism surged in support of foreign missions in 1898–99 with the Spanish-American War, especially with regard to the Philippines.[23] Anti-Roman Catholic sentiment was also a factor. In an article on "The Philippine Islands" in the *Christian Advocate* for September 1898, the Reverend R. G. Hobbs appealed to fellow Methodists: "Break the clutch which Rome has put upon those people, and give then a chance for a civilization which is something more than Christianized paganism."

The faith that America's course of action had approval of divine Providence seemed to be confirmed by the swift and complete triumph of American arms in Manila.[24] Rudyard Kipling urged Americans to "Take up the white man's burden." Religious leaders saw parallels between the American victories and those of Israel in biblical times. The editor of *Christian and Missionary Alliance* said that the story of Admiral Dewey's victory "reads almost like the stories of the ancient battles of the Lord in the times of Joshua, David, and Jehoshaphat." Alexander Blackburn, writing in the *Standard*, a Baptist publication, said, "The magnificent fleets of Spain have gone down as marvelously, I had almost said, as miraculously, as the walls of Jericho went down," and he maintained that the nation now had a duty "to throw its strong protecting arms around . . . the Philippine Islands" and to practice an "imperialism of righteousness."

Within a few weeks after Dewey's victory a Presbyterian writer could say that the religious press was practically unanimous "as to the desirability of America's retaining the Philippines as a duty in the interest of human freedom and Christian progress." Methodist Bishop Hurst concurred: "The missionary aspirations of the American Church will add this new people to its map for conquest. . . . Never before has there fallen, at one stroke of the bell of destiny, such a burden upon the American people." The *Baptist Union* agreed that "The conquest by force of arms must be followed by conquest for Christ." Anticipating the acquisition of the Philippines by the United States, the Methodist editors of *World-Wide Missions* rejoiced that "we are no longer compelled to go to a foreign country to seek raw heathen. When patriotism and evangelism can go hand in hand, the one strengthens the other. . . . How glorious it would be to think that we have one Mission in the heathen world with the starry flag afloat above it."

On the side of government, President William McKinley (who once said, "I am a Methodist and nothing but a Methodist") was not indifferent to this sentiment. To a delegation from the general missionary committee of the Methodist church that called on him in his office in November 1899, the President described how he had arrived at his decision—despite opposition and controversy—to retain the Philippines as a mission of "benevolent assimilation."

> I walked the floor of the White House night after night until midnight; and I am not ashamed to tell you, gentlemen, that I went down on my knees and prayed Almighty God for light and guidance more than one night. And one night late it came to me this way—I don't know how it was, but it came: . . . that there was nothing left for us to do but to take them all, and to educate the Filipinos, and uplift and civilize and Christianize them, and by God's grace do the very best we could by them, as our fellow-men for whom Christ died.

Senator Albert J. Beveridge delivered a Senate speech in January 1900, upon his return from a tour of the Philippines and the Far East, in which he concluded that "God marked the American people as His chosen nation to finally lead in the regeneration of the world." Not only was the Christian mission linked with national purpose, but the mission to America became subservient to the mission of America, and the nation replaced the church as the new Israel.[25] Clearly the mood at the turn of the century in both church and state was forward-looking in terms of progress and expansion, with a triumphant expectation that this would be "the Christian century."

Other Voices and Views

A rather unusual self-critical note was sounded by William Newton Clarke, a prominent liberal theologian at Colgate Theological Seminary in Hamilton, New York, in his *Study of Christian Missions* published in 1900. Clarke affirmed that "Christianity deserves possession of the world. It has the right to offer itself boldly to all men, and to displace all other religions, for no other religion offers what it brings. It is the best that the world contains" (19). But, he cautioned, "Mankind has entered one of its periods of passion and unrest. . . . The present atmosphere of the world is not inspiring to missionary zeal: it is too full of something opposite" (193–94). Further, it was Clarke's judgment that there was a "crisis in missions . . . a sense of pause . . . signs of weakening . . . and of uncertainty. . . . Something has happened, to chill the ardor" (170–71). Criticism was rife, financial support was wanting, retrenchment was diminishing the work. The problems were created, he said, by romantic, unrealistic expectations of a swift and complete triumph of the gospel (172–73), by material interests, a warlike spirit, racial antagonisms, and national ambitions in a period of passion and unrest. "What we occidentals call civilization," Clarke observed, "too often carries to heathen people the wrong gift" (243) Renewal of commitment in this "period of great transition" required a recognition that the task of missions—especially to overcome the ancient non-Christian religions—was "a far greater undertaking than our fathers thought" (185). To recover momentum in missions, American Christians needed to requicken their faith, to simplify the Christian message, and to adopt "the long and exacting work of making Christianity the religion of the world." While he had appreciation for those who were motivated by the SVM watchword, he had questions about its meaning and goal. "It might be as difficult to tell when the world has been evangelized," he said, "as to know when the present generation is past. . . . It is quite impossible that within the lifetime of a generation Christ should become intelligently known by all men" (73–74).

In contrast, John R. Mott in 1900 wrote his classic text, *The Evangelization of the World in This Generation*, in which he defined and defended the SVM watchword, then surveyed the possibilities and resources for accomplishing the task. The watchword, he said, "means the giving to all men an adequate opportunity of knowing Jesus Christ as their Saviour and of becoming His real disciples" (4). This is what Christ implied in the Great Commission. It means preaching the gospel to those who are now living; it does not mean the conversion of the world, according to Mott. There were approximately 15,000 Protestant missionaries throughout the world in 1900. Mott proposed there was a need for one missionary to every twenty thousand heathen; therefore he called for an increase in the missionary task force from 15,000 to 50,000—though he agreed with Professor Gustav Warneck that there was no need for more than the 537 mission agencies already in existence.

Robert E. Speer began his remarkable forty-six year tenure as secretary of the Board of Foreign Missions of the Presbyterian Church in the U.S.A. in 1891. Profoundly influenced during student days at Princeton College by Pierson and Moody, Speer was an SVM traveling secretary for one year following graduation from Princeton in 1889, then attended Princeton Seminary for a year, but never graduated. Like Mott, he was never ordained, and never served as a foreign missionary; they were "detained volunteers." Yet his influence in American missions—and beyond—in the first third of the century would be enormous. A prolific author (sixty-seven books and countless articles) and eloquent speaker, Speer was a preeminent intepreter of foreign missions. While Mott was the missionary statesman, Speer was the prophet.[26] His leadership of the Presbyterian board "contributed to an increase in Presbyterian foreign missionaries from 598 when he joined the board in 1891 to a peak of 1606 in 1927," and at 1356 shortly before he retired in 1937 it was the largest of any American agency at that time.[27] John A. Mackay, later president of Princeton Seminary and himself an influential figure in American missions, testified that Speer was "one of the greatest figures in American Christianity. Judged by any standard intellectual or spiritual, Dr. Speer was incomparably the greatest man I have ever known."[28] The Robert E. Speer Library building at Princeton Seminary is a tribute to his legacy.

Speaking in 1900, Speer said that "the aim of foreign missions [is] to make Jesus Christ known to the world with a view to the full salvation of men, and their gathering into true and living churches." There should be no confusion of the aim with the methods and results of missions. It is a "mischievous doctrine," he said, to suggest that missions "must aim at the total reorganization of the whole social fabric"; this may be a result, but it is not the aim of missions.[29]

Along with Mott and Speer as a major figure in this period and later was George Sherwood Eddy. Eddy graduated from Yale in 1891 with Henry W. Luce (father of the founder of *Time*) and Horace T. Pitkin. The three of them were student volunteers, they were roommates at Union Theological Seminary, and they planned to spend their lives in China. Pitkin went and was beheaded during the Boxer Rebellion in 1900. After finishing his seminary studies at Princeton with Eddy, Luce went to China and eventually became vice-president of Yenching University. But Mott prevailed on Eddy to go to India with the YMCA. After fifteen years in India, Eddy served another fifteen years as YMCA secretary for Asia doing student evangelistic work, then went on to become an influential world citizen as lay evangelist and advocate of the social gospel, socialism, and pacifism, in his lectures, travel seminars, and thirty-six books. In his autobiography, Eddy testified that his conversion under Moody at Northfield, and his association with Mott and Speer, were dominant in shaping his life. It was difficult for students in later generations, he said, "to realize how impelling was the appeal of the Volunteer Movement for us in those days."[30]

Ecumenical Missionary Conference, 1900

In planning for the Ecumenical Missionary Conference to be held in New York City in 1900, William E. Dodge expressed a common conviction, "We are going into a century more full of hope, and promise, and opportunity than any period in the world's history. We want to seize upon these opportunities."[31] The ten-day conference in April 1980 "was the largest missionary conference that has ever been held,"[32] with 200 mission societies from Europe, Britain, and the United States represented, and nearly 200,000 people attending the various sessions. Those who could not get into sessions at Carnegie Hall went to overflow meetings at nearby Calvary Baptist Church, Central Presbyterian Church, and other churches. President William McKinley, at the opening, spoke of "the missionary effort which has wrought such wonderful triumphs for civilization."[33] He was followed on the program by the governor of the state of New York, Theodore Roosevelt, and former President Benjamin Harrison, who was honorary president of the conference.

The Ecumenical Missionary Conference of 1900 was indicative of the momentum in support of interdenominational cooperation in missions, at home and abroad, that had been developing especially since the 1880s—to avoid competition, to realize better stewardship of resources, and to provide more effective witness to non-Christians. For instance, the Intercollegiate YMCA Movement, founded in 1877 with Luther D. Wishard as the first secretary, was a pioneering effort, and the Interseminary Missionary Alliance (later the Interseminary Movement), founded in 1880, "prepared the ground for the Mount Hermon awakening in 1886" and was the forerunner of the SVM.[34]

Of special significance for comity and cooperation was the formation in 1893 of the Interdenominational Conference of Foreign Missionary Boards and Societies in the United States and Canada (became the Foreign Missions Conference of North America in 1911, later the Division of Foreign Missions of the National Council of Churches in 1950, and the Division of Overseas Ministries, NCC, in 1965).[35] This was followed by a number of ecumenical organizations that were founded for coordination and cooperation in support of missions. Some of the more important were the Central Committee on the United Study of Foreign Missions, 1900; the Young People's Missionary Movement, 1902 (became the Missionary Education Movement in 1911); and the Laymen's Missionary Movement, 1907 (which some church officials at the time declared was "the most epoch-making [movement] that has occurred in the Christian world since the Protestant Reformation"), that was absorbed in 1919 by the Interchurch World Movement, and collapsed a year later in a financial fiasco.[36]

The number of American Protestant overseas missionary personnel increased dramatically from a relatively small number prior to 1880, to 2,716 in 1890, to 4,159 in 1900, to 7,219 in 1910, and over 9,000 in 1915.[37] Participation in foreign missions had become "an identifying mark of mainstream Protestantism."[38] Mott announced in 1910 that it was "the decisive hour of Christian missions," that there was a "rising spiritual tide" in the non-Christian world, and that "on the world-wide battlefield of Christianity . . . victory is assured if the present campaign be adequately supported and pressed."[39]

Women in Mission

In addition to the significant contribution of the SVM was the remarkable role of women in the American missionary enterprise. Women undergirded the missionary movement with prayer, study, financial support, personnel, and diffusion of information. Their periodicals included the Congregationalist *Light and Life for Heathen Women* (became *Life and Light for Women*, 1876), the Methodist *Heathen Woman's Friend* (became *Woman's Missionary Friend*, 1896), both founded in 1869, the Free Baptist *Missionary Helper* (1878), the Presbyterian *Woman's Work for Woman* (1871; merged with *Our Mission Field*, 1886; name changed to *Woman's Work*, 1905), the Southern Methodist *Woman's Missionary Advocate* (1880), the United Brethren *Woman's Evangel* (1881), the Methodist Protestant *Woman's Missionary Record* (1885), and the United Presbyterian *Woman's Missionary Magazine* (1887). However, the women faced opposition, discrimination, and lack of recognition by men. When Rufus Anderson, foreign secretary of the American Board and one of the outstanding American mission strategists of the nineteenth century, retired in 1866, he told his successor, "I cannot recommend bringing women into this work; but you are a young man, go and do it if you can."[40] In response to this situation, women formed their own mission boards, such as the Woman's Union Missionary Society of America for Heathen Lands (1860). At the Centenary Conference of 1888 in London, American women—led by Abbie Child—initiated the formation of the World's Missionary Committee of Christian Women, which has been described as "the first international ecumenical missionary agency."[41] In connection with the Columbian Exposition at Chicago in 1893, there was a Congress of Missions for Women and also a Conference of Women's Missionary Societies. The first meeting of the Interdenominational Conference of Woman's Boards of Foreign Missions of the United States and Canada was held in 1896 (became Federation of Woman's Boards of Foreign Missions in 1916; merged with the Foreign Missions conference in 1934). It was a parallel organization to the Interdenominational Conference of Foreign Mission Boards from which the women's boards were excluded.[42]

By 1890 there were 34 American women's societies supporting 926 missionaries in various fields, and together with the married women of the general missionary boards, they composed 60 percent of the total American missionary force.[43] By 1900 there were 41 women's agencies supporting over 1,200 single women missionaries. In 1910 the women's foreign missionary movement claimed a total supporting membership of 2,000,000.[44] While their general concern was for all people, their particular focus was on work with women and children. As the number of women missionaries outnumbered the men on many fields, the women's movement came to be viewed as a threat to the general boards, and women were reminded to keep their proper place. The prevailing sentiment was expressed in 1888 by the secretary of the American Baptist Missionary Union: "Woman's work in the foreign field must be careful to recognize the headship of man in ordering the affairs of the Kingdom of God."[45] After 1910, most of the women's agencies were gradually merged into the general denominational boards, where they came under more ecclesiastical control and were dominated by men.[46] This led eventually to "the destruction of the women's foreign missionary movement," because—as R. Pierce Beaver has observed—"the voluntary principle is essential to world mission," whereas denominational and ecumenical structures "frown upon spontaneous action and establishment of direct relationships which they do not initiate or administer."[47]

Black Americans in Mission

An aspect of American missions that is not widely recognized is the pioneering role and contribution of Black Americans. "Although the golden age of Black foreign missions did not come until the late 1870s," according to Gayraud S. Wilmore, "as early as 1782 former slaves such as David George, George Liele, Amos Williams, and Joseph Paul sought to transplant their churches from South Carolina and Georgia to Nova Scotia, Sierra Leone, Jamaica, and the Bahamas. . . . These men became the first unofficial Afro-American missionaries before the American foreign missionary movement had been solidly launched."[48] Lott Carey and Colin Teague were sent to Liberia in 1820 by the black Baptists of Richmond, and numerous other initiatives were taken by black Americans in missions during the nineteenth century, especially to Africa.[49] After the "Great Century," however, "with the struggle against virtual genocide in an era of racial hatred and violence at home, together with the distractions of World War I and the Great Depression, black church support of missions gradually declined and much was left in disarray."[50] A notable continuing black mission agency is the Lott Carey Baptist Foreign Mission Convention, founded in 1897, with headquarters in Washington, DC, that is an ecumenical mission serving denominations of Baptist tradition.

Textbooks

Books by Speer and William Owen Carver in the first decade of the century became standard texts for the study of missions. Staunchly evangelical, ecumenical, and sensitive to new insights, Speer published in this decade *Missionary Principles and Practice* (1902), *Missions and Modern History* (2 vols., 1904), and *Christianity and the Nations* (1910).

Carver, professor of missions at the Southern Baptist Theological Seminary in Louisville since 1899, published *Missions in the Plan of Ages* (1909) and *Missions and Modern Thought* (1910). Of his twenty-one published books, *Missions in the Plan of Ages*—described by R. Pierce Beaver as "representative of American thought on the eve of the Edinburgh Conference"—was Carver's most important and influential book.[51]

Edinburgh 1910

The milestone event at this early point in the century was the World Missionary Conference at Edinburgh in 1910, where American leaders such as Mott, Speer, James L. Barton, Harlan Beach, Bishop Charles H. Brent, Arthur Judson Brown, Henry Sloane Coffin, Sherwood Eddy, Douglas Mackenzie, Frank Mason North, Bishop James Thoburn, J. Campbell White, and Samuel Zwemer were prominent. It came at a time of high enthusiasm in the missionary endeavor, and the missionary obligation was considered a self-evident axiom to be obeyed, not to be questioned. Edinburgh was primarily concerned with strategy, consultation, and cooperation to complete the task of evangelizing the world; the Great Commission of Christ was the only basis needed for missions. Speer challenged the assembly at the opening service to prepare for "the immediate conquest of the world." Ten days later in his closing address Mott said, "The end of the conference is the beginning of the conquest." A Continuation Committee was appointed, with Mott as chairman, and in 1921 at Lake Mohonk, New York, it formed the International Missionary Council (IMC, merged with the World Council of Churches in 1961). This became the major international forum and vehicle for ecumenical cooperation in Protestant missions.

Two important journals were launched following Edinburgh 1910: the *Moslem World* began publication in 1911 with Zwemer as editor, and the *International Review of Missions* started in 1912. Another remarkable fruit of Edinburgh was the founding in 1914 of the Missionary Research Library in New York City under the leadership of Dr. Mott. Initial funding came from John D. Rockefeller, Jr., and in 1914 Mott wrote to Charles H. Fahs, who was to be the secretary (later changed to curator) of the new library, "We are now ready to go ahead full steam on the plan to secure the most complete and serviceable missionary library and archives in the world. I desire it to be thoroughly interdenominational, ecumenical, and international. It should be preeminently rich in source material." In 1929, when larger quarters were needed, Union Theological Seminary agreed to house the library in partnership with the Foreign Missions Conference of North America, and for years the library ranked as the best collection of its kind in the world.[52]

The Teaching of Missions

At the Ecumenical Missionary Conference in 1900, Charles Cuthbert Hall, president of Union Theological Seminary, reported that "the study of missions is slowly rising to the rank of a theological discipline."[53] By the time of the Edinburgh Conference there were four professorships for the teaching of missions in American seminaries: Episcopal Theological Seminary (Cambridge, Massachusetts), Omaha (Presbyterian) Theological Seminary (Nebraska), Southern Baptist Theological Seminary (Louisville, Kentucky), and Yale Divinity School.[54] In the decade following Edinburgh, six new professorships were established: Bethany Biblical Seminary in Chicago, Boston University School of Theology, Candler School of Theology at Emory University, and Union Theological Seminary in New York. In the 1920s eleven more seminaries established professorships of missions.[55] In 1911 the Hartford School of Missions was founded, later known as the Kennedy School of Missions of the Hartford Seminary Foundation (1913), where "for decades the greatest concentration of missions scholars were found."[56]

About 1917 informal meetings of those teaching missions and related subjects were started along the eastern seaboard, which became the Fellowship Professors of Missions of the Middle Atlantic Region.[57] But missiology would not be recognized in North America as a proper theological discipline for another fifty years. At this early stage, says James A. Scherer, missions instruction was "plagued by a certain immaturity and obscurity with regard to definition, methodological basis, and objectives. In retrospect, it appears that the credibility of the claims of world missions to a rightful place in theological education was weakened by a failure to think through the nature and requirements of the infant discipline and the manner in which these were to be represented in the curriculum. Was world missions merely an appendage to ecclesiology or practical theology? . . . Or did world missions have a solid theoretical and methodological basis which allowed it to challenge and to interact with other disciplines? What were the aims of the new subject? Were they related primarily to motivation and training, or did they have basic theological understanding as their object?"[58] As yet there was no consensus.

End of the "Great Century"

The outbreak of World War I marked the beginning of a new era in the missionary enterprise. Kenneth Scott Latourette maintained that the twentieth century, in the sense of a distinct change from the nineteenth century, really began in 1914 with the outbreak of the World War of 1914–18, and it marked the end of the "Great Century" of Christian expansion.[59] The break, of course, did not happen overnight, and some of the earlier trends continued to fruition in the new era. The general spirit of confidence, however, in the capacities of humanity, of inevitable progress in history, and in the scientific method as the key to the solution of evil in the world was increasingly replaced by skepticism, cynicism, and pessimism.

Following the disruption of the war, the sending and support of overseas missionary personnel came to a point of culmination. "Most of the major sending agencies reached a peak in the number of missionaries in the field during the early 1920s which was not approached again until after World War II."[60] Similarly the predepression high point in North American foreign mission contributions was reached in 1921.[61] The growth was impressive. In 1911 only one-third of the 21,000 Protestant foreign missionaries scattered around the world came from North America (including Canada).[62] By 1925 there were over 29,000 Protestant missionaries, and approximately half of them came from North America (there were more than 3,300 American missionaries in China alone). Income for foreign missions from living donors of fifteen major denominations in the United States soared from $5,300,100 in 1901 to $21,288,749 in 1919.[63]

Some prewar negative trends also continued to confront the missionary enterprise. Criticism of missions from secular sources escalated with charges of cultural and political imperialism. Issues that came out in the debate over the annexation of the Philippines, and the controversy surrounding the Boxer Rebellion of 1900, were carried forward by critics who cast aspersions on the motives and methods of foreign missions.

Debate over the theology of missions—fueled by the fundamentalist-modernist controversy—also became more serious and led to fragmentation. Two articles that appeared in the *Harvard Theological Review* in 1915 by James L. Barton and J. P. Jones, both of the American Board of Commissioners for Foreign Missions, were indicative of the changes in missionary thinking occurring in those churches and agencies that came under the sway of liberal theology and the social gospel movemment. The articles came to these general conclusions: (1) there was a change in the attitude of missionaries to the non-Christian religions that are no longer thought to be entirely false but instead have elements of truth in them; (2) there was a change of emphasis in missions from the individual to society, with less stress upon the number of admissions to the church than on the leavening influence of Christian truth in the community as a whole; (3) there was a broader range of activities for the missionary that meant less direct preaching of the gospel and more attention to the transformation of one's life as well as one's heart; and (4) there was a change of emphasis in the missionary message that formerly stressed salvation in the world to come but now laid more stress on salvation for life in the present world.[64]

Faith Missions

In contrast to the main-line denominational mission agencies that reflected these theological developments were the conservative faith missions that formed the Interdenominational Foreign Mission Association (IFMA) in 1917 as a "fellowship of missions without denominational affiliation" and with a statement of faith adhering to "the fundamental doctrines of the historic Christian faith." Among the founding agencies of the IFMA were Africa Inland Mission, Central American Mission, China Inland Mission, South Africa General Mission, and Sudan Interior Mission. The theologically conservative faith missions flourished and numerous new agencies were established, such as Orinoco River Mission (1920), Latin America Mission (1921), Iran Interior Mission, Oriental Boat Mission, and Gospel Mission of South America (all in 1923), West Indies Mission (1928), and the India Mission (1930). Bible institutes—especially at Moody, Toronto, Providence, and Los Angeles—provided large numbers of personnel for the conservative missions.

Theological controversy led to schism in the work of the United Christian Missionary Society (Disciples of Christ) in the Philippines in 1926; the formation in 1927 of the Association of Baptists for Evangelism in the Orient (later Association of Baptists for World Evangelization) by personnel formerly related to the American Baptist Foreign Mission Society; and the organization of the Independent Board for Presbyterian Foreign Missions in 1933 by J. Gresham Machen and his followers in their dispute with the Presbyterian Board of Foreign Missions. The resignation of Pearl S. Buck in 1933 as a Presbyterian missionary in China because of critical attacks on her theological views from fundamentalist sources was widely publicized.[65]

Decline of the SVM

The Student Volunteer Movement was in decline and the watchword was in the twilight of its influence. Mott had resigned as chairman in 1920; it was the end of an era. Nearly 13,000 Volunteers actually sailed for overseas service, it was claimed, between 1886 and 1936. But questions about missions and a desire for a broader approach to Christian internationalism affected the SVM. At a student conference under the auspicies of the SVM at Northfield in 1917, the participants asked, "Does Christ offer an adequate solution for the burning social and international questions of the day?" There was a growing sense that foreign missions were not the only channel through which Christians should work to bring about the healing of the nations. "A radical reorientation in the thinking and methods of the SVM" occurred at conventions in 1919 and 1923 where students called for "a radical change in the assumptions and methods underlying future SVM activity and conventions," to accommodate "the students' new-found interest in issues of race, war, and the social order."[66]

The *Christian Century* reported that at the SVM Convention in Detroit at the end of 1927, Sherwood Eddy "finally and publically repudiated that famous war-cry: 'The evangelization of the world in this generation.' No one challenged him; no one attempted to maintain that what is still needed is—to use the Eddyian phrase—'a Paul Revere's ride across the world.' "[67] Other factors in the decline of the SVM, says Clifton J. Phillips, included the growing fundamentalist-modernist split, the Great Depression of the 1930s that undercut the financial support of foreign missions, the rising secularism in American higher education, the spread of the social gospel, "and perhaps most important of all, a developing crisis in missionary thinking, which in the 1920s and later shifted even farther away from evangelization of the non-Christian world by Americans and Europeans in the direction of partnership and cooperation among the older and younger churches in the building of a Christian world order."[68]

As the SVM declined and changed its orientation in the 1930s, evangelicals formed the Student Foreign Missions Fellowship in 1936 (exactly fifty years after Mount Hermon 1886), and in 1939 the first Inter-Varsity Christian Fellowship chapters in the United States were established. In 1945 the two movements merged and the SFMF became the missionary arm of the IVCF.[69] They sponsored a student missionary convention at Toronto in 1946, where Samuel Zwemer reminded participants of the watchword and the earlier student movement. Two years later a second missionary convention was held on the campus of the University of Illinois at Urbana. The Inter-Varsity Urbana conventions became triennial events that would attract as many as 17,000 students, who claimed the tradition of the SVM and the watchword as their own.

The crucial issues in missions that had emerged since Edinburgh 1910 were debated at the Jerusalem meeting of the International Missionary Council in 1928 where the focus of discussion was on "The Christian Life and Message in Relation to Non-Christian Systems of Thought and Life." Secularism and syncretism were seen as the two major challenges to missions. In addition to Mott and Speer, Americans who were prominent at Jerusalem included Ralph Diffendorfer, E. Stanley Jones, Rufus Jones, William Ernest Hocking, Bishop Francis J. McConnell, John A. Mackay, Luther A. Weigle, and Samuel Zwemer. The European participants were generally critical of the Americans on two points: their emphasis on social concerns, i.e., the "social gospel," and their allowance for the possibility of revelation in non-Christian religions. One of the lessons learned at the Jerusalem meeting, according to John A. Mackay, was that "the missionary movement must become more theological, not primarily for those to whom missionaries go, but for the Church herself and the missionaries who represent her."[70]

Daniel Johnson Fleming, former missionary in India and professor of missions at Union Theological Seminary in New York City since 1918, dealt with the missionary attitude and approach to people of other faiths in his books *Attitudes Toward Other Faiths* (1928), and *Ways of Sharing with Other Faiths* (1929). Fleming—an influential liberal theoretician of missions—urged a sympathetic approach to people of other faiths, with a desire to share the knowledge of Jesus and his spirit, but he placed little emphasis on the need for conversion. By contrast, Samuel M. Zwemer, professor of missions at Princeton Seminary and regarded as the "Apostle to Islam," held to a staunchly evangelical position of "salvation in no other name" in his numerous publications.

The Hocking Report

The most significant event of the period in terms of creating controversy in American missions was the publication in 1932 of *Re-Thinking Missions*, the Report of the Commission of Appraisal of the Laymen's Foreign Missions Inquiry, edited by the chairman of the commission,

William Ernest Hocking, professor of philosophy at Harvard University. The report was the culmination of a massive survey and research project funded by John D. Rockefeller, Jr. While the report did not deny that missions should continue, it suggested that important changes had taken place that required the missionary enterprise to reconsider its motives, methods, message, and aims. These changes were: an altered theological outlook, the emergence of a basic world culture, and the rise of nationalism. The report proposed that the aim of missions should be "to seek with people of other lands a true knowledge and love of God, expressing in life and word what we have learned through Jesus Christ"; that "the Christian will regard himself as a co-worker with the forces which are making for righteousness within every religious system"; that "the relation between religions must take increasingly hereafter the form of a common search for truth"; and that the missionary "will look forward, not to the destruction of these [non-Christian] religions, but to their continued co-existence with Christianity, each stimulating the other in growth toward the ultimate goal, unity in the completest religious truth."

This was a radical departure from the traditional concept of missions, the role of the missionary, and the relation of Christianity to other religions. As such, the report provoked basic rethinking of the issues but was itself widely criticized for its tone of optimism and relativism, and was not representative of American thinking on missions. Robert E. Speer and John A. Mackay published critiques that rejected the theological views of the report. Mackay said it presented a theological viewpoint that was already outdated—"the sunset glow of nineteenth-century romanticism."[71] The only mission board in America to respond favorably to the theological tone of the report was the American Board of Commissioners for Foreign Missions. Hocking later elaborated on his thought about the way toward a single world faith—not by means of "radical displacement" but by "synthesis" leading to "reconception"—in his book *Living Religions and a World Faith* (1940).

Among the few mission scholars who were sympathetic with the viewpoint of the Hocking Report were Archibald G. Baker at the University of Chicago and Hugh Vernon White, secretary of the American Board of Commissioners for Foreign Missions. Baker, in his book *Christian Missions and a New World Culture* (1934), presented a position of nearly complete religious relativism. His justification for missions was that the experiments of Christianity with the problems of life had been more fruitful than the experiments of other religions. Therefore Christianity had a mission to share the results of this cultural experiment with other cultures by means of "the interpenetration or cross-fertilization of cultures" (293).

White, in *A Theology for Christian Missions* (1937) and *A Working Faith for the World* (1938), affirmed the position of the Laymen's Inquiry and said that "the Christian mission should be a man-centered enterprise," with "the service of man as the regulative aim of Christian missions."

The malaise in mission theology—reflected in Hocking, Baker, and White—was matched by a decline in financial support for foreign missions. By the mid-1930s the economic depression "threw the whole Protestant missionary enterprise in reverse."[72] It was symptomatic of the "American religious depression," described by Robert Handy as "a nationally observable spiritual lethargy evident in the 1920s and 1930s."[73] More specifically, as Charles W. Forman has observed, "the story . . . of the '20s and '30s suggests that missiology failed to meet the test. Instead of holding together and going deeper in response to many new challenges, it seemed to become shallower and to wander off into vague uncertainties or else to react defensively."[74]

Reaction to Hocking

In 1938, on the eve of World War II, the International Missionary Council met at Madras. In preparation for the conference, the Dutch missiologist Hendrik Kraemer published *The Christian Message in a Non-Christian World* which was said to have been "provoked by, and written in direct refutation of, the thought of Professor W. E. Hocking of Harvard."[75] Kraemer took the position that Christianity was "*the* religion of revelation" (23), and he stressed a radical discontinuity between the realm of what he called "biblical realism" (which critics said was neither biblical nor realistic) and the whole range of non-Christian religious experience. All non-Christian religions, philosophies, and world views, he said, are merely "the various efforts of man to apprehend the totality of existence," and are doomed to failure (111–12). The only point of contact between non-Christian religions and Christian revelation is "the disposition and the attitude of the missionary" (140).

Kraemer's view's were vigorously debated at the conference—and for a generation following—regarding the relationship between Christianity and other faiths, and the role of the church. After the conference there was a spirited exchange between E. Stanley Jones and Henry P. Van Dusen in the pages of the *Christian Century* that indicated both a vitality of thought and strategy among missionaries overseas and a sharp difference of perspective between this veteran missionary and this North American seminary professor who had no overseas experience. Jones—a Methodist missionary in India who was well known for his books *The Christ of the*

Indian Road (1925; sold over 600,000 copies in twelve languages) and *Christ at the Roundtable* (1928)—said that "Madras missed the way" because it had used the church as its starting point instead of the kingdom of God.[76] Van Dusen, who had been chairman of Section I at Madras, wrote a stinging rebuke, "What Stanley Jones Missed at Madras." He maintained that Jones had missed the proper church emphasis at Madras and that the conference had given appropriate attention to the kingdom, but not in the sense of being an instrumentality for a new social order, such as Jones advocated. Many "sincere students of the New Testament," according to Van Dusen, would "deny that [the kingdom] has any direct and indisputable implication for economic and international life," whereas "almost every Christian movement for radical social reform has come out of the heart of the church."[77] Jones, in his reply, acknowledged that he missed the church at Madras.

> I missed a church which started from where Jesus started, the Kingdom of God, and found instead a church which started with itself, and therefore largely ended with itself and with the saving of its fellowship.
> . . . I missed a church which, while conscious of its mission as the chief instrument of the Kingdom of God, also was humble enough to rejoice that God was using other instruments to bring in the Kingdom.[78]

A kingdom perspective in mission, such as Jones was urging, would come more than forty years later at the World Mission Conference sponsored by the World Council of Churches at Melbourne in 1980 under the theme "Your Kingdom Come."

The most important contribution to mission theory to appear during the war years was *The Philosophy of the Christian World Mission* by Edmund Davison Soper, a former Methodist missionary, who was professor of missions at Garrett Biblical Institute in Evanston, Illinois, when the book was published in 1943. Soper, representing the prevailing view in North America, took a middle position between Hocking and Kraemer. He affirmed the absolute uniqueness of the revelation in Christ as over against the relativism of Hocking, yet recognized the spiritual values in other religions as over against the radical discontinuity of Kraemer. He aptly described Kraemer's position as "uniqueness without continuity" and Hocking's as "continuity with doubtful uniqueness," then set forth his own position of "uniqueness together with continuity" (223, 225 ff.).

Also published in this period was Kenneth Scott Latourette's monumental seven-volume study, *A History of the Expansion of Christianity* (1937–

45). After graduation from Yale, Latourette—a Baptist—served as traveling secretary for the SVM, then briefly as a missionary in China until poor health forced his return to the States in 1912. His teaching career at Yale (1912–53) as professor of missions and Oriental history was marked by a steady stream of publications that established his international reputation as a leading historian and apologist of Christian missions. The thesis of his study of the expansion of Christianity was that

> throughout its history it has gone forward by major pulsations. Each advance has carried it further than the one before it. Of the alternating recessions, each has been briefer and less marked than the one which preceded it. This has been the case by whichever of the criteria the advance and recession have been measured—geographic extent, the new movements issuing from Christianity, or the influence upon the human race.[79]

It was Latourette's judgment that "in A.D. 1944 Christianity was affecting more deeply more different nations and cultures than ever before." Yet "when he died in the late 1960s," says one of his students, "he was not prepared to say whether the period of history from 1914 to 1960 was a period of missionary 'advance' or 'retreat.' "[80]

Postwar Renewal

After World War II a new wave of missionary vitality surged through the American churches. The immediate task was that of getting missionaries back to the field. In 1946 the American President Ship Lines allotted over 1,000 spaces on two former troop ships to be prorated among the various boards belonging to the Foreign Missions Conference of North America for transporting missionaries back to Asia. Main-line boards began to rebuild after a twenty-year period of decline and disruption, but they would never fully recover. For instance, the peak year of the Presbyterian Board before the depression was 1926 with 1,606 missionaries. That number had gradually decreased until 1942, when there were only 1,134 on the roll. During 1946–47, 100 new missionaries were commissioned and the total rose to 1,209.[81]

It was also a period of rapid growth for conservative evangelical missions, both in the existing agencies, and with a proliferation of new agencies: Missionary Aviation Fellowship (1944), Far East Broadcasting Company (1945), United World Mission (1946), Far Eastern Gospel Crusade (1947), Greater European Mission (1949), and Overseas Crusades

(1950). Another conservative evangelical association of mission agencies, the Evangelical Foreign Missions Association (EFMA), was formed in 1945 by the National Association of Evangelicals (established in 1942), to serve and foster the work of conservative denominational missions as well as some of the independent groups.[82]

Three influential scholars of conservative evangelical missions at the time were Robert Hall Glover, director for North America of the China Inland Mission, Harold Cook, director of the missions department at Moody Bible Institute, and Harold Lindsell, dean of Fuller Theological Seminary. Glover's book *The Progress of World-Wide Missions* (1924) was still widely used as a text in Bible institutes and colleges; *The Bible Basis of Missions* (1946) was published the year before he died. Both his books were viewed as classics by evangelicals. Cook's *Introduction to the Study of Christian Missions* (1954) was a standard textbook, and his *Missionary Life and Work* (1959) went through twenty-four printings. Lindsell's *A Christian Philosophy of Missions* (1949) and *Missionary Principles and Practice* (1955) were pioneering, systematic expositions of conservative evangelical mission theory and strategy. From an uncritical biblocentric perspective, Lindsell maintained that all those who have either rejected Jesus Christ or never heard of him are doomed to eternal hell. The only way to salvation, he said, is through faith in Jesus Christ; there are no real values in the non-Christian religions.

In 1952 there were 18,599 North American Protestant missionaries working overseas, which was more than half of the total Protestant missionary task force worldwide. By 1956 the number of North American personnel increased 25 percent to 23,432. The Methodist Board was the largest with 1,513 foreign missionaries.[83] In less than fifty years the North American percentage of the total Protestant missionary task force was reversed. "Whereas in 1911 about two-thirds of the foreign missionaries came from outside North America, in 1956 it was the other way around."[84] But a shift in the configuration of the North American missionary force was taking place. Whereas in 1952 the main-line boards related to the National Council of Churches supplied 50 percent of North American Protestant missionaries, by 1958 it was only 41 percent, while the percentage of personnel sent by other associations and independent groups, unrelated to the NCC, increased nearly 9 percent.[85] The trend in both directions would continue precipitously.

In 1952 the Associated Missions of the International Council of Christian Churches (TAM-ICCC) was formed, representing extreme right wing fundamentalism, inspired by Carl McIntire. Several agencies withdrew from TAM in 1969 and formed a new association known as the Fellowship of Missions (FOM). Both are small separatist associations that are militantly antiecumenical and do not associate with any other groups.

A New Context

There was a radically new context for world mission in the post-1945 period, with the resurgence of non-Christian religions, the shift of cultural and political power, and the emergence of indigenous national churches in nearly ever country of the world. The first postwar meeting of the IMC at Whitby, Canada, in 1947, called for "partnership in obedience"—a new relationship between Western mission agencies and the indigenous "younger churches." The Whitby meeting, followed by the inaugural assembly of the World Council of Churches at Amsterdam in 1948, marked the end of the "Vasco de Gama Epoch," the era of Western penetration and domination. The Communist revolution in China in 1949 and the expulsion of all missionaries were dramatic evidence of the new reality. The change was clear, but the way forward was less clear. At the next meeting of the IMC in Willingen, Germany, in 1952, Max Warren of the Church Missionary Society acknowledged the difficulty: "We know with complete certainty that the most testing days of the Christian mission in our generation lie just ahead. . . . We have to be ready to see the day of missions, as we have known them, as having already come to an end."[86]

In preparation for the Willingen meeting on the theme "The Missionary Obligation of the Church," a series of studies was commissioned by the Division of Foreign Missions of the NCC under the direction of the Committee on Research in Foreign Mission. More than fifty papers were prepared by mission executives and seminary professors from the United States and Canada on five subjects: (1) the biblical and theological basis of mission; (2) the missionary vocation; (3) North American mission boards and their task; (4) the missionary task in the present day; and (5) policy for today. Each subject was assigned to a commission to prepare papers and a report. Charles W. Forman, a member of the commission on policy, says, "Nothing so ambitious was ever attempted before—or since—in the way of mission studies, and the product of that effort may well stand as a landmark, an Ebenezer, for American missiology of 150 years."[87] Of special interest and importance is the report of Commission I, chaired by Paul Lehmann, entitled "Why Missions?" It defined the aim of mission as "the obligation to make God as He is revealed in Jesus Christ so known as to be faithfully served by all men" (1:2). A study of the messages and statement of the great church/missionary conferences from Edinburgh to Amsterdam, they said, showed that "the missionary movement in the twentieth century has . . . been following its apostolic prototype in the trinitarian direction of its thought and life. . . . From vigorous Christo-centricity to thoroughgoing trinitarianism—this is the direction of missionary theology, missionary strategy, and missionary obligation" (1:6). The report sounded a cautionary note, however, on the task of mission:

> Missionary obligation, grounded in the reconciling action of the triune God, is not the duty to save souls (after all only God does that, *ubi et quando visum est Deo*) but the sensitive and total response of the church to what the triune God has done and is doing in the world. It is the business of the Christian missionary to "make a straight in the desert a highway for our God" (Is. 40:3), not blow Gabriel's horn. Obviously, this does not mean that theological formulae, secretarial administration, and saving of souls are expendable. It only means that they are peripheral and must remain so, if the missionary movement is not to become something else.(1:6)

The inability of the Willingen conference to adopt an agreed statement on "The Missionary Obligation of the Church" was not surprising; it was an indication of the depth of disagreement over the direction of mission. To one participant it was another symptom of "a disastrous failure of nerve in the western missionary movement. . . . The sickness, however diagnosed, was essentially spiritual."[88]

Ecumenical Challenge and Change

If "the day of missions" was at an end, it was the beginning of a new day for the one mission of the church. With the home base for mission everywhere the church existed around the world, mission was no longer a one-way enterprise from the Western churches to Asia, Africa, and Latin America (a three-continent view); rather mission was the whole church, with the whole gospel, to the whole world (a six-continent view).[89] The integration of the IMC with the World Council of Churches at New Delhi in 1961 was endorsed by main-line mission boards in the United States as symbolizing in structure a theological view of mission as integral to the nature of the church. A similar structural change had already occurred in the United States in 1950 when the Foreign Missions Conference of North America joined the newly created National Council of Churches as the Division of Foreign Missions.

The Theology of the Christian Mission, an ecumenical symposium edited by Gerald H. Anderson, which appeared on the eve of the New Delhi Assembly of the WCC, presented a broad range of international scholarship on crucial issues—in biblical and historical perspective—that anticipated future developments. In addition to Barth, Cullmann, Kraemer, Warren, and others from Europe and Britain, the twenty-five contributors included an imposing array of Americans across the theological spectrum from Tillich to Lindsell, together with Orthodox, Roman Catholic, and Third World voices. Bishop Lesslie Newbigin, general secretary of the IMC, wrote the foreword. In his introduction, Anderson traced the progressively deepening thrust of mission theology among Protestants in the twentieth century, from the point of asking simply "How missions?" at the time of Edinburgh 1910, to the point of asking "What is the Christian mission?" at the time of the Ghana meeting of the IMC in 1957.[90] *Christianity Today* magazine (24 April 1961) viewed the volume with such alarm that it devoted an eleven-page article by the editors—"A New Crisis in Foreign Missions?"—to a critique of the book, because, they said, it "discloses far-reaching influences now divergently shaping the philosophy of the Christian mission around the world" and "inevitably raises searching questions for the Protestant ecumenical movement," at a time when "discussion of contemporary mission strategy promises to dominate the theological horizon" (2–3). Comparing it to the earlier works by Hocking and Kraemer, the editors said the new volume "may rock the Christian world missionary venture afresh." Especially the essays on the relation of Christianity to other faiths, they said, would make the volume "a center of debate for some time," and it would be "required reading . . . even for fundamentalist critics" (3–4). Despite the fact that "it contains some first-rate biblical theology," the editors worried that "the book could significantly influence reformulation of missions: 1. by its tenuous connection of the missionary task to a nebulous trinitarian theology; 2. by relating the ideal completion of mission to the WCC-IMC-identified Church; and 3. by viewing Christianity as the fulfillment (rather than antithesis) of pagan religions" (4). By way of final appraisal, *Christianity Today* assailed the volume because, in the judgement of this conservative evangelical journal, "confidence in the Hebrew-Christian religion as the one true and saving religion is being shattered; Christianity and other world religions are viewed . . . as different in degree rather than in kind" (13).

Other indications of foment in ecumenical perceptions of mission occurred at the 1960 conference of the World Student Christian Federation (WSCF), in Strasbourg. Students at the conference felt there was "too much speaking about the life of the church; what students wanted was action in the world. And there seemed to be too much mission; what students wanted was a welcome to this world."[91] Hans Hoekendijk—later professor of missions at Union Theological Seminary in New York—urged the participants at Strasbourg "to begin radically to desacralize the church" and to recognize that Christianity is "a secular movement," not "some sort of religion."[92] It was the decade of the secular, and the world set the agenda of the church. The struggles for justice, liberation, and human development not only were part of the ecumenical definition of mission, but seemed to take precedence over the need for people to be converted, baptized and brought into the church.[93]

The radical challenge was voiced on the American scene by M. Richard Shaull, former Presbyterian missionary in Latin America, in his installation address as professor of ecumenics at Princeton Seminary in 1963:

> Theologically speaking, the church may be a missionary community. In actual fact, however, it has become a major hindrance to the work of mission. . . . Our ecclesiastical organizations are not the most striking examples of dynamic and flexible armies which direct their energies primarily toward witness and service to those outside. Missionary boards and organizations, in their justified desire to turn over increasing responsibility to their daughter churches, have become so bound to relatively static ecclesiastical organizations that, with rare exceptions, they have shown little possibility of thinking imaginatively about the vast new frontiers of mission or becoming engaged in new ventures on them.[94]

Another American voice calling for radical changes was Keith R. Bridston, former Lutheran missionary in Indonesia and staff member of the World Council of Churches. In his book *Mission Myth and Reality* (1965), Bridston predicted that "the latter half of the twentieth century . . . may prove to be as radical in its implications for the missionary outlook of the Christian church as the Copernican revolution was for the scientific cosmology of its day."(13) Traditional forms of mission, he said, "embody a response to a world that no longer exists and express a theological understanding of the relation of the world to God that is now felt to be fallacious" (17). The vocational category of "foreign missionary" was, he suggested, "irrelevant and theologically unjustified," and mission boards were "sociologically anachronistic and ecclesiologically questionable" (18). The church was "still at the first stage of discovering the right questions— in considering the nature and form of the Christian mission today" (18).

Norman A. Horner was right when he observed in 1968 that "the

Protestant missionary enterprise has undergone more radical change in the last fifteen years than in the previous century."[95]

Conservative Evangelical Resurgence

Conservative evangelicals were distressed by developments in the ecumenical movement that they felt were compromising—if not replacing—the task of evangelism in mission and calling into question the continuing mandate of the Great Commission. In a series of major conferences, evangelicals rallied around a revival of the SVM watchword.[96] In 1960, at the IFMA Congress on World Missions at the Moody Church in Chicago, evangelicals saw themselves in continuity with Edinburgh 1910, affirmed that "the total evangelization of the world may be achieved in this generation," and issued a call for 18,000 additional missionaries.[97] Similarly, in 1966 at Wheaton, Illinois, a joint EFMA/IFMA Congress on the Church's Worldwide Mission declared, "We . . . convenant together . . . for the evangelization of the world in this generation, so help us God!" Also in 1966, the World Congress on Evangelism in Berlin, sponsored by *Christianity Today* magazine, with Billy Graham as honorary chairman, concluded, "Our goal is nothing short of the evangelization of the human race in this generation." For conservative evangelicals the spirit of Edinburgh 1910 was alive and well in 1966—a crucial year of new dynamism.

In 1968 the Association of Evangelical Professors of Missions was organized. Of the evangelical missiologists, the most productive author was J. Herbert Kane at Trinity Evangelical Divinity School, who had served with China Inland Mission. After revising and enlarging Glover's *Progress of Worldwide Missions* in 1960, Kane published *A Global View of Christian Missions* (1971), *Understanding Christian Missions* (1974), *Christian Missions in Biblical Perspective* (1976), *A Concise History of the Christian World Mission* (1978), *Life and Work on the Mission Field* (1980), and others that were used extensively as texts in evangelical schools.

After publishing *The Bridges of God* (1955) and *How Churches Grow* (1959), on strategies that lead to quantative church growth in missionary situations, Donald A. McGavran—graduate of Yale Divinity School and longtime missionary in India—established the Institute of Church Growth at Northwest Christian College in Eugene, Oregon, in 1961. His Institute moved to Fuller Theological Seminary in 1965 where it became the School of World Mission. By the 1980s this evangelical school had developed into the largest graduate faculty of missiology in North America. Following McGavran's emphasis on evangelism for church growth among people groups (homogenous units)—formed along lines of ethnic, caste, racial, and other existing social relationships—the school is noted for its study of strategies to foster success in discipling converts and multiplying churches among those who are receptive to the gospel. Spin-offs from McGavran's movement include the *Global Church Growth Bulletin* (which he edits), Ralph Winter's U.S. Center for World Mission that focuses on "reaching unreached people groups," Win Arns' Institute for American Church Growth, and several church growth research centers in Third World countries. Critics of the emphasis on establishing homogenous churches as a strategy for church growth, such as René Padilla in Argentina, maintain that it has no biblical foundation, that it is contrary to the New Testament emphasis on breaking down barriers and building up unity in the body of Christ, and that it reinforces the status quo.[98] Others worry that concern for social justice is secondary, and warn that the pragmatic emphasis of the church growth movement is in danger of turning it into a mere "spiritual technology."[99]

A growing appreciation for the insights of linguistics and anthropology among missionaries—especially evangelicals—was influenced by the pioneering work of Eugene A. Nida, secretary for translations in the American Bible Society, through his books *God's Word in Man's Language* (1952), *Customs and Cultures* (1954), *Message and Mission: The Communication of the Christian Faith* (1960), and *Religion Across Cultures* (1968). In the 1950s, Nida gave encouragement and contributed to the development of the journal *Practical Anthropology*, edited by William Smalley, for missionaries with special interests in anthropology.[100]

The Pentecostal and charismatic movements are another vital stream in American evangelical missions. The Assemblies of God, founded in 1914 with lineage to the Azusa Street, Los Angeles, revival of 1906–9, is the largest Pentecostal denomination in the United States. With a strong emphasis on missions (1,300 missionaries in 1986), the Assemblies had nearly ten times as many members in Latin America as in North America by the mid-1980s. Melvin L. Hodges—field director for Latin America and later professor of missions at the Assemblies of God Theological Seminary in Springfield, Missouri—expounded their emphasis on indigenous-church principles and a Pentecostal perspective on missions in his books *The Indigenous Church* (1953) and *A Theology of the Church and Its Mission* (1977).[101]

Confusion and Transition

By 1973, evangelical agencies were providing 66.5 percent of the funds and 85 percent of the personnel for American Protestant overseas missions.

Meanwhile, main-line boards were in a period of painful transition. It was "a theological transition with notable operational consequences," says W. Richey Hogg.

> The shift marks a move away from a Western Christian evangelistic crusade to the world and toward an engagement with the world in what is regarded as a total evangelistic response to the world's needs and the religious beliefs of its people. . . . It views the North American role in world mission not in terms of large numbers of professional missionaries, but rather through fewer skilled specialists and particularly through the work and witness of the worldwide lay Christian diaspora in secular posts.[102]

There was confusion, however, about what it meant exactly to speak of mission in terms of "engagement with the world" in "a total evangelistic response to the world's needs." People in the pews were getting mixed messages about the future of the missionary enterprise. Bishop Stephen Neill warned that "if everything is mission, nothing is mission." Adding to the confusion in the early 1970s was a call for a moratorium on Western missionaries by some ecumenical church leaders in the Third World,[103] and a new anti-Americanism in many parts of the world fueled by the war in Vietnam. A neo-isolationism in American society led to a wave of defeatism and a loss of momentum in mission boards of denominations in the National Council of Churches.

This affected the teaching of mission in main-line, ecumenical seminaries as well. In addition to the earlier Fellowship of Professors of Missions of the Middle Atlantic Region (now the Eastern Fellowship),, a national Association of Professors of Missions (APM) was founded in 1952[104] and a Midwest Fellowship of Professors of Missions began to meet informally sometime during the 1950s and was formally organized in 1957. By 1968, however, R. Pierce Beaver—professor of missions at the University of Chicago Divinity School—could report that "students are now cold, even hostile, to overseas missions"; that the place of missiology as a discipline in the seminary curriculum "is most precarious, and I expect its rapid decline and even its elimination from most denominational seminaries."[105] Only sixteen professors attended the meeting of the national APM in 1970. The decade 1963–73 saw the demise of mission studies and training at the Kennedy School of Missions at Hartford Seminary, at Scarritt College for Christian Workers in Nashville, at the Missionary Orientation Center in Stony Point, New York, and at the Lutheran School of Missions near Chicago.

GERALD H. ANDERSON

Revitalization of Missiology

In response to this situation, an *ad hoc* gathering of mission leaders and academicians in 1972 founded the American Society of Missiology (ASM) as a broadly inclusive professional society for the study of world mission. In 1973 the ASM began publishing a new quarterly, *Missiology*, that incorporated the journal *Practical Anthropology*. The ASM—bringing together conservative evangelicals, conciliar Protestants, and Roman Catholics in remarkable fashion—fostered a renewal of missology and facilitated the recognition of the discipline by the academic community in North America.[106] By 1986 the ASM had over five hundred members, the various associations of professors of mission had taken on new life, and *Missiology* journal had a circulation in excess of 2,200. Also contributing to the revitalization of missiology were the *Evangelical Missions Quarterly*, published by IFMA and EFMA since 1964; the *International Bulletin of Missionary Research* (successor to the *Occasional Bulletin* from the Missionary Research Library, 1950), published by the Overseas Ministries Study Center; Orbis Books, the publishing imprint established in 1970 by Maryknoll; the Missions Advanced Research and Communication Center (MARC) of World Vision; William Carey Library, an evangelical missions publishing firm in Pasadena, California, founded in 1969; the Billy Graham Center, established at Wheaton College in 1974; new graduate schools of mission and evangelism at Trinity Evangelical Divinity School, Columbia (South Carolina) Graduate School of Bible and Missions, and Asbury Theological Seminary; and approval by the Association of Theological Schools in 1986 of standards for offering the Doctor of Missiology (D.Miss.) as a professional academic degree. A survey of doctoral dissertations on mission topics for the Ph.D., Th.D., S.T.D., and Ed.D. degrees, revealed nearly 1,000 dissertations accepted at theological schools and universities in the United States and Canada in the period 1945–81, with Boston University, University of Chicago, and Columbia University leading the list. An increase from 211 dissertations accepted in 1960–69, to 462 dissertations in 1970–79, was further evidence of revitalization.[107]

In a 1985 survey of missiology as an academic discipline in American seminaries, James A. Scherer reported "a qualitative improvement in the climate for the teaching of missions, and a quantitative increase in programs and activities, especially in the decade from 1975 to 1985." He concluded that the discipline of missiology "is at last respectable, possesses a birth certificate, has gained some peer recognition, and shows signs of a promising future."[108] Those teaching in the discipline in the mid-1980s, as reported by Scherer, saw the contribution of missiology as being "an integrating and permeating role"—a catalyst—within the theological curriculum, "to keep theological education open to the whole world, and to keep the world's needs at the heart of seminary life"; to increase "awareness of the role and contributions of churches in the two-thirds world"; and to give leadership "in the dialogue with people of other faiths."[109]

It was a remarkable turnaround in less than two decades from Beaver's alarming forecast, and Beaver himself—the doyen of American missiologists in the period—contributed much to help bring about the change. After missionary service in China with the Evangelical and Reformed Church, and internment by the Japanese during World War II, he taught missions at Lancaster Theological Seminary, then was director of the Missionary Research Library for seven years, and professor of missions at the University of Chicago Divinity School from 1955 until his retirement in 1971, after which he served as director of the Overseas Ministries Study Center for three years. A prolific author, several of Beaver's books were pioneering studies that became standard references: *Ecumenical Beginnings in Protestant World Mission: A History of Comity* (1962), *Pioneers in Mission: The Early Missionary Ordination Sermons, Charges, and Instructions* (1966), *Church, State, and the American Indians* (1966), and especially his *All Loves Excelling: American Protestant Women in World Mission* (1968; rev. 1980, title *American Protestant Women in World Mission*). A large symposium he edited for the ASM in 1976, *American Missions in Bicentennial Perspective*, was judged by Robert T. Handy to be "one of the most important books in the field of religion to arise out of the bicentennial celebration . . . a landmark in the development of missiology in America."[110] Like Latourette—warmly evangelical, yet firmly ecumenical, a historian with impeccable academic credentials—Beaver was trusted across the theological spectrum and served as a "bridge person" in bringing scholars together to advance the cause of missiology. *The Future of the Christian World Mission* (1971), a festschrift in his honor, was testimony to his effectiveness. Beaver maintained that "every seminary needs a professor of missions, whatever his personal discipline may be, to be a living symbol of the church's worldwide mission and to be the agent who summons students and faculty to engagement in it."[111] It was the case that most of those who taught missiology in university theological faculties in the postwar period were historians.

Ecumenical and Evangelical Crosscurrents

The impact of the postwar transition and the contrast between ecumenical and evangelical missions is described by Wilbert R. Shenk:

That part of the missionary movement most closely identified with the Christendom thrust of the Great Century rapidly lost momentum after 1945, while independent and Free Church groups surged forward. The latter often acted as if they were still living in the nineteenth century. They treated sociopolitical issues simplistically and interpreted the missionary call as the simple and unambiguous action of saving souls.[112]

The situation for evangelicals began to modify, however, following the International Congress on World Evangelization at Lausanne in 1974 (a sequel to the 1966 Berlin Congress on Evangelism), the Consultation on World Evangelization, sponsored by the Lausanne Committee at Pattaya, Thailand, in 1980, and the Consultation on Evangelism and Social Responsibility in 1982 at Grand Rapids, Michigan—jointly sponsored by the Lausanne Committee and the World Evangelical Fellowship. In response to a challenge largely from Third World and young evangelicals, it was acknowledged within the Lausanne movement and the World Evangelical Fellowship, that evangelism and social action are integrally related in mission, though a debate continues as to whether evangelism has *priority*. Arthur P. Johnston of Trinity Evangelical Divinity School, in his book *The Battle for World Evangelism* (1978), disagreed with these developments and warned that it was a drift toward the "evangelistic sterility in the WCC" (18). He argued that "historically the mission of the church is evangelism alone" (18), and he criticized members of the Lausanne Committee and other evangelicals who redefine mission in terms of holistic evangelism that includes social action.

In contrast to this debate among evangelicals, ecumenical mission theology maintains that it is artificial and unbiblical to dichotomize or prioritize the witness of word and deed to the single reality of the reign of God.[113] Especially as Christians encounter oppression under authoritarian regimes, they are aware—once again—that evangelism is inseparable from concerns for justice and peace, and that faithfulness in mission is measured as much by the *quality* of discipleship as it is by the *quantity* of disciples.

The scandal of divided witness among Protestants (not to mention other Christian traditions) continues to plague the missionary endeavor. This was highlighted on a global scale in 1980 when two world mission conferences were held within thirty days of each other; one by the WCC at Melbourne, Australia, and the other by the Lausanne Committee at Pattaya, Thailand. The modern ecumenical movement had its genesis in the missionary movement of the nineteenth century—as recounted by William Richey Hogg in his definitive study, *Ecumenical Foundations* (1952)—

but convergent forces are more than matched by divergent forces, so that unity in mission remains elusive.

Historical Research in American Missions

John King Fairbank in 1968 lamented "the neglect of missionaries in American historiography," and described the missionary as "the invisible man of American history."[114] Historical research in American missions is a goldmine for exploring scholars, yet—as Pierce Beaver once observed—"most writing in the history of missions is not being done by church historians, but by general historians and area experts in the universities and colleges."[115] A selection of studies published in the 1980s indicates that this situation largely continues: Suzanne Wilson Barnett and John King Fairbank, eds., *Christianity in China: Early Protestant Missionary Writings* (1985); Adrian A. Bennett, *Missionary Journalist in China: Young J. Allen and His Magazines, 1860–1883* (1983); Nancy Boyd, *Emissaries: The Overseas Work of the American YWCA, 1895–1970* (1986); Kenton J. Clymer, *Protestant Missionaries in the Philippines: 1898–1916* (1986); Patricia R. Hill, *The World Their Household: The American Woman's Foreign Mission Movement and Cultural Transformation, 1870–1920* (1985); Jane Hunter, *The Gospel of Gentility: American Women Missionaries in Turn-of-the-Century China* (1984); William R. Hutchison, *Errand to the World: American Protestant Thought and Foreign Missions* (1987); Sylvia M. Jacobs, ed., *Black Americans and the Missionary Movement in Africa* (1982); and Walter L. Williams, *Black Americans and the Evangelization of Africa: 1877–1900* (1982). James Eldin Reed chides church historians for their "scholarly neglect" of the history of missions, and says, "No doubt the religious core of the missionary movement will remain invisible until (and unless) the church historian comes to the rescue. Until then, . . . we will be forced to view the inner meaning of the missionary enterprise as through a glass darkly."[116]

Another problem in the history of missions as an academic discipline is that up to this point most of it has been written by Western scholars. It has been written, says Stephen Neill, "far too much from the side of the operators and far too little from that of the victims. . . . We know fairly well what it feels like to be a missionary; we know much less of what it feels like to be the object of the missionary's attentions."[117] In a similar vein, African theologian John Mbiti says to Western church historians, "We feel deeply affronted [that you have] more meaningful . . . academic fellowship with heretics long dead than with living colleagues of the church today in the so-called Third World."[118]

Missionary Personnel

There were more North American Protestant missionaries serving overseas in 1986 than ever before—over 39,000 career persons and nearly 28,000 short-termers—from 764 agencies with income in excess of $1 billion. The growth in missionary personnel was uneven, however, as shown in the following table prepared by Robert T. Coote, based on data in the thirteenth edition of the *Mission Handbook: North American Protestant Ministries Overseas* (1986), compared with data from earlier editions of the *Mission Handbook.*[119]

North American Overseas Protestant
Career Missionary Personnel Totals

Affiliation	1953	1968	1985
National Council of Chs./DOM	9,844	10,042	4,349
Can. Council of Chs./CWC	572	1,873	234
EFMA	2,650	7,369	9,101
IFMA	3,081	6,206	6,380
Independent/Unaffiliated	3,565	11,601	19,905
(less doubly affiliated)	−1,113	−2,941	−660
Total	18,599	34,150	39,309

The continuing decline of personnel in main-line—or old-line—boards related to the DOM/NCC (11.5 percent of the total in 1984), was more than offset by the continuing increase of personnel in evangelical agencies, though that is also a mixed picture. In his analysis of the data, Coote shows that for EFMA/IFMA taken as a whole, 1968 marked the beginning of a plateau, and this plateau has prevailed for almost two decades.[120] The really dramatic growth in evangelical personnel occurred in unaffiliated evangelical or fundamentalist agencies, especially the three largest—Southern Baptist Foreign Mission Board (1984, 3,346 career missionaries), Wycliffe Bible Translators (3,022, Canadian personnel included), and New Tribes Mission (1,438). In 1985 the annual Lottie Moon Christmas offering in Southern Baptist churches for support of foreign missions amounted to nearly $67 million (toward a total foreign missions budget of $162 million in 1986), and 429 new Southern Baptist missionaries were named.

Agenda of Issues

The place of persons in mission is an issue that faces mission agencies with increasing urgency as many areas of the Third World become closed to North American missionaries. While sending men and women to proclaim the gospel in cross-cultural situations may be an abiding reality at the heart of mission, it does not necessarily follow that "more missionaries mean more mission"; faithfulness in mission is measured in larger terms than the number of missionaries sent. The need to reconceptualize the role of the missionary is high on the agenda for the future, taking into account the increasingly significant role of Third World mission agencies with more than 20,000 non-Western Protestant missionaries in 1986.[121]

Also on the agenda for further investigation is the theology of mission—the basic presuppositions and underlying principles that determine, from the standpoint of Christian faith, the motives, message, methods, strategy, and goals of mission.[122] Of particular importance for this task is the contribution of Third World scholars, such as Orlando E. Costas at Andover Newton, Kosuke Koyama at New York's Union Theological Seminary, Samuel Escobar at Eastern Baptist, Lamin Sanneh at Harvard, Tite Tienou at Alliance Seminary, and C. S. Song at Pacific School of Religion, as well as those who are overseas.

The most critical aspect of this task deals with the Christian attitude toward religious pluralism and the approach to people of other faiths. In ecumenical scholarship it is generally recognized that Christ is present and active among non-Christians, but the crucial question is whether Christ is present in non-Christian religions as such, and whether they may thereby be considered ways of salvation. It is one thing to recognize that Christ is present in other faiths; it quite something else to say that this provides salvific efficacy to other faiths, and that people of other faiths may be saved *in* their religions or even *through* their religions, without explicit affirmation of faith in Christ. Since Vatican Council II, Protestants have been pressed in this direction by Catholic scholars, such as Paul F. Knitter in his book *No Other Name? A Critical Survey of Christian Attitudes Toward the World Religions* (1985). Related to this discussion is the role of dialogue versus evangelism in mission to people of other faiths—an increasingly controversial topic. Conservative evangelical scholars are only beginning to address these issues with fresh thinking.

Evangelicals have given leadership, however, in attention to issues of gospel and culture, and contextualization in mission, especially in the work of missionary anthropologists, such as Charles Kraft and Paul Hiebert at Fuller Seminary, Linwood Barney at Alliance Seminary, Donald Larson and William Smalley at Bethel College, Charles Taber at Emmanuel School of Religion, and Darrell Whiteman at Asbury Seminary.[123]

A Shifting Center of Ecclesiastical Gravity

Of special significance for the study and understanding of mission in the remaining years of the twentieth century is the fact that the center of ecclesiastical gravity in the world is shifting from the northern to the southern hemisphere. The Swiss Catholic missiologist Walbert Bühlmann, in his book *The Coming of the Third Church* (1977), observed that whereas at the beginning of this century 85 percent of all Christians lived in the West, there has been a shift in the church's center of gravity so that by the year 2000 about 58 percent of all Christians—and about 70 percent of all Catholics—will be living in the Third World. Bühlmann considers the coming of this church of the Third World and the third millennium—the so-called Third Church—to be "*the* epoch-making event of current church history."[124]

Once again the old centers of strength and influence in the church are becoming the new peripheries, as the areas of greatest church growth and theological creativity are found in the Third World. This suggests that we are in one of the most important periods of church history—a period of ferment and transition. In certain respects, as Tracey K. Jones, Jr., has observed, "The Christian mission around the world today is in colossal confusion." Rather than despair, however, this should be seen as a sign of vitality and hope, says Jones, because "untidiness and confusion have characterized the great periods of missionary expansion."[125] To paraphrase something that Wilfred Cantwell Smith once said about Islam, we could say that the most exciting chapter in church history is the one that is currently in the process of being written.

The Unfinished Task

Reliable data about the whole church in the whole world are now available—for the first time—in the *World Christian Encyclopedia* (1982), a fact-filled, 1,010-page volume, edited by David B. Barrett, former Anglican missionary in Africa, now serving as a research consultant for the Southern Baptist Foreign Mission Board. While Barrett's work documents the dramatic expansion of Christianity around the world, especially during the last one hundred years, it gives no basis for complacency. There were approximately 1.6 billion Christians in a world of 5 billion people in 1986, but the percentage of Christians in the world's population has decreased by two percent since the beginning of this century—from 34.4 percent to 32.8 percent in 1980—and half of that decrease occurred between 1970 and 1980.[126] With far more non-Christians in the world in 1986 than on the day when Jesus was crucified, the unfinished task of world evangelization is immense. The stated goal of some American evangelical agencies is to establish work among the 17,000 so-called unreached people groups in the world by the year 1995, and to achieve "A Church for Every People by the Year 2000."

Can the West Be Converted?

There is a serious "missionary problem" in the United States, however, as in Britain and Western Europe. It is the spread of nominalism in the church and secularism in society. An American Lutheran theologian has observed that "the single most striking fact in the life of main-line U.S. churches over the last twenty years is the rapid erosion of concern about whether people believe in Jesus. . . . The point is not that people no longer believe in Jesus. It is rather that those who do believe seem to care much less than they did twenty years ago about whether those who do not believe come to the place where they do. And this lack of care," he says, "is no simple thoughtlessness; it is an energetic rejection of such care."[127]

In his Warfield Lectures at Princeton Theological Seminary in 1984—titled "Can the West Be Converted?"—Lesslie Newbigin said, "Surely there can be no more crucial question for the world mission of the church than the one I have posed. Can there be an effective missionary encounter with *this* culture—this so powerful, persuasive, and confident culture which (at least until very recently) simply regarded itself as 'the coming world civilization.' "[128] Similarly, recognizing the spiritual crisis in churches of the West, Australian Methodist evangelist Alan Walker says, "The Western world is now the toughest mission field on earth. The whole church must come to the aid of stricken, declining Western churches. . . . Now the missionary age is moving into reverse, and the rest of the world must reach out to the West."[129] With nearly one hundred million unchurched people, the United States is not only one of the toughest but one of the largest mission fields in the world.

The Christian mission is simultaneously directed to "Jerusalem . . . and to the ends of the earth."[130] That mission to all the nations includes—for all the nations—the United States. This is a fruit, in part, of what American Protestants in pursuit of mission have helped to bring about—a world church for world mission.

Notes

1. Cf. Clifton J. Phillips, "The Student Volunteer Movement and Its Role in China Missions, 1886–1920," in *The Missionary Enterprise in China and America,* ed. John K. Fairbank (Cambridge, MA: Harvard University, 1974), 93–98.

2. Cf. R. Pierce Beaver, "Missionary Motivation through Three Centuries," in *Reinterpretation in American Church History,* ed. Jerald C. Brauer (University of Chicago Press, 1968), 141 ff.

3. Quoted by Edward McNall Burns, *The American Idea of Mission: Concepts of National Purpose and Destiny* (New Brunswick, NJ: Rutgers University Press, 1957), 1, from Melville's *White-Jacket.*

4. John Edwin Smylie, "National Ethos and the Church," *Theology Today* 20, no. 3 (1963): 314.

5. See Gerald H. Anderson, "Providence and Politics behind Protestant Missionary Beginnings in the Philippines," *Studies in Philippine Church History* (Ithaca, NY: Cornell University Press, 1969), 280.

6. W. Richey Hogg, "The Role of American Protestanism in World Mission," in *American Missions in Bicentennial Perspective,* ed. R. Pierce Beaver (South Pasadena, CA: William Carey Library, 1977), 364.

7. Anson Phelps Stokes, *Church and State in the United States* (New York: Harper and Brothers, 1950), 2:311. See also James Eldin Reed, "American Foreign Policy, The Politics of Missions and Josiah Strong, 1890–1900," *Church History* 41, no. 2 (1972): 230–45.

8. P.11. References to *Our Country* are taken from the revised edition of 1891, as reprinted and edited by Jurgen Herbst (Cambridge, MA: Belknap Press of Harvard University Press, 1963).

9. Ibid., 200–202.

10. Dana Lee Robert, "Arthur Tappan Pierson and Forward Movements of Late-Nineteenth-Century Evangelism" (Ph.D. diss., Yale University, 1984), 165.

11. John R. Mott, *History of the Student Volunteer Movement for Foreign Missions* (Chicago: SVMFM, 1892), pamphlet, 6–11.

12. Quoted by Mott, *History of the Student Volunteer Movement for Foreign Missions,* 29. Cf. Clarence P. Shedd, *Two Centuries of Student Christian Movements* (New York: Association Press, 1934), 267.

13. Dana L. Robert, "The Legacy of Arthur Tappan Pierson," *International Bulletin of Missionary Research* 8, no. 3 (1984): 120; also Robert, "The Origin

of the Student Volunteer Watchword: 'The Evangelization of the World in This Generation,' " *International Bulletin of Missionary Research* 10, no. 4 (1986): 146 ff.

14. Dana L. Robert, " 'The Crisis of Missions': Premillennial Mission Theory and the Origins of Evangelical Missions" (Paper delivered at conference on A Century of World Evangelization: North Americn Evangelical Missions, 1886–1986, Wheaton College, Wheaton, IL, 17 June 1986), 9; also Robert, "Arthur Tappan Pierson and Forward Movements," 305–12, and "The Legacy of Adoniram Judson Gordon, *"International Bulletin of Missionary Research* 11, no. 4 (1987).

15. Robert, " 'The Crisis of Missions,' " 15.

16. Robert L. Niklaus, John S. Sawin, and Samuel J. Stoesz, *All for Jesus: God at Work in The Christian and Missionary Alliance Over One Hundred Years* (Camp Hill, PA: Christian Publications, 1986), 68 ff.

17. Robert, "The Crisis of Missions," 15.

18. C. Howard Hopkins, *John R. Mott, 1865–1955: A Biography* (Grand Rapids, MI: Eerdmans, 1979), 83–86.

19. Mott, *History of the SVMFM*, 28–33.

20. James S. Dennis, *Centennial Survey of Foreign Missions* (New York: Fleming H. Revell, 1902), 1. See also Harlan P. Beach, *A Geography and Atlas of Protestant Missions*, 2 vols. (New York: Student Volunteer Movement for Foreign Missions, 1902–6); James S. Dennis, Harlan P. Beach, and Charles H. Fahs, eds., *World Atlas of Christian Missions* (New York: Student Volunteer Movement for Foreign Missions, 1911); Harlan P. Beach and Burton St. John, eds., *World Statistics of Christian Missions* (New York: Committee of Reference and Counsel of the Foreign Missions Conference of North America, 1916); Harlan P. Beach and Charles H. Fahs, eds., *World Missionary Atlas* (New York: Institute of Social and Religious Research, 1925).

21. Paul A. Varg, "Motives in Protestant Missions, 1890–1917," *Church History* 23 (1954): 75, 77.

22. Hopkins, *John R. Mott*, 104, 107.

23. The definitive study is Kenton J. Clymer, *Protestant Missionaries in the Philippines, 1898–1916: An Inquiry into the American Colonial Mentality* (Champaign: University of Illinois Press, 1986).

24. For discussion and documentation on clergy sentiments about taking possession of the Philippines, see Anderson, "Providence and Politics," 284 ff.; also Winthrop S. Hudson, "Protestant Clergy Debate the Nation's Vocation," *Church History* 42 (1973): 110–18.

25. Cf. Charles L. Chaney, *The Birth of Missions in America* (South Pasadena, CA: William Carey Library, 1976), 298.

26. Sherwood Eddy, *Pathfinders of the World Missionary Crusade* (Nashville: Abingdon-Cokesbury Press, 1945), 260.

GERALD H. ANDERSON

27. James Alan Patterson, "Robert E. Speer and the Crisis of the American Protestant Missionary Movement, 1920–1937," (Ph.D. diss., Princeton Theological Seminary, 1980), 185.

28. Quoted by H. McKennie Goodpasture, "Robert E. Speer's Legacy," *Occasional Bulletin of Missionary Research* 2, no. 2 (1978): 38. See also R. Pierce Beaver, "North American Thought on the Fundamental Principles of Missions During the Twentieth Century," *Church History* 21 (1952): 348, and Patterson, "Robert Speer," 185 ff.

29. Robert E. Speer, "The Supreme and Determining Aim," *Ecumenical Missionary Conference, New York, 1900: Report* (New York: American Tract Society, 1900), 1:74–78.

30. Sherwood Eddy, *Eighty Adventurous Years: An Autobiography* (New York: Harper and Brothers, 1955), 29.

31. *Ecumenical Missionary Conference: Report,* 1:11.

32. William Richey Hogg, *Ecumenical Foundations: A History of the International Missionary Council and Its Nineteenth-Century Background* (New York: Harper and Brothers, 1952), 45; also Charles W. Forman, "Evangelization and Civilization: Protestant Missionary Motivation in the Imperialist Era: The Americans," *International Bulletin of Missionary Research* 6, no. 2 (1982): 54.

33. *Ecumenical Missionary Conference: Report,* 1:39.

34. Hogg, *Ecumenical Foundations,* 84.

35. Samuel McCrea Cavert, *Church Cooperation and Unity in America: A Historical Review, 1900–1970* (New York: Association Press, 1970), 52, 202.

36. Valentine H. Rabe, *The Home Base of American China Missions, 1880–1920* (Cambridge, MA: Council on East Asian Studies, Harvard University, Harvard University Press, 1978), 26, 30.

37. Edwin Munsell Bliss, ed., *Encyclopaedia of Missions* (New York: Funk and Wagnalls, 1891), 2: 626; Dennis,, *Centennial Survey,* 257; Hogg, "The Role of American Protestanism in World Mission," 369.

38. R. Pierce Beaver, *American Protestant Women in World Mission: History of the First Feminist Movement in North America,* rev. ed. (Grand Rapids, MI: William B. Eerdmans Publishing, 1980), 87. First published in 1968 under the title *All Loves Excelling: American Protestant Women in World Mission.*

39. Mott, *The Decisive Hour of Christian Missions* (London: SVM Union, 1910), 78–79, 112.

40. Quoted by Beaver, *American Protestant Women,* 87.

41. Ibid., 145.

42. Ibid., 149–54.

43. Jane Hunter, *The Gospel of Gentility: American Women Missionaries in Turn-of-the-Century China* (New Haven: Yale University Press, 1984), xiii.

44. Patricia R. Hill, *The World Their Household: The American Woman's Foreign Mission Movement and Cultural Transformation, 1870–1920* (Ann Arbor: University of Michigan Press, 1985), 195.

45. Quoted by Beaver, *American Protestant Women*, 114, and Hunter, *Gospel of Gentility*, 14.

46. Beaver, *American Protestant Women*, 184 ff.

47. Ibid., 205.

48. Gayraud S. Wilmore, "Black Americans in Mission: Setting the Record Straight," *International Bulletin of Missionary Research* 10, no. 3 (1986): 98.

49. Ibid, 98 ff. See also Sylvia M. Jacobs, ed., *Black Americans and the Missionary Movement in Africa* (Westport, CT: Greenwood Press, 1982), and Walter L. Williams, *Black Americans and the Evangelization of Africa, 1877–1900* (Madison: University of Wisconsin Press, 1982).

50. Wilmore, "Black Americans," 100.

51. Beaver, "North American Thought," 347. See also Hugo H. Culpepper, "The Legacy of William Owen Carver," *International Bulletin of Missionary Research* 5, no. 3 (1981): 119–22.

52. R. Pierce Beaver, "The Missionary Research Library and the Occasional Bulletin," *Occasional Bulletin of Missionary Research* 1, no. 1 (1977): 2; also Hopkins, *John R. Mott*, 425.

53. *Ecumenical Missionary Conference: Report*, 1:151.

54. World Missionary Conference, 1910, *Report of Commission VI: The Home Base of Missions* (New York: Fleming H. Revell, 1910), 175. It was reported at the Edinburgh conference that "at Yale University the 'Courses of Study of the Missionary Department' number one hundred-and-three items under thirteen heads!" (W. H. T. Gairdner, *"Edinburgh 1910": An Account and Interpretation of the World Missionary Conference* [Edinburgh: Oliphant, Anderson and Ferrier, 1910], 227). Olav Guttorm Myklebust lists only three professorships at the time of Edinburgh in vol. 1 (71) of his study, but lists four in vol. 2 (373) of his work, *The Study of Missions in Theological Education*, 2 vols. (Oslo: Egede Instituttet, 1955, 1957).

55. Myklebust, *Study of Missions*, 2:71–72.

56. R. Pierce Beaver, "The Meaning and Place of Missiology Today in the American Scene" (Paper given at the European Consultation on Mission Studies, Selly Oak Colleges, Birmingham, England, April 1968), 3. Beaver adds this critical judgment about Hartford: "That school, however, consistently rejected responsibility for theoretical and theological concern in missions."

57. Myklebust, *Study of Missions*, 2:71, 185. As the source of his information Myklebust cites a typescript by Daniel J. Fleming, "History of the Fellowship of Professors of Missions," and a letter from R. Pierce Beaver, dated 29

November 1955. In response to my inquiry in November 1986, the library at Union Theological Seminary, New York, reported that there is no copy of the Fleming typescript in the Fleming file or papers. In response to a similar inquiry, Professor Myklebust wrote in a letter dated 10 December 1986, "I am afraid I have to disappoint you. The documents to which you refer are not in the archives of the Egede Institute. The secretary and the librarian have searched the files, but in vain. . . . Neither Fleming's 'History' or Beaver's letter of Nov. 29, 1955 are there. However, I can assure you that the quotations from Fleming's 'History' are through and through correct." Cf. R. Pierce Beaver, "The American Protestant Theological Seminary and Missions: An Historical Survey," *Missiology* 4, no. 1 (1976): 84.

58. James A. Scherer, "Missions in Theological Education," in *The Future of the Christian World Mission: Studies in Honor of R. Pierce Beaver,* ed. William J. Danker and Wi Jo Kang (Grand Rapids, MI: Eerdmans, 1971), 145.

59. See Kenneth Scott Latourette, *A History of the Expansion of Christianity,* vol. 4, *The Great Century in Europe and the United States of America, A.D. 1800–A.D. 1914* (New York: Harper and Brothers, 1941), 7.

60. Valentine H. Rabe, "Evangelical Logistics: Mission Support and Resources to 1920," in Fairbank, ed., *The Missionary Enterprise in China and America,* 71.

61. Ibid., 388, n. 80.

62. Frank W. Price and Kenyon, E. Moyer, "A Study of American Protestant Foreign Missions in 1956," *Occasional Bulletin from the Missionary Research Library* 7, no. 9 (1956): 1.

63. Rabe, "Evangelical Logistics," 88.

64. James L. Barton, "The Modern Missionary," *Harvard Theological Review* 8 (January 1915): 1–17, and J. P. Jones, "The Protestant Missionary Propaganda in India," ibid., 18–44. The articles are summarized in *International Review of Missions* 4 (April 1915): 308–9.

65. *Christian Century,* 23 November 1932, 1434.

66. Shedd, *Two Centuries,* 405.

67. "Youth and Missions," editorial in the *Christian Century,* 12 January 1928, 40.

68. Phillips, "Student Volunteer Movement," 109.

69. David M. Howard, *Student Power in World Missions,* 2d ed. (Downers Grove, IL: InterVarsity Press, 1979), 110. See also H. Wilbert Norton, *To Stir the Church: A Brief History of the Student Foreign Missions Fellowships, 1936–1986* (Madison, WI: Student Foreign Missions Fellowship, 1986).

70. John A. Mackay, "The Evangelistic Duty of Christianity," *The Christian Life and Message in Relation to Non-Christian Systems of Thought and Life,* vol. 1 of *The Jerusalem Meeting of the International Missionary Council, March 24–April 8, 1928* (New York: IMC, 1928), 390.

71. "The Theology of the Laymen's Foreign Missions Inquiry," *International Review of Missions* 22 (1933): 178.

72. Beaver, "The American Protestant Theological Seminary and Missions," 84. This was more true of the main-line denominated mission agencies than of the faith missions. Between 1929 and 1931 China Inland Mission sent out over two hundred new missionaries; World Radio Missionary Fellowship was founded in 1931; and Wycliffe Bible Translators was founded in 1934.

73. Robert T. Handy, "The American Religious Depression, 1925–1935," *Church History* 29, no. 1 (1960): 13.

74. Charles W. Forman, "A History of Foreign Mission Theory in America," in *American Missions in Bicentennial Perspective,* ed. R. Pierce Beaver, 103.

75. Henry P. Van Dusen, "The Missionary Message Since Madras," *Christendom* 9 (1944): 27.

76. E. Stanley Jones, "Where Madras Missed Its Way," *Christian Century,* 15 March 1939, 351.

77. *Christian Century,* 29 March 1939, 411.

78. Ibid., 31 May 1939, 707.

79. Latourette, *A History of the Expansion of Christianity,* vol. 7, *Advance Through Storm: A.D. 1914 and After, With Concluding Generalizations* (New York: Harper and Brothers, 1945), 494.

80. Tracey K. Jones, Jr., "History's Lessons for Tomorrow's Mission," *International Bulletin of Missionary Research* 10, no. 2 (1986): 51. See also E. Theodore Bachmann, "Kenneth Scott Latourette: Historian and Friend," in *Frontiers of the Christian World Mission Since 1938: Essays in Honor of Kenneth Scott Latourette,* ed. Wilber C. Harr (New York: Harper and Brothers, 1962), 231–80; K. S. Latourette, "My Guided Life," ibid., 281–93 (with select bibliography of his published writings); and Latourette, *Beyond the Ranges: An Autobiography* (Grand Rapids, MI: Eerdmans, 1967).

81. W. Reginald Wheeler, ed., *The Crisis Decade: A History of the Foreign Missionary Work of the Presbyterian Church in the U.S.A., 1937–1947* (New York: Board of Foreign Missions of the Presbyterian Church in the U.S.A., 1950), 285–86.

82. Harold Lindsell, "Faith Missions Since 1938," 219 ff.

83. Price and Moyer, "Study of American Protestant Foreign Missions in 1956," 2.

84. Harold Lindsell, "An Appraisal of Agencies Not Co-operating with the International Missionary Council Grouping, "*International Review of Missions* 47 (1958): 202.

85. Frank W. Price, "World Christian and Missionary Statistics," *Occasional Bulletin from the Missionary Research Library* 9 (6 May 1958); Frank W. Price and Clara E. Orr, "North American Protestant Foreign Missions in 1958," *Occasional Bulletin from the Missionary Research Library* 9 (8 December 1958).

86. M. A. C. Warren, "The Christian Mission and the Cross," in *Missions Under the Cross: Addresses Delivered at the Enlarged Meeting of the International Missionary Council at Willingen, in Germany, 1952,* ed. Norman Goodall (New York: Friendship Press, 1953), 40. R. Pierce Beaver said, "World War II marked the end of the old order of overseas missions," ("The American Protestant Theological Seminary and Missions," 84).

87. Charles W. Forman, "A History of Foreign Mission Theory in America," 109.

88. Max Warren, *Crowded Canvas: Some Experiences of a Life-time* (London: Hodder and Stoughton, 1974), 154.

89. W. Richey Hogg, "New Thrusts in the Theology and Life of the Christian Mission," in *Christian Mission in Theological Perspective,* ed. Gerald H. Anderson (Nashville: Abingdon Press, 1967), 207.

90. Gerald H. Anderson, "The Theology of Mission Among Protestants in the Twentieth Century," in *The Theology of the Christian Mission* (New York: McGraw-Hill, 1961), 4–7.

91. David L. Edwards, "Signs of Radicalism in the Ecumenical Movement," in *The Ecumenical Advance: A History of the Ecumenical Movement, 1948–1968,* ed. Harold E. Fey (Philadelphia: Westminster Press, 1970), 400.

92. Hans Hoekendijk, "Christ and the World in the Modern Age," *Student World,* 54, nos., 1–2 (1961): 75, 81–82.

93. This was the judgment of Lesslie Newbigin, a prominent participant in the ecumenical missionary events of that decade, in his *Unfinished Agenda: An Autobiography* (Grand Rapids, MI: Eerdmans, 1985), 198.

94. M. Richard Shaull, "The Form of the Church in the Modern Diaspora," *Princeton Seminary Bulletin* (March 1964), reprinted in *New Theology No. 2,* ed. Martin E. Marty and Dean G. Peerman (New York: Macmillan, 1965) 266–67.

95. Norman A. Horner, ed. *Protestant Crosscurrents in Mission: The Ecumenical-Conservative Encounter* (Nashville: Abingdon Press, 1968), 10.

96. See Denton Lotz, *"The Evangelization of the World in This Generation": The Resurgence of a Missionary Idea Among the Conservative Evangelicals,* Th.D. diss., University of Hamburg, Germany, 1970 (privately printed), 231 ff.

97. Arthur F. Glasser has described the "the IFMA parochialism" at the Chicago Congress as "the last attempt of dispensationalist-separatists to dominate the American missionary movement. And it fell far short of being a success . . . . a curious mixture of triumphialism and pessimism . . . the platform was dominated by the old guard. It was a depressing scene." (Arthur F. Glasser and Donald A. McGavran, *Contemporary Theologies of Mission* [Grand Rapids, MI: Baker Book House, 1983], 117–18). See also Arthur F. Glasser, "The Evolution of Evangelical Mission Theology since World War II," *International Bulletin of Missionary Research* 9, no. 1 (1985): 9–13.

98. C. René Padilla, "The Unity of the Church and the Homogeneous Unit Principle," *International Bulletin of Missionary Research* 6, no. 1 (1982): 29–30.

99. See Tim Stafford, "The Father of Church Growth," cover story on Donald McGavran in *Christianity Today,* 21 February 1986, 19–23; reprinted with comments and response by McGavran and Ralph D. Winter in *Mission Frontiers* 8, no. 1 (1986): 5–10; also McGavran,, "My Pilgrimage in Mission," *International Bulletin of Missionary Research* 10, no. 2 (1986): 53–58.

100. See Matthew Black and William A. Smalley, eds., *On Language, Culture, and Religion: In Honor of Eugene A. Nida* (The Hague: Mouton, 1974).

101. See Gary B. McGee, "Assemblies of God Mission Theology: A Historical Perspective," *International Bulletin of Missionary Research* 10, no. 4 1986): 166–70; McGee, *This Gospel Shall Be Preached: A History and Theology of Assemblies of God Foreign Missions to 1959* (Springfield, MO: Gospel Publishing House, 1986); and L. Grant McClung, Jr., ed., *Azusa Street and Beyond: Pentecostal Missions and Church Growth in the Twentieth Century* (South Plainfield, NJ: Bridge Publishing, 1986).

102. W. Richey Hogg, "The Role of American Protestantism in World Mission," 388.

103. See Gerald H. Anderson, "A Moratorium on Missionaries?" *Christian Century,* 16 January 1974, 43–45.

104. Beaver is mistaken when he says that the APM "came into existence in 1950" ("The American Protestant Theological Seminary and Missions," 85); also James Scherer (when he cites Beaver), "The Future of Missiology as an Academic Discipline in Seminary Education: An Attempt at Reinterpretation and Clarification," *Missiology* 13, no. 4 (1985): 448. See Norman A. Horner, who was present at the founding meeting in Louisville in 1952 and was elected the first secretary-treasurer of the APM ("The Association of Professors of Missions in North America: The First Thirty-five Years, 1952–1987," *International Bulletin of Missionary Research* 11, no. 3 [1987]).

105. Beaver, "The Meaning and Place of Missiology Today in the American Scene," 4–5.

106. When the Council on the Study of Religion voted to accept the American Society of Missiology as one of its constituent member societies, effective 1 January 1976, Louis J. Luzbetak, S.V.D., then-president of the ASM, declared, "This is a historic landmark; on this day 'missiology' becomes a fully recognized academic discipline in North America" ("Missology Comes of Age," *Missiology* 4, no. 1 [1976]: 11. See also the discussion of this event and developments in the years that followed, by James Scherer, "The Future of Missiology," 455 ff.

107. "Doctoral Dissertations on Mission," *International Bulletin of Missionary Research* 7, no. 3 (1983): 97 ff.

108. James Scherer, "The Future of Missiology," 455.

109. Ibid., 457–58.

110. *Occasional Bulletin of Missionary Research* 2, no. 1 (1978): 28.

111. R. Pierce Beaver, "The Meaning and Place of Missiology Today," 5.

112. Wilbert R. Shenk, "The 'Great Century' Reconsidered," *Missiology* 12, no. 2 (1984): 142.

113. See Lesslie Newbigin, "Cross-currents in Ecumenical and Evangelical Understandings of Mission," *International Bulletin of Missionary Research* 6, no. 4 (1982): 146 ff., with responses by Paul G. Schrotenboer and C. Peter Wagner and reply by Newbigin.

114. John King Fairbank, "Assignment for the '70's," *American Historical Review* 74 (1969): 876–79.

115. Editorial Foreword, *Mo Bradley and Thailand* by Donald C. Lord (Grand Rapids, MI: Eerdmans, 1969), 7.

116. James Eldin Reed, "American Foreign Policy," 245.

117. S. C. Neill, "The History of Missions: An Academic Discipline," in *The Mission of the Church and the Propagation of the Faith,* ed. G. J. Cuming (London: Cambridge University Press, 1970), 160.

118. John S. Mbiti, "Theological Impotence and the Universality of the Church," in *Mission Trends No. 3: Third World Theologies,* ed. Gerald H. Anderson and Thomas F. Stransky (New York: Paulist Press; Grand Rapids, MI: Eerdmans, 1976), 17.

119. Robert T. Coote, "Taking Aim on 2000 A.D.," in *Mission Handbook: North American Protestant Ministries Overseas,* ed. Samuel Wilson and John Siewert, 13th ed. (Monrovia, CA: MARC, World Vision International, 1986), 39. Copyright © 1986 by Missions Advanced Research and Communication Center. Reprinted by permission.

120. Ibid. See also Robert T. Coote, "The Uneven Growth of Conservative Evangelical Missions,," *International Bulletin of Missionary Research* 6, no. 3 (1982): 118–23.

121. Larry D. Pate and Lawrence E. Keyes report that "there are over 20,000 non-Western missionaries today," and they anticipate "there will be more than 100,000 . . . by the year 2000" ("Emerging Missions in a Global Church," *International Bulletin of Missionary Research* 10, no. 4 [1986]: 156). See also Keyes, *The Last Age of Missions* (Pasadena, CA: Willliam Carey Library, 1983).

122. See Rodger C. Bassham, *Mission Theology: 1948–1975* (Pasadena, CA: William Carey Library, 1979), and James A. Scherer, *Gospel, Church and Kingdom: Comparative Studies in World Mission Theology* (Minneapolis: Augsburg Publishing House, 1987).

123. See also the papers and report from the Willowbank Consultation on Gospel and Culture, sponsored by the Lausanne Committee in 1978, *Down to Earth: Studies in Christianity and Culture,* ed. John Stott and Robert T. Coote (Grand Rapids, MI: William B. Eerdmans Publishing, 1980).

124. Walbert Bühlmann, *Courage, Church!* (Maryknoll, NY: Orbis Books, 1978), 131. See also Bühlmann, *The Church of the Future: A Model for the Year 2001* (Maryknoll, NY: Orbis Books, 1986).

125. Tracey K. Jones, Jr., "History's Lessons for Tomorrow's Mission," 50.

126. David B. Barrett, "Annual Statistical Table on Global Mission: 1986," *International Bulletin of Missionary Research* 10, no. 1 (1986): 23.

127. James H. Burtness, "Time for Change," *Lutheran Standard,* 7 October 1983, 4. An expanded version appeared in *Dialog* (Summer 1982) under the title "Does Anyone Out There Care Anymore Whether People Believe in Jesus?"

128. Lesslie Newbigin, "Can the West Be Converted?" *International Bulletin of Missionary Research* 11, no. 1 (1987): 2. See also Newbigin, *The Other Side of 1984* (Geneva: World Council of Churches, 1983), and *Foolishness to the Greeks: The Gospel and Western Culture* (Grand Rapids, MI: Eerdmans, 1986).

129. Alan Walker, *World Parish* (November 1985). Quoted by Coote, "Taking Aim on 2000A.D.," 57.

130. Acts 1:8 See R. Pierce Beaver, *The Missionary Between the Times* (Garden City, NY: Doubleday, 1968), 12.

Liturgical and Credal Studies

Aidan Kavanagh, O.S.B.

THERE is no doubt that liturgical and credal studies have had a significant impact on the lives of Western Christians during the century celebrated by this volume. With few exceptions the Western churches have undertaken far-reaching reforms in their patterns of worship, particularly over the last twenty-five years. Nothing indicates that the undertaking is complete. The purpose of this essay is not to evaluate the undertaking but to account for its existence and to point out some of its major features. For the reform in Western worship did not spring from nowhere, and its major features have contexts that are not always remarked upon.

The Background

The one thing without which modern reforms in liturgical worship could not exist is the still increasing body of liturgical studies begun during the Renaissance. Indeed it is only in the sixteenth century that the word "liturgy," from the Greek *leitourgia* meaning a work done for the commonweal,[1] enters the Western vocabulary, gradually replacing the old Latin term *officium*.[2] This change was sparked by the Renaissance emphasis on antiquity, an emphasis that carried over into the religious realm in the rediscovery and teaching of biblical languages, in particular Greek. Renaissance resourcement was thus the proximate genesis of liturgical studies along with that equally Renaissance ferment north of the Alps for church reform. By the time of the Reformation such studies had not proceeded very far, and they were soon warped by theological polemics as Reform and Counter-Reform settled in.

Liturgical studies was a nascent effort in need of method and focus. Medieval and sixteenth-century students of liturgy emphasized for the most part what they considered to be the *meaning* of received rites. Theological polemic between Catholic and Protestant concerning liturgy during the sixteenth century and after simply continued this search for, and interpretation of, meaning. This way of going about things had serious short-

216

comings. Its method was almost entirely theological, and as the Western schisms gathered strength it became increasingly confessional. As it analyzed texts received from various quarters, it had no dependable way of determining where those texts ultimately came from or the degree of their integrity. Nor did many of the original Reformers particularly care, so overwhelming was their sense of urgent theological a priori. Cleaving to correct doctrine was the liturgical method of the Reformers, and it often overwhelmed historical considerations. As Archbishop Thomas Cranmer put it in 1553, his English Service in the Book of Common Prayer of 1552 was "more pure and according to God's words, than any other that hath been used in England these thousand years." It was indeed "the same that was used fifteen hundred years past."[3] In saying this, Cranmer was being no more nor less historically naive than his medieval scholastic forebears who had built sacramental theories on spurious statements attributed to premedieval popes. Sixteenth-century attempts at liturgical reform were largely based on theological *parti pris* and innocent of history.

Only toward the end of the century did this situation begin to change. Many of the liturgical reforms instigated by the Council of Trent (1545–63), not to be finally completed until 1614, were based on surprisingly good, if limited, historical research.[4] An example of this is the immense work done in researching the reform of the *Rituale* by J. A. Santori.[5] But other work that had little directly to do with official liturgical reform had also begun to seek out the roots and recover the texts of Christian worship scattered and buried in libraries all over Europe. Already G. Cassander in 1558, and Jacques de Joigny, called Pamelius, had in 1571 published significant works on liturgy, using the word in its modern sense for the first time.[6] These attempts at resourcement set in motion an astonishing endeavor over the next two centuries that not only recovered old texts and founded the historiographical disciplines of paleography, diplomatics, sigillography, and numismatics but also induced the long-term process of cataloging European libraries. Modern liturgical studies, no less than those of patristics, biblical exegesis, and historical theology owe their origin to these scholars and their successors, especially G. Bona (1674),[7] the Maurists J. Mabillon (1632–1707) and E. Martène (1654–1734),[8] L. Muratori (1672–1750),[9] G. Tommasi (1649–1713),[10] and the canonist G. D. Mansi (1692–1769).[11] The later work in liturgical studies as well as the reform and reunion movements in the Western Christian churches that this essay will treat, all stand upon the shoulders of scholars such as these.

During the hardening of confessional lines following the mid-sixteenth century, when the apologetics and confessional theology being elaborated in the academies of Western Christianity was supreme, studies such as those initiated by these scholars were demonstrating several matters that would qualify, if not undermine, the emerging status quo in liturgy and creed. For one thing, their research revealed the rich diversity in which Christians of earlier centuries had worshiped in both East and West. The notion that all early Christians had worshiped according to a single, pure, biblical rite was shown not to have been the case. The coming to uniformity was late and never total in the East, despite the great influence of Orthodox Constantinople. It was even later in the West, despite the enormous prestige of Roman usage, which was itself observed variously around Europe until well after Trent.[12] Diversity turned out to be primitive and normal in the common tradition; uniformity late and abnormal. The tradition is at home with diversity, but it is warped by the imposition of uniformity because at that point the worship of a people passes out of its own hands into those of experts, lawyers, members of centralized ecclesiastical bureaucracies, and parliaments—as in the England of Thomas Cranmer or, later, the Rome of Pius V and his successors.

At the same time historical liturgical studies, especially as they began to compare distinct families of Christian liturgies whose texts could be recovered, began to shed light on the function of tradition as distinct from a coercively imposed and uniform status quo. Liturgy prior to the sixteenth century was carried not by a legal system but by a much more complex and sophisticated web of habit, repetition, memory, and regular enactment that formed the locale of people's religious sentiments and daily lives. Liturgical sources serve as tidewater marks of this tradition, and being able to read these marks over a considerable period of time gives one insight into the forces that were at work in the religious culture of the mass of people underneath the intellectual searches and theoretical endeavors of educated elites. What one encounters in liturgical sources are articulations of spiritual power and sociocultural pressures rather than theological arguments or random didactic theories and aesthetic urges.[13]

Recognizing diversity and the function of tradition were but two of the long-term results of the invention of liturgical studies from the late sixteenth through the nineteenth centuries. But these two results have been overarching in the past hundred years so far as modern liturgiology and church reform are concerned. They have enabled church reform to be both more radical and more conservative of tradition than the reforms or counterterreforms of the sixteenth and seventeenth centuries. Something of this began to be detected early on in England as serious discrepancies between the liturgical reforms of Thomas Cranmer, retained in the English Prayer Book of 1662, and the deeper tradition of Western usage being revealed by subsequent liturgical research came to light. The detection of discrepancies resulted in a spate of both private and public liturgical alternatives produced by Jeremy Taylor in 1658, Edward Stevens, William Whiston, John Henley, the Nonjurors, Thomas Rattray, and the Church of Scotland in 1764.[14]

Among Roman Catholic scholars a similar detection of discrepancies between the Counter-Reformation liturgical settlement and older Roman forms was gradually taking place. Sources prior to those used by the post-Tridentine reformers of the late medieval Roman liturgy were increasingly coming to hand, as were texts of liturgies other than the Roman in both East and West. This burgeoning repertoire of texts, together with the elaboration of a methodology for dating and interpreting them, made it possible to mount an initial taxonomy of Christian liturgies according to type, family, region, and derivation.[15] Until the mid-nineteenth century this scholarship remained exclusively in European academies, having little if any effect on the rigidified and somewhat defensive polity of Counter-Reformation Catholicism.

At that time, in reaction to Enlightenment rationalism, state absolutism, the early stages of the Industrial Revolution and the alienation of the masses from the churches, significant movements began almost simultaneously in several areas of Christian Europe. These movements, while viewed by many at the time as liberal or "modernist," were in fact invariably conservative in that they sought to restore some degree of historic integrity and pastoral vitality to churches weakened by human accommodations and under pressure from aggressive modern states. These movements opposed the purely moralistic confines into which the Enlightenment and the states influenced by it wished to push religion, making it an arm of government meant to pacify the masses and keep them in line (whence Marx's diagnosis of religion as the opiate of the people). Hence the concern of these movements for tradition as a genetic view of the present that reaffirms people's sense of tradition and solidarity with the past, giving them a firm base from which to move into the future. Hence their emphasis on the more-than-rational dimensions in human knowing and the priority they gave to the aesthetic not as the center of mere feeling but also of moral perception and the source of will; the place where knowing, feeling, and willing become one act. Hence then their rediscovery of the importance of Christian worship, with its symbolism, poetry, music, art and ceremony as faith and experience transacted in common.

To construe as Romantic or as mainly aesthetic the motives of these movements—the Tractarian in England,[16] the Grundtvigian in Denmark,[17] the ecclesiological in Germany,[18] and the monastic and liturgical in France—is to underestimate one of the most powerful movements of the nineteenth century. Standing on the shoulders of that strong scholarly resourcement noted previously, the movement was portentous. Its liturgical aspect, for example, was most overtly developed at Solesmes in France by Prosper Guéranger.[19] Reacting against a perceptible alienation of the masses from the church as a result of dislocations in family and community caused by the Industrial Revolution, Guéranger proposed to reintegrate those masses by restoring to them active participation in the Roman liturgy, an historic expression of unity that could become a focal point of Christian values transcending the conflicting claims of state and industry on people's lives. He thus advocated the austere monody of plain chant and the simple elegance of authentic Roman ceremonial in order to give the people easier access to fundamental Christian values. As a sort of laboratory in which this might be worked out, Guéranger refounded the small monastery of Solesmes. It became the first center for practicable liturgical reform in all its phases for the next several generations.[20] The historical scholarship of the seventeenth and eighteenth centuries in matters liturgical was enriched and made more urgent by the development of this new dimension, which foresaw the application of scholarship to current theological and pastoral concerns. The Reformation and Counter-Reformation regard for liturgy as one arena for polemics began to wane.

Due to its scholarly depth and sense of responsible urgency this new sort of resourcement began to have wide-ranging results in the highest levels of Roman Catholicism, despite opposition in many quarters. Pope Leo XIII proposed Thomism as the fundamental style of theological inquiry[21] and called for new efforts in biblical research, founding the Pontifical Biblical Commission to oversee the process in 1902.[22] His successor, Pius X, furthered these policies by addressing the liturgy and its music in 1903.[23] This address was subsequently regarded as the first formal commendation of the nascent "liturgical movement," even though Pius IX had already approved the Cecilian movement's intention to restore liturgical music in 1870. But the statement of Pius X in 1903, coming when it did, had effects that went far beyond its own specific concerns. If nothing else, it signaled that the state of worship was a matter of major concern in the largest of the Western churches. It also heralded a flood of papal statements on liturgy and allied matters to be issued with increasing frequency over the next half century.[24]

This spreading concern for liturgical restoration and repristination— it could not yet be called a program for bold reform of the liturgy—was thus not something unto itself, nor was it the creation solely of pedants and aesthetes. It rested on a large and still-growing body of research into the origins and growth of Christian liturgy carried on since the sixteenth century by scholars both Protestant and Catholic. It reflected a profound sense of unease over the state of society and of church as both of these reeled beneath the hammer blows of political and technological revolutions after the middle of the eighteenth century in Europe. There was an initial sense that the center was no longer holding. To reinforce the middle ground meant that its foundations had to be rediscovered and a new polity evolved. Pusey and Newman in England, Grundtvig in Denmark, Möhler in Germany, Guéranger in France, and those influenced by them began to perceive that the roots of a repristinated Christian polity somehow intersected in communal worship. They also perceived that communal worship was not merely an act of expediency whose justification was that it might make people both politically and morally "better." They began to approach worship not in terms of liturgy's utility but in theocentric terms, asking how the divine presence by faith, grace, word, and sacrament in communal worship might rehabilitate the world according to criteria that transcended current issues.

The shift was from the moralistic, the polemic, and the anthropocentric to the theological. It begot an approach to liturgical worship that was, paradoxically, able to forge a much closer relationship between liturgy, with all its historical, theological, spiritual, and aesthetic aspects, and those cultural and social matters that were so divisive at the time. The growing emphasis on what Pius X's 1903 statement on liturgy and music called the *actuosa participatio*, or active participation, of the people, repeated in Pius XI's *Divini Cultus* of 1928 and Pius XII's *Mediator Dei* of 1947, carried with it the corollary of the people's *actuosa participatio* not only in the building up of the church but of civil society as well.[25] Papal statements on the liturgy and on the contemporary social order thus went hand in hand. They expressed a conceptual unity based on the inalienable rights of all those who participate in social endeavors such as work, politics, and divine worship to their own proper role and dignity in those endeavors. This conceptual unity was often overlooked by those who opposed or were unconcerned about liturgical repristination and, later, reform.

But it was not lost on the advocates of what came to be called the "liturgical movement" in Europe and America. Lambert Beauduin (1873–1960) had been a diocesan priest in Belgium engaged in social work for eight years before becoming a monk in order to devote himself fully to working out how the liturgy formed the Christian basis for such work. Not only was he the first great intellectual leader of the liturgical movement prior to the First World War,[26] but the formal beginning of the movement is usually dated from his address to a conference at Malines in 1909.[27] Beauduin stressed concern for the working masses and the need to look to the liturgy's future rather than its past, thus setting the stage for moving beyond Guéranger's earlier avowed program of restoration and repristination and on toward reform of the rites received from the past, something Beauduin almost lived to see begun in the Second Vatican Council (1962–65).

Romano Guardini's seminal books, *Vom Geist der Liturgie* (1918), *Vom Sinn der Kirche* (1922), and *Liturgische Bildung* (1923), outlined the scope of the liturgical problem in terms that were no less social and cultural than they were theological and pastoral. The first two of these books[28] compelled an American, Virgil Michel (1890–1938), to begin studying liturgy in the early twenties, a labor that took him to Europe as a student of Beauduin in Rome. Michel, a Benedictine monk, returned to his abbey in Minnesota and founded *Orate Fratres*, now *Worship*, as a journal of liturgical and social advocacy. He wrote an astonishing array of books and articles on these matters from 1926 until his early death in 1938.[29]

From its very first volume, in 1927, *Orate Fratres* evidenced yet another strand that the liturgical movement had woven into itself from its inception, namely, ecumenism. Ecumenism had been an increasing concern as scholarly research in the history of liturgy and in patristics had developed during the previous three hundred years. In the rediscovery of early texts these scholars slowly rose beyond the confessional polemics spawned in the sixteenth century by asking themselves less *how* certain issues were to be interpreted than *what* it was that was being interpreted. This resulted in scholarly convergence across sharply defined confessional lines concerning basic Christian phenomena. As the Western churches were buffeted by the Enlightenment and by the industrial and political revolutions of the eighteenth and nineteenth centuries this convergence on matters basic to Christian survival increased, showing up in the shift from anthropocentric to theological emphases in the several nineteenth-century movements on the Continent and in England mentioned above.

How all this came to rest in Virgil Michel is typical and instructive. Orestes Brownson (1803–76), about whom Michel wrote his doctoral dissertation in 1918, was an American ecumenist and Catholic convert whose views Michel knew well and shared.[30] Michel's other great mentor in ecumenism was Lambert Beauduin, through whom was transmitted to Michel a vision of the reunion of Eastern and Western churches that had already received Vatican support from the late nineteenth century.[31] In 1925 Beauduin had also taken part in the Malines Conversations (1921–25) between Catholics and Anglicans at the invitation of Cardinal Mercier. Beauduin's interests became Michel's interests, and these were reflected in the pages of *Orate Fratres* as well as in his work in Anglican and Orthodox dialogues with Roman Catholics in the United States during the 1930s.[32]

All this was contributing to the gathering force of what later would be called the ecumenical movement. Sporadic reunion movements among various churches had increased in tempo and intensity during the nineteenth century, particularly in England. These began to coalesce into two international forums beginning in the nineteen twenties. One was Life and Work, concerned with the social aspects of Christian life and faith, which met in Stockholm in 1925 and Oxford in 1937. The other was Faith and Order, concerned with theological and ecclesiological matters between the churches, which met in Lausanne in 1927 and Edinburgh in 1937. The union of the two, begun in Utrecht in 1938, became the World Council of Churches a decade later.[33]

It is difficult to overemphasize the synchrony of liturgical and ecumenical movements both in their roots and in their convergence in our own day. When one reads the 1981 Faith and Order statement made in Lima, Peru, on baptism, eucharist, and ministry,[34] one is rarely aware that such concerns are historically anything but the narrow obsessions of those afflicted only with ecclesiastical tastes. A generation before the American Civil War Johann Adam Möhler, of the Roman Catholic Tübingen school, was arguing that the church, so far from being grounded in the hierarchy or the state, was the sum total of the communal life of all believers. This life was shot through with regular if deeply mysterious encounters between God in Christ and redeemed humanity. Liturgical worship was, for Möhler, the chief arena of human participation in the redemptive course, for which reason what would later be called *actuosa participatio* was incumbent upon all members of a worshiping community. For this reason Möhler was against private masses by singular clergy, called for the restoration of communion by both bread and cup to all the people at a time when communion was infrequent and always under the species of bread alone, and advocated vernacular languages in the Latin liturgy.[35] After 1830, as a result of state attacks on the church, Möhler came to appreciate that only in a free and united religious community possessing a definite transcendental dimension could full humanism be guaranteed. "If there will be no higher power than the state in Europe, then human freedom will have come to an end," he wrote in 1837.[36] He thus elaborated a strong christocentric ecclesiology that was to display itself in the regular and accessible practicality of divine worship in the eucharist. Here each Christian consummates membership in the community. "This linking of corporate worship to the concrete institutions of the church and Möhler's phrase 'the church as the mystical body of Christ' came to stand behind the thinking of almost all French and German liturgists."[37]

The ecumenical propensity of all this is obvious, even at a time of strongly defined confessional differences. Nor was it only an academic reality. In the same year that Möhler made the statement about the state and human freedom just quoted, Wilhelm Löhe became pastor of the Lutheran parish in Neuendettelsau, a Bavarian village south of Nürnberg, where he would remain for nearly forty years.[38] During that time he led liturgical reform in his denomination, a reform that touched all aspects of Christian living—worship, service, mission, and theology. In tension with the Protestant *Landeskirche* in ways similar to the tension between Tractarians and the established church in England, Löhe strove to recover from the Reformation what he called "sacramental Lutheranism," holding that while the Reformation may have been complete in doctrine, it was "incomplete in the consequences of doctrine . . . in churchly consciousness, life, and work."[39] Not only did Löhe study and reform the worship of his parish according to the classic Lutheran *Kirchenordnungen* broadened by his knowledge of earlier Christian practice and of Roman Catholic, Anglican, and Eastern traditions. He also trained and supported nearly two hundred missionaries for work among Lutheran immigrants to North America, some of whom helped found the Missouri Synod and Wartburg Theological Seminary in Dubuque, Iowa. Through these people Löhe's liturgical orders found use not only in Bavaria but in the United States as well.[40]

Like Möhler the Catholic academic, Löhe the Lutheran pastor began his reflections on the church "with the notion of fellowship as the ground and goal of human existence, clarified in the relationship of humanity with God."[41] In the liturgy this fellowship comes into accessible and practical expression throughout Christian history, becoming in the process a catholic community that, unlike the *Landeskirche*, transcends territorial boundaries and even confessional differences.[42] In his liturgical work, consequently, Löhe "could borrow freely from other liturgical traditions in order to preserve these traces of the one Church for the churches of the Lutheran confession."[43] The same could be said, *mutatis mutandis*, for all subsequent liturgical reform movements, whether Protestant or Catholic, down to our own day. But it is important to remember that the methodology of borrowing from other traditions was not merely an example of ad hoc antiquarianism. It was held in focus by a broad and increasingly nuanced understanding of membership in the visible-invisible church. This can be seen in Möhler, Pusey, Newman, and Löhe; it is an ecclesiological understanding, deeply ecumenical in potency, which is similar to the "evangelical

Catholicism" of Philip Schaff (1819–93) and to the "radical catholicity" of John Williamson Nevin (1803–86).

No less than any of the others just mentioned, these two representatives of the German Reformed tradition in America were drawn to historical forms of worship. Schaff, like Löhe, held that these forms were not displaced by the Reformers but only "cleansed from sin and perversions,"[44] and that the liturgical freedom of the Reformation should not be construed as unrestricted license to produce forms of worship wholly without precedent.[45] The history of liturgical development in Roman Catholicism and of liturgical reform in Anglicanism from the sixteenth century onward is laden with a similar attitude, and it is one with which Luther and Calvin would have agreed. But generations of polemic, aliturgical Pietism, and the kind of revivalism that accompanied the moving frontier in America had blurred the attitude and blunted its perception in more than one Protestant group. Nevin, indeed, had noted this in his first book, *The Anxious Bench* (1844), which stirred controversy in German Reformed circles just as Philip Schaff arrived in America to join him on the seminary faculty at Mercersburg, Pennsylvania. Together, Nevin and Schaff developed what has been called "Mercersburg Theology," with strong liturgical and sacramental emphases similar to those that we have already seen developing in Europe.

But their work was not merely theoretical. They collaborated in the beginnings of a fundamental return to basics in liturgical reform among the German Reformed churches in America amid no less controversy than greeted Nevin's *The Anxious Bench* of 1844. A "Provisional Liturgy" was produced in 1857–58, revised in 1866 as the *Order of Worship*, underwent modification in 1869, and finally received approval in 1884 and 1887 as the *Directory of Worship for the Reformed Church in the United States*. Having said this, however, one must note that Nevin and Schaff's liturgical return to basics was governed by several factors. In reaction, like Guéranger, to eccentric individualism, Nevin developed a sacramental anthropology based on post-Kantian idealism in *The Mystical Presence* (1846), which he used to reinterpret not only Calvin but the liturgical sources he invoked so freely as antidotes for sectarianism.[46] "It was Nevin's hope, one shared by Schaff, that the objective and 'churchly' expressions of the *Provisional Liturgy* would, if used consistently by the people, triumph over the subjective eccentricities of sectarian pluralism and the 'free prayer' tradition" that had gained such hold among the German Reformed in America.[47]

For his part Philip Schaff stressed the moderate Hegelian principle of organic development in doctrine and church life and honored the theological formulations of traditional orthodoxy. While he admired August Neander's Pietist motto, *Pectus est quod theologum facit*, he was critical of Pietism's failure to recognize the objective character of Christianity in the church and of its refusal to admit the evolutionary nature of doctrinal development. The notion of organic development is a basic factor in Schaff's own view of church history in his *What Is Church History?* (1846) and in the introductory essay to his *History of the Apostolic Church* (1851).[48] But another essay in the present volume treats Schaff in the detail he deserves.[49]

The Disciplines

Looking back over the panorama of influences that stand behind the modern phase of liturgical and credal studies, the proposal made by some critics that these influences can be characterized as "Romantic" is hard to take seriously. Where one finds an undeniable Romanticism is in some advocates of Puginesque architecture and in some enthusiasts for late Italianate ceremonial and piety. But such extravagances were at best tertiary by-products of a far deeper movement whose roots stretched back into the Renaissance and whose flowering had already begun quite prior to the nineteenth century.

This deeper movement tracked far larger game than the revival of Gothic architecture or the elaboration of intricate ceremonial. Liturgical and credal studies represent, in academical manifestations, responses to pressures that bore on Western Christianity from the fifteenth to the present centuries, and each response has had its own specific method geared to a specific pressure. Identifying each of these may help classify certain monuments in the literature of liturgical studies since the beginning of this century.

First was *the development of historical method*, especially in the seventeenth and eighteenth centuries, the effect of which was to make it possible to distinguish allegation from fact, structure from interpretation. Painstaking historical work over four centuries has made it clear that, whatever else may be said about the liturgical work of major Reformers such as Luther, Cranmer, and Calvin, their reforms in Western worship proceed from theological motives that were scarcely informed by history. The discovery of a mass *ordo* by the Lutheran theologian Matthias Flacius, called "Illyricus" (1520–75), and published by him in 1557 as representative of early Western eucharistic usage free of medieval Roman corruptions, caused a sensation among contemporary theologians.[50] Only later was the "Missa Illyrica" shown to be an eleventh century *ordo* of Roman usage composed for a bishop in northern Germany, something that rendered the text useless for the polemical purposes to which it had been put. Historical method has had the effect of calling polemic ahistorical sorts of theological interpretation of liturgical tradition, and Pietism in all its denominational permutations, to account. And in the development of liturgical and credal studies historical method has consistently served as the fundamental check and balance against interpretative excess and a certain pious obscurantism.

Philip Schaff was as good a practitioner of this general method as anyone of his time. The reaction to his and Nevin's liturgical work among the German Reformed in America, as we have seen, was not untypical of the reaction to historical criticism met by others around the same time and after, particularly in Roman Catholicism. The critical work of the Bavarian church historian Johann Ignatz von Döllinger (1799–1890) led to his excommunication in 1871 and set the stage after the First Vatican Council for official regard of such work as "liberal" or "modernist." The work of Pierre Batiffol (1861–1929) on the eucharist, which appeared in 1905, was put on the Index of Forbidden Books.[51] And the eminent director of the French School in Rome, Louis Duchesne (1843–1922), who edited the *Liber Pontificalis* and wrote *Origines du Culte chrétien*, endured bitter attacks for his critical attitude toward conventional legends that had little or no basis in historical fact.[52] To the same era belong Ferdinand Probst (1816–99) in Germany and Edmund Bishop (1846–1917) in England.[53]

Major inheritors of this tradition of close historical work were Anton Baumstark (1872–1948), Hans Lietzmann (1875–1942), Gregory Dix (1901–52), and the encyclopedists Fernand Cabrol (1855–1937) and Henri Leclercq (1869–1945) who were mainly responsible for the great reference work *Dictionnaire d'archéologie chrétienne et de liturgie* (1903–53). Each of these scholars produced large bodies of work (Baumstark alone 546 items), but each is remembered for a seminal work that has since been regarded as monumental for the discipline. On method, Baumstark's *Liturgie comparée* (1940) called for comparing Western and Eastern rites in order to perceive common underlying structures.[54] Lietzmann's *Messe und Herrenmahl* is the most erudite and sustained study of the Christian eucharist yet written, first appearing in 1926 and finally in English in 1979 less as a book than as a body of continually revised research published in fascicules.[55] Not nearly attaining to the erudition of Lietzmann, Gregory Dix's treatment of the eucharist, *The Shape of the Liturgy* (1945), made liturgical scholarship brilliantly available to popular readership, especially in England and America, and may well be regarded as the most influential piece of liturgical writing by an Anglican during this century.[56] Less successful on the scholarly level were Dix's writings on confirmation[57] and eucharistic reservation.[58] The latter work was destroyed by criticism[59] but the former still exercizes some influence to this day.

One other scholar deserves mention in the context of historical studies: Josef Andreas Jungmann. His works were widely influential throughout Europe, England, and America due to their wide translation into English, especially *Die Stellung Christi im liturgischen Gebet* (1925)[60] and the masterful *Missarum Sollemnia: Eine genetische Erklärung der römischen Messe* (1949),[61] which gave definitive shape to studies in the sources of the Roman eucharist. *Missarum Sollemnia* in particular demonstrated conclusively that no liturgical system can adequately be grasped without first recovering its sources and then putting them in historical perspective. For a liturgical system as ancient and varied as the Roman, this has been a long effort stretching back, as noted, into the Renaissance. In the light of Jungmann's work, the same sort of effort has been undertaken for the Byzantine liturgical system by his Jesuit colleagues at the Pontifical Institute of Oriental Studies in Rome. The institute's long-standing series of monographs (*Orientalia Christiana Analecta*) and papers (*Orientalia Christiana Periodica*) publish its research not only on Byzantine[62] but also other Eastern Christian liturgical systems.[63] Thus for Eastern Christian worship and allied matters, the Oriental Institute, not yet generally well known in this country, is becoming a focal point for such studies and of deep exumenical importance.

Although historical studies do not remove all difficulties or answer fully all questions touching liturgical worship, they at least tell us with some clarity where we have been and what has been done or not done in the past. History cleanly done does not allow theological interpreters to fantasize the past for polemical purposes. A well-laid-out body of historical facts also provides a framework for discussing further problems in the present. So far as Christian liturgy is concerned, two other problematic pressures in addition to the historical have been the nature of symbolic discourse and the general anthropology of ritual behavior.

The nature of symbolic discourse has been a liturgical problem that churches in the modern era have had among themselves, where it has assumed strongly theological dimensions, and that those same churches have had with their secular milieux, where it has been cast in a more philosophical mold. How one discourses symbolically, and to what purpose, is an issue forced to a critical point by the development of other forms of modern discourse such as those employed by the natural sciences and, more recently, by certain types of political critique, namely revolutionary dialectic and its offspring, revisionist "scholarship." These forms of discourse, when combined with the genial materialism of consumer economics, have called into question on the most fundamental level whether symbolic discourse is useful beyond, perhaps, therapeutic contexts such as those elaborated by Freud and Jung. These contexts, it may be worth noting, are personal, individual, and largely subjective—characteristics that secular societies increasingly require religion of whatever sort to assume.[64] What results from all this is a social presumption that a literalist and revisionist discourse is the *lingua franca* of human affairs, best expressed in amassed statistics whose interpretation is governed by largely politicized ideology. This social presumption concerning the nature of public discourse is, of course, inimical not only to religion but to culture and all their combined aspects—artistic, literary, political, theological, philosophical, and liturgical.

Christian thinkers began to sense this shift as secular absolutist states began to establish themselves in Europe after the French Revolution. As already noted, nineteenth-century writers like Möhler, Newman, and Pusey, and reformers like Guéranger, turned their attention to giving the social masses easier and more vital access to the vast symbolic reservoir represented in their cultural and religious heritage through restoration of their liturgical worship, a worship intended to build up civil society no less than the churches. Hence the social concern that has accompanied liturgical reform since its pastoral phase began almost a century ago.[65] Hence also the work of Löhe, Nevin, and Schaff in the nineteenth century; of Beauduin, Michel, and the Second Vatican Council in this century.

J. A. Möhler's *Symbolik* raised the matter of symbolic discourse in broad theological terms as early as 1832, as we have seen, and in 1846 J. W. Nevin elaborated a post-Kantian view of symbolic discourse applied to the eucharist in *The Mystical Presence*, a work that lay at the heart of the Mercersburg Theology and its thrust toward liturgical reform. On a broader plane, Rudolf Otto (1869–1937), following the general directions of Schleiermacher, raised the category of the "holy" in symbolic discourse in his *Das Heilige* (1917).[66] But perhaps the boldest address of the matter in strictly liturgical and sacramental terms has been the controversial work of Dom Odo Casel (1886–1948) in what he called "theology of Mysteries" (*Mysteriengegenwarttheologie*), meaning that Christ the great sacrament or *mysterium* continues to be present to save in the church through the liturgy.[67] This approach gave a new twist to Roman Catholic sacramental theology, represented in the influential book of E. Schillebeeckx, *Christ the Sacrament of the Encounter with God* (1963).[68] In a more generally philosophical context the problem of symbolic discourse has been addressed by Paul Ricoeur[69] and by Mircea Eliade in a context of the history of religions.[70]

More specifically liturgical addresses of the problem of symbolic discourse have tended to separate into two modes, both theologically orientated, which I would call "mystagogical" and "systematic." The mystagogical type generally tends to expound the liturgy from within the received structures and symbolisms themselves, emphasizing their internal grammar and seeking their own native coherence. This literary genre has a long and durable history, reaching back to the explanatory sermons of what had occurred in baptism preached to the newly baptized by Cyril of Jerusalem, John Chrysostom, Ambrose, and others in the fourth century. These developed into more extensive commentaries on the liturgy, particularly the eucharist, usually composed by bishops, in both East and West—commentaries that became the standard mode of understanding the liturgy throughout the medieval period.[71] The purpose of liturgical mystagogies, present no less than past, has been not to analyze or speculate but to reflect upon, explain, and commend the liturgy to those who participate in it either actually or by desire. Romano Guardini's *Spirit of the Liturgy* (1930), Louis Bouyer's *Liturgical Piety* (1955), Alexander Schmemann's *Introduction to Liturgical Theology* (1967), and my own *On Liturgical Theology* (1984) represent this genre in different modern styles and from different points of view.[72]

Systematic theological studies of the liturgy, on the other hand, tend to analyze and interpret content as expressed in liturgical texts, and to do this from a stance that is usually taken up outside the liturgical tradition being analyzed. These studies frequently view the liturgy *in globo* rather than as a congeries of distinct and sometimes differing ritual languages whose very differences contain flashes of insight no less than do their frequent samenesses. Such studies increasingly adapt methodologies generated elsewhere in modern academia and bring them to bear on liturgical texts, producing results that have little or no basis in any or some of the traditions under analysis. What such studies necessarily do is interpret the liturgy in general according to methods native to academia for audiences ecumenical and ministerial that are in closest proximity to, and dependent on, the academy. These audiences are prone to translate such studies into actual liturgical events that are synthetic, even syncretistic, largely verbal, rather antiseptic, and often ideologically charged, representing no particular community of faith but giving most of them brief moments of euchological "equal time" in respect of ecumenical fairness.

The advantage of such studies is that they can often bring into sharp focus certain doctrinal themes and shifts that may not be noticed by worshipers deeply involved in a particular liturgical tradition. Methods of analysis native to academia can also afford historical perspective to largely ahistorical participation in received liturgical rites and to mystagogical commentary on the same rites. But such studies never justify liturgical endeavors, nor do they make them possible except in an evanescent and synthetic mode. This is so because the urge to worship proceeds from a response of faith to religious revelation, not from intellectual agreement with systematizing liturgical and theological data. Yet system can certainly assure and clarify the habit of worshiping for those who need such clarity and assurance. This in itself is an important, if somewhat limited, pastoral function such studies may perform. Two of the most significant systematic theological studies of liturgy current are C. Vagaggini's *Theological Dimensions of the Liturgy* (1976) and Geoffrey Wainwright's *Doxology* (1980).[73]

A general anthropology of ritual behavior, although it does not yet exist in full form, was called for in a work specifically devoted to liturgical study first by Ernest B. Koenker in 1954.[74] Yet serious address of ritual behavior goes back at least to Arnold van Gennep's trailblazing work on rituals of passage at the beginning of this century,[75] and to Emile Durkheim beginning somewhat later.[76] In the 1950s anthropologists such as Lévi-Strauss and Geertz,[77] along with sociologists such as Erving Goffman and Peter Berger,[78] began to relate their disciplines to the study of religion and its ritual functions. Specifically regarding ritual phenomena, the papers of the Royal Society of London on ritualization among animals and humans, which appeared in 1966,[79] were a stimulus to further investigations by such well-known and religiously sympathetic anthropologists as Victor Turner and Mary Douglas.[80] This growing body of work made it possible to hold an initial conference on liturgy as ritual at the University of Notre Dame and the publication in 1973 of nine of the papers delivered there.[81] This and subsequent literature has begun to be given taxonomic form by Ronald L. Grimes,[82] and a new *Journal of Ritual Studies*, sponsored by the University of Pittsburgh's Department of Religious Studies, began publication in 1986.

Although anthropological findings concerning the genus ritual, of which liturgy is a species, are now generally acknowledged by liturgical scholars in this hemisphere (less so, perhaps, in Europe), few yet work consciously in the *anthropology* underlying their craft. This may be due to the long-standing gravitational pull of the more classical modes of liturgical study such as history and theology. It also has something to do with the concern, during the recent decades of liturgical reform, with practical matters of commending changes, and of making changes that were commendable, to various ecclesiastical constituencies with identifiable statistical standings. Writers who address themselves especially to the latter concern can sometimes be found referring to one or another work on ritual anthropology. But such references are more often than not extrinsic and made in passing. They rarely exhibit much more than a superficial awareness of the methods or concerns that have produced the results cited. And the more ideological the essay commending this or that reform, the more difficulty is found with anthropological results, which often recommend caution, patience, continuity, repetition, and other characteristics an ideology of liberalization in liturgical usage finds illiberal or "conservative."[83]

This is unfortunate because some knowledge of anthropology can, as Koenker suggested in 1954, help connect liturgical studies with other areas that with increasing frequency are seen to be involved in or in competition with regular liturgical behavior in churches—areas such as the rituals of secular society and civil religion, not to say the small and intricate ritual patterns each individual constructs in order to shape reality for one's responses to it, particularly during certain crucial phases of life.[84] Enriching the anthropological dimension in liturgical studies seems an important way of helping those studies avoid lapsing into the strategic infecundity of historicism or theologism on the one hand, or of a highly ideologized advocacy for constant reform on the other. Liturgy, like ritual and even codes of belief, can stand only certain kinds of reform in certain quantities and at a certain speed before it modulates into some other sort of endeavor.[85]

Conclusion

This essay began by noting the massive reforms in liturgical worship that have been undertaken by Western churches in recent years. The studies that have made these reforms possible began with the Renaissance and expanded rapidly after the Reformation and Counter-Reformation had set in. Early liturgical scholars were obsessed with resourcement not because they were antiquarians but because the polemical atmosphere of the times made the search for precedent and continuity a requisite for claiming integrity in usage against attacks by opponents.

Although this effort began in apologetics, as sources were recovered and as methodologies were invented to handle what had been recovered liturgical studies gradually moved away from theological interpretation and became more rigorously historical. These studies discovered a greater richness and diversity in the liturgical traditions of both East and West than had previously been imagined, something that slowly began to moderate overwrought theological claims on both sides of the sixteenth-century Western schism.

With the advent of the Enlightenment and its increasingly absolutist states, followed by the political and technological revolutions of the nineteenth and early twentieth centuries, the Western churches faced crises of survival for which history alone could not provide all the answers. To avoid losing the masses, the liturgy had to be restored as a reservoir and catalyst of Christian values more easily accessible to ordinary people. This implied liturgical reform beginning first with repristinization and simplification. But such a reform could not go very far without a new and more sympathetic theology that would go quite beyond what Reform and Counter-Reform had in place. Credal and liturgical studies began to dance cheek to cheek, and a vast new ecumenical consensus on church and worship slowly evolved along with a deepening sense of social concern. The consensus converged on liturgy not as something separate from church and society but as the place where both regularly intersect in an act that is deeply symbolic and effective for its participants. Nevin and Schaff, no less than Möhler, Pusey, Newman, Guéranger, and Löhe, perceived this in their own times. So did the Second Vatican Council, when it took up as its first matter of business a Constitution on the Sacred Liturgy, *Sacrosanctum Concilium* (1963), a document that triggered reforms in Roman Catholic worship that in their depth and extent are unparalleled in the history of the church. These in turn encouraged other Western churches to similar boldness in reform.

Historical studies have been at the core of all this, as have studies in the nature of symbolic discourse both philosophical and theological. Systematic theology has begun to clarify the results of such study, and the ancient genre of mystagogy has been revived to expound liturgical content in a manner more congenial to modern perception. Finally, a potentially fruitful cross-fertilization between anthropological work on ritual behavior and liturgical studies has recently begun. Centers for the formal academic study of liturgy on the graduate level now exist at the University of Notre Dame; St. John's University, Collegeville, Minnesota; the Catholic University of America in Washington, DC; and at Drew University in New Jersey. Two major professional organizations of liturgical scholars have been formed, the North American Academy of Liturgy and Societas Liturgica.[86]

In addition to the anthropological dimensions of liturgy, three other areas of research seem to need emphasis by modern scholars in the discipline. First, the study of non-Western Christian liturgies is seriously under-represented among liturgical scholars in this country. This is not only ecumenically unfortunate but also produces a parochial outlook among scholars and restricts their knowledge and vision to Western forms, making comparative liturgical studies difficult if not impossible. No competent liturgical scholar can afford to know only one liturgical system any more than an architect can afford to know only draftsmanship but not engineering or mathematics. Furthermore, many of the forms such a scholar studies in fact originate in Eastern liturgical systems, only later to be adopted in the West, and in their native environment carry on an often different life of their own to this day. From this divergence comparative liturgics can learn much about how what it studies functions at the deepest level.[87] Second, studying the genesis of Christian liturgical forms in late Judaism has hardly begun, and no Christian scholar has yet come close to the originality of J. Heinemann's *Prayer in the Talmud: Forms and Patterns* (1977)[88] or L. Hoffman's *Canonization of the Synagogue Service* (1979). Third, close internal analysis of the origin and often confusing growth of individual liturgical units on their own terms and without later theological a priori reasoning needs to be more frequently done. Rather than force anachronistic concerns on liturgical origins, one must ask the various families of rites East and West themselves to tell us what, say, the anointings in baptism are there to do, what the many and extensive dismissals one finds in early liturgies exist for and how they affect the divisions within a service, and what "confirmation" originally was in the West and how it came to be altered and reinterpreted during and after the fifth century, leading to confusion in the twentieth.[89]

The agenda for scientific liturgical studies is by no means over. After the reforms of the past generation, indeed, questions not previously forseen have arisen and the agenda has expanded rather than shrunk. Liturgics is a much more interdisciplinary field demanding greater erudition and discipline than ever before.

Notes

1. The frequent explanation of *leitourgia* as always meaning a work done *by* the people is mistaken. The term originated in secular Greek to denote a public service or utility done by an individual, such as endowing a theater, keeping up a section of roadway, or paying taxes. In the last sense it is used by Aristotle *(Politics* 7.9.7) of a people's obligation to the gods, a sense known also by the Septuagint (Numbers 8:25) and applied in rabbinical literature to the synagogue service. *Leitourgia* used in this way is best translated as Divine Service. See "Liturgies," *The Westminster Dictionary of Church History* (Philadelphia: Westminster Press, 1971), 504–6.

2. Medieval treatises entitled *De Divinis Officiis* are thus not commentaries solely on the liturgy of the hours but on the liturgy generally, in particular on the eucharist.

3. *Writings and Disputations of Thomas Cranmer, Archbishop of Canterbury, Martyr 1556, relative to the Sacrament of the Lord's Supper,* ed. J. E. Cox (Cambridge: Parker Society, 1844), 429.

4. In its final session, Trent turned the execution of these reforms over to the papacy on the understanding that the guiding principle of the work would be not to change the liturgy according to theological principles but to restore it *ad pristinam orandi regulam* or *ad pristinam sanctorum Patrum normam.* See P. Jounel, "La réforme liturgique suscitée par Le Concile de Trente (1562–1614)," in *L'Eglise en Prière,* ed. A. G. Martimort (Paris: Desclée, 1961), 43–7.

5. J. A. Santori, *Rituale sacramentorum Romanum* (Rome ca. 1584). See B. Löwenberg, *Das Rituale der Kardinals Julius Antonius Sanctorius: Ein Beitrag zur Entstehungsgeschichte des Rituale Romanum* (Munich, 1937).

6. G. Cassander, *Liturgica de ritu et ordine dominicae coenae quam celebrationem Graeci liturgiam, Latini missam appelarunt* (1558); Jacques de Joigny "Pamelius," *Liturgica latinorum,* 2 vols. (Cologne, 1571). Also C. de Sainctes, *Liturgiae sive missae sanctorum patrum, etc.* (Anvers, 1562); M. Hittorp, *De catholicae ecclesiae divinis officiis* (1591). See J. P. Dolan, *The Influence of Erasmus, Witzel, and Cassander in the Church Ordinances and Reform Proposals . . . of the 16th Century* (Münster: Aschendorff, 1957).

7. G. Bona, *Rerum liturgicarum libri duo* (Rome, 1671).

8. J. Mabillon, *Musaeum Italicum,* 2 vols. (Paris, 1687, 1689), and *De Re Diplomatica* (Paris, 1681); E. Martène, *De antiquis ecclesiae ritibus libri tres* (Rouen, 1700).

9. L. Muratori, *Liturgia Romana vetus* (Rome, 1748).

10. G. Tommasi, *Responsoralia et antiphonaria Romanae ecclesiae* in his *Opera Omnia,* vol. 4 (Rome, 1749), 330ff.

11. Mansi was mainly an editor and organizer of the work of others. Nonetheless the great collections of conciliar and patristic texts bearing his name contain much liturgical material that continue to be useful even in the present century.

12. See S. J. P. van Dijk and J. Hazelden Walker, *The Origins of the Modern Roman Liturgy* (Westminster, MD: Newman Press, 1960).

13. This attitude informs and is given brilliant exposition across a larger front by Ramsay MacMullen, *Christianizing the Roman Empire: A.D. 100–400* (New Haven: Yale University Press, 1984).

14. W. Jardine Grisbrooke, *Anglican Liturgies of the Seventeenth and Eighteenth Centuries*, Alcuin Club Collection 40 (SPCK, London 1958). Also H. B. Porter, *Jeremy Taylor Liturgist (1613–1667)* (London: Alcuin Club/SPCK, 1979).

15. The absence of such a taxonomy is what led Mattheus Flacius Illyricus, the Lutheran theologian and scholar (1520–75), to categorize a Mass text he discovered as a most antique Western liturgy from which the Roman liturgy had departed and degenerated. In fact, the text and the liturgy it contains is eleventh century, probably from Minden in Westphalia, representing a local variant of Roman usage. For the "Missa Illyrica," see n. 50, below.

16. Centered from 1833 on John Keble (1792–1866), Edward Bouverie Pusey (1800–82), and John Henry Newman (1801–90), about whom the literature is vast and increasing.

17. Centered on Nikolai Grundtvig (1783–1872), and not without effects on Soren Kierkegaard (1813–55). See A. M. Allchin, "Grundtvig: An English Appreciation," *Worship* 58 (1984): 420–33; *N. F. S. Grundtvig, Tradition and Renewal*, ed. C. Thodberg and A. P. Thyssen (Philadelphia: Nordic Books, 1983).

18. Centered on Johann Adam Möhler (1796–1838) of Tübingen, and especially on his book *Symbolik, oder Darstellung der dogmatischen Gegensatze der Katholiken und Protestanten nach ihren öftentlichen Bekenntisschriften* (1832; English trans. 1843). On the context, see Thomas F. O'Meara, "The Origins of the Liturgical Movement and German Romanticism," *Worship* 59 (1985): 326–42.

19. The restored monastery of St. Pierre at Solesmes, near Paris, was opened in 1833 by Prosper Guéranger (1805–75). Solesmes soon became the continental center of monastic and liturgical renewal, Guéranger himself contributing to the latter with his *Institutions Liturgiques*, 3 vols. (1840–51), and *L'Année Liturgique*, 9 vols. (1841–66). See B. Capelle, "Dom Guéranger et l'esprit liturgique," *Les Questions liturgiques et paroissiales* 22 (1937): 131–46. The attack on Guéranger by Louis Bouyer, *Liturgical Piety* (University of Notre Dame Press, 1955), has been seriously questioned by R. W. Franklin in a series of articles in *Worship* 49 (1975): 318–28; 50 (1976): 146–62; 51 (1977): 378–99; 53 (1979): 12–39.

20. Under Solesmes' influence other monasteries took up similar work: Beuron and Maria Laach in Germany, Maredsous in Belgium with its famous Irish abbot Columba Marmion, and at Buckfast in England under Abbot Ansgar Vonier. On this monastic dimension see R. W. Franklin, "Humanism and

Transcendence in the Nineteenth Century Liturgical Movement," *Worship* 59 (1985): 342–53.

21. In the encyclical *Aeterni Patris*, 4 August 1879.

22. In the enclyclical *Providentissimus Deus*, 18 November 1893.

23. In the "motu proprio" *Tra le sollecitudini*, 22 November 1903, the feast day of St. Cecilia, patron saint of musicians.

24. See *Official Catholic Teachings: Worship and Liturgy*, ed. J. Megivern (Wilmington, NC: Consortium-McGrath, 1978). For a reprise of the ideology concerning liturgical music which developed from 1903 until the Second Vatican Council, see J. Gelineau, *Voices and Instruments in Christian Worship*, trans. C. Howell (Collegeville, MN: Liturgical Press, 1964). For problems latent in this ideology, which became evident after the council, see *Crisis in Church Music* (Washington, DC: Liturgical Conference, 1967).

25. See Theodor Filthaut, *Learning to Worship*, trans. Ronald Wells (London: Burns and Oates, 1965), 33–34.

26. See Louis Bouyer, *Liturgical Piety* (University of Notre Dame Press, 1955), 58–64; *Lambert Beauduin, un homme d'Eglise* (Paris: Casterman, 1964).

27. See *The Study of Liturgy*, ed. C. Jones, G. Wainwright, and E. Yarnold (New York: Oxford Unviersity Press, 1978), 38. Also, more fully, *L'Eglise en Prière*, ed. A. G. Martimort (Paris: Desclée, 1961), 52–53; O. Rousseau, *Histoire du movement liturgique. Esquisse historique depuis le début du XIXᵉ siècle jusqu'au pontificat de Pie X* (Paris: Editions du Cerf, 1945); H. Schmidt, *Introductio in Liturgiam Occidentalem* (Rome: Herder, 1960) 164–208, with good bibliography. An excellent study by a Lutheran scholar is E. B. Koenker, *The Liturgical Renaissance in the Roman Catholic Church* (University of Chicago Press, 1954). Guéranger was the first to use the phrase "liturgical movement" in *Institutions Liturgiques*, vol. 3 (Paris, 1851).

28. The books were published together in English as *The Church and the Catholic and the Spirit of the Liturgy* (New York: Sheed and Ward, 1935); *The Spirit of the Liturgy* (New York: Benziger, 1931).

29. Michel was closely associated with Peter Maurin, Dorothy Day, and the Catholic Worker movement. Its paper, *The Catholic Worker*, Michel called "an excellent apology for the liturgical revival and its efforts to bring the liturgy into the lives of *all* Catholics"; *Orate Fratres* 8 (1934): 277. See Paul B. Marx, *Virgil Michel and the Liturgical Movement* (Collegeville, MN: Liturgical Press, 1957); Jeremy Hall, *The Full Stature of Christ: The Ecclesiology of Virgil Michel, O.S.B.* (Collegeville, MN: Liturgical Press, 1976); Aidan Kavanagh "Spirituality in the American Church: An Evaluative Essay," in *Contemporary Catholicism in the United States*, ed. Philip Gleason (University of Notre Dame Press, 1969), 197–214, esp. 210–13.

30. See Jeremy Hall, *The Full Stature of Christ*, 3–12.

31. Ibid., 12–21. Leo XIII and his successors gave this reunion work particularly to Benedictine monks in the foundation of the international college of

Sant'Anselmo at Rome in 1887 and, later, in backing Beauduin's own monastic foundation of Amay in Belgium in 1925, later moved to Chevetogne, and its review *Irenikon*.

32. For a résumé see Hall, 154–64; Paul B. Marx, *The Life and Work of Virgil Michel*, 380–81.

33. The literature on the modern ecumenical movement is immense. Major works on its inception and ideology are *Union of Christendom*, ed. K. D. MacKenzie (London: SPCK, 1938); M. J. Congar, *Chrétiens dèsunis* [1937], English trans. *Divided Christendom* (London: G. Bles, 1939); H. R. T. Brandreth, *Unity and Reunion: A Bibliography* (London: A. and C. Black, 1945); G. K. A. Bell, *Documents on Christian Unity* (London: Oxford University Press, 1948); R. M. Brown, *The Ecumenical Revolution* (Garden City, NY: Doubleday, 1967); *A History of the Ecumenical Movement, 1517–1948*, ed. R. Rouse and S. C. Neill (Philadelphia: Westminster Press, 1967); *A History of the Ecumenical Movement II, 1948–1968*, ed. H. E. Fey (Philadelphia: Westminster Press, 1967–70) 2 vols.

34. *Baptism, Eucharist, Ministry*, Faith and Order Paper 111 (Geneva: W.C.C., 1982). This statement was preceded by *One Baptism, One Eucharist, and a Mutually Recognized Ministry*, Faith and Order Paper 73 (Geneva: W.C.C., 1978).

35. See R. W. Franklin, "Humanism and Transcendence in the Nineteenth Century Liturgical Movement," *Worship* 59 (1985): 347.

36. J. A. Möhler, "Ueber die neueste Bekampfung der katholischen Kirche," *Gesammelte Schriften* 2 (Regensburg, 1839–40) 229; quoted by R. W. Franklin, "Humanism and Transcendence," 347.

37. Thus Franklin, "Humanism and Transcendence," 348.

38. See Thomas H. Schattauer, "Sunday Worship at Neuendettelsau under Wilhelm Löhe," *Worship* 59 (1985): 370–84.

39. See *Wilhelm Löhe: Three Books about the Church*, trans. James L. Schaaf (Philadelphia: Fortress Press, 1969), 152–55; Schattauer, "Sunday Worship," 373.

40. The principal orders are in Löhe's *Gesammelte Werke* 7:1 and 2, ed. Klaus Gansert (Neuendettelsau: Freimund, 1953), in particular his *Agende für christliche Gemeinden des lutherishen Bekentnisses*, 1844, 1853–59; Schattauer, "Sunday Worship," 373.

41. Schattauer, "Sunday Worship," 383. See *William Löhe: Three Books about the Church*, 48–51.

42. *Three Books*, 57–61, 92–96.

43. Schattauer, "Sunday Worship," 384.

44. *Three Books*, 177.

45. The attitudes of Schaff and Nevin on worship have been thoroughly analyzed and put in their European and American context by Nathan Mitchell, "Church, Eucharist, and Liturgical Reform at Mercersburg: 1843–1857" (Ph.D. diss., University of Notre Dame, 1978). See also Jack M. Maxwell, *Worship and*

Reformed Theology: The Liturgical Lessons of Mercersburg (Pittsburgh: Pickwick Press, 1976); the two studies of James H. Nichols, *Romanticism in American Theology: Nevin and Schaff at Mercersburg* (University of Chicago Press, 1961), and *Corporate Worship in the Reformed Tradition* (Philadelphia: Westminster Press, 1968).

46. John W. Nevin, *The Mystical Presence* [1846]. ed. B. Thompson and G. H. Bricker, Lancaster series on the Mercersburg Theology, vol. 4 (Philadelphia: United Church Press, 1966).

47. Nathan Mitchell, 637. The same tendency can be seen among English Congregationalists in the second half of the nineteenth century. See Horton Davies, *Worship and Theology in England, 1850–1900* (Princeton, 1962); B. Spinks, "The Liturgical Revival amongst Nineteenth-Century English Congregationalists," *Studia Liturgica* 15 (1982-83): 178–87.

48. Mitchel, 633–34. Philip Schaff, *What Is Church History?* trans. J. W. Nevin (Philadelphia: J. Lippincott, 1846); *The History of the Apostolic Church*, trans. E. D. Yeomans (New York: Scribner, 1853).

49. See David W. Lotz, "Philip Schaff's Idea of Church History," chap. 1 in this volume.

50. The text is in E. Martène, *De Antiquis Ecclesiae Ritibus* vol. 1 (Rouen, 1700), 481–513; J. P. Migne, *Patrologia Latina*, vol. 138, cols. 1305–36.

51. Batiffol published, in addition to numerous works on church history, the first scholarly study on the Roman breviary, *Histoire du Bréviaire romain* (Freiburg im Br., 1895), subsequently expanded in 1905 and 1911.

52. *Liber Pontificalis: texte, introduction et commentaire*, 2 vols. (Paris, 1886 and 1892); *Origines du Culte chrétien. Etude sur la liturgie latine avant Charlemagne* (Paris, 1889). Duchesne and Battifol together should be regarded as the founders of modern scientific historical study of Christian worship. In this they gave shape to gathering momentum in France, Germany, and especially Italy, where the first liturgical journal, *Ephemerides Liturgicae* began publication in 1887 and has lasted until today. See Enrico Cattaneo, *Il culto cristiano in occidente: Note storiche* (Rome: C. L. V. Edizioni Liturgiche, 1984), 452–86.

53. Probst published voluminously on early liturgies from 1870 to 1896. Bishop was a self-taught layman who was the main initiator of scientific liturgical studies in English. His essay on "The Genius of the Roman Rite" (1899) is still quoted and can be found in the collection of his papers, *Liturgica Historia* (Oxford, 1918). A younger collaborator, Richard Hugh Connolly (1873–1948), established the Hippolytan authorship of the Apostolic Tradition in *The So-Called Egyptian Church Order* (1916), edited the *Didascalia Apostolorum* (1929), and showed Ambrose as author of *De Sacramentis* (1942).

54. Anton Baumstark, *Liturgie comparée: Principes et methodes pour l'étude historique des liturgies chrétiennes* (Chevetogne, 1940). New edition by Bernard Botte 1953, translated into English by F. L. Cross 1958.

55. The English is probably the fullest edition: *Mass and Lord's Supper: A Study in the History of the Liturgy*, trans. Dorothea H. G. Reeve with introduction and supplementary essay by R. D. Richardson (Leiden: E. J. Brill, 1979).

56. Gregory Dix, *The Shape of the Liturgy* (London: Dacre Press, 1945). See Kenneth W. Stevenson, *Gregory Dix: Twenty-five Years On* (Bramcote, Nottinghamshire: Grove Books, 1977) esp. 23–35.

57. Gregory Dix, *Confirmation or Laying on of Hands* (London: SPCK, 1936); *Theology of Confirmation in Relation to Baptism* (London: Dacre Press, 1946). Dix's notion that confirmation adds the Holy Spirit to baptism led him, typically, to force evidence in his edition of *The Treatise on the Apostolic Tradition of St. Hippolytus of Rome* (London: SPCK, 1937), 2d ed. Henry Chadwick, ed. (1968). This elicited a closely argued response by G. W. H. Lampe, *The Seal of the Spirit. A Study in the Doctrine of Baptism and Confirmation in the New Testament and the Fathers* (London: SPCK, 1967). See Kenneth W. Stevenson, 4–10. Better than Dix's edition of Hippolytus is Bernard Botte's *La Tradition Apostolique du Saint Hippolyte* (Münster: Aschendorff, 1963), and the best study of its origins is J. M. Hanssens, *La liturgie d'Hippolyte* (Rome: Pontifical Oriental Institute, 1959).

58. Gregory Dix, *A Detection of Aumbries* (London: Dacre Press, 1942).

59. S. J. P. Van Dijk and J. H. Walker, *The Myth of the Aumbry* (London: Burns and Oates, 1957). See Kenneth W. Stevenson, *Gregory Dix*, 20–22.

60. (Münster, Aschendorff), 2d German ed., 1962, translated into English as *The Place of Christ in Liturgical Prayer* (London: G. Chapman, 1965).

61. (Vienna, Herder), 2 vols.; 5th ed. 1962, English trans. *The Mass of the Roman Rite: Its Origins and Development*, by Francis A. Brunner, 2 vols. (New York: Benziger, 1950, 1955).

62. Of particular interest are the monographs which will do for the Byzantine eucharistic liturgy roughly what Jungmann's work did for the Roman: J. Mateos, *Célébration de la Parôle dans la liturgie byzantine* (Rome: OCA 191, Pontifical Oriental Institute, 1971), dealing with the fore-mass; R. Taft, *The Great Entrance. A History of the Transfer of Gifts and Other Pre-Anaphoral Rites of the Liturgy of St. John Chrysostom* (Rome: OCA 200, Pontifical Oriental Institute, 1975), dealing with preparations for the eucharistic prayer. A final study of the last section of the service, including the eucharistic prayer and communion, is now in preparation by Taft.

63. Notable are S. Y. H. Jammo, *La structure de la messe chaldéene du début jusq'à l'anaphore. Etude historique* (Rome: OCA 201, Pontifical Oriental Institute, 1979); G. Winkler, *Das Armenische Initiationsrituale. Entwicklungsgeschichtliche und liturgievergleichende Untersuchung der Quellen des 3. bis 10. Jahrhunderts* (Rome: OCA 217, Pontifical Oriental Institute, 1982).

64. This privatization of religion has most recently been noted by Richard John Neuhaus, *The Naked Public Square: Religion and Democracy in America* (Grand

Rapids, MI: Eerdmans, 1984), and by myself in *On Liturgical Theology* (New York: Pueblo Publishing, 1984).

65. See e.g., the essays in *Liturgical Foundations of Social Policy in the Catholic and Jewish Traditions*, ed. Daniel F. Polish and Eugene J. Fisher (University of Notre Dame Press, 1983). Also my own "The Politics of Symbol and Art in Liturgical Expression," in *Symbol and Art in Worship*, ed. Louis Maldonado and David Power, Concilium series 132 (New York: Seabury, 1980), 28–39.

66. English trans., *The Idea of the Holy*, by John W. Harvey [1923] (London: Oxford University Press, 1950).

67. Casel's main works are *Das christliche Kult Mysterium* (Regensburg: Pustet, 1960); English trans., *The Mystery of Christian Worship* (Westminster, MD: Newman Press, 1962); and *Mysterium der Ekklesia* (Mainz: Matthias-Grünewald, 1961). Both these works are in fact collections of essays and lectures, updated and rewritten, extending back to 1924. The best overview of the controversies generated by Casel's work is Theodore Filthaut, *Die Kontroverse über die Mysterienlehre* (Warendorf, 1947). A full bibliography of Casel is in *Vom christlichen Mysterium*, ed. A. Mayer, J. Quasten, B. Neunheuser (Düsseldorf: Patmos Verlag, 1951), 363–75, running to 211 titles.

68. (New York: Sheed and Ward, 1960). This is a partial translation of the first part of *De sacramentele Heilseconomie* (1952), which draws also on Heidegger, Merleau-Ponty, and others.

69. Paul Ricoeur, "Structure-Word-Event," *Philosophy Today* 4 (1960): 196–207; *The Symbolism of Evil* (Boston: Beacon Press, 1967); *Interpretation Theory: Discourse and the Surplus of Meaning* (Fort Worth: Texas Christian University Press, 1976).

70. E.g., Mircea Eliade, *Birth and Rebirth: The Religious Meanings of Initiation in Human Culture*, trans. W. R. Trask (New York: Harper and Row, 1958); *Cosmos and History: The Myth of the Eternal Return*, trans. W. R. Trask (New York: Harper and Row, 1959); *Images and Symbols*, trans. P. Mairet (New York: Sheed and Ward, 1961); *Rites and Symbols of Initiation*, trans. W. R. Trask (New York: Harper and Row, 1965).

71. The main such commentary in the East was that of Patriarch Germanus of Constantinople (ca. 730), preceded by the *Mystagogy* of Maximus Confessor (ca. 630) and followed by the commentary of Nicholas Cabasilas (ca. 1350) representing the final synthesis of Byzantine practice and understanding. See R. Bornert, *Les commentaires byzantins de la Divine Liturgie du VII au XV siecle* (Paris: Archives de l'Orient chrétien 9, 1966); R. Taft, "The Liturgy of the Great Church: An Initial Synthesis of Structure and Interpretation on the Eve of Iconoclasm," *Dumbarton Oaks Papers* 34/35 (1982): 45–75.

The most influential western commentary was that of Amalarius of Metz (ca. 780–850). See *Amalarii, Opera Omnia Liturgica*, ed. J. M. Hanssens, 3 vols. (Rome, 1948–50).

72. For Guardini see n. 28. Louis Bouyer, *Liturgical Piety* [British title *Life and Liturgy*] (University of Notre Dame Press, 1955); Alexander Schmemann. *Introduction to Liturgical Theology* (Portland, ME: American Orthodox Press, 1966); Aidan Kavanagh, *On Liturgical Theology* (New York: Pueblo Publishing, 1984).

73. C. Vagaggini, *Theological Dimensions of the Liturgy* 2 vols. (Collegeville, MN: Liturgical Press, 1976), Geoffrey Wainwright, *Doxology: The Praise of God in Worship, Doctrine, and Life* (New York: Oxford University Press, 1980).

74. Ernest Benjamin Koenker, *The Liturgical Renaissance in the Roman Catholic Church* (University of Chicago Press, 1954). This remarkable book by a Lutheran scholar provides a wide-ranging look at the origins and state of the liturgical movement in Roman Catholicism prior to the Second Vatican Council. In view of its prognosis for the future, it is even more interesting to read now, a generation later.

75. Arnold van Gennep, *The Rites of Passage* [1909], trans. M. B. Vizedom and G. L. Caffee (University of Chicago Press, 1960). See Max Gluckman, "Les Rites de Passage," *Essays on the Ritual of Social Relations*, ed. Max Gluckman and C. D. Forde (Manchester University Press, 1962), 1–52. Van Gennep's distinction of rites of passage into phases of separation, liminality, and incorporation has been influential on the work of Victor Turner, e.g., "Passages, Margins, and Poverty: Religious Symbols of Communitas," *Worship* 46 (1972): 390–412, 482–94. Also Urban T. Holmes, "Liminality and Liturgy," *Worship* 47 (1973): 386–99.

76. Emile Durkheim, *The Elementary Forms of the Religious Life* [1915], trans. J. W. Swain (New York: Free Press, 1963).

77. E.g., Claude Lévi-Strauss, *Structural Anthropology* [1956], trans. C. Jacobsen and B. G. Schoepf (New York: Basic Books, 1963); *Totemism*, trans. R. Needham (Boston: Beacon Press, 1963); *The Savage Mind*, trans. G. Weidenfeld and Nicholson, Ltd. (University of Chicago Press, 1968). Also Clifford Geertz, "Ethos, World-View and the Analysis of Sacred Symbols," *Antioch Review* 17 (1957–58): 421–37; "Religion as a Cultural System," *Anthropological Approaches to the Study of Religion*, ed. M. Banton (London: Tavistock, 1966).

78. Erving Goffman, *The Presentation of Self in Everyday Life* (New York: Doubleday, 1959); *Behavior in Public Places: Notes on the Social Organization of Gatherings* (New York: Macmillan, 1963); *Interaction Ritual: Essays on Face-to-Face Behavior* (New York: Doubleday, 1967). Also Peter Berger, *The Noise of Solemn Assemblies* (New York: Doubleday, 1961).

79. *Philosophical Transactions of the Royal Society of London*, ser. B., vol. 251, no. 772 (1966).

80. E.g., Victor Turner, *The Ritual Process: Structure and Antistructure* (Chicago: Aldine, 1969); *Dramas, Fields and Metaphors* (Ithaca: Cornell University Press, 1974), and see n. 75; Mary Douglas, *Natural Symbols: Explorations in Cosmology* (New York: Pantheon, 1970).

81. *The Roots of Ritual*, ed. James Shaughnessy (Grand Rapids, MI: Eerdmans, 1973). Subsequently, a participant in the conference published a short introduction, especially for seminarians, to the ritual nature of liturgy; Leonel L. Mitchell, *The Meaning of Ritual* (New York: Paulist Press, 1977).

82. Ronald L. Grimes, *Beginnings in Ritual Studies* (Washington, DC: University Press, 1982); "Ritual Studies," *The Encyclopedia of Religion*, ed. Mircea Eliade (New York: Free Press, 1987).

83. The commendations of solemn high mass in Latin by Victor Turner (see n. 75), and the comments by Mary Douglas (see n. 80) on the adverse effects for socioreligious bonding of so apparently simple a matter as the liberalization of fast and abstinence laws in Roman Catholicism, are examples. Representative recent manuals of liturgical studies contain no bibliography on the anthropology of ritual behavior, and the category "Ritual" does not appear in their indexes. See *The Study of Liturgy*, ed. C. Jones, G. Wainwright, E. Yarnold (New York: Oxford University Press, 1978); Herman Wegman, *Christian Worship in East and West* [1976], trans. Gordon W. Lathrop (New York: Pueblo Publishing, 1985); E. Cattaneo, *Il culto Cristiano in occidente* [1978] (Rome: Edizione Liturgische, 1984); *Anamnesis: Introduzione storico-teologica alla Liturgia*, ed. S. Marsili, 3 vols. (Casale Monferatto: Marietti, 1974–83); see K. Seasoltz's review in *Worship* 60 (1986): 84–87.

84. See Eric H. Erikson, "Ontogeny of Ritualization in Man," *Philosophical Transactions of the Royal Society of London*, ser. B, vol. 251, no. 772, (1966) 337–50; Aidan Kavanagh, "The Role of Ritual in Personal Development," *The Roots of Ritual*, ed. James Shaughnessy (Grand Rapids, MI: Eerdmans, 1973), 145–60.

85. Some examples of ritual anthropology's being taken seriously in writings about liturgy are Marion Hatchett, *Sanctifying Life, Time, and Space: An Introduction to Liturgical Study* (New York: Seabury, 1976); *Liturgy and Cultural Religious Traditions*, ed. H. Schmidt and D. Power, Concilium series 102 (New York: Seabury, 1977); George S. Worgul, *From Magic to Metaphor: A Validation of the Christian Sacraments* (New York: Paulist Press, 1980). For liturgy's influence on an anthropologist, see Roy Rappaport, *Ecology, Meaning, and Religion* (Richmond, CA: North Atlantic Books, 1979). For a broadening notion of worship, see Ninian Smart, *The Concept of Worship* (New York: St. Martin's Press, 1972); Geoffrey Parrinder, *Worship in the World's Religions* (Totowa, NJ: Littlefield, 1976); Jonathan Z. Smith, *Imagining Religion: From Babylon to Jonestown* (University of Chicago Press, 1982). Also Allen Guttman, *From Ritual to Record: The Nature of Modern Sports* (New York: Columbia University Press, 1978); Gregor T. Goethals, *The TV Ritual: Worship at the Video Altar* (Boston: Beacon Press, 1981). The leading student of ritual in American civil religion remains Robert Bellah, *The Broken Covenant: American Civil Religion in a Time of Trial* (New York: Seabury, 1975).

86. The North American Academy of Liturgy meets yearly in January, Societas Liturgica every other year in August either in Europe or in America. Pro-

ceedings of NAAL appear annually in a summer edition of *Worship*, those of Societas Liturgica irregularly in its own journal *Studia Liturgica*.

87. E.g., Robert F. Taft, *Beyond East and West: Problems in Liturgical Understanding* (Washington DC: Pastoral Press, 1984).

88. See Thomas J. Talley, "The Literary Structure of Eucharistic Prayer," *Worship* 58 (1984): 404–20.

89. See Robert F. Taft, "The Structural Analysis of Liturgical Units: An Essay in Methodology," *Worship* 52 (1978): 314–29. A broader example illustrating such analysis of origins is Thomas J. Talley, *Origins of the Liturgical Year* (New York: Pueblo Publishing, 1986). On the confirmation question see my "Confirmation: A Suggestion from Structure," *Worship* 58 (1984): 386–95, an essay I have expanded as *Confirmation: Origins and Reform* (New York: Pueblo Publishing, 1988).

Ecumenical Studies

John T. Ford

H E advocated the reunion of Christendom"[1]—these words, which formed the concluding phrase of Philip Schaff's memorial inscription, characterize one of his most important professional endeavors and one of his deepest theological commitments. The reunion of Christians figured prominently in his inaugural lecture on *The Principle of Protestantism*, which he delivered in Reading, Pennsylvania, on 25 October 1844 before the synod of the German Reformed church in his capacity as its newly appointed professor of biblical literature and ecclesiastical history at Mercersburg Seminary.[2] Almost half a century later, ecumenism was again a major concern in the lecture that he delivered at the Parliament of Religions in Chicago, on 22 September 1893; disregarding the advice of physicians and friends, who feared the exertion of the trip would kill him, Schaff declared: "I was determined to bear my last dying testimony to the cause of Christian union in which I have been interested all my life."[3] His lecture on *The Reunion of Christendom* indeed proved to be his "dying testimony"; Schaff died less than a month later on 20 October 1893.[4]

Schaff's lifelong interest in Christian union seems to have been part of his personal "ecumenical pilgrimage." Baptized in the Reformed Church in Switzerland, he was confirmed in the Lutheran church during his student days in Germany; after accepting the synodal call to come to America to teach theology at Mercersburg, he became a member of the German Reformed church; later after being invited to teach at Union Theological Seminary in New York, he transferred to the Presbyterian church. However, such formal ecclesiastical ties pale in comparison to Schaff's other ecumenical contacts that ranged from conversations with church leaders and theologians of every persuasion, through attendance at the services of many different churches, to participation in numerous interdenominational conferences. "It seems to have been Dr. Schaff's good fortune to be associated with almost every important gathering for a generation that is prominently associated with Christian union and toleration."[5]

Yet Schaff was not merely an ecumenical activist but a convinced ecumenist, whose commitment derived from his understanding of the church, its history, and especially its historical development.

> For him the concept of the Church, the theory of Church history, and the ecumenical concept of Evangelical Catholicism were a unfied whole, in which one followed from the other, one determined the other, and none could be understood without the other. It was the concept of the Church as the visible body of Christ, which posited the ecumenical problem; he found the solution to this problem in the romantic-idealistic concept of organic-dialectical development.[6]

An organic-dialectical interpretation of church history convinced Schaff that "Christianity can be identified only with its first historical form, the Apostolic Church"; subsequent "forms of Christianity were merely necessitated by the special historical conditions of their times and must, therefore, be regarded as transitional stages of Christianity."[7] Accordingly, Schaff regarded Protestantism and Catholicism as transitional stages; and, in Hegelian fashion, "he looked for a new synthesis of the two positions which should include the best aspects of Protestantism and the finest parts of Catholicism."[8] Schaff was persuaded that the dialectic of historical development would lead to the emergence of "Evangelical Catholicism" and believed that "Christ will yet appear to gather the separated members of His church once more together." While unwilling to predict the eventual shape of this coming together, Schaff insisted that "Church unity is not a vague spiritual unity, but a visible and attainable reality"; consequently, "a living outward intercommunication between all Christian churches must give practical proof that they are not only one in spirit, but one body also."[9]

The belief that Christians must become not only spiritually one but also visibly one, led Schaff to espouse two positions that were markedly different from those of many of his American Protestant contemporaries. First, he emphatically disavowed Protestant denominationalism: "Away with human denominations, down with religious sects! Let our watchword be: One Spirit and one body! One Shepherd and one flock! All conventicles and chapels must perish, that from their ashes may arise the One Church of God, phenix-like [sic] and resplendent with glory, as a bride adorned for her bridegroom."[10] Such apocalyptic language reveals Schaff's conviction that "one of the greatest tragedies in the history of the Church was the spread of the sectarian attitude to all Protestant churches" with the unfortunate result that "too many Protestant communions are unwilling to sacrifice their own private interests for the betterment of the Kingdom of God."[11] In Schaff's mind, "the Church was too large and too great to be restricted to any particular denomination."[12]

A second divergence from prevailing nineteenth-century American Protestant attitudes was Schaff's surprisingly favorable view of Roman Catholicism. Instead of considering the Reformation as the repudiation of Catholicism, Schaff held that *"The Reformation is the legitimate offspring, the greatest act of the Catholic Church; and on this account of true catholic nature itself, in its genuine conception."*[13] Indeed, it was Schaff's "conviction that true Protestantism has more in common with Roman Catholicism, as represented by Moehler, for instance, than with the Protestantism of many so-called Protestants."[14] More cognizant than most Americans of the rise of rationalism in the German universities, "Schaff felt that the more dangerous enemy of the church was not Roman Catholicism but the peril from the rationalists within the confines of Protestantism."[15]

Flowing from this appraisal of Catholicism were several important ecumenical consequences. In particular, Schaff was prompted to criticize those who considered ecumenism merely as a means of forging "a union of Protestants as a ready weapon against Roman Catholicism and Romanizing tendencies in Protestantism"; those who failed to see the unity of the church as a goal in itself effectively "debased the ecumenical quest for unity to a mere instrument in the service of a party motive;" consequently, Schaff "considered a conception of union which excluded the Roman Catholic and the Greek Orthodox Churches as 'altogether too contracted.'"[16]

Schaff's rejection of denominationalism and his favorable appraisal of Roman Catholicism were not so unusual in the German university milieu with which he was familiar, as such views were at that time in the United States.[17] As would prove to be the lot of many other ecumenists, Schaff's ecumenical outlook was suspect among many of his American co-religionists, some of whom went so far as to accuse him of heresy. Though other immigrants might have been deterred by such opposition, Schaff, as "an American by the call of Providence and by free choice with all my heart,"[18] envisioned the United States as a land of ecumenical opportunity:

> God has great surprises in store. The Reformation is not by any means the last word He has spoken. We may confidently look and hope for something better than Romanism and Protestantism. And free America, where all the churches are commingling and rivalling with each other, may become the chief theatre of such a reunion of Christendom as will preserve every truly Christian and valuable element in the various types which it has assumed in the course of ages, and make them more effective than they were in their separation and antagonism.

The denominational discords will be solved at last in the concord of Christ, the Lord and Saviour of all that love, worship, and follow Him.[19]

While Schaff felt that "the theology of the future will be a theology of love," which "will give new life to the Church and prepare the way for the reunion of Christendom,"[20] he did not think it mandatory or possible to resolve all doctrinal issues. For example, his address at the Bonn Union Conference in 1875, indicated that "a full agreement in the theological conception of the Holy Spirit and the inexhaustible mystery of the Trinity seemed to him impossible and unnecessary," insofar as "the church has no right to go beyond the Scriptures in her doctrinal symbols."[21] However, Schaff's proposal "that we should agree in adopting certain statements in S. John's Gospel and S. Paul's Epistles and leave everything else to take care of itself" was apparently not well received.[22]

Similarly, exception was taken in Episcopalian circles to Schaff's views on the "historic Episcopate," which he considered as "the stumbling-block to all non-Episcopalians" and one that "will never be conceded by them as a condition of Church unity, if it is understood to mean the necessity of three orders of the ministry and of episcopal ordination in unbroken historic succession;" accordingly he predicted that that "the non-Episcopal Churches will never unchurch themselves and cast reproach upon their ministry."[23]

Schaff was more successful in defending the irrepeatability of baptism; in 1885, when the General Assembly of the Presbyterian church was debating whether to recognize the validity of Roman Catholic baptisms, Schaff's argument convinced the participants: "if converts from the Roman Catholic Church are to be rebaptized, then we must dig up the bones of Calvin and Zwingli and Luther and sprinkle them over again."[24] This incident illustrates Schaff's great talent as an ecumenical rhetorician who was able to demolish what he considered sectarian stances by a combination of historical erudition and humorous *reductio ad absurdum*.

Schaff's persuasive abilities reached their height in fostering ecumenical cooperation on such scholarly projects as a common translation of the Bible and a series of denominational histories, which he hoped would "not only be a valuable authentic contribution to our theological and historical literature, but also tend to remove ignorance and prejudice and to bring Christians nearer together."[25] Schaff believed that ecumenical understanding would be nurtured by the study of church history: "When it is pursued with 'malice toward none but with charity for all,' it will bring the denominations closer together in an humble recognition of their defects and a grateful praise for the good which the same Spirit has wrought in them and through them."[26]

Schaff's ecumenical effectiveness lay preeminently in what he once described as his "providential mission" of being "a sort of international theological nuncio and mediator."[27] This self-description was corroborated in the remarks of Thomas Joseph Shahan at a memorial session of the American Society of Church History, two months after Schaff's death:

> On different occasions Dr. Schaff, it is remembered with gratitude by Catholics, corrected misstatements of their doctrines and rebuked exaggerated and false notions concerning them. . . . while the Catholic historian and theologian finds much from which he must dissent in the writings of Dr. Schaff, still, when he considers his natural and acquired abilities, his earnest zeal, his manliness, his astounding productivity, he is tempted to exclaim:
> *"Talis cum sis, utinam noster esses."*[28]

Schaff's ecumenical talents seem to have been less those of the creative theologian and more those of the pragmatic diplomat. "His distinction did not lie in developing new ideas, but in grasping and combining the ideas of others, and in his literary presentation and practical application of them."[29] At times, this ability proved to be visionary as in his proposal for a "federal or confederate union" of churches resembling the "political confederation of Switzerland, the United States, and the Modern German Empire." In words prophetically descriptive of the councils of churches that would be formed in the twentieth century, Schaff proposed a "voluntary association of different Churches in their official capacity, each retaining its freedom and independence in the management of its internal affairs, but all recognizing one another as sisters with equal rights and co-operating in general enterprises, such as the spread of the gospel at home and abroad, the defence of the faith against infidelity, the elevation of the poor and neglected classes of society, works of philanthropy and charity, and moral reform."[30]

Schaff's advocacy of "conciliar ecumenism" was one more instance of his ecumenical vision—a vision that stemmed from his ecclesiological conviction that Christian unity is not merely spiritual and eschatological but necessarily visible and attainable. On the theological level, his ecumenical vision led him to disavow denominationalism and to espouse an inclusive catholicism. On the practical level, his ecumenical vision prompted his extraordinary involvement in ecumenical conferences and inter-denominational projects. And with characteristic immigrant fervor, Schaff asked what better place for realizing such an ecumenical vision than in the democratic climate of the United States?

If, in retrospect, one might feel that Schaff was overly optimistic in minimizing both the serious doctrinal issues that need to be resolved and the numerous practical obstacles that need to be surmounted before any comprehensive reunion of Christians can take place in America or elsewhere; nonetheless, "one might say that some of the most important themes and achievements of the ecumenical movement of the twentieth century were in part already touched upon, in part anticipated by Schaff."[31] Such ecumenical vision was unusual in Schaff's day, and is still all too uncommon in our own: "In the English-speaking world, at least, it would be hard to equal the intensity of Schaf's [*sic*] expectancy with regard to the ecumenical church."[32]

Schaff then might justifiably be considered "an ecumenical prophet," both pointing to and calling for the reunion of all Christians.

The Emergence of "Ecumenical Studies"

In the theological schools of Schaff's day, there was comparatively little space for ecumenism, let alone for "ecumenical studies" as a distinct academic discipline. Schaff was an ecumenist in the sense that his repeatedly enunciated concern for the "reunion of Christendom" was a leitmotif in his other theological pursuits.

Recent theologians tend to share Schaff's conviction and have incorporated an ecumenical perspective into their treatment of biblical, systematic, historical, and applied theology. Indeed, some theologians feel that insofar as an ecumenical orientation can be embodied within the traditional areas of theology, there is little or no need for ecumenical studies as a separate theological pursuit. In contrast, many other theologians argue that even if an ecumenical dimension can and should enhance all branches of theology, "Christian unity" is still such a fundamental issue that it deserves to be addressed separately. In their judgment, the question is not the need for but the nature of "ecumenical studies."

While a few theologians have attempted to make ecumenical studies a separate branch of systematic theology,[33] a more common pattern is the use of a historical approach focused on (though not necessarily limited to) the history of the ecumenical movement in the twentieth century. Within this historical framework, the doctrinal issues, as well as the nontheological factors, that have been instrumental in creating and continuing divisions among Christians can be clarified and compared.

Such a method has considerable value both as a way of conceptualizing the barriers to Christian union and as a means of comparing the doctrinal differences between Christian traditions. Also, such a method has sometimes proved successful in showing that doctrinal differences that once were considered divisive are more semantic than substantive. Yet such a comparative historical approach has occasionally shown the reverse: doctrinal differences once presumed to be superficial can be deeper than most theologians previously supposed. Thus, instead of serving as a bridge between different viewpoints, comparative dogmatics can also reveal how deeply divided Christians really are.

The discovery of differences that are apparently irresolvable through a comparative historical methodology effectively raises the question of the purpose of ecumenical studies. Should ecumenism be pursued as a discipline that analyzes and compares the theological differences separating Christians? Or should ecumenism be pursued as a study that seeks to formulate practical strategies and procedures that will help lead churches to union? Or should ecumenism be conceived as a discipline that searches for a theological synthesis that will enable Christians to resolve their denominational differences?

Schaff seems to have been comfortable in pursuing all these options. In a way extraordinary for his day, he fostered cooperative endeavors to produce a comparative history of different denominations,[34] attended conferences concerned with proposals for church union, and prophesied that the antithetical relationship between Protestantism and Catholicism would eventually be subsumed in a future synthesis that would combine what was authentically Christian in both traditions. Although few ecumenists today would espouse an Hegelian dialectic, popular in the German universities of Schaff's student days, as the basis for a modern ecumenical synthesis, nonetheless, his proposal has a number of parallels in recent ecumenical thought.

The most obvious commonality is the quest for visible unity, which ecumenists currently describe in such terms as "conciliar fellowship" or "a communion of communions." Such proposed forms of unity are frequently portrayed in process terminology; for example, unity is envisioned as a gradual process of mutual reconciliation through a reciprocal sharing of spiritual gifts. While such a description sounds more appealing (at least to many present-day ecumenists) than Schaff's Hegelian-style synthesis, such a proposal is not without its own difficulties: first is the presumption that the issues originally causing the separation are no longer relevant, or at least can be surmounted by a process of reconciliation; secondly it presumes that the spiritual gifts to be shared are compatible, not contra-dictory. This theoretical questionableness, or at least the pragmatic need to test such assumptions as part of the ecumenical pilgrimage, indicates that "as Christians move toward visible unity, they will need to clarify what exactly is the unity they seek."[35]

Another contemporary parallel to Schaff's vision is found in the quest for "doctrinal consensus." Once again there is need for precise definition and systematic clarification. For some, "consensus" implies univocal agree-ment about all substantive issues while allowing for variant interpretations of secondary matters. Yet, even if it is possible to distinguish the substantive from the secondary (and such a distinction is easier to make on paper than to formulate in practice), others feel that "univocal" agreement is philo-sophically impossible.

In effect, while ecumenists can formulate generic consensus statements (such as confessions of faith, doctrinal agreements, and plans for church union) that Christians of different denominational backgrounds are willing to accept, almost inevitably their interpretations of these consensus state-ments will be different and possibly at some point irreconcilably so. Not surprisingly, critics raise the question, What is the purpose of formulating consensus statements, if they are open to divergent, and even conflicting, interpretations?

In response, ecumenists point out that in the apostolic church there were not only different observances but also different theologies and even-tually different doctrinal expressions. Insofar as differences in doctrine and discipline were allowed in the early church, similar differences should be allowable today. However, even though diversity was tolerated in the early church, limits were eventually set, with the result that some dissenting individuals were expelled from the Christian community. In effect, while this biblical-historical analogy establishes the legitimacy of doctrinal diver-sity, what must still be determined are the mandatory extent of convergence and the permissible degree of divergence.[36]

Christian diversity today is much more extensive than at any previous time in history. The very success of Christianity in reaching people of many different cultures and nations has not only meant an increase in the number of languages into which the gospel must be translated but also an increase in the philosophical perspectives in which the gospel can be understood. In effect, if the one gospel is proclaimed throughout the world, that proclamation is interpreted in many different ways. But is there a fundamental unity undergirding this apparent diversity?

In response, some point out that it is still possible to find credal statements that most Christians can affirm; others, however, note that a univocal interpretation of these statements is practically impossible in a world of philosophical pluralism. Moreover, this same philosophical pluralism makes it impossible to construct a single normative "ecumenical theology" as the philosophical basis for ecumenical studies. From a theoretical viewpoint, then, the maximum that ecumenists can hope to achieve is the specification of a set of consensus theses to which most Christians could subscribe while simultaneously interpreting these theses from different philosophical perspectives.[37]

Thus, while contemporary ecumenists seem more or less willing to share Schaff's optimism about finding a future ecumenical consensus, they have been unable to find an adequate philosophical/theological replacement for his Hegelian-style dialectic.[38] Some, of course, feel that ecumenical studies are at such an early stage of development that it is presently premature to expect doctrinal consensus. Others, however, feel that ecumenical studies is necessarily a process discipline until such time as union among Christians is actually achieved; only then will it be possible to propose a systematic ecumenical synthesis. Still others observe that if and when Christians manage to achieve union, ecumenical studies would presumably no longer be necessary, except as an interpretation post factum.

Although these substratal philosophical-theological problems are recognized, most ecumenists, at least those in the United States, have tended to pursue ecumenical studies from an historical perspective that is simultaneously practical, critical, and irenic. The practical emphasis in contemporary ecumenism stems from the desire of ecumenists to achieve some actual type of Christian union in the not-too-distant future. The critical focus of ecumenism is the contribution of scholars whose participation in ecumenical dialogue has introduced many recent developments in biblical, theological, and historical scholarship. Consequently, a new irenicism has emerged; in contrast to the past, when denominational histories were generally written from an apologetic, even a polemic, stance, ecumenically minded historians now try to interpret church-dividing events with both historiographical integrity and Christian fair-mindedness.[39]

This combination of professional exactitude and charitable concern has been accompanied by a shift away from denominational defensiveness toward an emphasis on what Christians have continued to hold in common in spite of their separation. This current ethos in ecumenical studies might well be described in the patristic phrase espoused by Pope John XXIII: *In necessariis unitas, in dubiis libertas, in omnibus caritas*—a position advocated by Schaff as well as by Martin Luther.[40]

253

Introductions to the Ecumenical Movement

Although the emergence of ecumenical studies as a distinct historical-theological discipline is a comparatively recent phenomenon, there is no shortage of literature on ecumenism. In fact, there is such a flood of ecumenically related publications that even professional ecumenists have trouble tracking, much less reading, them all. Consequently, those unfamiliar with the ecumenical movement may wonder where to begin, while those whose chief interests are in other areas of theology may wonder what to read in order to acquire an overall view of the ecumenical movement.

The following bibliographical survey has been prepared with the different interests of readers in mind. Specifically, an effort has been made to mention three types of publications: those of primary usefulness to ecumenical novices, those of likely interest to theological readers who have some familiarity with ecumenism, and those of special importance for experienced ecumenists. Such typecasting is obviously a discretionary enterprise and certainly one subject to revision in light of the continually changing ecumenical scene; moreover, such a listing can only sample a small portion of the resources available in English.

Given the vast quantity of literature on ecumenism, where should an ecumenical novice begin? For those seeking an overview of contemporary ecumenism, a good place to start reading is with William Rusch's *Ecumenism: A Movement Toward Church Unity*.[41] This small volume provides a clear, concise introduction to the current trends and major issues of the ecumenical movement: the biblical and theological bases for church unity; a brief history of the ecumenical movement, with special attention given to the National Council of Churches and the World Council of Churches; a synopsis of selected bilateral dialogues (Anglican-Roman Catholic, Anglican-Lutheran, Lutheran-Roman Catholic, Lutheran-Reformed); and a representative summary of the ecumenical involvement of four churches (Episcopal church, Lutheran Church in America, Orthodox Church in America, Roman Catholic church). Although some sections focus on specifically Lutheran issues that may not be of interest to other readers, on the whole, this book is an excellent survey of of contemporary ecumenism for readers who possess a basic understanding of current theology and some familiarity with church history.

Another introductory volume, which many readers will find fascinating because of its travelogue approach, is Thomas Ryan's *Tales of Christian Unity: The Adventures of an Ecumenical Pilgrim*.[42] To prepare for his appointment as associate director of the Canadian Centre for Ecumenism,

Ryan spent a year of study and dialogue at such ecumenically important sites as Cairo, Jerusalem, Constantinople, Mount Athos, Bossey, and Canterbury. Ryan's "tales," like their Chaucerian counterparts, employ a mix of personal impression, geographical description, historical information, ahd doctrinal discussion as the matrix for his candid questions and reflections on ecumenical problems and possibilities. There is, however, one inherent drawback to Ryan's geographical format: topics tend to be treated impressionistically rather than systematically and some important topics are not treated at all. Nonetheless, novice ecumenists should find this book a readable way of beginning their own ecumenical pilgrimage, and even ecumenical veterans may find this volume a stimulus for reminiscing about their personal ecumenical experiences.

For readers who wish a more systematic and historical introduction to the ecumenical movement, one of the best surveys is Robert McAfee Brown's *The Ecumenical Revolution: An Interpretation of the Catholic-Protestant Dialogue*,[43] which appeared soon after the Second Vatican Council (1962-65). In a highly readable style, Brown examined the change in climate that prompted Christians to move "from diatribe to dialogue," reappraised the Reformation in a way that challenged Protestants to move toward union, and highlighted the ecumenical breakthrough that Roman Catholicism achieved at Vatican II. Brown did not hesitate to treat such ecumenically sensitive issues as religious liberty ("toleration is not enough"), Jewish-Christian dialogue (including the controversial question of "the conversion of the Jews"), and worship in common (including the problem of "intercommunion"). Although there have been many changes in the ecumenical scene in the two decades since this book's original publication, most of the material, even if now somewhat dated, remains useful for its thorough coverage of ecumenical history and theology; indeed, this volume is still an excellent source for readers who want to garner a better appreciation of the ecumenical progress that has been made, as well as a better understanding of the historical background to current ecumenical issues. It would be a blessing for ecumenism if an updated paperback edition were published.

For readers who want even greater depth and detail, encyclopedic information about virtually every aspect of the ecumenical movement prior to 1968 is available in the two volumes of *A History of the Ecumenical Movement*.[44] Granted that the sheer length of these two volumes—the text alone is in the neighborhood of twelve hundred pages—tends to be formidable, dedicated readers will find an impressive wealth of historical information, biographical data on influential persons, thought-provoking synopses of theological trends, as well as numerous bibliographical references. Since many of the chapters were written by people who were participants in the history they describe, there is a personal dimension to this collaborative publication that other historical accounts do not have; simultaneously, the authors, aware that personal proximity can be a hermeneutical liability, have tried to be as objective as possible in their interpretations.

The first volume covers the period from 1517 (the year of Luther's Ninety-five Theses) to 1948 (the date of the first assembly of the World Council of Churches). After a survey of the search for Christian unity prior to the Reformation and a consideration of the "ecumenical idea" as it emerged during, and continued after, the Reformation, the major portion of the volume is devoted to ecumenism in the nineteenth and twentieth centuries. While there were proponents of, and proposals for, Christian reunion in the sixteenth, seventeenth, and eighteenth centuries, the most forceful ecumenical impetus came from an unexpected source: the missionary movement of the nineteenth century.

In that era of exploration and colonization, missionaries from Europe and North America went to Africa and Asia with the intention of winning souls for Christ, at the same time that their compatriots in the military and the government were claiming territories in the name of the home country. With the proclamation of the gospel, so to speak, following the flag, Christianity became identified with the colonizing country; thus, in practice, conversion to Christianity not only implied aceptance of the gospel but frequently included the added incentive of educational, social, and political advantages. Moreover, not only was Christianity in the so-called mission countries imbued with the cultural and ethnic patterns of the parent countries, but the numerous divisions among Christians in Europe and North America were exported as well. As a result, Christianity in Africa and Asia frequently took on a "crazy quilt" appearance: Africans who accepted the doctrines of German Lutherans, Asians who patterned their worship after High Church Anglicans, Chinese who adopted the devotions of French Roman Catholics, and so on.

The missionary proclamation of the gospel was not only vested in nationalistic and denominationalistic dress but was also vitiated by an un-Christian rivalry that reflected both the contention among the colonial powers for political hegemony and the denominational conflicts that the missionaries had brought with them from their home countries. Indeed, missionary rivalry was frequently encouraged by mission boards that gauged their level of support according to the number of converts at each mission station under its auspices. Such ecclesiastical entrepreneurship had many deleterious effects; for example, cities in colonial countries tended to have a surfeit of competing missionary groups, while the less populous and less accessible backcountry had few missionaries. Simultaneously, missionary rivalry created both competition for, and confusion among, prospective converts: sometimes, indigenous people were tempted to comparative shopping for the most enticing membership benefits offered by competing churches; simultaneously, the "native people" were confused by missionaries, who proclaimed a gospel of love, yet were at odds among themselves.

Eventually, in order to reduce the detrimental effects of competition, as well as to exercise better stewardship of limited resources, mission-sponsoring societies entered into arrangements of "comity," whereby a particular area was exclusively assigned to one denomination. Such agreements were only partially successful, insofar as some denominations were unwilling to accept such a division of territory. Nonetheless, such cooperative agreements did reflect the fact that many of the new Christians in mission countries were not particularly interested in preserving the divisions that had alienated their denominationally divided patrons and parents. In addition to such pragmatic motives, there gradually emerged the conviction, described at the World Missionary Conference in Edinburgh in 1910, that it is "the aim of all missionary work to plant in each non-Christian nation one undivided Church of Christ."[45]

Even its contemporaries hailed the Edinburgh Conference "as a major occurrence"; subsequently, church historians have considered it "the birthplace of the modern ecumenical movement."[46] Historically speaking, this gathering of official delegates from missionary societies was more denominationally inclusive than earlier missionary meetings. And while their differences had the potential for fomenting divisiveness among the delegates, such did not happen: "At Edinburgh Christians of very different allegiances found that uninhibited discussions could be carried on in an atmosphere of common worship, that in a fellowship knit together and deepened by prayer conscientiously-held differences could be clearly stated and transcended without surrender, and that the unity of Christ's Church in the midst of differences could be clearly felt."[47]

The experience of Edinburgh helped generate two other movements: the first, the World Conference on Faith and Order, was primarily interested in the long-term goal of resolving divisive doctrinal issues and in reconciling discordant ecclesiastical structures; the second, the Universal Christian Council for Life and Work, was more concerned about the immediate task of applying Christian principles to contemporary social, economic, and political problems, as well as alleviating human suffering, especially crisis situations that surpassed the resources of any single church and thus called for interchurch cooperation. These two movements have come to symbolize two different ecumenical strategies: Faith and Order represents the quest for unity through doctrinal agreement, while Life and Work represents the search for unity through collaborative work on practical problems.

Pursued separately, however, these two different orientations can easily become one-sided. On the one hand, the concern of Faith and Order about resolving doctrinal and disciplinary differences as a prerequisite for church union not only tended to downplay the many other human factors that impede Christian unity but also seemingly assumed that the search for agreement is more important than an appreciation of differences and an acceptance of diversity.[48] On the other hand, the apparent assumption of Life and Work that "doctrine divides, but service unites" tended to overlook the fact that different ethical judgments about specific social and political problems can be just as divisive as doctrinal disputes;[49] moreover, "at times large sections of its [Life and Work] supporters seemed to proclaim the view that social and political reform would prove the panacea for all human ills."[50]

By 1936, however, leaders in both movements were convinced of the need "to take two radical decisions: to bring together Life and Work and Faith and Order and to set up a fully representative assembly of the churches."[51] The following year in separate world conferences, the delegates of Life and Work in Oxford, and subsequently the delegates of Faith and Order in Edinburgh, agreed to unite to form the World Council of Churches. Although preliminary plans were made for holding the first assembly of the World Council in August 1941, "because of World War II and its aftermath, the period of formation and provisional existence lasted for ten years."[52]

The World Council of Churches

After World War I, several ecumenical leaders proposed the formation of a "League of Churches." Just as the newly constituted League of Nations hoped to foster human unity by furnishing a forum for resolving international tensions and, above all, for avoiding future wars, so it was hoped that a "League of Churches" would further ecclesial community by lessening denominationally based hostilities and by resolving the issues that separated Christians.[53] In fact, it was nearly three decades later, and only after another even more disastrous world war, that the long-awaited World Council of Churches formally came into existence.

The first assembly of the World Council met in Amsterdam from 22 August through 4 September 1948. In attendance were 351 official delegates of 147 churches from 44 countries.[54] While some representatives from Asia, Africa, and Latin America were present, European and North American participants predominated. Moreover, the first assembly had a definitely Protestant flavor, since only a few Orthodox churches were represented and the Roman Catholic church declined to send a delegation.

The discussion of the assembly's theme, "Man's Disorder and God's Design," revealed a diversity of viewpoints that reflected not only denominational differences but also postwar political divisions; nonetheless the participants were able to express "their common readiness and their conviction that they should bear witness of God's design as a factor bringing order into a disordered and disrupted world."[55] The contrast between divine design and human disorder was particularly evident within the universal church. On the one hand, the assembly acknowledged that "God has given to His people in Jesus Christ a unity which is His creation and not our achievement"; on the other hand, the churches found the realization of this fundamental unity "faced by some stubborn problems," so that "it is not always easy to reconcile our confessional and ecumenical loyalties."[56]

In retrospect, this awareness of "the universal church in God's design" seems to have provided the ecclesiological foundation for the ecumenical commitment of the churches. If, in the past, ecumenism had been the work of a few dedicated individuals, whose efforts were not infrequently suspect within their own churches, what was significant about the Amsterdam Assembly was that "the Churches themselves accepted the responsibility for the ecumenical movement and, conversely, that the ecumenical movement received a firm foundation in the continuous life of the Churches."[57]

At Amsterdam, although the member churches "covenanted with one another in constituting this World Council of Churches,"[58] relatively little was said about the council's ecclesiological significance. The need for addressing ecclesiological questions quickly became urgent in the face of accusations that the World Council aimed at becoming a "Super-Church" that would eventually dominate the member churches and destroy their cherished traditions. Replying to such misrepresentations was not easy; the council was faced with the question of "how one can formulate the ecclesiological implications of a body in which so many different conceptions of the Church are represented, without using the categories or language of one particular conception of the Church."[59]

Recognizing the need for clarifying the ecclesiological significance of the council, yet acknowledging that membership in the council "does not imply the acceptance of a specific doctrine concerning the nature of Church unity," the World Council's Central Committee, meeting in Toronto in

1950, published a description of eight ecclesiological "assumptions underlying the World Council": (1) Christ is the Divine Head of the Body; (2)
the Church of Christ is one; (3) the membership of the Church of Christ
is more inclusive than the membership of any individual church body; (4)
membership in the World Council does not imply that a member church
must regard other member churches as churches in the true and full sense
of the term; (5) member churches recognize elements of the true church
in the other churches; (6) member churches are willing to consult together;
(7) the member churches both assist each other and refrain from actions
that are incompatible with fellowship; (8) member churches enter into a
spiritual relationship through which they seek to learn from, and give help
to, each other.[60]

While the Toronto Statement eventually came to be regarded as "a
landmark in the World Council's thinking about itself and its relation to
work for unity,"[61] the question of the council's ecclesiological significance
continued to be discussed. For example, in its statement on "The Calling
of the Church to Mission and Unity," the Central Committee, meeting
in Rolle, Switzerland, in 1951, noted both the consensus that "unity is of
the essence of the Church" and the continued lack of agreement "as to
the visible forms in which this unity is to be expressed."[62]

The possibility of exiting from this ecclesiological impasse emerged
the following year at the third World Conference on Faith and Order in
Lund, Sweden. "At Lund an era of study in comparative ecclesiology
ended."[63] The participants recognized that "we can make no real advance
toward unity if we only compare our several conceptions of the nature of
the Church and the traditions in which they are embodied;" the participants
also recognized that "we cannot build the one Church by cleverly fitting
together our divided inheritances."[64] Lund then acknowledged the need
"to explore more deeply the resources for further ecumenical discussion
to be found in that common history which we have as Christians and
which we have discovered to be longer, larger, and richer than any of our
separate histories in our divided churches"; accordingly, in place of comparative ecclesiology, the conference recommended a christological and
pneumatological approach: "it is of decisive importance for the advance
of ecumenical work that the doctrine of the Church be treated in close
relation both to the doctrine of Christ and to the doctrine of the Holy
Spirit."[65]

The Lund Conference also recognized that the World Council had
reached "a crucial point in our ecumenical discussions," namely, the need
to give "clearer manifestation" to the unity that the churches had already

experienced together; accordingly, the churches were asked "whether they are doing all they ought to do to manifest the oneness of the People of God" and "whether they should not act together in all matters except those in which deep differences of conviction compel them to act separately?"[66]

Two years after Lund, the World Council held its second assembly in Evanston, Illinois; in attendance were 502 delegates from 161 member churches, including an increased presence of "younger churches." Similar to the experience at the first assembly in Amsterdam,, the discussion of the conference theme, "Christ, the Hope of the World" revealed that the Old World and the New had different theological outlooks: "The concept of the Christian hope held by the European Churches tended to be eschatological, whereas the concept of the American Churches was more optimistic and more concerned with the Christian's hope in this world here and now."[67]

Evanston recognized not only that theological differences are sometimes geographically based, but also that "old confessional divisions are being criss-crossed by new lines of agreement and disagreement"; nor is it easy to resolve such divisions, rather, overcoming disunity "may require obedience unto death"; in concrete terms, the churches may "have to be prepared to offer up some of their accustomed, inherited forms of life in uniting with other churches without complete certainity as to all that will emerge from the step of faith."[68] However, just as the participants at Amsterdam stated that they intended "to stay together," those at Evanston prayed that Christ would "enable us to grow together."[69]

The growth of the council during the next half-dozen years was evident at the meeting of the third assembly in New Delhi in 1961. In attendance were 577 delegates from a membership that had grown to 198 churches, including the Orthodox churches of Eastern Europe and many "younger churches," and for the first time, Roman Catholics attended an assembly as official observers. The New Delhi Assembly, whose theme was "Jesus Christ—the Light of the World," approved two important changes, one structural, the other constitutional. First, the International Missionary Council was incorporated into the World Council, thereby integrating the three organizations whose life histories were indebted to the missionary conference at Edinburgh in 1910.[70] Secondly, the New Delhi Assembly adopted an explicitly trinitation basis for membership: "The World Council of Churches is a fellowship of Churches which confess the Lord Jesus Christ as God and Saviour according to the Scriptures and therefore seek to fulfill together their common calling to the glory of the one God, Father, Son and Holy Spirit."[71]

The New Delhi Assembly also addressed an issue of long standing by approving a statement that challenged the churches to move toward visible and concrete unity on the local level.

> We believe that the unity which is both God's will and his gift to his Church is being made visible as all in each place who are baptized into Jesus Christ and confess him as Lord and Saviour are brought by the Holy Spirit into one fully committed fellowship, holding the one apostolic faith, preaching the one Gospel, breaking the one bread, joining in common prayer, and having a corporate life reaching out in witness and service to all and who at the same time are united with the whole Christian fellowship in all places and all ages in such wise that ministry and members are accepted by all, and that all can act and speak together as occasion requires for the tasks to which God calls his people.[72]

The question of unity figured prominently again at the fourth World Conference on Faith and Order in Montreal in 1963. On the one hand, the attempt to develop a better ecumenical understanding of "the Church in the Purpose of God" made little progress over what had been previously formulated; on the other hand, the discussion on the local church in the light of the New Delhi statement, though surfacing a diversity of viewpoints, produced both new insights and new directions for the future.[73] For example, the local church was seen as "the proving ground of unity," either the place where "the scandal of Christian disunity is particularly conspicuous and injurious," or the place where "the local church realizes that it is the Church Universal in a particular place."[74]

Since the life and witness of local churches are frequently damaged by denominationalism, prejudice, discrimination, and institutional self-interest, the Montreal Conference summoned "all in each place" to "the serious recognition that through baptism we are one people serving the one Lord" and so to a "growing partnership" in mission and ministry.[75] In a somewhat ambivalent and more or less unexpected way, Montreal provided a change in direction for the ecclesiological concerns of the World Council:

> Whereas previously the dominant theme of the Faith and Order movement had been ecclesiology in the strict sense, the Montreal delegates suddenly saw this theme in a new light. Was not the search for church unity basically only a secondary question? Should not attention be concentrated mainly on the Church's proving itself to be the Church

in the modern world? At least the connection between the concern for unity and this self-authentication of the Church in the world must be demonstrated.[76]

The relationship between the church and the modern world again occupied center stage at the World Council's fourth assembly at Uppsala, Sweden, in 1968. In attendance to consider the assembly's theme, "Behold, I make all things new," were not only 704 delegates from 235 member churches, as well as observers from 43 nonmember churches, church councils, and other organizations, but also a sizable contingent of young people (including 127 "youth participants" and 345 stewards) whose interventions were "welcomed by some of the delegates" but "less happily received by others."[77] Symbolic of the anguished concern at Uppsala over such societal issues as discrimination and human rights was the fact that the preacher at the opening service was a substitute for the assassinated Martin Luther King, Jr., who had originally been scheduled to preach.

As the assembly's report on "the Holy Spirit and the Catholicity of the Church" acknowledged, "it seems to many, inside and outside the Church, that the struggle for Christian unity in its present form is irrelevant to the immediate crisis of our times."[78] Indeed, the quest for unity is related to the church's "Catholicity," envisioned not only as "a gift of the Spirit" but also as "a task, a call and an engagement" that demands that the church "express this catholicity in its worship by providing a home for all sorts and conditions of men and women; and in its witness and service by working for the realization of genuine humanity."[79] The World Council, however, should be concerned not only about present problems but also "should work for the time when a genuinely universal council may once more speak for all Christians, and lead the way into the the future."[80]

Seven years later, when the World Council met in Nairobi, Kenya, "no overwhelmingly important issue, new or old, had emerged to preoccupy the [fifth] Assembly and polarize its passions."[81] Rather, the 676 voting delegates representing 286 member churches were confronted with considerable diversity, not only in theological and political viewpoints, but also in styles of worship. More than ever, the participants, who considered the theme—"Jesus Christ frees and unites"—were challenged to enunciate "what unity requires": "The one Church is to be envisioned as a conciliar fellowship of local churches which are themselves truly united. In this conciliar fellowship, each local church possesses, in communion with the others, the fullness of catholicity, witnesses to the same apostolic faith, and therefore recognizes the others as belonging to the same Church of Christ and guided by the same Spirit."[82]

The assembly's vision of unity as "conciliar fellowship" has both strengths and weaknesses. On the one hand, there is a vagueness about what structures would be required to achieve "conciliar fellowship," possibly due to a fear that "bureaucratic structures [are] incompatible with spiritual freedom and personal community."[83] In addition, it is unclear how the unity of the church can be maintained while advocating "diversity in the Church as something to be not only admitted but actively desired."[84] On the other hand, there is a prophetic quality in the awareness that "for the sake of witnessing to the gospel of Christ the Church is free to ground itself firmly in the culture and life style of every people to whom it is sent," yet simultaneously a realistic warning that "no church should become so identified with its own or another particular culture, present or past, as to frustrate its critical dialogue with that culture."[85]

The Nairobi Assembly ratified this basic commitment to seek "visible unity" in an important constitutional revision of the World Council's description of its "functions and purposes": "The World Council of Churches is constituted. . . . to call the churches to the goal of visible unity in one faith and in one eucharistic fellowship expressed in worship and in common life in Christ, and to advance towards that unity in order that the world may believe."[86]

This passage was cited, eight years later at the sixth assembly of the World Council in Vancouver, as "our central ecumenical goal," as furnishing the "single vision [that] unites our two profoundest ecumenical concerns: the unity and renewal of the Church and the healing and destiny of the human community."[87] As Vancouver's "message" emphasized, previous assemblies had made commitments, first "to stay together," then "to grow together," and "to struggle together." In line with its theme, "Jesus Christ—the Life of the World," the sixth assembly's 847 voting delegates—who represented "four hundred million people of three hundred member churches" confessed that "we are called to live together."[88]

What do such commitments mean in concrete terms? Vancouver pointed out that "a strong Church unity, affirmed in words, lived in deeds, relevant and credible to the problems of human community, would properly have at least three marks which the divided churches do not yet share": first, "a common understanding of the apostolic faith"; second, "a full mutual recognition of baptism, the eucharist and ministry"; and third, "common ways of decision-making and ways of teaching authoritatively."[89] While such a goal will be difficult to achieve, these "marks" do help to clarify the agenda for the future.

Whether the World Council will be able to work through such an agenda is an open question. From the preceding sketch of the council's search for its ecclesiological self-identity, many different tensions are evident; some of these are primarily intramural, as for example, the tension between the doctrinal focus of Faith and Order and the practical concerns of Life and Work, or tension between the denominational traditions of the older churches and the dynamic indigenous development of the younger churches. Simultaneously, other tensions within the World Council replicate the polarities of the modern world—East versus West, Northern Hemisphere versus Southern, male versus female, capitalist versus Communist, white versus nonwhite, authority versus liberation, etc.

The council's history indicates that the dimensions of these tensions also change. For example, an interesting study by Ans J. van der Bent in *From Generation to Generation: The Story of Youth in the World Council of Churches*[90] shows that some of the problems of youth vis-à-vis the World Council are (or at least sound) perennial, while other tensions seem in tandem with the times. For example, between the end of World War I and the Vancouver Assembly (1983), the attitudes of youth toward the ecumenical movement went through five different stages: an initial period of partnership, followed by a sense of world Christian youth community, and the participation of youth in the mission and service of the church, then an abrupt change to intergenerational conflict, which recently seems to have been replaced with a mutual tolerance allowing youth to witness and work in their own ways. Since ecumenical leadership has tended to come from the ranks of the Christian youth leaders of the preceding generation, it will be interesting to see what influence the present generation's spirit of tolerance will have in resolving ecumenical problems in the future.

At least for the predictable future, however, it is likely that the World Council will continue to experience a number of long-standing tensions. Structurally, the World Council sometimes appears as a complex bureaucracy that is victimized by its own internal conflicts that defy effective control; whatever the truth to this charge, the World Council is certainly a diversified organization that defies easy coordination.[91] Theologically, the World Council sometimes appears as an amorphous aggregation of churches speaking with such dissonant voices that its message is confusing if not contradictory; yet, if the World Council has difficulty in achieving unanimity, its consensus statements certainly represent a broad spectrum of Christian belief and practice.[92] However, such tensions are hardly unique to the World Council; similar ecumenical strains have appeared in parallel endeavors on the national, regional, and local levels.[93] Perhaps the primary challenge confronting the World Council on the international level, and its counterparts on other levels, is that of learning to channel these tensions in creative and productive ways.

Finally, it must be recognized that the World Council has not yet succeeded in attracting all Christian churches to its membership; among the nonmembers are many so-called evangelical and fundamentalistic churches and the Roman Catholic church (whose ecumenical development will be considered in the next section). Nonetheless, even if "the ecumenical movement is more than the World Council of Churches,"[94] still by serving as a forum where churches can meet together in faith and fellowship, the World Council seems to be realizing Schaff's vision of a "confederate union" of churches.

Vatican II and Roman Catholic Ecumenism

Although Schaff's historical dialectic furnished him with a vision of the inevitable interaction of Protestantism and Catholicism, he presumably would have been surprised at how radical a reorientation the Roman Catholic church would experience in the twentieth century. For the first half of this century, the official ecumenical policy of the Roman Catholic church was symbolized by the encyclical, *Mortalium Animos*, issued by Pope Pius XI in 1928, in response to the first World Conference of Faith and Order held the previous year in Lausanne, Switzerland: "There is but one way in which the unity of Christians may be fostered, and that is by furthering the return to the one true Church of Christ of those who are separated from it."[95]

In light of this "ecumenism of return" mandated by the Roman Catholic church's understanding of itself as the only true church, the Holy Office in 1948, published a monitum reminding Roman Catholics that canon law prohibited their attendance at "mixed gatherings" without prior permission from the Vatican; in fact, such permission was not granted to any of the Roman Catholics who had been invited to attend the first assembly of the World Council in Amsterdam, as "unofficial observers," although "a few Roman Catholic theologians were able to follow the Assembly's proceedings, unobtrusively."[96]

This policy was partially modified by the provisions of *Ecclesia Catholica* in 1949, which expressed the Roman Catholic church's interest in the ecumenical movement and allowed Roman Catholics, with specific permission, to participate in ecumenical gatherings. A year later, the World Council's Toronto Statement that "membership does not imply that each

Church must regard the other member Churches as Churches in the true and full sense of the word"[97] removed a major doctrinal barrier to Roman Catholic participation in ecumenical meetings. Roman Catholic observers subsequently attended the Faith and Order Conference at Lund in 1952, but no Roman Catholics were given permission to attend the World Council's second assembly at Evanston in 1954. Officially designated Roman Catholic observers were again present at the Faith and Order Conferences at Oberlin, Ohio, in 1957, and St. Andrews, Scotland, in 1960. At New Delhi the following year was the first time that the Roman Catholic church was officially represented at an assembly of the World Council.

During the first half of the century, the groundwork for later ecumenical theology and practice was laid by a few courageous pioneers, whose efforts were frequently viewed with suspicion. One of the earliest Roman Catholic ecumenists in Europe was Fernand Portal, whose friendship with Lord Halifax, led to the promising, but ultimately ill-fated, Malines conversations with representatives of the Church of England.[98] One of the earliest theologians to advocate ecumenism was Yves Congar, whose book on *Divided Christendom* attempted to specify a theological basis for Roman Catholic participation in the ecumenical movement.[99] Simultaneously, on the pastoral level, Abbé Paul Couturier promoted "the unanimous prayer of all Christian groups that he [Christ] may reunite them when and in what manner he wills."[100]

In the United States, a week of prayer for the reunion of Christians, the "Chair of Unity Octave," established in 1908 by Paul (Lewis Thomas) Wattson, a priest of the Episcopal church, was continued after he and the other members of the Society of the Atonement, the religious community that he founded as an Episcopalian, transferred to the Roman Catholic church.[101] Yet such efforts were comparatively isolated until mid-century, when many American Roman Catholics began to be influenced by the lectures and writings of ecumenists like the two official Roman Catholic observers at Oberlin, John Sheerin, the editor of the *Catholic World*, and Gustave Weigel, a professor at Woodstock College.[102] While such pioneering endeavors might have gradually moved the Roman Catholic church toward greater participation in the ecumenical movement, involvement in ecumenism was tremendously accelerated by Pope John XXIII and the Second Vatican Council.

On 28 October 1958, the conclave of cardinals elected Angelo Roncalli, as the successor of Pius XII, whose pontificate had lasted nearly two decades. The newly elected pontiff, who surprised people by selecting the name John XXIII,[103] was just short of his seventy-seventh birthday, and so it was widely presumed that the cardinals had chosen him as a "caretaker pope," who, so to speak, would tend the church for a few years. Few people expected an energetic, much less an innovative, papacy.

Less than two months after his election, John XXIII again surprised the world by announcing a general council of the bishops of the Roman Catholic church—an unexpected decision, since it had been nearly ninety years since the previous general council (the First Vatican Council, 1869–70). After months of extensive preparation, the Second Vatican Council convened in St. Peter's Basilica in Rome on 11 October 1962; in addition to over two thousand prelates of the Roman Catholic church, in attendance were many officially invited observers from other Christian communions. Although John XXIII only lived long enough to witness the first session of the council, his pastoral concern for an *aggiornamento* (bringing-up-to-date) of the church was continued during the remaining three sessions that met during the pontificate of his successor, Pope Paul VI.[104]

Most of the council's discussions and decisions were concerned with the intramural renewal of the Roman Catholic church; nonetheless, as the "Decree on Ecumenism" asserted, "the restoration of unity among all Christians is one of the principal concerns of the Second Vatican Council."[105] In words reminiscent of the International Missionary Conference at Edinburgh in 1910, Vatican II acknowledged that disunity among Christians is unacceptable, because "such division openly contradicts the will of Christ, scandalizes the world, and damages that most holy cause, the preaching of the Gospel to every creature."[106]

Describing the ecumenical movement as "fostered by the grace of the Holy Spirit, for the restoration of unity among all Christians,"[107] Vatican II espoused an ecumenism of "reunion" in contrast to the Roman Catholic church's previous insistence on the "return" of other Christians to the "one true church." This change in policy was based on an important shift in ecclesiology: instead of identifying the "unique church of Christ" with the Roman Catholic church, the council pointed out that the Church of Christ "subsists in the Catholic Church,"[108] thereby allowing for an acknowledgment of the ecclesiological significance of other churches: "some, even very many of the most significant elements and endowments, which together go to build up and give life to the Church itself, can exist outside the visible boundaries of the Catholic Church."[109]

And in contrast to the previous canonical restrictions on the participation of Roman Catholics in ecumenical meetings, Vatican II encouraged "all the Catholic faithful to recognize the signs of the times and to take an active and intelligent part in the work of ecumenism."[110] Specifically, the council encouraged Catholics to overcome the prejudices of the past and recommended that Catholics cooperate with other Christians in humanitarian projects. Vatican II also gave its approval to joint prayer with other Christians, though sacramental sharing was still restricted.[111]

However, what subsequently has proved to be ecumenically productive for the resolution of long-standing doctrinal controversies was the council's recommendation for dialogue "between competent experts from different Churches and Communities."[112] Recognizing that Roman Catholic doctrine had formerly been expressed in such a monolithic way that it was "an obstacle to dialogue," Vatican II advised Catholic theologians to "remember that in Catholic doctrine there exists an order or 'hierarchy' of truths, since they vary in their relation to the foundation of the christian faith."[113] This conciliar recommendation (as will be seen in the following section) led to the official establishment of "bilateral conversations" between the Roman Catholic church and other confessional traditions on the international, national, and regional levels.

In analogous fashion, a Joint Working Group was established with the World Council of Churches; simultaneously, Roman Catholics became official members of the Faith and Order Commission and other World Council bodies. However, the question of Roman Catholic membership in the World Council continues to pose problems for both sides: on the one hand, since representation on conciliar committees and other units of the World Council is proportional to a church's membership, the fact that the total number of Roman Catholics is greater than the combined membership of all the member churches of the World Council would presumably require a major revision of the World Council's structures; on the other hand, to some Roman Catholics, membership in the World Council "would seem tantamount to a rejection of the petrine function as foundation and preserver of unity" as well as "a denial of the Catholic Church's universality (catholicity), identity, and of its self-image of being a sacrament of Christ."[114]

In addition to the ecclesiological and organizational differences between the World Council as a representative body of churches and the Roman Catholic church as a single worldwide communion, there are also fundamental methodological differences between the more existentialistic approach of the World Council and the more essentialistic tradition of Roman Catholicism.[115] It is presently unclear how a wide variety of problems, ranging from ecclesiology to ethics, can be resolved.

What does seem clear, however, is that the public credibility of the Roman Catholic church's entry into the ecumenical movement owes much to the council's "Declaration on Religious Liberty," which was the only conciliar document addressed to the entire world.[116] It was also the most controversial of all the documents at Vatican II, for it represented a notable revision of previous church-state teaching: previously, many theologians had claimed religious freedom for Roman Catholics in countries where they are in the minority but had insisted that Roman Catholics should enjoy a privileged position in countries where they are in the majority—with the adherents of other religions at a proportionate disadvantage. This issue had long plagued Protestant-Catholic relations in the United States,[117] and it was appropriately an American professor of theology, John Courtney Murray,[118] who was the leading advocate and architect of the principles at the heart of this "Declaration." Vatican II understood religious freedom as a fundamental human right, based not on the subjective attitude of an individual but on the dignity of the human person; consequently, a government can never justly suppress the freedom of religious profession and practice, which should be guaranteed within appropriate constitutional bounds. Similarly, from a theological perspective, the church should never infringe on the religious freedom of those who do not accept its teaching, whether they are Christians or non-Christians.

The "relation of the Church to non-Christian religions" was the subject of a separate declaration, which also created considerable controversy, in part because of the political situation in the Middle East.[119] In particular, this "Declaration" repudiated anti-Semitism, although less emphatically than many in the Jewish world desired. In a more general sense, the "Declaration," in contrast to the traditional teaching that there is "no salvation outside the church," rejected discrimination against all "non-Christians" and asserted that all peoples of the earth, with their various religions, form one human community, whose spiritual, moral, and cultural values are respected by the church. However, since the term "non-Christians" has a negative connotation, it would have been preferable to have spoken in a more positive way, for example, of "believers of other faiths." Although this "Declaration" was a radical departure from earlier stances, still it can only be regarded as "seminal" or "preliminary" for the difficult task of both Jewish-Christian dialogue and the broader interreligious dialogue.[120]

Interconfessional Dialogue

Already during Philip Schaff's lifetime, churches belonging to the same confessional tradition began holding international meetings. Though "Anglicans deny that theirs is a confessional grouping and they did not in fact develop a continuing organization until after 1958," the first conference of bishops of the Anglican Communion was held at Lambeth in

1867.[121] The "Alliance of Reformed Churches Throughout the World holding the Presbyterian System" was organized in 1875 and held its first meeting two years later. Subsequently, with greater or less organizational formality, most of the major national and regional churches have become affiliated with what were formerly termed "world confessional families" but have more recently been called "world Christian communities."

The emergence of these international organizations has not only facilitated dialogue among their member churches and enabled them to rediscover neglected or forgotten aspects of their confessional heritage, it has also provided unexpected opportunities for interconfessional conversations on the worldwide level. For example, the Roman Catholic church, as a way of implementing the Second Vatican Council's recommendation for ecumenical dialogue among theologians, has jointly arranged with other world Christian communities for the establishment of international bilateral conversations consisting of officially appointed representatives from each side. This pattern has also been employed by other world confessional bodies and has led to the formation of well over a hundred different official conversations on the international, national, and regional levels.[122]

The world Christian communities are sometimes criticized for being competing elements in the ecumenical movement;[123] similar criticisms have occasionally been used to play one bilateral conversation against another or against the multilateral endeavors of the World Council. This is not to say that the bilaterals are without problems; for example, there is some danger that a bilateral may become so focused on resolving the divisive issues separating the two participating confessional traditions that it will lose sight of the broader ecumenical picture; there is also the possibility that when a church sponsors more than one bilateral conversation, the conclusions achieved in one bilateral may not be consistent with the conclusions reached in another; but the most common problem is that one bilateral may be unaware of, and thus duplicate, what another bilateral has already accomplished.[124]

In fact, such problems of coordination and communication have been relatively minor in comparison with the surprising theological agreement achieved by the bilaterals. While some bilaterals have made much greater progress than others, on the whole, their discussions have given a different perspective to church-dividing issues. The orientation of a specific bilateral is usually influenced by the historical relationship of the sponsoring churches. For example, some bilaterals, such as the Anglican-Roman Catholic, have been primarily concerned with long-standing historical differences; other bilaterals, such as the United Methodist-Roman Catholic, have devoted considerable attention to contemporary pastoral concerns.[125] Some bilaterals, such as the Lutheran-Roman Catholic dialogue in the United States, have systematically investigated long-standing doctrinal problems;[126] other bilaterals, such as the international Evangelical-Roman Catholic Dialogue on Mission, have focused on the implications of a central biblical theme.[127]

Yet, even when different bilaterals treat the same topic, they tend to develop distinctive orientations. For example, while both the Lutheran-Roman Catholic and the United Methodist-Roman Catholic dialogues in the United States have discussed the topic of ordained ministry, their focus was different: in the former, on the relationship of eucharist and ordained ministry, in the latter, on the spirituality of the ordained ministry.[128] Although the reports of both bilaterals contain common elements, the results of one bilateral can not simply be transferred en bloc to the other.

While the bilateral conversations are probably the most feasible way of resolving the divisive issues between two confessional traditions, if unity among all Christians is ever to be achieved, a multilateral approach is ultimately necessary. Admittedly, the very thought of an ecumenical dialogue involving the whole spectrum of Christian churches for the purpose of attaining doctrinal agreement seems immensely difficult, if not practically impossible. Yet, surprisingly, such a multilateral convergence has been achieved on the crucially important topics of *Baptism, Eucharist and Ministry* by the Faith and Order Commission of the World Council of Churches at its meeting in Lima, Peru, in 1982.[129]

The so-called Lima Report is the climax to a lengthy process of ecumenical discussion that originated at the first international conference of Faith and Order at Lausanne, Switzerland, in 1927. The more immediate origins, however, are "three agreed statements" on "One Baptism, One Eucharist, and a Mutually Recognized Ministry" that the Faith and Order meeting in Accra, Ghana, in 1974 "submitted to the churches for consideration and comment."[130] After revision in light of such comments, the Lima Report was unanimously approved by the Faith and Order Commission; this unanimous acceptance was a particularly significant instance of theological convergence among a broad range of Christian traditions— from Orthodox and Catholic, through mainline Reformation, to Adventist and Pentecostal.

The convergence achieved in the Lima document is not simply the least common denominator of possible agreement; rather, "the agreed text purposely concentrates on those aspects of the theme that have been directly or indirectly related to the problems of mutual recognition leading to unity." Nor does the Lima statement merely ask the churches for further study and comment in light of their own doctrine and discipline; rather, the Faith and Order Commission invited the churches to give an "official response to this text at the highest appropriate level of authority"; as part of such a "process of reception," the churches were asked to inform the commission about four specific dimensions of the Lima Report:[131]

> -the extent to which your church can recognize in this text the faith of the Church through the ages; -the consequences your church can draw from this text for its relations and dialogues with other churches . . . ; -the guidance your church can take from this text for its worship, educational, ethical, and spiritual life and witness; -the suggestions your church can make for the ongoing work of Faith and Order as it relates the material of this text . . . to its long-range research project "Towards the Common Expression of the Apostolic Faith Today."[132]

In contrast to many other ecumenical documents, which have been read by a very limited audience, and "despite the predictions that a theological text of this kind could no longer grip the attention of ordinary Christians," the Lima document has become a "bestseller" that has already been translated into twenty-six languages, with still other translations pending.[133] While the interest of theologians in this document was to be expected,[134] what is unusually significant is the grass-roots interest that suggests that many church members are not interested simply in cooperative endeavors among Christians but also hope to find some way of resolving the long-standing doctrinal issues that have divided Christians.[135]

If Philip Schaff would presumably have been gratified that Christians with a great diversity of denominational backgrounds have accepted the Lima Report as a basic statement of their faith, he might have been surprised by the recommendation that "the threefold ministry of bishop, presbyter and deacon may serve today as an expression of the unity we seek and also as a means for achieving it."[136] While recognizing that "the New Testament does not describe a single pattern of ministry which might serve as a blueprint or continuing norm for future ministry in the Church" and while acknowledging that "the threefold pattern [of bishops, presbyters, and deacons] stands evidently in need of reform," the Lima Report challenged "churches not having the threefold pattern . . . to ask themselves whether the threefold pattern does not have a powerful claim to be accepted by them."[137]

This specific question, along with similar ones, forms part of the much larger issue of the "reception" of ecumenical statements. From a legal point of view, "reception" can be understood as the very minimal act of acknowledging the arrival of a document; and while practically all churches have some more or less well defined process for approving their own intramural statements, procedures are not nearly so clear when it is a question of "receiving" ecumenical statements. Moreover, from an ecclesiological viewpoint, "reception," understood as making a doctrinal statement part of the life of a church, is really the highest form of recognition possible, thus a type of approbation to be given only after serious deliberation. In effect, by challenging the churches "to receive" the Lima Report at their highest official levels, the World Council has set the stage for a new ecumenical phenomenon: "reception" as a process of corporate decision-making among churches.[138]

While the ultimate results of this process of "reception" remain to be seen, the official responses to the Lima Report have started to appear. On the whole, the responses are surprisingly favorable in recognizing that the Lima document represents "the faith of the Church through the ages." Yet some basic reservations have been expressed, particularly in the area of ministry, where some (usually nonepiscopal churches) feel that the report has gone too far, and others (usually sacramental churches) feel that it has not gone far enough. While all of the responses delineate some of the divergences between the Lima text and their own denominational positions, a few respondents seem rather resistant about allowing the Lima document really to challenge their own church's doctrine and discipline. Thus the initial round of responses gives a better sense of how the Lima text relates to the denominational past and present, than how it provides possibilites for an ecumenical convergence in the future.[139]

While the Faith and Order Commission does not presently intend to revise the Lima Report, it does intend to report on the responses received, as well as to continue working on two additional and complementary projects that are currently under study: one on "the common expression of the apostolic faith," the other on "the unity of the Church and the renewal of human community."[140] The commission hopes to formulate reports on both these topics for consideration and comment by the churches.

United and Uniting Churches

Philip Schaff's hope that the United States would be "the chief theatre" for the "reunion of Christendom" suggests the image of a play that has started and is presently in progress with the ending still in suspense. Since Schaff's day, the United States has been the scene of a number of church unions, most of which have tended to be within the same confessional family or between churches of different traditions whose doctrines and polity were similar.[141] Although transconfessional unions, bringing together churches with notably different doctrinal backgrounds and ecclesiastical structures, have occurred in other countries,[142] this has yet to happen among the major denominations in the United States.

The challenge to work toward such a comprehensive church union received compelling expression in 1960 in "A Proposal Toward the Reunion of Christ's Church" by Dr. Eugene Carson Blake, then stated clerk of the United Presbyterian Church in the U.S.A. and later secretary general of the World Council of Churches.[143] In substance, Blake proposed that his own church enter into a quadrilateral discussion in view of organic union with the Episcopal church, the Methodist church, and the United Church of Christ. Although these four churches had previously collaborated on various projects, their respective ecclesiastical histories and confessional traditions were so different that their corporate union seemed to many to be unfeasible, if not impossible.

Nonetheless, Blake's proposal elicited a favorable response. In 1962, representatives of the four churches established the Consultation on Church Union for the purpose of exploring "the possibility of the formation of a Church, truly catholic, truly reformed, truly evangelical."[144] After the initial meeting, membership invitations were sent to three other churches that already had ecumenical links to one of the original four; two of these churches accepted: the Evangelical United Brethren (which in 1968 united with the Methodist church to form the United Methodist church) and the Christian Churches-Disciples of Christ (which was in union conversations with the United Church of Christ); the Polish National Catholic Church (which was then in full communion with the Episcopal church) declined. Other American churches were invited to send observer consultants to future plenary meetings of the consultation.

In 1965, the consultation invited these other churches to become full participants. Subsequently, five churches responded affirmatively: the (southern) Presbyterian Church in the United States (which in 1983 united with the northern United Presbyterian Church in the U.S. to form the Presbyterian church), the National Council of Community Churches, and three predominantly black churches, the African Methodist Episcopal Church, the African Methodist Episcopal Zion Church, and the Christian Methodist Episcopal Church. Other churches have continued to send observer consultants to the meetings of the consultation.

By 1970, the consultation had prepared *A Plan of Union for the Church of Christ Uniting* for study and response by its member churches.[145] The *Plan* consisted of two parts: first, a doctrinal statement about the basis for union, the nature of the church and its membership, scripture and tradition, worship and ministry; second, a set of organizational provisions for the uniting church's transitional and permanent structures. A decade after Blake's proposal, reunion seemed to be on the horizon.

The *Plan*, however, quickly succumbed under an avalanche of objections. Apparently it had been overly optimistic to presume that "if we take our theological assumptions seriously, the organizational conclusions would pretty well take care of themselves."[146] Rather, the reverse was true: an analysis of the responses to the *Plan* revealed "general agreement on matters of faith, worship and the basic nature of the Church's ministry, but a general unreadiness to accept the organizational structures proposed for a united church."[147] In effect, the reactions to the *Plan* made it apparent that unless and until the members of the participating churches acquired an ecumenical vision and experienced ecumenical fellowship, they would not really be motivated to support church union. Thus, the consultation recognized the importance of sharing its vision of a uniting church and providing ecumenical experience among all the members of the participating churches.

The consultation then made a twofold decision: on the one hand, it decided to continue redrafting the *Plan* in light of the responses received; on the other hand, it began implementing a process of growing together at the local and regional levels. Among the means utilized in this process were the establishment of "interim eucharistic fellowships"—clusters of local congregations that meet regularly for celebration of the eucharist—and "generating communities"—groupings of local congregations that covenant for a period of time to share specific aspects of their church lives; these specially selected fellowships and communities constituted a set of ecumenical laboratories, where church union could be tested at the local level.

Simultaneously, the consultation attempted to address a number of other church-dividing issues, such as institutional racism and the exclusion of women and young people from full participation in the church— issues that are sometimes greater barriers to church union than doctrinal differences.[148] Since discrimination and exclusivism are sometimes practiced more implicitly than explicitly, the consultation underscored the need for churches to confront these problems candidly and directly. Nonetheless, while attention to such issues is a praiseworthy attempt to address long-standing sources of alienation that stand in the way of reconciliation within and between churches, these additions to the consultation's agenda have also complicated and slowed the process of union. However, many feel that such issues must be resolved if church union is really to effect renewal in the life and worship of the uniting churches.

By 1976, the consultation had prepared a revised statement of its "emerging theological consensus," *In Quest of a Church of Christ Uniting*;[149] this document retained in revised form the theological sections of the *Plan* but omitted the structural provisions that had aroused so much opposition. The sections on the nature of unity, the church and membership, and faith and worship occasioned comparatively little difficulty; the chapter on ministry created considerable debate, particularly about the nature of the diaconate and the constitutional framework for the episcopacy in the uniting church.[150] Underlying the debate on the threefold ministry was a collision of two different mind-sets: on the one hand were those who interpreted the statements on ministry with an organizational-constitutional-juridical mentality; on the other hand were those who focused on the personal-pastoral-sacramental aspects of ministry. In effect, the interpretation of *In Quest* implicitly raises what has increasingly become a central hermeneutical issue in ecumenical dialogue: what degree of doctrinal consensus is necessary for church union?

The consultation has chosen to answer this question by challenging its member churches to commit themselves to a covenant to live and work together until some sort of visible union takes place. By implication, this proposed covenanting embodies three facets of the consultation's pilgrimage: first, the acceptance of a theological consensus; second, the need for expressing this consensus in liturgical celebration and interchurch cooperation on every level; third, the designing of organizational structures that would align the different denominational administrations into a uniting church. Of these three tasks, the one furthest along is the work on *The COCU Consensus*, whose chapter on ministry has been revised in light of the ecumenical convergence expressed in the Lima Report.[151] The work on the other two tasks will necessarily be a long and involved process; indeed, it may well prove easier for theologians to formulate consensus statements, than it is for ecclesiastical administrators to amalgamate their respective bureaucracies or for local churches to relinquish some of their autonomy.

In effect, the history of the consultation seems to indicate that attention to process is as necessary to the viability of church union efforts as attention to theological consensus. Nonetheless, while there is much to be said for understanding church union as a process of living and working together as a way of growing together, there is also a definite danger of protracting the process. Problems once thought to have been solved may easily be resurrected in new form once the original problem solvers are no longer on the scene. Agreements once thought to be firm may easily come unraveled once the consensus-negotiators are no longer at hand.

New problems and new questions that were not initially at issue may arise, or even be contrived by those opposed to union, to stalemate the process of uniting. If the quest for church union is a pilgrimage in faith as well as a process of growth, there comes a time when a commitment must be made, even though all questions are not answered, even though all problems are not resolved.

Reflections

Reflecting on contemporary ecumenism in light of Philip Schaff's ecumenical outlook and endeavors shows some striking similarities. Like Schaff, many contemporary ecumenists find themselves criticized by their co-religionists for their ecumenical commitment; denominational loyalties are still a deterrent to ecumenism. And like Schaff, many ecumenists find that their statements of doctrinal consensus and their proposals for church union are rejected (sometimes indirectly through a request for further study) by many members of their churches.

Contemporary ecumenists have had to contend with a puzzling lack of interest in their efforts to resolve long-standing doctrinal controversies in order to achieve church union. Perhaps this lack of interest is due to the failure of many to understand the significance of the doctrinal consensus that has been achieved or perhaps a failure to perceive any need for visible union among Christians. Or perhaps this lack of interest is due to a lacuna in ecumenical experience; those who merely read consensus statements or union proposals have had no share in the experiential process of those who prepared them and so no investment in their acceptance. In effect, the mere texts of consensus statements and plans of union are incapable of communicating the ecumenical experiences that helped the participants arrive at agreement. Thus, contemporary ecumenists seemingly could use more of Schaff's evangelical fervor in communicating their commitment to the "reunion of Christendom."[152]

In addition to recognizing the need to replicate Schaff's ecumenical energy and enthusiasm, contemporary ecumenists are increasingly coming to share his view that the "reunion of Christendom" does not require the resolution of all doctrinal issues. The participants in recent official ecumenical dialogues have taken their work so seriously that they have not only found basic areas of agreement, they have also concluded that the extent of their consensus is sufficient to warrant, indeed to require, that their churches take concrete steps toward realizing some type of visible unity.

One theological delineation of this doctrinal mandate for church union has been presented by Heinrich Fries and Karl Rahner in *Unity of the Churches: An Actual Possibility.*[153] In the authors' judgment, the dual threat of contemporary atheism and secularism implies that "the ecumenical task has become an urgent matter of survival for Christianity and the churches"; furthermore, church union is theologically warranted because the doctrinal basis for Christian unity is already available in "the fundamental truths of Christianity, as they are expressed in Holy Scripture, in the Apostles' Creed, and in that of Nicaea and Constantinople"; in addition to scripture and these creeds, "no explicit and positive confession in one partner church" should be imposed as "dogma obligatory for another partner church."[154]

Based on such a combination of "common confession" and "epistemological tolerance," Fries and Rahner envision the "one Church of Jesus Christ" as consisting of many "regional partner churches," each retaining its own organization, liturgy, and theology. In such a union, Protestant Christians would not have to subscribe to many of the doctrinal statements that Catholics regard as binding in faith, provided that these Catholic doctrines were not specifically denied. For example, in regard to the papacy, Protestant churches would be asked to "acknowledge the meaning and right of the Petrine service of the Roman pope to be the concrete guarantor of the unity of the Church in truth and love"; this recognition of the papacy would then be reciprocated by the pope who "explicitly commits himself to acknowledge and to respect the thus agreed upon independence of the partner churches."[155]

While the authors may have been excessively optimistic in their proposals—which have already become the object of considerable debate[156]—still they seem on target in highlighting a number of critical questions: what is the essential basis for the unity of the churches? If scripture and the creeds are not a sufficient basis for unity, what more is required? And if Christians do manage to find a basic unity in faith and fellowship, how much diversity is allowable?

This last question has been answered by the veteran ecumenist, Yves Congar in a way that might have surprised and delighted Philip Schaff. From his analysis of the New Testament and the early church, Congar concludes that "diversity has always been accepted in the unity of faith."[157] In Congar's appraisal of the present ecumenical situation, "no church or communion has succeeded in convincing the rest that it is in possession of *the* truth"; thus, a single church can no longer conceive of unity as the return, or "the reduction of the others to itself."[158] Such a conclusion prompts Congar to ask whether a church should "make it a condition of union" that other churches must accept the "dogmas defined by it in the absence of others?"[159] Many ecumenists today would agree with Congar that one church "cannot impose dogmas defined without the participation of others and without any root in their tradition as a *sine qua non* for communion."[160]

Like Schaff, contemporary ecumenists are committed to the task of trying to determine what is really necessary for visible unity, while allowing for legitimate diversity and expressing mutual love within the Christian community: *In necessariis unitas, in dubiis libertas, in omnibus caritas.*

Notes

1. D. Schaff, *The Life of Philip Schaff, in Part Autobiographical*. (New York: Charles Scribner's Sons, 1897), 497; hereafter cited as *Life*.

2. The lecture, originally delivered in German, was first published as *Das Princip des Protestantismus* (Chambersburg, PA: Druckerei der Hochdeutsch-Reformierten Kirche, 1845) and later made available in an expanded version, translated by Schaff's colleague, John Williamson Nevin (1803–86), under the title, *The Principle of Protestantism as Related to the Present State of the Church* (Chambersburg, PA: "Publication Office" of the German Reformed Church, 1845); hereafter cited as *Principle*.

3. D. Schaff, *Life*, 486.

4. Schaff's paper was published in *The World's Parliament of Religions*, ed. J. H. Barrows (Chicago, 1893) 2:1192–1201 and in an expanded version, *The Reunion of Christendom* (New York, 1893); cf. G. Shriver, *Philip Schaff: Christian Scholar and Ecumenical Prophet* (Macon, GA: Mercer University Press, 1987), 102–6.

5. D. Schaff, *Life*, 275.

6. K. Penzel, *Church History and the Ecumenical Quest: A Study of the German Background and Thought of Philip Schaff*. (New York: Union Theological Seminary, 1962), 222; hereafter cited *Church History*.

7. K. Penzel, *Church History*, 338.

8. L. Binkley, *The Mercersburg Theology*. Franklin and Marshall College Studies 7 (Manheim, PA: Sentinel Printing House, 1953), 63.

9. D. Schaff, *Life*, 111.

10. P. Schaff, *Principle*, 121.

11. L. Binkley, *Mercersburg Theology*, 61.

12. Ibid., 70–71.

13. P. Schaff, *Principle*, 49; italics in original.

14. K. Penzel, *Church History*, 50; Johann Adam Möhler (1796–1838) was an ecumenically minded Roman Catholic theologian who once taught at Tübingen, where Schaff studied.

15. L. Binkley, *Mercersburg Theology*, 58.

16. K. Penzel, *Church History*, 330–31.

17. Cf. K. Penzel, *Church History*, 91; L. Binkley, *Mercersburg Theology*, 52.

18. D. Schaff, *Life*, 92.

19. P. Schaff, *Church and State in the United States or the American Idea of Religious*

Liberty and Its Practical Effects (New York-London: G. P. Putnam's Sons, 1888/New York: Arno Press, 1972), 83.

20. P. Schaff, Introduction to Emanuel V. Gerhart, *Institutes of the Christian Religion* (New York: A. C. Armstrong and Son, 1891) 1: xv.

21. D. Schaff, *Life*, 279–80; the statement of his son and biographer, David, that Philip Schaff spoke "at Döllinger's request" (279) is at variance with the recollections of another participant, Alfred Plummer, whose notebook recorded that Schaff "came forward and almost insisted upon being heard" (*Alfred Plummer, Conversations with Dr. Döllinger, 1870–1890*, ed. R. Boudens, Bibliotheca Ephemeridum Theologicarum Lovaniensium 67 [Leuven: University Press, 1985], 134).

22. *Alfred Plummer*, 134, recorded that Döllinger, the conference host, remarked after Schaff's address: "If his opinions are shared by the other members of the Conference, it follows that we all of us should have done far more wisely if we had remained at home." On Döllinger's role at the (Second) Bonn Union Conference in 1875, cf. P. Neuner, *Döllinger als Theologe der Oekumene*, Beiträge zur ökumenischen Theologie 19 (Paderborn-Munich-Vienna-Zurich: Ferdinand Schöningh, 1979), 197–219.

23. P. Schaff, *The Reunion of Christendom*, as cited by C. C. Tiffany, "Dr. Schaff and the Episcopal Church," *Report and Papers of the Sixth Annual Meeting of the American Society of Church History* (New York, 27, 28 December 1893), 21. Schaff's comments were prompted by the adoption of the "Four Anglican Articles of Reunion," the "Quadrilateral" approved by the convention of the Episcopal church at Chicago in 1886 and subsequently adopted in modified form by the Lambeth conference in 1888.

24. D. Schaff, *Life*, 391.

25. D. Schaff, *Life*, 465.

26. P. Schaff, *The Reunion of Christendom*, 35, cited by D. Schaff, *Life*, 460.

27. Schaff to Alexander F. Mitchell, 12 February 1887, in response to the announcement of the conferral of an honorary doctorate by St. Andrews University, in D. Schaff, *Life*, 409

28. T. Shahan, "Dr. Schaff and the Roman Catholic Church," *Report and Papers of the Sixth Annual Meeting of the American Society of Church History* (New York, 27, 28 December 1893), 26–28; the unidentified Latin phrase can be translated: "Since you are so distinguished, would that you were one of us."

29. K. Penzel, *Church History*, 194; cf. similar remarks on 69, 345–6. 30. P. Schaff, *The Reunion of Christendom*, as cited by D. Yoder, "Christian Unity in Nineteenth-Century America," in *A History of the Ecumenical Movement, 1517–1948*, ed. R. Rouse and S. Neill (Philadelphia: Westminster Press, 1954), 256.

31. K. Penzel, *Church History*, 347,

32. J. Nichols, *Romanticism in American Theology: Nevin and Schaff at Mercersburg* (University of Chicago Press, 1961), 136; Nichols frequently uses the variant

spelling, "Schaf"; according to B. Thompson and G. Bricker, eds. of *The Principle of Protestantism* (Philadelphia-Boston: United Church Press), 235, n. 2: "Schaff's manuscripts prepared in Germany prior to his arrival in America illustrate that he spelled his name inconsistently as 'Schaff,' and 'Schaf' "; G. Shriver, *Philip Schaff: Christian Scholar and Ecumenical Prophet*, I, n. I, notes that "named Philipp Schaaf at birth, in about 1847 he changed the spelling to Philip Schaff."

33. E.g., John Mackay, *Ecumenics: The Science of the Church Universal* (Englewood Cliffs, NJ: Prentice-Hall, 1964), 27, considered "ecumenics" as "the science of the Church Universal, conceived as a World Missionary Community." A comprehensive historical-systematic approach to ecumenism is offered in the three volumes of the *Handbuch der Oekumenik* edited by Hans-Jörg Urban and Harald Wagner (Paderborn: Bonifatius); the first volume (1985) discusses the "unity of the People of God" in its biblical perspective and the history of the church through the nineteenth century; the second volume (1986) treats the ecumenical movement in the twentieth century; the third volume is to deal with the ecumenical problematic of Christian theology.

34. Cf. P. Schaff, H. Potter, S. Jackson, et al. the American Church History Series, 13 vols. (New York: Christian Literature, 1893–97).

35. M. Fahey, "Twentieth Century Shifts in Roman Catholic Attitudes toward Ecumenism," in *Catholic Perspectives on Baptism, Eucharist, and Ministry*, ed. M. Fahey (Lanham-New York-London: University Press of America, 1986), 36.

36. This problem surfaced at the fourth World Council on Faith and Order (Montreal, 1963) in the contrasting interpretations proposed by E. Käsemann, "Unity and Diversity in New Testament Ecclesiology," *Novum Testamentum* 6 (1963): 290–97, and R. Brown, "The Unity and Diversity in New Testament Ecclesiology," ibid., 298–308.

37. E.g., J. Lochman, *An Ecumenical Dogmatics: The Faith We Confess* (Philadelphia: Fortress Press, 1984) successfully provides "an ecumenical sketch of the faith we confess as the people of God" through a series of theological reflections on the Apostles' Creed; yet not all would agree that the author has succeeded in providing "an ecumenical dogmatics."

38. P. Avis, *Truth Beyond Words: Problems and Prospects for Anglican-Roman Catholic Unity* (Cambridge, MA: Cowley Publications, 1985), 82–93, 112–16, describes some of the crucial ecumenical implications of pluralism.

39. One recent example of a notable historiographical shift is furnished by the converging Protestant and Roman Catholic assessments of Luther; cf. R. Stauffer, *Luther vu par les catholiques: l'évolution des recherches sur Luther dans le catholicisme du début du siècle à nos jours* (Neuchâtel-Paris: Delachaux et Niestlé, 1961); B. Marthaler, "The Luther Image," *Homiletic and Pastoral Review* 66 (1966): 317–25.

40. This Latin phrase, which can be translated "In essentials, unity; in nones-

sentials, liberty; in all things, charity," was one of the three mottoes of Schaff's life; cf. G. Shriver, *Philip Schaff: Christian Scholar and Ecumenical Prophet*, 110, n. 1; also cf. Y. Congar, *Diversity and Communion* (Mystic, CT: Twenty-Third Publications, 1985), 108;

41. Philadelphia: Fortress Press, 1985. Another excellent introduction to the ecumenical movement is Peter Neuner's *Kleines Handbuch der Oekumene* (Düsseldorf: Patmos, 1984); also helpful is *Oecuménisme* by Francis Frost (Paris: Letouzey and Ané, 1984), which is an extract from the encyclopedia *Catholicisme: Hier-Aujourd'hui-Demaine*.

42. New York/Ramsey: Paulist Press, 1983.

43. Garden City, NY: Doubleday, 1967; the revised and expanded (paperback) edition (1969) includes three additional chapters on postconciliar Roman Catholicism, *Humanae Vitae* and the crisis of authority in Roman Catholicism, and "secular ecumenism" that were not in the original (hardback) edition.

44. *A History of the Ecumenical Movement, 1517–1948*, vol. 1, ed. R. Rouse and S. Neill (Philadelphia: Westminster Press, 1954), and *The Ecumenical Advance, A History of the Ecumenical Movement*, vol. 2 (1948–68), ed. H. Fey (Philadelphia: Westminster Press, 1970); these two volumes, reissued by the World Council of Churches (Geneva, 1986), will hereafter be cited *HEM* with the appropriate volume number.

45. K. Latourette, "Ecumenical Bearings of the Missionary Movement and the International Missionary Council," *HEM* 1:359.

46. Ibid., 355, 362.

47. Ibid., 360.

48. Cf. T. Tatlow, "The World Conference on Faith and Order," *HEM* 1:405–41; a particularly useful resource is *A Documentary History of the Faith and Order Movement, 1927–1963*, hereafter cited *Documentary*, ed. L. Vischer (St. Louis: Bethany Press, 1963).

49. N. Karlström, "Movements for International Friendship and Life and Work, 1910–1925," *HEM* 1:540.

50. N. Ehrenström, "Movements for International Friendship and Life and Work, 1925–1948," *HEM* 1:595.

51. W. Visser't Hooft, *The Genesis and Formation of the World Council of Churches* (Geneva: World Council of Churches, 1982), 39–40; this volume, hereafter cited *Genesis*, with its candid descriptions of the difficulties attendant upon the formation of the World Council replaces the author's earlier treatment in "The Genesis of the World Council of Churches," *HEM* 1:697–724, which he confessed "does not deal adequately with the period in which the first proposals were made, and requires elaboration at many other points" (*Genesis*, vii).

52. W. Visser't Hooft, *Genesis*, 58.

53. Ibid., 1–17.

54. W. Visser 't Hooft, *HEM* 1:719 and *Genesis*, 63; however, H. Krüger, "The Life and Activities of the World Council of Churches," *HEM* 2:37, gives the number of churches as 145.

55. H. Krüger, *HEM* 2:38.

56. L. Vischer, *Documentary*, 76, 79, 81: excerpts from the "Report of Section I" on "the Universal Church in God's Design."

57. W. Visser 't Hooft, *HEM* 1:721.

58. L. Vischer, *Documentary*, 75.

59. Ibid., 168–69.

60. Ibid., 171; the full text of the "assumptions" is given on 171–76; for a description of the preparation of the Toronto Statement, including Roman Catholic contributions, the debate at Toronto and subsequent discussion, cf. W. Visser 't Hooft, *Genesis*, 70–85.

61. Ibid., 82.

62. L. Vischer, *Documentary*, 179.

63. M. Handspicker, "Faith and Order 1948–1968," *HEM* 2:155.

64. L. Vischer, *Documentary*, 85, 90.

65. Ibid., pp. 96, 92.

66. L. Vischer, *Documentary*, 86.

67. H. Krüger, *HEM* 2:39.

68. L. Vischer, *Documentary*, 136, 137; the Orthodox delegates at Evanston, however, declared that "the whole approach to the problem of reunion [as formulated in the report on "Our Oneness in Christ and Our Disunity as Churches"] is entirely unacceptable" (ibid., 141).

69. Ibid., 141.

70. H. Krüger, *HEM* 2:41–44.

71. *The New Delhi Report: The Third Assembly of the World Council of Churches, 1961*, ed. W. Vissert 't Hooft (New York: Association Press, 1962), 37, 426; cf. 152–59.

72. *The New Delhi Report*, 116: the text, which is printed in bold-faced type, is also available in L. Vischer, *Documentary*, 144–45.

73. *The Fourth World Conference on Faith and Order, Montreal 1963*, ed. P. Rodger and L. Vischer (New York: Association Press, 1964), 21–23, 30–31.

74. Ibid., 80, 81, 84.

75. Ibid., 89.

76. L. Vischer, "The Ecumenical Movement and the Roman Catholic Church," *HEM* 2:333.

77. E. Blake, "Uppsala and Afterwards," *HEM* 2:416.

78. *The Uppsala Report 1968: Official Report of the Fourth Assembly of the World*

Council of Churches, July 4–20, 1968, ed. N. Goodall (Geneva: World Council of Churches, 1968), 12.

79. Ibid., 13, 14.

80. Ibid., 17.

81. *Breaking Barriers, Nairobi 1975: The Official Report of the Fifth Assembly of the World Council of Churches, Nairobi, 23 November–10 December, 1975*, ed. D. Paton (London: SPCK/Grand Rapids, MI: Eerdmans, 1976), 30.

82. Ibid., 60 (report of sec. 2: "What Unity Requires").

83. Ibid., 62; however, see 63: "there is no community without structure, but structure must serve and facilitate good church order, which is itself essentially and properly the expression of committed personal fellowship in Creed."

84. Ibid., 61.

85. Ibid., 64.

86. *The Constitution of the World Council of Churches*, 3 (i), in *Breaking Barriers, Nairobi 1975*, 317–18, cf. discussion on 189–90.

87. *Gathered for Life: Official Report, VI Assembly, World Council of Churches, Vancouver, Canada, 24 July–10 August, 1983*, ed. David Gill (Geneva: World Council of Churches/ Grand Rapids, MI: Eerdmans, 1984), 43–44.

88. Ibid., 1.

89. Ibid., 45.

90. Geneva: World Council of Churches, 1986.

91. For an interesting and informative overview of the work of the World Council, cf. L. Howell, *Acting in Faith: The World Council of Churches since 1975* (Geneva: World Council of Churches, 1982); for current information, see the World Council's publication, *One World*, which periodically carries a survey of the World Council's programs and activities (e.g., *WCC 1986* is a special enlarged issue for January-February 1986).

92. A helpful survey and bibliographical resource is available in *Major Studies and Themes in the Ecumenical Movement*, comp. Ans J. van der Bent (Geneva: World Council of Churches, 1981).

93. An excellent, though now somewhat dated, historical survey and bibliographical resource for the American ecumenical scene is provided in *Church Cooperation and Unity in America: A Historical Review: 1900–1970* by S. Cavert (New York: Association Press, 1970).

94. *Gathered for Life*, 51.

95. O. Tomkins, "The Roman Catholic Church and the Ecumenical Movement, 1910–1948," *HEM* 1:683.

96. L. Vischer, "The Ecumenical Movement and the Roman Catholic Church," *HEM* 2:316; cf. O. Tomkins, ibid. 1:689.

97. *Documentary*, 173.

98. Cf. H. Hemmer, *Fernand Portal (1855–1926): Apostle of Unity*, trans. and ed. A. Macmillan (London: Macmillan/New York: St. Martin's Press, 1961) and the more recent study by Régis Ladous, *Monsieur Portal et les siens* (Paris: Cerf, 1985).

99. M. J. Congar, *Divided Christendom: A Catholic Study of the Problem of Reunion* (London: Geoffrey Bles: Centenary Press, 1939) a translation of *Chrétiens Désunis: Principes d'un Oecumenisme Catholique* (Paris, 1937)

100. Cf. G. Curtis, *Paul Couturier and Unity in Christ* (London: SCM/ Westminster, MD: J. Eckenrode, 1964), 82.

101. Cf. C. Angell, C. LaFontaine, *Prophet of Reunion, The Life of Paul of Graymoor* (New York: Seabury, 1975).

102. Weigel's ecumenically oriented writings include: *A Survey of Protestant Theology in Our Day* (Westminster, MD: Newman, 1954), *A Catholic Primer on Ecumenism* (Westminster, MD: Newman, 1957), *Faith and Understanding in America* (New York: Macmillan, 1959), *American Dialogue* with Robert McAfee Brown (New York: Doubleday, 1960), *Churches in North America* (Baltimore: Helicon, 1961), *Catholic Theology in Dialogue* (New York: Harper, 1961).

103. The last officially recognized pope to bear the name "John" was John XXII (1316–34); however, a papal claimant during the Great Western Schism took the name "John XXIII" in 1410, but was deposed by the Council of Constance in 1415; by selecting the name, "John XXIII," Cardinal Roncalli categorically excluded this namesake from the official papal lineage.

104. While there are numerous contemporary accounts of the council, one of the most lively and widely read (as well as irreverent in the judgment of some) was that of Xavier Rynne (a pseudonym) in four volumes, subsequently published in a one-volume version as *Vatican Council II* (New York: Farrar, Straus and Giroux, 1968).

105. The "Decree on Ecumenism," approved by the council on 21 November 1964, is also known by its opening Latin words, *Unitatis Redintegratio*, hereafter cited *UR*, with the appropriate paragraph number: *UR* 1, for the passage cited above. The "Decree on Ecumenism" is available in English translation in *Doing the Truth in Charity: Statements of Pope Paul VI, Popes John Paul I, John Paul II, and the Secretariat for Promoting Christian Unity, 1964–1980*, ed. Thomas Stransky and John Sheerin (New York/Ramsey: Paulist Press, 1982), 18–33; as the title of this work suggests, this volume also provides an extensive selection of postconciliar ecumenical documents. The text of the "Decree on Ecumenism" is also available in *Vatican Council II: The Conciliar and Post Conciliar Documents*, ed. Austin Flannery (Collegeville, MN: Liturgical Press, 1975), 452–79; this volume also furnishes the texts of the other documents approved by the Council and selected postconciliar Vatican documents; additional postconciliar documentation is provided by *Vatican Council II: More Post-Conciliar Documents*, vol. 2, ed. Austin Flannery

(Northport, NY: Costello, 1982). The Stransky-Sheerin volume is the better source for ecumenical documentation; the more comprehensive documentation in the Flannery volumes is extremely useful in tracing postconciliar developments.

106. *UR* 1; among the many commentaries on the "Decree on Ecumenism" one of the most thorough in English is that of W. Becker and J. Feiner, "Decree on Ecumenism," *Commentary on the Documents of Vatican II*, ed. H. Vorgrimler (New York: Herder and Herder, 1968), 2:1–164. A historical introduction to the "Decree," including the interventions of American bishops, and a commentary by George Tavard, are available in *American Participation in the Second Vatican Council*, ed. V. Yzermans (New York: Sheed and Ward, 1967), 283–334. Also see the retrospective commentary of W. M. Brown, "Commentary on the Decree on Ecumenism, Unitatis Redintegratio," *The Church Renewed: The Documents of Vatican II*, ed. G. Schner (Lanham-New York-London: University Press of America, 1986), 37–54.

107. *UR* 1.

108. *Constitution on the Church (Lumen Gentium)* 8; cf. *UR* 3.

109. *UR* 3.

110. *UR* 4.

111. The question of sacramental sharing (*communicatio in sacris*) received further consideration and limited amplification in several postconciliar documents; cf. *Doing the Truth in Charity*, 115–30.

112. *UR* 4.

113. *UR* 11; for a discussion of the "hierarchy of truths," cf. Y. Congar, *Diversity and Communion* (Mystic, CT: Twenty-Third Publications, 1985), 126–33, and the extensive bibliography on 212.

114. J. McDonnell, *The World Council of Churches and the Catholic Church* (New York and Toronto: Edwin Mellen, 1985), 371. While this volume is a useful resource for data, its presentation is excessively restricted to documentary comparison and its interpretation tends to be narrowly traditional; nonetheless, its critique of the relationship between Geneva and Rome needs to be seriously considered.

115. Cf. T. Der, *Barriers to Ecumenism: The Holy See and the World Council of Churches on Social Questions* (Maryknoll, NY: Orbis, 1983).

116. This declaration, also known by its introductory Latin words, *Dignitatis Humanae*, is available in *Vatican Council II*, ed. A. Flannery, 1:799–812. Among the many commentaries on the "Declaration" are *Religious Liberty: an End and a Beginning*, ed. J. Murray (New York: Macmillan/ London: Collier-Macmillan, 1966), and *Conflict and Consensus: Religious Freedom and the Second Vatican Council* by R. Regan (New York: Macmillan/ London: Collier-Macmillan, 1967).

117. A short historical survey is provided by L. Curry, *Protestant-Catholic Relations in America: World War I through Vatican II* (Lexington: University of Kentucky Press, 1972).

118. For a perceptive analysis of the development of Murray's thought, cf. T. Love, *John Courtney Murray: Contemporary Church-State Theory* (Garden City, NY: Doubleday, 1965).

119. This declaration, also known by its introductory Latin words, *Nostra Aetate*, is available in *Vatican Council II*, ed. A. Flannery, 1:738–42. An excellent set of commentaries is provided by *Twenty Years of Jewish-Catholic Relations*, ed. E. Fisher, A. J. Rudin, M. Tanebaum (New York/Mahwah: Paulist Press, 1986).

120. Cf. *Christian Faith in a Religiously Plural World*, ed. D. Dawe and J. Carman (Maryknoll, NY: Orbis, 1978), *Christ's Lordship and Religious Pluralism*, ed. G. Anderson and T. Stransky (Maryknoll, NY: Orbis, 1981), and *Interreligious Dialogue: Facing the Next Frontier*, vol. 1: *Modern Theological Themes: Selections from the Literature*, ed. R. Rousseau (Scranton, PA: Ridge Row Press, 1981)

121. H. Fey, "Confessional Families and the Ecumenical Movement," *HEM* 2:117.

122. Currently, the most comprehensive list of these official dialogues is *A Bibliography of Interchurch and Interconfessional Theological Dialogues* (Rome: Centro pro Unione, 1984), prepared by J. Puglisi and S. Voicu; in addition to listing the individual meetings of over a hundred different officially sponsored dialogues in various parts of the world, this volume provides information (where available) about published reports and interpretive articles. An older and thus dated, but still useful, resource is the directory of M. Ehrenström and G. Gassmann, *Confessions in Dialogue: A Survey of Bilateral Conversations among World Confessional Families, 1959–1974*, 3d rev. ed. (Geneva: World Council of Churches, 1975).

123. Cf. the contentious critique of U. Duchrow, *Conflict over the Ecumenical Movement: Confessing Christ Today in the Universal Church*, trans. David Lewis (Geneva: World Council of Churches, 1981).

124. For a critical survey of the Roman Catholic bilaterals in the United States, cf. "The Bilateral Consultations between the Roman Catholic Church in the United States and Other Christian Communions," *Proceedings of the Catholic Theological Society of America* 27 (1972): 179–232, and "The Bilateral Consultations between the Roman Catholic Church in the United States and Other Christian Communions (1972–1979)," *Proceedings of the Catholic Theological Society of America* 34 (1979): 253–85. For a discussion of "The Quest for Christian Consensus: Bilateral Theological Dialogue in the Ecumenical Movement," cf. the set of papers prepared by a study group of the Faith and Order Commission of the National Council of Churches in *Journal of Ecumenical Studies* 23 (1986): 361–544.

125. Cf. *Growth in Agreement: Reports and Agreed Statements of Ecumenical Conversations on a World Level*, ed. H. Meyer and L. Vischer, Faith and Order

Paper 108, (New York/Ramsey: Paulist Press; Geneva: World Council of Churches, 1984), 61–129, 307–87. This volume, which contains reports from a dozen different international conversations, is currently the most convenient source of information on international dialogue; a topical index facilitates the use of this book, so that it is relatively easy to compare what different dialogues have stated about specific issues. A companion volume containing similar material from interconfessional dialogues in the United States is in preparation.

126. The Lutheran-Roman Catholic Dialogue in the United States has been particularly productive; the series Lutherans and Catholics in Dialogue has published studies on *The Status of the Nicene Creed as Dogma of the Church* (1, 1965), *One Baptism for the Remission of Sins* (2, 1966), *The Eucharist as Sacrifice* (3, 1967), *Eucharist and Ministry* (4, 1970), *Papal Primacy and the Universal Church* (5, 1974), *Teaching Authority and Infallibility in the Church* (6, 1980), and *Justification by Faith* (7, 1985). Vols. 1–3 in a combined edition (1973) and vols. 5–7 were published by Augsburg Publishing House (Minneapolis); vol. 4 was jointly published by the U.S.A. National Committee of the Lutheran World Federation (New York) and the Bishops' Committee for Ecumenical and Interreligious Affairs (Washington, DC).

127. Cf. *The Evangelical-Roman Catholic Dialogue on Mission, 1977–1984, A Report*, ed. B. Meeking and J. Stott (Grand Rapids, MI: Eerdmans/Exeter: Paternoster, 1986).

128. *Eucharist and Ministry* (Lutherans and Catholics in Dialogue 4) 7–33, with "Holiness and Spirituality of the Ordained Ministry: Report on the United Methodist-Roman Catholic Dialogue—1976" (Washington, DC: U.S. Catholic Conference, 1976).

129. The Lima Report was originally published as Faith and Order Paper 111 (Geneva: World Council of Churches, 1982) and has been republished in many places, including *Growth in Agreement*, 465–503; hereafter the text will be cited *BEM* with references to the paragraphs of the report.

130. *One Baptism, One Eucharist, and a Mutually Recognized Ministry: Three Agreed Statements*, Faith and Order Paper 73 (Geneva: World Council of Churches, 1975).

131. *BEM*, preface (ix, x); the minutes and addresses of the Lima meeting are available in the first volume of *Towards Visible Unity: Commission on Faith and Order, Lima, 1982*, ed. Michael Kinnamon; also of interest are the study papers and reports in the second volume, which indicate the projected work of the Faith and Order Commission on two pivotal topics, "the common expression of the apostolic faith today" and "the Unity of the Church and the renewal of human community;" these two topics may eventually be worked into convergence-statements similar to the Lima Report (Faith and Order Papers 112, 113 [Geneva: World Council of Churches, 1982]).

132. Ibid., x; the original text appeared in italics.

133. *Churches Respond to BEM: Official Responses to the "Baptism, Eucharist and Ministry Text*, vol. 1, ed. Max Thurian, Faith and Order Paper 129 (Geneva: World Council of Churches, 1986), 1.

134. Among the recently available theological commentaries on *BEM* are the following: *Ecumenical Perspectives on Baptism, Eucharist and Ministry*, ed. M. Thurian, Faith and Order Paper 116 (Geneva: World Council of Churches, 1983); *The Search for Visible Unity: Baptism, Eucharist, Ministry*, ed. J. Gros (New York: Pilgrim Press, 1984; simultaneously co-published in *Journal of Ecumenical Studies* 21 [1984]: 1–146); *Orthodox Perspectives on Baptism, Eucharist, and Ministry*, ed. G. Limouris and N. Vaporis, Faith and Order Paper 128 (Brookline, MA: Holy Cross Orthodox Press, 1985; simultaneously published in *The Greek Orthodox Theological Review* 30 [Summer 1985]); *Catholic Perspectives on Baptism, Eucharist and Ministry: A Study Commissioned by the Catholic Theological Society of America*, ed. M. Fahey (Lanham-New York-London: University Press of America, 1986).

135. A helpful booklet for parish-level use in discussing the Lima Report is William Lazareth's *Growing Together in Baptism, Eucharist and Ministry: A Study Guide*, Faith and Order Paper 114 (Geneva: World Council of Churches, 1982).

136. *BEM* 22.

137. *BEM* 19, 24, 25.

138. On the question of "reception," see T. Rausch, "Reception Past and Present," *Theological Studies* 47 (1986): 497–508, and L. Vischer, "The Process of 'Reception' in the Ecumenical Movement," *Mid-Stream* 23 (1984): 221–33.

139. *Churches Respond to BEM*, ed. M. Thurian, presents the initial set of responses from a diversity of ecclesial traditions and geographical locations: Lutheran (LCA, North Elbian), Anglican (Ireland, South America), Baptist (Britain, Ireland), Methodist (New Zealand), Presbyterian/Reformed (Cameroon, Scotland, United Kingdom), Disciples of Christ, and Orthodox (the results of the symposium published in *Orthodox Perspectives on Baptism, Eucharist, and Ministry*, ed. G. Limouris and N. Vaporis, 159–68).

140. Cf. *Faith and Renewal: Reports and Documents of the Commission on Faith and Order, Stavanger 1985, Norway*, ed. T. Best, Faith and Order Paper 131, (Geneva: World Council of Churches, 1986).

141. Cf. S. Neill, "Plans of Union and Reunion, 1910–1948," *HEM* 1:445–95; an appendix (496–505) gives a list of "plans of union and reunion, 1910–1952." For current information, cf. the "narrative bibliography" found in *Called to Be One in Christ: United Churches and the Ecumenical Movement*, ed. M. Kinnamon and T. Best, Faith and Order Paper 127, (Geneva: World Council of Churches, 1985), 73–77; the major portion of this volume contains papers and case studies from a consultation sponsored by the Faith and Order Commission of the World Council of Churches: *Growing Towards Consensus*

and Commitment: Report of the Fourth International Consultation of United and Uniting Churches, Colombo, Sri Lanka, Faith and Order Paper 110 (Geneva: World Council of Churches, 1981).

142. Among the notable examples of transconfessional unions are the United Church of Canada (1925) that involved Presbyterian, Methodist, and Congregational churches, and the Church of South India (1947) involving Methodist, Anglican, and United churches.

143. E. Blake, "A Proposal Toward the Reunion of Christ's Church" *Christian Century* 77, 21 December 1960, 1508–11.

144. *Consultation on Church Union—The Reports of the Four Meetings* (Cincinnati: Forward Movement Publications, 1966), 18.

145. The text of the *Plan* is included in the *Digest of the Proceedings of the Ninth Meeting of the Consultation on Church Union,* ed. Paul A. Crow, Jr. (Princeton, NJ: Consultation on Church Union, 1970), 87–190; the *Plan* was also published as a separate booklet.

146. E. Blake, "A United Church: Evangelical, Catholic and Reformed," *Thought* 41 (1966): 56.

147. W. Boney, "COCU: Memphis and After," *Journal of Ecumenical Studies* 10 (1973): 654.

148. For a perceptive treatment of these "non-doctrinal" barriers, cf. *Christian Unity: Matrix for Mission* by Paul A. Crow, Jr. (New York: Friendship Press, 1982).

149. *In Quest of a Church of Christ Uniting: A Statement of Emerging Theological Consensus,* printed in *Mid-Stream* 16 (1977): 49–108, and also available as a separate booklet from the Consultation on Church Union (Princeton, 1976).

150. For a comprehensive treatment of the theological issues facing the consultation, cf. *Oneness in Christ: The Quest and the Questions* by Gerald Moede (Princeton: Consultation on Church Union, 1981).

151. *The COCU Consensus: In Quest of a Church of Christ Uniting,* ed. Gerald F. Moede (Princeton: Consultation on Church Union, 1985).

152. Unfortunately, little or no specific information is available about many ecumenical meetings (cf. the repeated instances noted by J. Puglisi and S. Voicu in *A Bibliography of Interchurch and Interconfessional Theological Dialogues*); thus, in addition to interpretive reports (such as those available on the Consultation on Church Union), it would be helpful to have more experiential histories of ecumenical conversations such as the "personal notes for a study" provided by Paul Empie, *Lutherans and Catholics in Dialogue,* ed. R. Tiemeyer (Philadelphia: Fortress Press, 1981).

153. Trans. R. and E. Gritsch (Philadelpia: Fortress Press; New York/Ramsey: Paulist Press, 1985).

154. Ibid., 1, 7 (cf. 13–41).

155. Ibid., 8 (cf. 59–92).

156. Cf. E. Herms, *Einheit der Christen in der Gemeinschaft der Kirchen: Die ökumenische Bewegung der römischen Kirche im Lichte der reformatorischen Theologie, Antwort auf den Rahner-Plan*, Kirche und Konfession 24 (Göttingen: Vandenhoeck and Ruprecht, 1984).

157. *Diversity and Communion*, the title of chap. 3, pp. 23–33.

158. Ibid., 161, 162.

159. Ibid., 172.

160. Ibid., 174.

The First Century

Institutional Development and Ideas about the Profession

Henry Warner Bowden

P HILIP Schaff exerted decisive influence in founding the American Society of Church History and in determining its early interests. As a scholar of international repute, associated with theological education as well as historical study, Schaff took the initiative in sponsoring an organizational meeting at his home on East Forty-third Street in New York City.[1] The recently formed American Historical Association may have encouraged church historians to think of organizing a society that coordinated activities among professionally trained individuals.[2] Whether stimulated by AHA precedent or not, thirty-nine seminary and college professors, ministers, and journalists responded positively to Schaff's invitation in the spring of 1888. They constituted the nucleus of a society dedicated to the principles of "cultivating church history as a science, in an unsectarian, catholic spirit" and of "facilitating personal intercourse among students of history as a means of mutual encouragement."[3] Later that year Schaff presided at the first annual meeting, held in Washington, DC, and delivered one of what turned out to be five presidential addresses. Institutional circumstances have changed considerably since that inaugural year, but the ASCH has persevered in cultivating the spirit of open-ended inquiry into matters related to Christian history.

Early members of the society included luminaries from Europe who occupied honorary positions in keeping with Schaff's notions of prestige and reciprocal favors. There seems to have been no discernible antagonism between this eclectic coterie and their counterparts interested in secular topics.[4] Early minutes show that the first governing council resolved to approach the AHA "for the purpose of effecting a union with that Association as an independent section."[5] Samuel M. Jackson, ASCH secretary, wrote Herbert B. Adams, AHA secretary, toward that end, but in that initial summer he hinted at possible differences between separate interests amid common pursuits. "It was the sentiment of the majority at our meeting on March 23rd that in as much as our general aims were one we should not be a rival organization in any sense but a part of your Association. At the same time we do not wish to be absorbed by you, but recognized as having independent existence."[6] Jackson and Adams traded views about their respective organizations before the ASCH officially convened in December 1888. Adams expressed doubts about the alliance as proposed, saying that it would be better to organize church historians as a "section within the Association than to annex an independent section." He also wanted to charge three dollars beyond ASCH dues as payment for AHA publications. Jackson countered by suggesting that the two groups meet simultaneously in the same city but not at identical hours or in the same buildings. He saw no need for extra fees. Reiterating his previous attitude, Jackson proffered: "Our membership would be thus enrolled in the AHA, but perhaps separately grouped as an independent section of it. The united body would have one president, one treasurer, perhaps one secretary."[7]

At its first annual meeting the ASCH council appointed a committee of conference "to discuss the proposed affiliation of the two Societies" with a similar AHA committee. Correspondence must have passed between the principals during the following year because Adams penned a cordial note to Jackson in October 1889:

In the early summer I forwarded your letter regarding the fusion of the two Associations, to the Hon. John Jay of New York City, requesting him to confer with you, at his leisure, regarding the proposed relation. It seems to me that such a fusion can be accomplished at the next meeting of the two Societies, upon some such basis as that which you proposed.[8]

No closer cooperation took place at the next meeting or for another seven years. Leading figures of the AHA promoted an ideology of historical inquiry aligned with natural science, whereas prominent spokesmen for the ASCH urged historians to employ Christian faith in order to understand churches adequately. Despite diverging perspectives and varying methods, the available evidence shows that leaders of both societies expressed interest in close cooperation. Still, something prevented this mutually attractive proposal from being realized. Adams spoke of "fusion," while Jackson mentioned only "affiliation." A sense of independence among church historians, who organized themselves without tangible aid from the larger body, may have figured as heavily as any vaguely sensed incompatibility between secular and religious historiography. No surviving statement illuminates reasons for continuing separation, and when institutional merger eventually occurred, new circumstances virtually required it.

Schaff died on 20 October 1893, but the ASCH did not find anyone who provided the leadership that he had given. The first president had been reelected annually for six years, and that practice continued with the Methodist bishop and educator, John F. Hurst. Schaff had contributed substantial papers to the society's proceedings each year; Hurst assumed a more modest administrative role. Instead of drawing on his own historical scholarship, he simply reviewed annual publication lists. From the beginning, he never intended to match Schaff's bravura performances:

> I want to do what is best about a brief opening address at our annual meeting. I do not care to take a place on the regular program, but perhaps a cursory record of the church historiography of the year would be in place. I would like your helpful suggestions. I have the *Critical Review* and *Theolog. Literatur-Zeitung,* but these are but partial helps.

Something was missing after 1893—energetic leadership, vigorous scholarship, or personal dynamism in stressing the importance of churches in their varied settings. Hurst acknowledged that the organization had lost its earlier momentum, "I am very anxious to do everything to promote its interests, and will be glad at any time to receive any suggestions bearing in that direction. I believe with you that the Society is passing through a crisis, but I think we can make amends for any losses by new accessions."[9]

A few new members joined, raising the first year's mark of 69 to a high of 177 in 1893, but this was not enough to pump new life into the faltering ASCH. Many church historians did not support the society because they balked at the idea of two organizations that divided loyalties in one discipline. The listless ASCH found that its low income could not pay for publishing all papers delivered at annual meetings. For a possible solution Hurst picked up an old theme: "As to relations with the American Historical Association," he wrote in 1894, "we might consider it seriously and decide later on." [10] Negotiations between ASCH and AHA continued sporadically after Schaff's death, and merger remained an option. Still, church historians were confident enough about separate activities as late as 1895 to suggest launching a national journal. Hurst expressed enthusiasm for the project. "I think it would be a most excellent plan to organize and put on the market a Review of Church History—a Quarterly. Our Society has earned its right to do this work, and our members can carry it out."[11] Such hopes foundered, however, on depleted funds and waning resolve.

The group decided in 1896 to forfeit independence and become part of the AHA umbrella organization. Church historians tried thereafter to conduct their affairs as a self-conscious group within the larger society. Those interested in ecclesiastical topics survived under a new aegis; they paid AHA dues, though, and their separate publications ceased.

From 1897 to 1906 the ASCH technically did not exist. As a section affiliated with the AHA, church historians met under the larger group's sponsorship, planning meetings and screening participants according to their own standards. We have little way of knowing what their sessions were like, who presented papers, or how many attended. Judging from remarks made by secular historians, the section's annual programs did not command much respect or generate wide interest. J. Franklin Jameson, editor of the *American Historical Review* for most of its first three decades, epitomized that patronizing attitude in 1901. Writing his friend Francis A. Christie, a church historian who later presided over a revived ASCH, Jameson scoffed: "By the way, are you going to the Washington meeting: I hope so, on general grounds of utility, though the Reverend Sam Jackson's programme for the Church History Section does not seem so alluring as to impel you to the journey."[12]

Whatever the quality of meetings and however good the contributions, church historians faced mounting difficulties. When Jackson recommended papers to be published, they were rejected. When he pronounced others to be unworthy, they were published over his objection.[13] Because the federal government printed AHA proceedings, some viewed this struggle as an episode in church-state relations. For church historians it boiled down to the simple question of who was in charge. By 1906 they had had enough and reasserted their independent standing. A separate institution, no matter how uncertain the future, seemed better than organizational and fiscal stability under arbitrary management.

The revived ASCH held its tenth annual session (and the first of this century) in December 1906, ending nine years of indeterminate status. Sixteen constituents met at the library of Columbia University in New York to plan for the future. They used the old society's constitution as a starting point and updated it as needed. After discussing matters for two hours they unanimously supported a revised document that remains the skeleton of guidelines in force today.

The original constitution had remained unchanged from 1888 through 1896. It contained ten articles that provided for governance, standard business procedures, and membership requirements. The revised constitution retained most of those articles, but its few changes indicated a new attitude about governance. Officers had originally numbered seven: president, four vice-presidents, secretary, and treasurer. Twentieth-century members cut that total to four by eliminating three vice-presidents and stipulating that all officers be elected by ballot. They also inserted this arresting phrase: "No president shall be elected to succeed himself."[14] One might read too much into that laconic statement, and it is only conjecture to suggest that the proviso rejected Schaff's hegemony or Hurst's ineptitude. But the revived society clearly separated itself from a deference to authority that had characterized procedures in the previous era. Honorary memberships were also dropped; a quorum of ten remained necessary for annual business; dues stayed at three dollars. And carried over virtually unchanged from the first constitution were these words that possibly offer a final clue to persistent tensions with officers of the AHA: "The Council shall be charged with the general interests of the Society including the election of members, the calling of meetings, the selection of papers, the arrangement of programs, the determination of papers to be published, and the auditing of the Treasurer's accounts."[15]

Minutes of the annual meeting in 1914 mentioned the matter of incorporation for the first time, and that new impulse required more extensive constitutional revision.[16] No one can say why the issue arose, but Samuel M. Jackson's death in 1912 might have been a relevant factor. Jackson had served as ASCH secretary from its inception. He was the strongest link with the past, and he probably evoked powerful memories of Schaff because the founder had been his exemplar and patron. A well-to-do bachelor, Jackson had also helped finance many of the society's projects. His passing may have notified members that they needed principles more than personalities for leadership and investments more than gifts for funding.

An incorporated society could provide the continuity previously supplied by Jackson. It also allowed for successive leaders and acted lawfully as a single person because, as personnel changed, the group continued indefinitely. Another feature of permanence was that incorporated societies collectively held property, incurred debts, and invested or expended funds as directors saw fit.[17] But a corporation needed both constitution and bylaws, and so the ASCH Council adopted enlargements in May 1915, with full membership approval following in December. The council's legal adviser then placed a notarized certificate of incorporation in the hands of a New York Supreme Court justice. On 30 March 1916 the New York legislature made the ASCH a legal corporation.[18]

Incorporation affected constitutional form more than practice. It occasioned a greatly expanded verbal structure that included bylaws for the first time, but those documents essentially recapitulated familiar activities. The original constitution and its modified 1906 version had designated "studies in the department of Church History" as the society's province. The text for incorporation announced an expanded intention "to promote and stimulate historical study and research generally, but particularly in the department of Church History." Routine duties now made explicit included holding conventions and publishing "papers, books, writings, reports, articles, and data" that featured work by society members. Other goals specified in 1915 entailed discovering, collecting, and preserving historical manuscripts, creating a depository library, and establishing scholarship funds. Monies for these purposes were to accrue through newly stated responsibilities: maintaining endowments, holding real or personal property acquired through purchase or gifts, and mortgaging, leasing, or selling those assets.[19]

Applying for membership was cumbersome for a time after 1915. The new constitution declared, with somewhat aristocratic overtones, that "members of each class shall have equal rights and privileges in the corporation." Uncertainty about "class" distinctions may have been eased by additional assurance that "all persons interested in Church History shall be eligible to membership," but vestiges of exclusivism could account for low enrollment figures during these years.[20] Applicants had to be nominated by one ASCH member and seconded by another. The secretary then sent the nominees' names to council members who commented on each in writing. Bylaws required council to meet once a year and screen applicants. Favorable "letters of approval" from a majority of council members cleared nominees for membership. In 1920 a constitutional change stipulated payment of dues as part of this process, warning also that those not paying dues for three years would find their names stricken from the roll.

There were few constitutional revisions after 1920. In 1943 the society adopted new bylaws that provided for several standing committees. Relieving the secretary and council, committees began to take care of programs and local arrangements for professional meetings. Multiplied responsibilities called for special expertise, and new committees emerged to supervise membership and investments. An editorial committee was given charge over all ASCH publications, and a research committee rounded out the list. Bylaws also empowered council to appoint special committees for limited purposes.[21] Minor adjustments in 1950 shifted some assignments from the secretary to the treasurer and created a committee on program and local arrangements for the Pacific Coast section of the ASCH.[22] An updated constitution was adopted in 1951 and revised again in 1983. A few recent changes include voice vote instead of ballots for president and a new stringency making presidents ineligible for reelection. Dues now have no fixed rate, and the quorum has risen from ten to twenty-five. Official duties have been expanded and specified; connections with the Council on the Study of Religion as well as with the American Subcommission of the International Commission for Comparative Church History are currently included. Supervision of all prize competitions has been assigned to the research committee.[23] But the most important change after 1950 occurred without a constitutional revision. In 1970 younger society members set machinery in motion to secure more democratic representation on the ASCH council.

The council had shared power with Schaff in the early days, and after renewed independence it controlled management and policy. During the first nine years there were eleven council members, the seven aforementioned officers plus four elected representatives. Five persons constituted a quorum. The renewed council in 1906 consisted of president, vice-president, secretary, treasurer, two other elected members, and all former presidents. Three sufficed for a quorum. ASCH incorporation stipulated that the body of "directors" be fifteen. So the 1915 constitution named its participants as before, and when former presidents made the total too large, those longest out of office ceased being members. If not enough former presidents filled council strength to fifteen, members from the ranks were elected to reach that total. The quorum once again became five.

There were no changes in council membership or quorum in the 1920 constitution, or in the 1943 and 1950 bylaws revisions. In 1951 the updated constitution adequately described arrangements: the council of fifteen consisted of four officers, five most recent former presidents, and other elected members necessary for maximum strength. The governing body also had to include at least one member from the Pacific region. Another provision allowed former presidents, retired from full membership on the council, to attend as observers without voting privileges.

By 1970 general membership had more than doubled since the last changes in governance. So steps were taken that year to democratize seating on the ASCH council. For one thing, its size increased from fifteen to eighteen. Vestiges of perennial control were removed by disfranchising the secretary, treasurer, and all former presidents. Such officers were welcomed thereafter as consultants, as were heads of all standing and special committees. One editor of *Church History* together with the president and vice-president (president-elect after 1973) were the only elected officers on council. The fifteen others consisted of members-at-large, three groups of five serving three years each.[24] Groups whose terms ended in 1971 and 1972 served less time, but since the "class of 1973" council has benefited from a stable rotation of one-third of its membership after full terms, with the nominating committee supplying another five-member group annually.

The quiet revolution of 1970 has made it possible for council to draw on fresh insights presented by this more inclusive participation.

Council responsibilities have always been central to ASCH activities. The first constitution (quoted on p. 298) stated its rather comprehensive duties. The 1906 constitution redefined membership on council but kept its duties the same. In 1915 council was empowered to suspend, expel, and restore members, with a clarification stating that the question of dues was the chief consideration in such actions. It was also authorized in 1915 to dispense corporate funds, providing no monies beyond actual resources could be spent except by written consent of every council member. Revised procedures in 1943 allowed council to devise and follow its own rules as long as they were consistent with the constitution and bylaws, requiring though that council report its activities at annual meetings. All other tasks related to programs, publications, membership, investments, nominations, and research were delegated to constitutionally sanctioned committees. Since 1943 the council has functioned more as a steering committee than a body directly responsible for specific duties. It receives annual reports from subgroups and forwards summarized reports to the whole ASCH. In addition to supervising standing committee work, it continues to serve as a forum for discussing ways of encouraging scholarship, a function that enhances policy improvement through open communication among a varied membership.

Membership grew slowly before 1950 and rose sharply thereafter. As mentioned earlier, 69 individuals joined in the founding year, while the rejuvenated society's first published roster (1908) listed only 61. Numbers fluctuated for the next two decades. In 1926 the total of ASCH constituents rose no higher than 177, the high point reached during Schaff's administration. The society has published forty-seven membership lists since its inception. Utilizing tabulations in decade segments, enrollments reflected these totals:

> 1895—160
> 1908—61
> 1915—154
> 1925—(177)[25]
> 1935—259
> 1945—444
> 1955—618
> 1965—983
> 1975—1,468
> 1985—1,295

Accounting for this growth pattern involves some speculation, but any reliable assessment must take cognizance of both the increased strength of midwestern church historians after 1920 and the augmented numbers of religion scholars in the 1960s. During the first two twentieth-century decades the revived ASCH had taken on the character of a parochial, eastern establishment. Meetings were always held in New York, with one exception, and few officers lived west of the Alleghenies. But midwestern membership was growing, and there were rumblings of discontent about too much eastern control. As early as 1916 minutes show that some Chicago historians had considered forming their own "Mississippi Valley Section" as a branch of the ASCH.[26] Those inclinations subsided, however, and most members favored expanding the existing society to include greater midwestern participation. They also brought fresh energy to ideas about a professional journal. The secretary's report for 1916 suggested as "One of the possibilities which should be considered . . . the foundation of an *American Journal of Church History*." While acknowledging the project as a "great desideratum," the report concluded that such an undertaking had to be postponed because it "cannot be realized without proper endowment."[27]

Nevertheless, confidence about more widespread representation and a possible new journal signaled institutional health, and midwesterners added strength to that trend. One of the most important persons in that development was Shirley J. Case, professor of early church history in the Divinity School at the University of Chicago and ASCH president in 1925. Case took the lead in nurturing church historical disciplines at Chicago, in generating such interests at other midwestern schools, and in recruiting members.[28] This was not a single-handed enterprise, of course, and many others cooperated in shifting the center of gravity westward. But it was probably Case who personally created a new ASCH feature, the annual spring conference. Beginning in June 1925, the society started holding "literary meetings," and all of them were held in the Midwest until 1939. Academic institutions in Chicago hosted more than half of those additional conventions as increased western vigor stimulated the society to move beyond its narrow base in New York. This gradual renovation may not have been actively opposed by easterners, as Case's biographer has asserted, but the fact remains that Case engendered a more national perspective by expanding activities to his region.

Membership figures climbed markedly after World War II. There were modest gains during the Great Depression and some fluctuation during the war years, but membership exceeded 400 by 1945 and accelerated thereafter. Many younger church historians were veterans who entered the field after studying under the GI Bill; postwar revivals probably attracted others to historical work. Lists in the 1950s indicate an average gain of 35 members annually, and increases during the 1960s jumped to over 100 each time a new list appeared. Several universities by then had begun new programs in religious studies that incorporated church history as part of training in the humanities. Graduates of those secular programs joined forces with products of more traditional theological education to swell ASCH ranks. Membership reached its highest total in 1977 with a figure of 1,558. Since then new members have not offset deaths, resignations, and vocational attrition among fresh Ph.D.'s. The current listing of 1,389 represents a winnowed but stable constituency that occupies professional posts throughout the country.

In 1967 the society surveyed its members for information on age, education, vocation, scholarly interests, religious affiliation, residence, and membership in other professional organizations. Questionnaires went to 1,256 people; 980 responded. The average age of ASCH members in that resulting profile was forty-two years. Those holding seminary degrees of some kind totaled 683, with 625 of them having earned a doctorate in either this country or Europe. Most ASCH members were teachers. Of the 731 ranked from instructor to retired professor, 278 of them taught in private or denominational liberal arts colleges, while another 229 held instructional posts at seminaries or university divinity schools. One hundred twenty-three others were employed by public universities or colleges, and 11 more taught at private universities. British and Continental universities claimed 3 each; 13 held posts in Canadian universities; 7 more in non-western theological schools rounded out the total. In the aggregate, college professors outnumbered seminary colleagues 431 to 236. Of those not involved in teaching, predominant vocations included pastors (127), school administrators (29), and denominational officials (25). Seventy-four percent of the ASCH membership was ordained in the Christian ministry in 1967.

Church historians in the survey indicated a spectrum of scholarly interests. Major divisions covered many subcategories, but general heading included 63 persons interested in the early church, 78 in medieval topics, 169 in the Renaissance and Reformation, 100 in modern Europe, and 276 in American churches. Religious affiliation ranged over sixty different ecclesiastical associations. Ignoring regional subgroups, the greatest number (132) of ASCH members was Lutheran. Other major affiliations were Presbyterian (125), Methodist (110), Baptist (95), Roman Catholic (85), Episcopalian (82), United Church of Christ (58), Disciples (37), Mennonite (17), and Evangelical United Brethren (15). All ASCH members resided in the United States except for 10 Canadians and 15 who lived abroad. Regions contained the following alignments: Midwest, 321; Northeast, 259; Southeast, 128; and West Coast, 100. Eighteen northeastern and midwestern states claimed more than 20 members each, while California proved to be the largest by registering more than 80. Members belonging to other learned societies listed the American Historical Association or the American Academy of Religion as top choices in a list covering over four hundred different groups.[29]

Another way of studying the society statistically is to concentrate on the ASCH presidency. Over the past hundred years there have been eighty-five presidents; Schaff and Hurst held multiple terms, while no one held office from 1897 through 1906. The total figure was increased by one in 1948 when two presidents served in that year, one resigning in April and his successor holding office for the next eight months (see Appendix A). The median age of presidents was fifty-three, with extremes ranging from seventy-seven to thirty-four. The oldest president was Edward T. Corwin (1911), and the youngest was Edward R. Hardy, Jr. (1942). Three pairs of fathers and sons have held the office. David S. Schaff, the founder's son, presided in 1917, and other tandems have been Robert H. Nichols (1920) and James H. Nichols (1950) together with Frederick W. Loetscher (1934) and Lefferts A. Loetscher (1962).

Education for 80 percent of all presidents has included a doctorate as the highest earned degree, most of them from a seminary or university in this country, with seven from Germany and one from Sweden to round out that number. Others completed a B.D. or S.T.B. degree after college, and several earned masters' degrees in the United States, England, or Germany. Teaching has been the major vocation for presidents, as it has for most ASCH members through the years. Most (46) held professorships of church history at denominational seminaries. A few others (9) taught at universities, but joint appointment at associated divinity schools makes classification difficult. Those exclusively in universities taught in either history or religion departments. Presidents have come from over fifty different institutions; those contributing more than any other have been the divinity schools of the University of Chicago (8) and Yale (7), with Union Theological Seminary in New York (5) a close third. Other presidents held seminary posts in something other than church history, taught undergraduates, or served a denomination in some capacity.

A centenary summary of presidential church preference lists 15 Presbyterians, 12 Episcopalians, 11 Baptists, 11 Methodists, 9 Lutherans, 8 Congregationalists, 4 Reformed, 4 Unitarians, 4 United Church of Christ, and 2 Roman Catholics. Records also indicate one each from among Moravians, Evangelical and Reformed, Mennonites, Disciples, and Quakers. As far as geographical distribution is concerned, presidents residing in the northeast dominated the society until 1925 when Shirley J. Case broke the pattern. Case's initiative in fostering midwestern influence bore fruit in many ways, and at the time of this centennial retrospective Illinois leads all states with a total of 17 presidents. Regional distribution showed heavy gravitation along the Atlantic seacoast. The Northeast (Massachusetts, Connecticut, New York, New Jersey, Pennsylvania, and District of Columbia) counted 48 presidents; the Midwest (Ohio, Indiana, Illinois, Wisconsin, and Missouri) tallied 25; the West Coast (California and Oregon) had 8; while the South (North Carolina and Texas) furnished 4.

Efforts to enhance the quality and increase production of church history have been the mainstay of ASCH existence. Ideas about what constitutes the best church history have changed over the years, and ways of fostering scholarship have varied too, but the society has continually involved itself with promoting research.

Initial volumes of ASCH *Papers* contained presidential addresses and other essays. The society also provided surveys of extant work on special topics and lists of recent publications. In addition to printing literary summaries, society leaders endorsed and even subsidized distribution of special monographs, book-length bibliographies, encyclopedias, and reprinted texts. The society supported publication of the American Church History series, a shelf of thirteen volumes that appeared between 1893 and 1897. Schaff instigated those studies whose pioneering investigation of twenty denominations has not been equaled. Such an ambitious publishing program was so intent on furnishing collected materials and fostering similar inquiries that it taxed limited resources. The consequent financial strain contributed to the society's demise in 1896.

The renewed ASCH issued a second series of *Papers*, an inferior set that appeared sporadically over three decades. Financial difficulties made it impossible to publish annual volumes, and many of them contained little more than minutes of meetings and presidential addresses. They were an inadequate outlet for research, and they reflected the stultified atmosphere that characterized societal affairs when they remained exclusively on the eastern seaboard.

Vigorous new scholarly impulses came from the Midwest, spearheaded by William W. Sweet, Case's colleague at the University of Chicago. In 1925, during its first spring meeting, the society created a special committee on research. Sweet became the dominant figure in that body, and one could say that he shaped the committee in his image, using ASCH auspices to supplement his personal efforts at Chicago. But it was a mutually agreeable relationship, and society minutes record repeated thanks to the committee for its accomplishments. Sweet was interested in collecting documents, and the ASCH research committee concentrated on that task. Between 1927 and 1933 committee members canvassed archives in at least eleven states to locate ecclesiastical records. Money from a University of Chicago research fund paid for the trips and allowed investigators to make a card index file of their inventories. If purchases were possible, documents were housed at Sweet's university. If materials could not be moved, a catalogue of widespread archival deposits with 5,000 entries was available to students. Sweet did the bulk of this labor, and his four-volume *Religion on the American Frontier* (1931-46) remains its most tangible result. Research committee reports discussed those volumes as virtually an ASCH project, and the entire society seems to have taken heart from the committee's practical achievements.[30]

While research committee work progressed, efforts in another direction finally culminated in the often-mentioned, long-awaited quarterly journal. In view of earlier caution about sufficient endowment, it is ironic that the journal appeared in what one editor called "the worst year of the current depression." Trepidations aside, in 1931 ASCH officials invited publishers to bid for printing the journal. They chose the Mennonite Publishing Company of Scottdale, Pennsylvania, from among twelve competitors. After several unexpected delays, *Church History* launched its first issue in March 1932, with a circulation of 285.[31] Journal editors based in Chicago did not, however, enjoy cordial relations with the Pennsylvania firm, and in the following year they reacted sharply to the printer's "dilatory methods." An early report mentioned "neither tranquil nor satisfactory" interaction and concluded that labor for the journal "cost a great amount of trouble and energy on the part of the Board."[32] Despite such annoyances, *Church History* quickly became a solvent, viable enterprise. By early 1934 it operated without a deficit. That same year editors employed new printers: Berne Witness Company of Berne, Indiana. That relationship proved to be more amenable, and the second firm served the society until 1976, when financial stringencies dictated moves to other publishers.

For half a century *Church History* has been the most outstanding feature of ASCH activities. The quality of its articles has made the journal a template for advances in research as well as the repository of exemplary scholarship. Editorial supervision has remained primarily in the Midwest, with executive offices housed at the University of Chicago. Initially there was one managing editor, a professor at the university, aided by a board consisting of one or two colleagues and the incumbent ASCH president. In postwar years the editorial board expanded to include scholars from as far away as Duke and Colgate-Rochester, but most activities still centered at Chicago. Editors have also relied on a panel of advisers, this group varying in size from two to ten. Managerial tasks have ranged from scholarly criticism to mundane problems such as updating mailing lists and enforcing deadlines. In 1950 one editor wrote about the less attractive side of his duties:

> Our biggest difficulty lies in the fact that I must coax whatever services I can out of the printers, read proofs that are all the way from amazing excellence to inconceivable carelessness, and sweat the issue out each time without knowing just what catastrophes are likely to strike, or when. Please don't take this as a tale of self-pity. It is just a realistic summation of affairs.[33]

The journal has enjoyed a succession of wise, discerning, and long-suffering editors. Their toil along with that of board members and outside consultants has made *Church History* arbiter of the state of the discipline in this country.

Other efforts to encourage scholarship have involved publications besides the journal. In the 1930s and early 1940s ASCH officials experimented with a series called Monographs in Church History and another entitled Studies in Church History. Substantial support for such ventures appeared in 1938, when Frank S. Brewer of Glen Ellyn, Illinois, donated $10,000 to the ASCH. Brewer wanted proceeds from the money to subsidize publication costs for manuscripts of high merit, preferably for studies of Congregational history. The earliest prize winner was Waldo E. L. Smith whose manuscript, *Episcopal Appointments and Patronage in the Reign of Edward II*, appeared in 1938 as volume three of the Studies series.

New bylaws in 1943 stated that the ASCH Council would choose Brewer Prize winners and make arrangements for resultant publications.[34] In 1950 the society announced that it could no longer manage publication of winning manuscripts, offering instead to assist any publisher with subvention funds.[35] Grants in aid of publication amounted to $1,000 until 1980, when the figure was doubled. Authors became responsible for securing their own publisher, and a time limit was imposed after which the prize reverted to ASCH accounts. Apparently the original intention of printing prize essays as volumes in the Studies series proved impracticable. Books did not sell in sufficient quantity, and the series quietly ended. After 1951 entrants for the Frank S. and Eliza D. Brewer Prize Essay of the American Society of Church History were judged by a panel of three society members named for that purpose. The jury made recommendations to editors of *Church History*, and a winner emerged only when a contestant received a majority of both panelist and editorial votes.[36] In more recent years selection procedures have devolved entirely upon the research committee, and several topics in addition to Congregational history have been accepted. Twenty-six authors have been named prizewinners since 1938 (see Appendix B), and almost all of them have succeeded in having their works published, displaying the Brewer Prize designation on their title pages.

At its annual meeting in 1976 the ASCH initiated another prize, a cash award to the author of a book originating in North America judged to be the best example of church history appearing within the two previous years.[37] ASCH archives preserve a letter from David Schaff that donated $500 to the society in centennial commemoration of his father's birth, 1 January 1819. The son stipulated in 1919 that the gift honoring his father could not be used to pay general ASCH expenses, and, should the society ever be disbanded, the bequest should transfer to Union Theological Seminary in New York.[38] Society archives mention no subsequent use of this deposit until 1976 when it served as seed money for inaugurating the Philip Schaff Prize competition. Since 1979 five authors have received this biennial award for distinguished research and interpretation in the diverse fields that comprise church history (see Appendix B).

A third prize was inaugurated in 1979, intended as with previous competitions to stimulate better results in historical study. Named for Sidney E. Mead, renowned essayist and graduate instructor at Chicago, Claremont, and Iowa, this prize pertains to those just entering the discipline. Young students of church history in, or recently graduated from, doctoral programs are encouraged to submit article-length manuscripts based on their primary research. Thus far, two winners have received a cash award and had their essays printed in *Church History*. In 1986 the Albert C. Outler Prize in Ecumenical Church History was created to encourage work in the broad fields cultivated by its namesake, an eminent scholar whose career enlivened the campuses of Yale, Duke, and Southern Methodist University. Research committee members conduct competitions for all these awards, hoping thereby to improve the quality of scholarship at all levels of the profession.

Historiographical patterns have changed over the past hundred years, and scholars within the ASCH have held various ideas about what constitutes good church history. Those ideas have supported divergent research methods, interpretive perspectives, and topical preferences. They championed varying objectives as the ones best served by historical knowledge. Different views on the craft have existed side by side, and no single viewpoint commanded universal assent. The society has encompassed a diverse constituency without dictating to it.

Presidential addresses have provided a recurring opportunity for expressing ideas about church history. During the society's ninety years of existence 85 presidents have held office, and 80 addresses have been printed under ASCH auspices. Ten meetings yielded no address: in 1893 the session was given over to commemorative services following Schaff's death; Hurst and Fisher made no formal presentations; three addresses mentioned in society minutes were never printed; medical problems prevented two presidents from delivering addresses; one president simply handed out a typed bibliography to accompany his informal remarks (see Appendix A). Summarizing the printed work, there have been 6 essays related to the early church, 4 considerations of medieval themes, 19 Reformation studies, 24 addresses on American topics, 14 articles related to modern European or international Christianity, and 13 reflections on problems of method and interpretation. Most presidents used their formal address to discuss topics they were currently studying. Few broached questions about the nature of church history or the relation of their craft to general historiographical issues.

One of those who did consider basic problems was George E. Horr whose 1919 address drew lessons from the recent war to make two observations. On the procedural side, Horr remarked that the conflict in Europe had made everyone appreciate more fully the complexity of historical relationships. Great events such as international conflicts did not stem from single causes or lend themselves to simple explanations. He reasoned that ecclesiastical movements resulted from mixed impulses too, including social, economic, and political forces alongside religious ideals. Without stressing mundane factors exclusively, Horr insisted that physical as well as spiritual categories were pertinent to historical explanation.[39] On the topical side, he observed that the war had raised new questions for historical investigation: freedom in democratic states, ecclesiastical leadership amid differing political philosophies, and mutual support for a league of nations. Church historians could shed light on these modern themes by demonstrating the influence of Christianity on current statecraft. The war had also replaced European provincialism with a wider perspective, and Horr thought church historians should expand their horizons to include Greek, Armenian, and Coptic churches. He hoped, futilely as it turned out, that historians would develop a new cosmopolitan perspective and investigate less familiar versions of shared Christian affirmations.[40]

In 1920 Robert H. Nichols summarized traditional ideas about the church historian's task as they had developed to his day. The subject was vitally connected with theological education in his view, and few inquiries into past ecclesiastical experience could thrive apart from programs that trained men for the Christian ministry. As part of this larger purpose, church history should not focus on changes in liturgy, doctrine, or polity, still less on the superiority of one denomination over others. Nichols held instead that "the thing we most want the students to get hold of is what Christianity has done in the world, how it has affected thought and action, what impression it has made on society." He thought church history should highlight past achievements, making it in effect a philosophy of social activism, teaching by example. Not one to quibble unduly about terminology, he held nevertheless that "a better name than Church History would be . . . Christianity in History."[41]

Besides reminding ministers that religion affected cultural contexts, Nichols recommended historical study as a discipline that led students to appreciate accuracy, to judge evidence by sifting causes and effects, and to avoid hasty conclusions. Church history could also broaden ministers' perspectives while it made them better analysts. Those reared in narrow religious contexts learned of diverse situations where Christian witness had influenced previous epochs. Contact with great Christian thinkers and activists in various times enriched personal experience. Nichols thought too that historical study gave students a more practical turn of mind. Knowledge of what had been done in the past made it easier to assess contemporary possibilities. A final benefit for pastor and people was that church history helped make the human condition intelligible. Preaching sought to explain life, and history afforded knowledge about human circumstances over the ages. Knowing what Christianity had meant in earlier times suggested what it could mean in the present.[42]

The burden of Nichols' presentation was that church history contributed to spiritual and intellectual progress insofar as people learned to live and think better. Ministers had to understand their religion from sources beyond the Bible and theology, learning from concrete examples what faith could and could not do. "For gaining such knowledge," he maintained, "obviously one necessity is instruction in what Christianity has been and has done." Factual knowledge about various phases and expressions of church life could help "grasp the essential truth of the religion."[43] So church history provided a basic component in sound ministerial training. It disciplined the intellect and enriched personality; it equipped people for effective preaching and leadership; it displayed truth and power in experiences that collectively formed the Christian heritage.

Presidential remarks made the following year opposed all previous ideas about the craft that subordinated it to religious utility. In 1921 Ephraim Emerton asserted that church history could not, by its very nature, serve churches or enhance theological convictions. Nichols had thought of the craft as a buttress to theological programs, but Emerton insisted that methodological procedures precluded any concern about religious consequences. Nichols had wanted church history to further ecclesiastical interests, but Emerton was concerned with making the discipline acceptable in secular universities. Whereas others considered faith a prerequisite for understanding religious affairs, Emerton held that church historians could focus on nothing beyond the human realm, using methods common to regular historical inquiry.[44]

Emerton began his 1921 address by saying that proper church history did not "rest upon emotion or dogma or propagandist bases, but, so far as possible, upon purely historical considerations." More emphatic than Horr, he grounded his work exclusively in mundane categories. "Church History," he maintained, "is nothing more nor less than one chapter in that continuous record of human affairs to which we give the name of history in general."[45] Treating the ecclesiastical past as part of general humanistic inquiries was for Emerton "the cornerstone of all dealing with our subject."

Historical narratives that invoked supernatural agents exceeded proper procedures, and Emerton rejected them. Once Providence intervened in human affairs, he argued, divine intervention would be continuously necessary. Historians looking at such a world would have to employ a double standard, with religious and secular entitites depending on irreconcilable factors and disparate evidence. Others defended that dualistic approach by saying that the church's past was at "tangled skein" of human and divine threads, and their task was to trace the golden thread of divine presence through successive ages. Emerton could not accept such a "spasmodic conception" of human experience. He considered that view wrongheaded because it misconstrued both the way events occurred and how historians studied them. Church history *was* a tangled skein because it shared complexities and multiple influences with other kinds of human experience. But providential historians just made matters worse by introducing their own faith assumptions into the record as imputed causes.

For Emerton, any narrative constructed to serve higher ends violated the rules for writing acceptable history and was guilty of "trimming the plain human record to suit [its] own fancy." The mundane quality of churches laid their records bare to the same methods of historical criticism used elsewhere. By not relying on supernatural elements, church historians could share with modern scholars a constricted but solid ground for understanding the human past where "no glamor of antiquity, no weight of tradition, no presumption as to good intentions can cover violation of those rules laid down by modern science as the unshakable foundations of historical certainty."[46] Relying on supernatural causation also outraged Emerton's idea of Providence as much as it did his concept of sound history. With theological overtones as well as methodological preferences in mind, he observed that "the divine presence is not to be thus catalogued and indexed to fit the limitations of us little men."[47]

A common naturalistic method could avoid much that discredited church history in the eyes of secular critics, but references to supernatural influences were still a problem because they existed in the empirical evidence. Emerton recognized this difficulty and admitted that church materials would always contain attributions that challenged human understanding. The easiest solution would be to deny them credence and write history after ruling out part of the record. But Emerton refused to define the problem out of existence as firmly as he opposed taking historical documents at face value. His moderating choice was to distinguish between human belief in providential events and divine intervention itself. Beliefs in the superhuman were authenticated facts in historical records and could be studied as factors affecting culture. The supernatural itself was a subject for metaphysics, an intangible quality beyond documentation. With ontological differences and consequent investigative strictures in mind, he argued that

> historical evidence concerns only such things as are perceptible to human powers and can be recorded by human means. Miracles—*all* miracles—are excluded from the historian's function, because no human evidence can establish the fact of miracle. Yet the fact of *belief* in miracle is as obvious a human phenomenon within Christianity as in every other religion. As such the historian is bound to deal with it, never for a moment with the object of proving or disproving the alleged miracle, but only to set the effects of this belief in their right place in the record he is trying to interpret.[48]

Emerton asked ASCH members to accept the new, secular definitions and rules of evidence that promised church history an honored place in the professional guild.

Five years later another presidential address rounded off this first cluster of conceptual reflections on church history. In 1926 William W. Rockwell raised questions about presuppositions, or distortions stemming from them, as obstacles to objective history. Thinking back on how propaganda had been used in the Great War, he noted ruefully that bias ruined impartial analysis. Alleged reports of atrocities and emotional appeals to nationalism had distorted a clear view of the facts. Patriotic fervor was manipulated to blunt the edge of discriminating judgment, and whenever feeling overruled calm thought, it "crashes heavenward in hymns of hate, earthward in shrapnel and poison gas. The balances of historic justice are weighted down by mudslinging." Biases obscured the truth, and Rockwell noted that investigators were victimized by predilections: "We are all drafted into the Light Brigade."[49] With recent examples of managed information in mind, he wondered if historians could circumvent bias in either the documents themselves or in interpreting them.

This proved to be a rhetorical question because, after surveying logical possibilities, Rockwell concluded that all historians incorporated presuppositions in their work.[50] His real concern in the address was to make church historians recognize that they used presuppositions, the better to control them. But improvement meant admitting there was a problem in the first place, and in his view too many church historians presumed on special benefit of clergy to analyze evidence in an unacceptably permissive way. So Rockwell enumerated what he considered the worst offenses against the modern historian's canon. At the heart of distortions in church history was the familiar but invidious distinction between secular and sacred, sometimes coupled with the galling claim that churches as heavenly agents could not fail in earthly ventures. Some historians clouded their narratives further by using dogma to substantiate fact or by holding miracles to be true by pointing to popular belief in them. Rockwell argued that such usages had no place in common historiographical procedures. Church history could not invoke the transcendental aspect of its subject matter in order to employ special investigative or interpretive techniques.

Secular historians had biases too, but Rockwell did not elaborate on them, claiming lack of space (in one of the longest of all presidential addresses). He did single out materialism and rationalism as crippling presuppositions, condemning them because they dogmatically held human categories to be the only standard for truth.[51] Choosing a middle ground, he acknowledged that complete objectivity was impossible, and beyond that he simply urged historians not to edit facts to suit their case. He ended with a gentle plea for tolerance: "If we have bias, let us . . . allow for it, as navigators must allow for the shifting deviations of the mariner's compass. Each man should know and discount his personal equation."[52] Rockwell urged ASCH members to accept each other with a cooperative spirit in hopes that church history might improve in quality over the next quarter century.

In 1950 James H. Nichols returned to fundamental issues with a sophistication that indicated how thought about the field had matured. His presentation was the first of three addresses that embodied a new emphasis on the church as a unique entity and on theological affirmations as important interpretive considerations. Each essayist in this middle cluster returned to issues raised previously, and in the more recent context their ideas about the discipline were noticeably congruent with neo-orthodox theology that influenced religious circles at that time.

Nichols began by asserting that church history was not contributing satisfactorily to religious thought in his day. He acknowledged that the craft had earned respect by using critical, scientific methods, but its emphasis on technical precision had allowed concern for interpretive patterns to lapse. Historical understanding had lost its ability to draw meaning from religious insight and in turn to substantiate confessional principles through tangible data. Nichols did not belittle the importance of accuracy, but he decried narratives without sufficient interpretation as flawed and deficient. Histories containing data devoid of proper explanation were barren, misguided, or noncommital results of what he called "the positivistic view." Church historians since Emerton's day had won intellectual respectability among professional colleagues, but while adopting critical methods and securing greater objectivity, they had also assimilated positivistic notions of historical meaning. By concentrating exclusively on the mundane qualities of human experience, they had lost sight, he said, of deeper meanings in the church they intended to study.[53]

In Nichols' estimation, church history had given away too much in becoming just one specialty among others. Those who thought of churches as human institutions confined themselves to usages compatible with other historical topics. For them all religious expressions were embedded in and explained by the complex relationships of mundane affairs. But empirical observation alone could not detect the sacred as it influenced human experience, and Nichols found such an orientation too limited: "all positivist history must be secular history, and cannot be a history of the Church as the work of redemption in human life. The Christian vision of history was only one of many unifying conceptions of historical meaning which were abandoned in an enthusiasm for misconceived scientific method." It was not enough to study churches as cultural institutions, no matter how important they might be, because secular definitions failed to retain "the conviction that in fact the life of the church was the focus of the meaning of history in general."[54] Lacking that vision, historians were reduced to studying Christian movements without asking if institutions embodied the real church or exhibited divine presence in their activities.

Nichols thought it was time for church historians to balance their respect for scientific accuracy with a renewed appreciation of ideological perspective. Positivist history did not supply an interpretive vantage point, and facts could not speak for themselves. Some historians in fields such as literature and art had begun admitting that they needed evaluative criteria to interpret their data, but Nichols wryly noted that few of these advanced thinkers belonged to the ASCH. As another case in point, it was a sad commentary on regnant standards that none of the best students of Puritanism in his generation was a church historian. Nichols aimed at a moderate objective in his "concern to recover the interpretive role of history without sacrificing critical method." He did not want to expose interpretations to competing ideologies where discussions persuaded only those already convinced. "We are all aware, of course, of the danger of falling off the razor edge on the other side, and reducing history to a tumult of publicists of various political, cultural, and religious views."[55] Too much emphasis on ideology could distort history as badly as evidence presented with no explanation at all, and Nichols advocated historiographical reform that blended the best aspects of method and insight. In view of standard approaches in his day, though, he had to stress the ideational side of the equation. Historians of every topic would not merit wide attention if they merely reproduced facts without commenting on their meaning and significance.

If plain historiographical need called for interpretation of bare fact, church historians received even further promptings from theologians to draw on religious ideas germane to their subject matter. Theological considerations allowed historians to stress once again the religious mission of ecclesiastical institutions and from that perspective to discern supernatural truth in human experiences. But Nichols knew that revitalized church history could not simply adopt a theological definition of the church and then celebrate its earthly career. Tracing the golden thread of divine presence was still difficult, especially if associated with one church's doctrine, rituals, and institutional forms. No church deserved exclusive attention as the focal point of divine action, and no claims to providential origins or authority could be taken at face value. Proper study of organized Christianity should avoid such minutiae in order to concentrate on salvation as the core experience possible in every church.

The redemptive experience gave meaning to all ecclesiastical organizations and reduced their external differences to secondary importance. With salvation as a unifying concept, church historians could honor rules of factual accuracy while focusing on the ecumenical significance of their topic. As a preliminary to answering such ultimate questions as "Where and what is the church?" the more immediate and practicable line of inquiry for those dealing with concrete phenomena was "how much of this belongs to the story of God's redemption of mankind?" Nichols did not elaborate on what he meant by salvation or how many different experiences could be relevant to that concept, but he affirmed that the church historian's task was "to trace the actualization of the Gospel in human history, to discern and describe the signs of the Kingdom, to reveal the subtle indications of the presence of the Risen Christ to his adopted brethren."[56] Theological awareness stimulated inquirers to think of ecclesiastical experience as episodes that disclosed providential influence. In this perspective praxis superseded ontology as the historian's instrumental criterion. Nichols suggested that salvation was amenable to both empirical verification and ideological comprehension. It offered an opportunity for the discipline to establish a category of intellectual significance to its findings and to enhance religious understanding at the same time.

In 1955 Leonard J. Trinterud advanced discussion along these lines and brought out additional nuances for fellow guildsmen to ponder. His ideas probed more deeply into relationships between faith and empiricism while also placing salvation at the center of both practical scholarship and interpretive priorities. In the first part of his address, however, Trinterud felt it necessary to defend his own specialty, religion in America. Noting that some thinkers confined "real" church history to European topics, he opted for a wider perspective, arguing that histories of Asia and the Americas were not simply "patched on" to Europe. Just as wider historical vistas were necessary to deal with the separate cultures of modern times, his discipline needed broader conceptions, "catholic enough and comprehensive enough to deal with the whole Church."[57] American churches and other non-European institutions were not stepchildren or foundlings. It was necessary for the profession to develop topical categories inclusive enough to allow these latter-day phenomena as legitimate components of a worldwide movement.

Trinterud drew on current ecumenical discussions to underscore the need for greater acceptance of different ecclesiastical forms. Many "younger churches" had departed from traditional patterns, raising the question of whether deviations from classical usage really belonged to the Christian heritage. Honest historical inquiry showed that no single ecclesiology could serve as a standard, excluding all others. "Either we must all go back to Jerusalem," he observed, "or else we must remember that redemption is of God, that the Church is the result of that redemption, and that God is free and sovereign in his choice and use of historical instruments." Historians should not insist that new groups adopt traditional categories; they should rather seek in them that quality which made all churches segments of the Church Catholic. Circumstantial differences should not trouble broad-minded historians because "variety within Christendom is not the same thing as divisiveness or disunity."

> The history of the American Church is not in essence different from the whole history of the Church Catholic. . . . it is not possible today to point to a truly "undivided church," even though one carries his quest back to the age of the Apostles. Either we must all write only "denominational" histories, or else we may all write "church" histories.[58]

An ecumenical common denominator based on theological insight could free students from ecclesiological provincialism and avoid confusion among the variety of institutional forms spawned by cultural pluralism.

But if historians could not locate the church in a creed, polity, or some other tangible vehicle, how did they determine where it was? Trinterud said that salvation experience was the distinguishing factor, even though he was not more explicit than Nichols in defining it. For him the church included all "people related to God by the redemption which comes through Jesus Christ." It manifested itself in all circumstances of historical existence, in every age, all situations. To conceive of the church in this way was admittedly to base one's definition on "a confession of faith and not a matter of historical investigation and proof." Using this perspective, historians should try to be open and tolerant rather than exclusive in choosing subjects for study. Trinterud held that "however odd a group or denomination may be, the church historian must deal seriously with this people's faith that God through Jesus Christ did redeem them." Church historians had a duty collectively to examine and expound the myriad examples of what redemption had meant to different people in the past. They could not separate true claims from false ones; their proper task was to show the historical character of redemption by giving the panoply of multiple voices a chance to express themselves.[59]

A final problem burdening Trinterud was how to write history based on this theological conception of its content. If the Church was the body of redeemed believers, and its history the work of God, did not one have to be a prophet or apostle to record what transpired? Modern scholarly criteria were predominantly secular, and this discouraged any wish to include religious criteria in historical procedures. So the juxtaposition posed a dilemma: "how can you write the history of what God is doing? The answer, of course, is that you cannot." This conflict between aspiration born of religious insight and critical scholarship limited to empirical method made Trinterud confess to having a "bad conscience."

> I assume I ought to present *church* history, but I end up with only the history of Christianity. What I do differs only by its lack of ability from the work of those in other historical disciplines who, in dealing with various aspects of the Christian Church in history, do so frankly disavowing my assumption about the Church. And from their works I have learned no small part of whatever I may know about the history of the Christian Church. What, then, shall I do?[60]

He tried to solve this dilemma by distinguishing between the restrictions placed on careful historians and the greater freedom among readers who could interpret data from wider viewpoints.

Narratives did not always communicate the ideas intended by authors. Historians interpreted data and presented their understandings of the evidence, but Trinterud took heart from the fact that readers screened narrative accounts with their own controlling assumptions, possibly finding additional or contrary meanings in a written report. Those who learned about past events through secondary accounts of historical scholarship were able to bring independent judgments to bear on their evidence. The nature of historical materials and the limits of investigative methods confined modern scholars to a narrow scope. But readers enjoyed an autonomy denied those who wrote history in modern times. Interpretive restrictions imposed on authors had no binding authority on readers who wished to think otherwise about historical materials. A nonbelieving historian might convey a skeptical report of miracles, but readers with an insight sustained by faith could see the work as a testimony to divine power. Another historian might accept miraculous accounts, but other readers could reduce his narrative to a set of human events. Each reader was free to apply his own viewpoint, and no set of conclusions necessarily followed from either the evidence or methods used to ascertain it.

Trinterud's distinction between the limits of scholarship and the license of readers posits a hopeless relativism in the historical enterprise. But, since he wished to make it possible for theology and confessional insight to regain a place alongside the noncommital results of professional research, it relieved him of his bad conscience. When readers did not grasp the transcendental significance behind an author's words, "the church historian may write worse than he thinks." In cases where believers interpreted secular accounts their own way, "the reader may read far better than he knows." The higher reaches of church history hinged on popular con-

sumption, not on original composition. For Trinterud the redeeming feature of church history was an option, not its entrapment in positivistic
reductionism or any successful method based on new procedures. It lay
outside the historian altogether. Some people could discern church history
in whatever they read, while others would see "only the history of Christianity" because of the differing expectations they brought to the same
material. Church historians could use secular tools for research and still
serve religious needs by trusting faithful readers to find higher meaning
in mundane evidence. They could honor methodological standards in the
profession and pass theological responsibility along to readers. Trinterud
considered this solution to be psychologically realistic and practicable, one
that served critical history and theological input without capitulating to
extreme demands from either side. It encompassed care for fact and concern
for faith, combining science with belief to achieve the only realistic objective
for which historical students could hope, to "know perhaps as much as
we ever shall know of the historical life of the Church Catholic."[61]

In 1964 Albert C. Outler rounded out ideas along these lines in an
address notable for its polished artistry and balanced analysis. In describing
the church historian's task he emphasized an initial and basic responsibility
to re-create "segments of the human past in an intelligible narrative based
on public data verified by scientific observation." But scientific observation
of the past disclosed that events in their combination possessed a fortuitous
character that prevented comprehensive or conclusive explanations. Historical understanding relied on factors at three different levels. First, there
were natural or universal processes that most observers relied on as "laws."
Human choices within those lawlike natural processes complicated matters
by introducing variant individual behavior based on personal motives. But
the truly imponderable factor was chance, a haphazard concatenation of
implausible occurrences that fell outside any rational calculus. Outler pointed
to such "accidents" as a reminder that all explanatory efforts failed to
account for everything that happened. He noted that by mid-century even
mathematics and physics had acknowledged some uncertainty in their
explanations of natural events. In the historical profession the principle of
uncertainty was pervasive, endemic to the methods of inquiry themselves.
Absolute certainty about the past was impossible for three reasons. Rec-
ollection could never fully recover what had been experienced; eyewitnesses
saw more than they could comprehend, and their retrospective descriptions
were edited versions of original experience; accidents defied verifiable generalizations. In light of these inevitable uncertainties historians faced the
predicament of supplying interpretive comments. While aiming at comprehensiveness and order in public data, they had to "present their inwardly

disciplined accounts of objective happenings in the full knowledge of the constant dialectic between event and interpretation in . . . historical narrative."[62]

Outler thought it was the beginning of wisdom to acknowledge that all historical knowledge contained uncertainties derived from both the partial nature of data and the restricted access of investigators. To admit this would free historians from slavishly copying scientific models and would yield them a greater "awareness of the instabilities of historical existence and the persisting equilibria of human experience." An awareness more open to possibilities also allowed historians to recognize aspects in human action that went beyond naturalistic frames of reference. For example, human history undeniably contained acts of deliberate self-transcendence. Such acts raised unavoidable questions about identifying the transcendental referent that was invoked on those occasions, and they called for an assessment of claims about superhuman influence in the mundane realm. The usual historical response to such questions in Outler's day was to deny validity to transcendental beings and to reject the possibility of any supernatural influence, even if the records bore witness. "The notion of 'providence' has simply dropped below the mental horizon of modern historiography," he observed. In its place modern scholars appear content with several "notions that are consistent only in their anthropocentrism" serving as "pseudo-scientific substitutes for discarded religious beliefs." But even though antitheological historians might scoff at the possibility of transcendental influences in history, Outler insisted that excluding them by naturalistic decree was insufficient. Mundane bias did no better in offering plausible explanations of chance happenings. Documentary references to providence made it a factor to reckon with, and the inability of secular interpretations to account satisfactorily for chance and for human motivations at least left the category open to serious consideration.[63]

Some sort of metahistorical element was clearly inescapable among historians who admitted the complexity of their task. To represent the human past adequately, historians had to be honest in portraying it as natural but not merely so, as public and social yet inward and personal as well. So, unlike Trinterud who avoided the issue, Outler held that the integrity of historiographical procedure forced investigators to grapple with "comments that exceeded the warrants of verifiability." Every combination of insights and judgments used to interpret the past functioned in the same way, he maintained, as a doctrine of providence. Perspectives on what constituted meaning in human events included many alternatives, but all of them implicitly recognized that history and metahistory were interdependent. The church historian's idea of providence, his "obligation to rehearse the Christian past in the light of the Christian world view," was simply a specific example of the larger problem. Unfortunately, many church historians had overemphasized the metahistorical side and made unacceptable assertions in their work:

> Explicit in their notions of God's providence . . . they were also committed to providing *causal* explanations of the implausible events in their stories—and for this it was all too easy to fall back on their doctrines of providence for attributions that are often glib and always unverifiable. In this way they confused . . . their understanding of the correlations between spiritual realities . . . with natural processes . . . In this way they not only flawed their narratives; they came near to spoiling the doctrine of providence. Thus presented, it persuaded few unbelievers, but it did give mischievous reinforcement to partisan pride . . . self-righteousness and triumphalism among Christians.[64]

Reacting to those bad metahistorical explanations, naturalistic historians rejected not only egregious references to providence but suppressed legitimate uses of the concept as well. Outler thought that secularization in church history had benefited the craft by narrowing the gap between his field and critical history in general. But he considered it a loss too in that church history had become unable to keep alive the wealth of theological insights into historical meaning and significance.

Regardless of whether or not church historians utilized theological categories to some degree, Outler held that no plausible account in their work, as historians, was possible without a responsible attitude toward basic Christian convictions. Students of past ecclesiastical activities had to develop competence in both scientific methods and theological knowledge. They had to show positive and negative correlations between beliefs and behavior, spiritual community and sociological institution. In that context each historian had to speak of providence, if only to decry traditional expressions of it as put forth in faulty causal explanations. But Outler argued for a perspective between complete rejection and overweening triumphalism. He pointed to a more sophisticated, less assertive meaning that affirmed "God's provision and maintenance of structures and processes of human possibility in the order of creation." Terming this divine resourcefulness "pronoia," he held that it did not entail predetermination of historical events or miraculous intervention into natural relationships. It constituted rather a pervasive supernatural presence in the world where natural laws operated and humans determined their own choices. Awareness of pronoia was Outler's definition of salvation. Redemption was perceiving and relying on God's presence, living with discernment and hope through the mutabilities of time. Using that attitude as a common denominator, church historians could investigate communities that had laid claim to it through the ages.

If one denies that it is the church that has survived these transitions, he has no further problems about *church* history, save as a chapter in the story of human illusions. If . . . he attempts to explain the church's survival by reference to the causal interventions of providence, he has as obviously renounced his interest in church *history*. The remaining alternative, one might think, is some sort of acknowledgment of the dynamic presence of the Holy Spirit in the church in history, leading men toward a knowledge of their true identity and their true community.

Outler hoped that some vision of God's pronoia could be conveyed in critical narratives without violating historiographical standards. He called for scholarship pursued with "modesty born of uncertainty and a confidence born of a glimpse of God at work not only in the Scriptures but in all succeeding ages."[65] Honest historical scrutiny, sustained by the real possibility of God's overarching presence, could deepen Christian self-understanding while it acknowledged the complexities involved in past occurrences and checked optimism about predicting future eventualities.

During the next decade two more presidents addressed themselves to historiographical questions, clarifying and updating issues that have vexed students of the ecclesiastical past. In 1973 William A. Clebsch provided a refined analysis of investigative procedures, with directives regarding the genre depending heavily on methodological strictures. He was familiar with the problems that had been raised since Rockwell's day regarding presuppositions and scientific objectivity. And in light of those conundrums Clebsch acknowledged that historians could never disown the individual mind-sets, personal objectives, and cultural conditioning that made each of their works distinctive. Given this current state of affairs among scholars, they could not hope "to arrive at a universal, objective stance for interpretation of documentary evidence." He hoped church historians would recognize the limits of their interpretive criteria, though, because such awareness was the first step in solving difficulties that had heretofore retarded the discipline. Clebsch suggested, in this prolegomenon to more extensive studies, nothing less than a plan for correlating different religious episodes into a unified narrative, an interpretive blueprint with which students could "fashion the pieces" according to some consistent pattern of historical meaning.[66] He moved beyond dated squabbles over scientific models and proceeded to describe a viewpoint that offered an integrative basis for understanding European Christianity. Drawing on humanistic studies for guidance in method and perspective, he hoped to render a better depiction of Christian expressions than the providentialist and naturalist versions that preceded him.

Clebsch pinpointed two specific approaches as inappropriate to his own conception of proper historical study. History of doctrine, where he placed all "church history," was disqualified because it based interpretations on internally generated, self-ascribed categories. This doctrinally determined viewpoint often accepted church teaching as a vehicle of divine revelation and elevated the church's founder to a miraculous being, neither action confining references to "the class of events fully amenable to historical investigation." Almost as prevalent and similarly unacceptable was history of religion, a perspective that either accommodated distinctive Christian patterns to universal types or abstracted Christianity to a version of general religiousness. Instead of letting beliefs preclude judgment or allowing universal forms to distort specific events, Clebsch insisted that the integrity of tangible historical occurrences had to be honored. Because knowledge was grounded in documented human events, he argued that the data themselves were the only proper basis for defining interpretive options. In an attempt to surmount earlier distortions, he seized on ideas drawn from the evidence and asserted that "only by understanding Christianity in terms of the life-styles by which it has come into concrete, human expression can we conceive historical interpretations capable of guiding our efforts to identify and explain the individual pieces."[67]

There was an alternative to taking the claims of Christian doctrine at face value or to accepting the characteristics of other religions as interpretive criteria. Clebsch held that understanding Christianity and gauging its impact on humanity should depend on concrete behavior, and guidelines for understanding the religion could change when new epochs established new spiritual norms. He also found that three categories survived as recurrent factors during the changing epochs. Times reshaped the content and expression of Christianity, but discrete religious witness by individuals always gave the best data for types of piety; actual practice disclosed genuine commitment better than did verbalized principles; energetic response to cultural crises more clearly exhibited vital religion than did traditional formulas. Personal example, pragmatic activism, and relevance—these were essential ingredients in every part of the Christian past. These constants served historians who sought continuity and comparative interpretations while everything else metamorphosed with the passage of time. They were also as close as Clebsch came in his address to supplying a definition of salvation. Such recurrent themes gave historians focal points for observing "how spiritual energies have formed varying . . . types of pragmatic piety." By going behind transcendental references to look at actual life-styles, historians could observe Christianity through the actions of datable, locatable persons. Moreover, they could interpret it through documents embedded in the realities of human living and see how it was expressed within this worldly contexts, even though many of those persons yearned for eschatological deliverance.[68]

Clebsch offered his alternative viewpoint as "one way in which church historians today may move beyond the confines of history of doctrine while still drawing our interpretive terms and themes from Christianity itself rather than from other religions." His carefully circumscribed attention to human experience, with its fascinating variation and common denominators, placed religious history squarely in the realm of humanistic studies. Christianity was what Christians had said and done over centuries in various contexts. References to spirit, miracles, self-transcendence, and ultimate destiny were human expressions of people who made use of such themes in their dynamic versions of faith as actually practiced.

Thinking ahead to the next stage of historiographical development, Clebsch raised greater possibilities for the field. General historians and phenomenologists of religion could not properly understand Christian activities, he said, because church historians distorted their perspective with doctrinal allegiance. If present-day scholars could break their preoccupation with history of doctrine and the intellectual limits thus entailed, they could view evidence with an open mind and write clearly about tangible events. Church history had more to bring to religious studies than many had thought possible or worthwhile. So Clebsch urged new contributory efforts based on a humanist perspective liberated from inconsequential theological questions. With the results of those untrammeled investigations church historians could, he hoped, further the move toward a general science of religions.[69]

In 1977 Lewis W. Spitz provided additional thoughts on historical methods and objectives, and as a counterbalance to Clebsch's one-sided exhortation he defended the legitimacy of theological values in the guild. Spitz did not quarrel with the obvious benefits of secular history; he suggested instead that critical procedures developed in the larger field were of immense value to students of the ecclesiastical past. Definition of the subject to be studied was a thorny problem, however, because "church" was a notoriously protean concept. In broadest terms it could encompass the whole of Christianity; more narrowly it involved dubious references to an ethnic group, political faction, or social class distinguished from Moslems or Jews. Spitz held that practical or usable definitions had to probe beneath superficial labels in order to focus on "all those who relate to Christ as his followers, no matter how cogent or how confused their religious conception of what being His may mean." This definitional preference placed religious norms alongside empirical ones in setting parameters for the field, and it included salvation history as a "hidden card" in scholarly activities. If one stressed the common core of Christian experience, then topical definition relied on predetermined expectations of what would be found in prior experience.

> To believing historians church history stands in a continuum with the religious history of Israel, its historicity rooted in the Incarnation, its message is the word of Christ's life and death for man's redemption, sealed by the resurrection, and culminating in the eschatological coming of the Kingdom of God.

This perspective retained an admittedly transcendental dimension by locating the conceptual sphere, if not the actual procedures, of church history in theology. As a hidden card, salvation history remained "an element necessary to genuine church history" because it preserved concern for higher ends in the discipline.[70]

Before explaining his own plan for correlating sacred and secular perspectives in historical work, Spitz described three less preferable alternatives. The first placed God's saving acts at the center of earthly events, with church history depicting a second ring of providential influences, and secular history forming an external shell. Believers might find the model acceptable, but purely secular historians could not accept its priorities. Another option allowed for autonomy where historians could either study churches positivistically as human institutions or concentrate on Christian expressions as devout responses to revelation. There was no necessary connection between such approaches, however, and there was no uniform way to combine findings from antipodal viewpoints. A third paradigm varied the pattern by overlapping the circles of concentration. As with autonomy it too made scholarly responsibility vulnerable to whim. Spitz preferred none of these but rather an arrangement he called the "SIMUL principle," a view that comprised providential action and mundane complexities at the same time. If salvation, church, and secular events existed simultaneously and coextensively, the ideal historian could "proceed with his scientific research and interpretive reconstruction without the need to adduce specious providential interventions. At the same time . . . he may well know and believe very deeply that the story of the church has its transcendental dimension."[71] By perpetuating a religious component stressed earlier by Nichols, Trinterud, and Outler, Spitz articulated the persistent reaffirmation of those who wish to blend confessionalism with exactitude.

The SIMUL principle offered a balance of faith and humanistic investigation, an approach that preserved professional standards without letting supernatural considerations interfere unduly. It meant that one could treat Christ as a moral exemplar and inquire into how his followers had affected various cultures. One could as readily see in Christ the prototype of God's plan to elevate humanity with transformed dignity. Spitz found these perspectives compatible and simultaneously viable. He saw no reason why a historian's confessionalism should "interfere with his honest, open, informed, . . . efforts to do good history accredited by any scientific historian." And at the same time there was room in scholarship for "the vibrant faith that built the church." Indeed, he was convinced that "no church historian can tell that story truthfully without taking that dimension fully into account." This defense of a historian's working faith a century after Schaff was no mere replication of the founder's perspective. It did not rely on providential intervention in the world's affairs as a component of narrative explanation or interpretive overview. Still, it was a fresh assertion that theological insights could mix beneficially with secular methods and that this combination could stimulate church historians to regard the evidence of research from two different points of view.[72] Spitz recommended SIMUL as a way of retaining religious meaning in humanistic studies. It allowed for a theological appreciation of history without binding scholars to any programmatic philosophy of history. It made it possible for labor in the intellectual marketplace to be a genuine vocation, activity wherein the historian's faith enriched pursuit of truth by secular means.

The presidents discussed here constituted a small fraction of those in the ASCH who grappled with fundamental issues in the church historical enterprise. Their addresses between 1919 and 1977 stimulated hundreds of colleagues who also pondered the use of critical methods in their chosen field. None of them advocated deliberate distortion of evidence to vindicate predetermined belief systems; none despaired of understanding their subject because relating its interstices was too difficult. Between those extremes modern church historians have developed a number of perspectives along a spectrum featuring two basic emphases. One side, encompassing most scholars in previous decades and a sizable number today, gives highest priority to theological considerations. These practitioners usually refer to a church as somehow retaining a modicum of divine origin and meaning. They insist that beliefs have a proper place in interpretations, and their ultimate objective includes appropriating the past as a support for contemporary religious understanding. On the other side, a smaller number of historians have tabled the question of religious authenticity in order to concentrate on secular method and themes of cultural importance. Humanists confine themselves to social aspects of religious activity, and they shun the view that beliefs should supplement a study of mundane institutions. Their objective is nothing less or more than making durable contributions to the secular store of human knowledge. Most present-day historians have moved toward the humanistic, secularist side of the spectrum, but scholars of every viewpoint continue to wrestle with the task of blending religious conceptions and earthly procedures. Their ingenuity in such enterprises make church historiography a perpetually fascinating study.

Summary

Several important patterns developed in the ASCH during its first hundred years. After early ambiguity regarding the AHA, a decade in limbo, and subsequent revival the society became in this century a body of professional specialists with increasing corporate stability. Obtaining a charter in 1916, the organization grew by attracting new members, especially in midwestern sections of the country. What began as a club in eastern cities metamorphosed into a more inclusive forum for scholars spread throughout the United States and Canada. Power initially wielded by a dedicated but exclusive clique was gradually distributed more widely. Council membership and committee activities today exhibit healthier democratic participation. Numerical growth has leveled off in recent decades. It remains to be seen whether the present total indicates a decline from irrecoverable heights or is simply a temporary plateau, anticipating greater membership in future years. Regardless of size, though, ASCH constituents have proved to all but a few doctrinaire antagonists that past ecclesiastical experience can be studied in ways that command intellectual respect.

As far as ideas are concerned, the society has encompassed an interesting variety of practitioners and theorists regarding the craft. Church historians have chosen to study a great many topics in different time periods, but within such diversity they have utilized two basic approaches to historical materials. They have tried in various ways either to blend faith affirmations with historical knowledge or to keep them separate categories. Historians have formulated many thoughtful solutions to this persistent question. No version dominates the field, and the problem of relating critical procedures with cumulative information is a constant one. Debates in the ASCH have repeatedly grappled with ways of linking natural and supernatural data, of integrating human sciences and theological traditions. This symmetrical pairing of ideas resembles a double helix wherein ideas about sacred and secular history face each other in spiraling counterpoise through successive generations. As a core concern to scholars this juxtaposition has been a perennial historiographical feature in the institution.

Those defending the place of religious insight in historical study have retained a perspective where spiritual referents add an explanatory dimension not found elsewhere. Their work is not just another form of confessionalism but rather an incorporation of ideas that round out human experience. Those wishing to exclude transcendental references have argued that strictures in historical method preclude mixing incompatible categories. Their work does not impugn the legitimacy of theology but rather attempts to protect history by establishing separate spheres where different norms and limits pertain. Considering the ASCH as a whole, ideas representing both points of view have manifested remarkable persistence. Like the double helix each side continues to mirror its counterpart, providing a matrix for fruitful interchange in the discipline. This situation nurtures creative combinations of ideas that stimulate historians as they contemplate further investigations during their society's second century.

Notes

1. David S. Schaff, *The Life of Philip Schaff, In Part Autobiographical* (New York: Charles Scribner's Sons, 1897), 465. See also *Papers of the American Society of Church History*, vol. 1 (New York: G. P. Putnam's Sons, 1889), v, xv. Hereafter cited as *PASCH*.

2. In an age of increased national consolidation and corporate participation, the AHA in turn had justified its formation by referring to the American Oriental Society (1842), American Social Science Association (1865), and American Philological Association (1869). See *Papers of the American Historical Association*, vol. 1 (New York: G. P. Putnam's Sons, 1885) 7–8.

3. *PASCH* 1: xv.

4. This author has previously implied such an antagonism in his *Church History in the Age of Science: Historiographical Patterns in the United States, 1876–1918* (Chapel Hill: University of North Carolina Press, 1971), 58–61. Further acquaintance with the evidence shows that it will not substantiate such an interpretation, no matter how much hindsight can tease out incompatible perspectives among protagonists.

5. *PASCH* 1: viii.

6. Letter dated 4 May 1888 from Jackson to Adams. S. M. Jackson Papers, New York University Archives, RG 36-1-2.

7. Letter dated 11 May 1888 from Adams to Jackson; letter dated 16 May 1888 from Jackson to Adams. S. M. Jackson Papers, RG 36-1-2.

8. Letter dated 31 October 1889 from Adams to Jackson. S. M. Jackson Papers, RG 36-1-24.

9. Letters dated 2 March 1894 and 20 October 1894 from Hurst to Jackson. S. M. Jackson Papers, RG 36-3-19.

10. Letter dated 9 January 1894 from Hurst to Jackson. S. M. Jackson Papers, RG 36-3-19.

11. Letter dated 17 July 1895 from Hurst to Jackson. S. M. Jackson Papers, RG 36-5-1.

12. Elizabeth Donnan and Leo F. Stock, eds., *An Historian's World: Selections from the Correspondence of John Franklin Jameson* (Philadelphia: American Philosophical Society,1956), 78.

13. See instances cited in Bowden, *Church History in the Age of Science*, 240–44.

14. *PASCH*, 2d ser., 1 (1913): v. For the original constitution see *PASCH* 1: ix–xi or any of the seven succeeding volumes that appeared through 1897.

15. *PASCH*, 2d ser., 1: vi; for slightly different wording of the earlier versions see

PASCH 1: x. The revived ASCH did not meet with the AHA again until 1917. That did not set a precedent, though, and the two societies did not meet together regularly or begin holding joint sessions until 1934.

16. *PASCH*, 2d ser., 5 (1917): xiii. It is worth noting in passing that the same page records this entry as well: "It was unanimously voted that women should be considered eligible for membership."

17. Theodore Burton, *Corporations and the State* (New York: D. Appleton and Co., 1911), 1–2, and Robert S. Stevens, *Handbook on the law of Private Corporations* (St. Paul: West Publishing, 1936), 15. In 1938 a Chicago attorney, Frank W. McCulloch, confirmed this interpretation by saying that the ASCH as a corporation could use money from sales of its publications to subsidize other publishing projects. As long as officers filed proper IRS forms, the society would remain tax-exempt. See ASCH Archives, Presbyterian Historical Society, RG 162-1-65. Since the AHA had been incorporated by the federal government in 1889, the ASCH action may have been another case of following precedent set by the larger professional organization.

18. *PASCH*, 2d ser., 5: xxv–xxvii, v–vi.

19. *PASCH* 1: ix and *PASCH*, 2d ser., 1: v contain the earliest statement of objectives; see *PASCH*, 2d ser., 5: vii for the expanded version.

20. *PASCH*, 2d ser., 5: vii–viii; wording about "class" was not deleted until the annual meeting of 27 December 1951.

21. *Church History* 13 (March 1944): 62–63. Hereafter cited as *CH*.

22. *CH* 20 (March 1951): 64–65. This probably followed AHA precedent as well, namely its founding a Pacific branch for general historians in 1904. The ASCH council, at the urging of Quirinus Breen, professor of history at the University of Oregon, agreed on 29 December 1944 to sanction annual meetings for Pacific Coast members: *CH* 14 (March 1945): 67. Regional sessions were held from 1945 until 1975 when lack of supporting interest made such meetings impracticable.

23. *CH* 23 (June 1984): 290–97. In deciphering reasons for constitutional changes, it may be worth noting that no twentieth-century president held office twice before the 1983 prohibition.

24. *CH* 40 (March 1971): 124; *CH* 43 (March 1974): 134.

25. There was no list for 1925, but the figure seems reasonable as an average between the closest reports: 166 for 1922 and 184 for 1927.

26. *PASCH*, 2d ser., 5: lxi. This too may have been another instance of copying general historians who organized the Mississippi Valley Historical Association in 1907.

27. Ibid., lxii.

28. Louis B. Jennings, *The Bibliography and Biography of Shirley Jackson Case* (University of Chicago Press, 1949), 33. It is important to recognize that midwestern dissatisfaction with eastern dominance did not fade away meekly. Council minutes of 30 December 1923 include a resolution to authorize separate ASCH

meetings for a subgroup in the central states. A special committee approved the idea's feasibility in 1924, and this support lay behind establishment of annual spring meetings, the first one being held at Chicago in June of 1925. See *PASCH*, 2d ser., 8 (1928): xx–xxi, xxix–xxx.

29. *CH* 37 (June 1968): 242–44.

30. ASCH Archives, RG 162-1-24. See also Sweet's summary report, "Church Archives in the United States," *CH* 8 (March 1939): 43–53.

31. ASCH Archives, RG 162-1-63.

32. Ibid.

33. Letter from Ray C. Petry to Winthrop S. Hudson, dated 16 January 1950, ASCH Archives, RG 162-1-65.

34. *CH* 13: 63.

35. *CH* 20: 64.

36. *CH* 21: 92.

37. *CH* 46 (March 1977): 134.

38. Letters dated 23 December 1918 and 4 January 1919, ASCH Archives, RG 162-1-67.

39. George E. Horr, "The Influences of the War Upon the Study of Church History," *PASCH*, 2d ser., 7 (1923): 28–30.

40. Ibid., 31, 35.

41. Robert H. Nichols, "Aims and Methods of Teaching Church History," *PASCH*, 2d ser., 7: 40–41.

42. Ibid., 42–46.

43. Ibid., 47.

44. For particulars on this early debate and Emerton's place in it, see chaps. 2 and 4 in Bowden, *Church History in the Age of Science*.

45. Ephraim Emerton, "A Definition of Church History," *PASCH*, 2d ser., 7: 56.

46. Ibid., 58–60.

47. Ibid., 57–58.

48. Ibid., 61–63.

49. William W. Rockwell, "Rival Presuppositions in the Writing of Church History: A Study of Intellectual Bias," *PASCH*, 2d ser., 9 (1934): 11.

50. Ibid., 12–14. Rockwell reviewed opinions on this question, especially those of Theodore Mommsen who called for a *voraussetzungs-lose Geschichtswissenschaft* and of Albert Koeniger who argued that a strictly presuppositionless history was impossible to achieve.

51. Ibid., 46–49.

52. Ibid., 51. On that page Rockwell pointed to the compromise position by quoting in an approving footnote: "What historians distrust . . . is really not hypotheses that invite investigation . . . but fixed theories that control inves-

tigation." See Allen Johnson, *The Historian and Historical Evidence* (New York: Charles Scribner's Sons, 1926), 160.

53. James H. Nichols, "The Art of Church History," *CH* 20 (March 1951): 3, 5–6.

54. Ibid., 6.

55. Ibid., 7.

56. Ibid., 8–9. In making this point Nichols utilized a quotation from Cyril C. Richardson. Since poor health had forced Richardson to resign the ASCH presidency in 1948, he never delivered an address. But an article published shortly thereafter probably embodied his intended address. In addition to the fact that Nichols used it, then, this passage merits inclusion for its own sake as part of the study of presidential ideas: "Church history will only be truly exciting and enter into its rightful place in our thinking, when we see that God speaks to us in its events and that they have as their meaning not only to explain our present, but to point to Christ and to reveal our very being. . . . Church history is the tale of redemption; . . . its central thread is the story of the Holy Community (known under various guises and found in manifold and surprising places) which is the bearer of revelation and through which God acts in human history." See Cyril C. Richardson, "Church History Past and Present," *Union Seminary Quarterly Review* 5 (November 1949): 13.

57. Leonard J. Trinterud, "The Task of the American Church Historian," *CH* 25 (March 1956): 3–5.

58. Ibid., 7–10.

59. Ibid., 10–12.

60. Ibid., 11–12.

61. Ibid., 13–15.

62. Albert C. Outler, "Theodosius' Horse; Reflections on the Predicament of the Church Historian," *CH* 34 (September 1965): 253–56.

63. Ibid., 256–57.

64. Ibid., 257–59.

65. Ibid., 258–61.

66. William A. Clebsch, "Toward a History of Christianity," *CH* 43 (March 1974): 5–6, 9.

67. Ibid., 6.

68. Ibid., 9–11, 15.

69. Ibid., 16, and footnote on 9.

70. Lewis W. Spitz, "History: Sacred and Secular," *CH* 47 (March 1978): 10, 16–17.

71. Ibid., 17–19.

72. Ibid., 19.

Appendixes

Contributors

Index

Appendix A

Centennial Retrospective

Key

Year   *Name*
(Life dates and places)
A. Sequential number
B. Highest earned degree, institution
C. Denomination
D. Ordained status
E. Position at time of Presidency
F. Age when President
G. "Presidential Address," *source*

1888–93   *Philip Schaff*
(1 January 1819, Chur, Switzerland–20 October 1893, New York, NY)
A. First
B. Lic. theol., University of Berlin
C. Presbyterian
D. Yes
E. Faculty member, Union Theological Seminary (NY)
F. 69–74
G1 "The Progress of Religious Freedom as shown in the History of Toleration Acts," *PASCH* 1 (1889): 1–126
G2 "Dante' s Theology," *PASCH* 2 (1890): 53–73
G3 "The Renaissance: The Revival of Learning and Art in the Fourteenth and Fifteenth Centuries," *PASCH* 3 (1891): 3–132
G4 "The Friendship of Calvin and Melanchthon," *PASCH* 4 (1892): 143–63
G5 "St. Thomas of Canterbury," *PASCH* 5 (1893): 3–33 (absent, but paper read by G. R. W. Scott).

G6 No address; meeting given over to memorial services for the deceased President.

1894–95   *John Fletcher Hurst*
(17 August 1834, Salem, MD–4 May 1903, Bethesda, MD)
A. Second
B. B.A. Dickinson College; studied at German universities.
C. Methodist
D. Yes
E. Bishop, M. E. church; Chancellor designate, American University.
F. 60–61.
G1 "President Hurst then delivered the annual address in which he reviewed the Church historical literature of the year 1894 in America, British Isles, and Continental Europe," *PASCH* 7 (1895): xiii
G2 "He then made a brief address upon the importance of parish histories, mentioned by name and characterized the more famous or valuable of such histories and alluded to the great stores of parochial history still in manuscript," *PASCH* 8 (1897): xiii

1896   *George Park Fisher*
(10 August 1827, Wrentham MA–20 December 1909, New Haven CT)
A. Third
B. B.D. Andover Theological Seminary
C. Congregationalist
D. Yes
E. Professor of Ecclesiastical History, Yale Divinity School
F. 69
G. No address; merger with the American Historical Association

1897–1906   No society, no President; reorganized 27 December 1906

1907   *Williston Walker*
(1 July 1860, Portland, ME–9 March 1922, New Haven, CT)
A. Fourth
B. Ph.D. University of Leipzig
C. Congregationalist

D. No
E. Professor of Church History, Yale University
F. 47
G. "The Current Outlook in Church History," *PASCH*, 2d ser., 1
(1913): 17–32

1908   *Henry Eyster Jacobs*
(10 November 1844, Gettysburg, PA–7 July 1932, Philadelphia, PA)
A. Fifth
B. M.A. Pennsylvania College; B.D. Lutheran Theological Seminary
C. Lutheran
D. Yes
E. Professor of Systematic Theology, Lutheran Theological Seminary (Philadelphia)
F. 64
G. "The Four Hundred and Four Theses of Dr. John Eck, published in 1530: A Contribution to the History of the Augsburg Confession," *PASCH*, 2d ser., 2 (1910): 21–81

1909   *Francis Albert Christie*
(3 December 1858, Lowell, MA–4 August 1938, Lowell, MA)
A. Sixth
B. A.B., Amherst College; studied at John Hopkins University and in German universities.
C. Unitarian
D. Yes
E. Professor of Church History, Meadville Theological Seminary (PA) (until 1926)
F. 51
G. "The Year 1909 in Church History," *PASCH*, 2d ser., 2 (1910): 153–73

1910   *Arthur Cushman McGiffert*
(4 March 1861, Sauquoit, NY–25 February 1933, Dobbs Ferry, NY)
A. Seventh
B. Ph.D., University of Marburg
C. Congregationalist
D. Yes

E. Professor of Church History, Union Theological Seminary (NY)

F. 49

G. "The President made his address, in the form of an unwritten report upon the literature on church history produced in 1910, supplemented by a typewritten bibliography distributed to members present," *PASCH*, 2d ser., 3 (1912): 1

1911   *Edward Tanjore Corwin*

(12 July 1834, New York, NY–22 June 1914, North Branch, NJ)

A. Eighth

B. M.A., City College of New York; B.D., New Brunswick Theological Seminary

C. Dutch Reformed

D. Yes

E. Retired church historian and minister; researcher on ecclesiastical records of NY for the Reformed church

F. 77

G. "The Ecclesiastical Condition of New York at the Opening of the Eighteenth Century," *PASCH*, 2d ser., 3 (1912): 81–115

1912   *Samuel Macauley Jackson*

(19 June 1851, New York, NY–2 August 1912, Washington, CT)

A. Ninth

B. M.A. City College of New York

C. Presbyterian

D. Yes

E. Professor of Church History, New York University

F. 61

G. "Servatus Lupus, A Humanist of the Ninth Century," *PASCH*, 2d ser., 4 (1914): 23–37; postumous presentation, read by William Walker Rockwell, the Secretary

1913   *Joseph Cullen Ayer, Jr.*

(7 January 1866, Newton, MA–15 April 1944, Philadelphia, PA)

A. Tenth

B. Ph.D., University of Leipzig

C. Episcopalian

D. Yes

E. Professor of Ecclesiastical History, Divinity School of the P. E. Church, Philadelphia.

F. 47

G. "On the Medieval National Church," *PASCH*, 2d ser., 4 (1914): 41–75

1914   *James Isaac Good*
(31 December 1850, York, PA–22 January 1924, Philadelphia, PA)
A. Eleventh
B. M.A., Lafayette College; B.D. Union Theological Seminary (NY)
C. German Reformed
D. Yes
E. Professor of Church History, Emeritus, Ursinus College; President, General Synod of the Reformed Church.
F. 64
G. "Reformation and the New World," not printed but mentioned in *PASCH*, 2d ser., 5 (1917): xiii

1915   *John Alfred Faulkner*
(14 July 1857, Grand Pre, Nova Scotia–6 September 1931, Madison, NJ)
A. Twelfth
B. M.A. Arcadia College; B.D., Drew Theological Seminary
C. Methodist
D. Yes
E. Professor of Church History, Drew Theological Seminary
F. 58
G. "The Reformers and Toleration," *PASCH*, 2d ser., 5 (1917): 3–22

1916   *Edward Payson Johnson*
(26 January 1850, Peru, IN–31 May 1924, New Brunswick, NJ)
A. Thirteenth
B. M.A., Wabash College; B.D., Auburn Theological Seminary
C. Presbyterian
D. Yes
E. Professor of Sacred and Ecclesiastical History, New Brunswick Theological Seminary

F. 66

G. "Christian Work among the North American Indians during the Eighteenth Century," *PASCH*, 2d ser., 6 (1921): 3–41

1917   *David Schley Schaff*
(17 October 1852, Mercersburg, PA–2 March 1941, Winter Park, FL)
A. Fourteenth
B. A.B., Yale College
C. Presbyterian
D. Yes
E. Professor of Ecclesiastical History and History of Doctrine, Western Theological Seminary
F. 65
G. "The Council of Constance: Its Fame and Its Failure," *PASCH*, 2d ser., 6 (1921): 45–69

1918   *Henry Bradford Washburn*
(2 December 1869, Worcester, MA–25 April 1962, Cambridge, MA)
A. Fifteenth
B. B.D., Episcopal Theological School; studied at German universities
C. Episcopalian
D. Yes
E. Professor of Ecclesiastical History, Episcopal Theological School
F. 49
G. "The Army Chaplain," *PASCH*, 2d ser., 7 (1923): 3–23

1919   *George Edwin Horr*
(19 January 1856, Boston MA–22 January 1927, Belmont, MA)
A. Sixteenth
B. A.B., Brown University; B.D., Newton Theological Seminary
C. Baptist
D. Yes
E. Professor of Church History, Newton Theological Seminary
F. 63
G. "The Influence of the War Upon the Study of Church History," *PASCH*, 2d ser., 7 (1923): 27–36

1920   *Robert Hastings Nichols*
(2 October 1873, Rochester, NY–18 July 1955, New York, NY)
A. Seventeenth
B. Ph.D., Yale University
C. Presbyterian
D. Yes
E. Professor of Church History, Auburn Theological Seminary
F. 47
G. "Aims and Methods of Teaching Church History," *PASCH*, 2d ser., 7 (1923): 39–51

1921   *Ephraim Emerton*
(18 February 1851, Salem, MA–3 March 1935, Cambridge, MA)
A. Eighteenth
B. Ph.D., University of Leipzig
C. Unitarian
D. No
E. Professor of Church History, Emeritus, Harvard Divinity School
F. 70
G. "A Definition of Church History," *PASCH*, 2d ser., 7 (1923): 55–68

1922   *William Nathaniel Schwarze*
(2 January 1875, Chaska, MN–14 March 1948, Bethlehem, PA)
A. Nineteenth
B. Ph.D., Moravian College
C. Moravian
D. Yes
E. Professor of Homiletics and Church History, Moravian College and Theological Seminary
F. 47
G. "Early Moravian Settlements in America," *PASCH*, 2d ser., 7 (1923): 71–88

1923   *James Coffin Stout*
(25 November 1869, Irvington, NY–14 March 1930, Bronxville, NY)
A. Twentieth
B. B.D., Princeton Theological Seminary

C. Dutch Reformed

D. Yes

E. Minister and Professor of Church History, Bible Seminary (NY)

F. 54

G. "The Early Christian Sarcophagi of the Lateran Museum and their Historical Suggestiveness," *PASCH*, 2d ser., 8 (1928): 3–15

1924   *Henry Jacob Weber*

(31 August 1854, Newark, NJ–27 October 1933, Bloomfield, NJ)

A. Twenty-first

B. Ph.D., University of Pennsylvania

C. Presbyterian

D. Yes

E. Professor of Theology and Church History, Bloomfield Theological Seminary

F. 70

G. "The Formal Dialectical Rationalism of Calvin," *PASCH*, 2d ser., 8 (1928): 19–41

1925   *Shirley Jackson Case*

(28 September 1872, Hatfield Point, New Brunswick, Canada–5 December 1947, Lakeland, FL)

A. Twenty-second

B. Ph.D., Yale University

C. Baptist

D. No

E. Professor of the History of Early Christianity, University of Chicago

F. 53

G. "The Acceptance of Christianity by the Roman Emperors," *PASCH* 2d ser., 8 (1928): 45–64

1926   *William Walker Rockwell*

(4 October 1874, Pittsfield, MA–30 May 1958, New York, NY)

A. Twenty-third

B. Ph.D., University of Göttingen

C. Congregationalist

D. Yes

E. Librarian and Associate Professor of Church History, Union Theological Seminary (NY)

F. 52

G. "Rival Presuppositions in the Writing of Church History: A Study of Intellectual Bias," *PASCH*, 2d ser., 9 (1934): 3–52

1927   *George Warren Richards*

(26 April 1869, Farmington, PA–11 June 1955, Lancaster, PA)

A. Twenty-fourth

B. Ph.D., University of Heidelberg

C. German Reformed

D. Yes

E. President and Professor of Church History, Reformed Theological Seminary (Lancaster, PA)

F. 58

G. "Zwingli's Commentary on True and False Religion," not printed in *PASCH*, but incorporated in *The Latin Works of Huldreich Zwingli* (Philadelphia: Heidelberg Press, 1929), 3: 1–42

1928   *Winfred Ernest Garrison*

(1 October 1874, St. Louis, MO–6 February 1969, Houston, TX)

A. Twenty-fifth

B. Ph.D., University of Chicago

C. Disciples of Christ

D. Yes

E. Associate Professor of Church History, University of Chicago

F. 54

G. "Interdenominational Relations in America before 1837," *PASCH*, 2d ser., 9 (1934): 59–93

1929   *Edward Strong Worcester*

(14 April 1876, South Orange, NJ–25 June 1937, New Brunswick, NJ)

A. Twenty-sixth

B. B.D., Hartford Theological Seminary

C. Congregationalist

D. Yes

E. Professor of Systematic Theology, New Brunswick Theological Seminary

F. 53

G. [The President] "opened the literary session of the Society with his Presidential Address. W. W. Rockwell discussed the paper," not printed; *PASCH*, 2d ser., 9 (1934): xli

1930   *William David Schermerhorn*
(23 October 1871, Lincoln, KS–19 April 1942, Evanston, IL)
A. Twenty-seventh
B. M.A., University of Chicago; S.T.B., Garrett Bible Institute
C. Methodist
D. Yes
E. Professor of Church History and Missions, Garrett Bible Institute
F. 58
G. "Doctrinal Attitudes of the Rising Younger Churches," *PASCH*, 2d ser., 9 (1934): 97–118

1931   *Abdel Ross Wentz*
(8 October 1883, Black Rock, PA–19 July 1976, Rockford, IL)
A. Twenty-eighth
B. Ph.D., George Washington University
C. Lutheran
D. Yes
E. Professor of Church History, Lutheran Theological Seminary (Gettysburg, PA)
F. 48
G. "Permanent Deposits of Sectionalism in American Christianity," *CH* 1 (March 1932): 3–13

1932   *William Warren Sweet*
(15 February 1881, Baldwin, KS–3 January 1959, Dallas, TX)
A. Twenty-ninth
B. Ph.D., University of Pennsylvania
C. Methodist
D. Yes
E. Professor of American Christianity, University of Chicago
F. 51
G. "The Churches as Moral Courts of the Frontier," *CH* 2 (March 1933): 3–21

1933　　　　*Conrad Henry Moehlman*
(26 May 1879, Meridan, CT–19 September 1961, Avon Park, FL)
A. Thirtieth
B. Ph.D., University of Michigan
C. Baptist
D. Yes
E. Professor of the History of Christianity, Colgate-Rochester Divinity School
F. 54
G. "The Christianization of Interest," *CH* 3 (March 1934): 3–15

1934　　　　*Frederick William Loetscher*
(15 May 1875, Dubuque, IA–31 July 1966, Princeton, NJ)
A. Thirty-first
B. Ph.D., Princeton University
C. Presbyterian
D. Yes
E. Professor of Church History, Princeton Theological Seminary
F. 59
G. "St. Augustine's Conception of the State," *CH* 4 (March 1935): 16–42

1935　　　　*John Thomas McNeill*
(28 July 1885, Elmsdale, Prince Edward Island, Canada–6 February 1975, Middlebury, VT)
A. Thirty-second
B. Ph.D., University of Chicago
C. Presbyterian
D. Yes
E. Professor of European Christianity, University of Chicago
F. 50
G. "Asceticism versus Militarism in the Middle Ages," *CH* 5 (March 1936): 3–28

1936　　　　*Wilhelm Pauck*
(31 January 1901, Laasphe, Germany–3 September 1981, Palo Alto, CA)
A. Thirty-third
B. Lic. theol., University of Berlin

C. Congregationalist

D. Yes

E. Professor of Church History, Chicago Theological Seminary

F. 35

G. "The Nature of Protestanism," *CH* 6 (March 1937): 3–23

1937   *Herbert Wallace Schneider*
(16 March 1892, Berea, OH–15 October 1984, Claremont, CA)

A. Thirty-fourth

B. Ph.D., Columbia University

C. Methodist

D. No

E. Professor of Philosophy and Religion, Columbia University

F. 45

G. "The Intellectual Background of William Ellery Channing," *CH* 7 (March 1938): 3–23

1938   *Reuben Elmore Ernest Harkness*
(27 October 1884, Sarnia, Ontario, Canada–16 February 1973 New London, CT)

A. Thirty-fifth

B. Ph.D., University of Chicago

C. Baptist

D. Yes

E. Professor of Church History, Crozer Theological Seminary

F. 54

G. "The Development of Democracy in the English Reformation," *CH* 8 (March 1939): 3–29

1939   *Charles Harold Lyttle*
(16 July 1884, Cleveland, OH–2 May 1980, Chicago, IL)

A. Thirty-sixth

B. Th.D., Meadville Theological School

C. Unitarian

D. Yes

E. Professor of Church History, Meadville Theological School, Chicago, IL

F. 55

G. "Historical Bases of Rome's Conflict with Freemasonry," *CH* 9 (March 1940): 3–23

1940   *Roland Herbert Bainton*
(30 March 1894, Ikeston, England–13 February 1984, New Haven, CT)
A. Thirty-seventh
B. Ph.D., Yale University
C. Congregationalist
D. Yes
E. Professor of Ecclesiastical History, Yale Divinity School
F. 46
G. "The Struggle for Religious Liberty," *CH* 10 (June 1941): 94–124

1941   *Francis William Buckler*
(10 August 1891, Groby, England–4 August 1960 Cambridge, England)
A. Thirty-eighth
B. M.A., Cambridge University
C. Episcopalian
D. No
E. Professor of Church History, Oberlin College
F. 50
G. "Barbarian and Greek–And Church History," *CH* 11 (March 1942): 3–32

1942   *Edward Rochie Hardy, Jr.*
(17 June 1908, New York, NY–26 May 1981, Cambridge, England)
A. Thirty-ninth
B. Ph.D., Columbia University
C. Episcopalian
D. Yes
E. Fellow and Tutor, General Theological Seminary (NY)
F. 34
G. "Servant of the Servants of God." *CH* 12 (March 1943): 3–27

1943   *Harold Stauffer Bender*
(19 July 1897, Elkhart, IN–21 September 1962, Chicago, IL)
A. Fortieth

B. Th.D., University of Heidelberg
C. Mennonite
D. Yes
E. Professor of Bible and Church History, Goshen College
F. 46
G. "The Anabaptist Vision," *CH* 13 (March 1944): 3–24

1944   *Percy Varney Norwood*
(3 January 1884, Salem, MA–1 May 1982, Cincinnati, OH)
A. Forty-first
B. Ph.D., Northwestern University
C. Episcopalian
D. Yes
E. Professor of Ecclesiastical History, Seabury–Western Theological Seminary
F. 60
G. "A Victorian Primate," *CH* 14 (March 1945): 3–16

1945   *Kenneth Scott Latourette*
(9 August 1884, Oregon City, OR–26 December 1968, Oregon City, OR)
A. Forty-second
B. Ph.D., Yale University
C. Baptist
D. Yes
E. Professor of Missions and Oriental History, Yale Divinity School
F. 61
G. "A Historian Looks Ahead; The Future of Christianity in the Light of Its Past," *CH* 15 (March 1946): 3–16

1946   *Matthew Spinka*
(30 January 1890, Stitary, Czechoslovakia–23 October 1972, Claremont, CA)
A. Forty-third
B. Ph.D., University of Chicago
C. Congregationalist
D. Yes
E. Professor of Church History, Hartford Theological Seminary

F. 56

G. "Berdyaev and Origen: A Comparison," *CH* 16 (March 1947): 3–21

1947   *Ernest George Schwiebert*
(17 October 1895, Deshler, OH–)
A. Forty-fourth
B. Ph.D., Cornell University
C. Lutheran
D. No
E. Professor of History, Wittenberg College
F. 52
G. "The Reformation from a New Perspective," *CH* 17 (March 1948): 3–31

1948   *Cyril Charles Richardson*
(13 June 1909, London, England–16 November 1976, New York, NY)
A. Forty-fifth
B. Th.D., Union Theological Seminary (NY)
C. Episcopalian
D. Yes
E. Associate Professor of Church History, Union Theological Seminary
F. 39
G. Resigned by letter 23 April 1948; reasons of health

1948   *Winthrop Still Hudson*
(28 August 1911, Schoolcraft, MI–)
A. Forty-sixth
B. Ph.D., University of Chicago
C. Baptist
D. Yes
E. Professor of the History of Christianity, Colgate-Rochester Divinity School
F. 37
G. "Puritanism and the Spirit of Capitalism," *CH* 18 (March 1949): 3–17

1949   *Massey Hamilton Shepherd, Jr.*
(14 March 1913, Wilmington, NC–)
A. Forty-seventh
B. Ph.D., University of Chicago
C. Episcopalian
D. Yes
E. Professor of Church History, Episcopal Theological School
F. 36
G. "The Place of the Prayer Book in the Western Liturgical Tra-
   dition," *CH* 19 (March 1950): 3–14

1950   *James Hastings Nichols*
(18 January 1915, Auburn, NY–)
A. Forty-eighth
B. Ph.D., Yale University
C. Presbyterian
D. Yes
E. Federated Theological Faculty, University of Chicago
F. 35
G. "The Art of Church History," *CH* 20 (March 1951): 3–9

1951   *Ray C. Petry*
(2 July 1903, Eaton, OH–)
A. Forty-ninth
B. Ph.D., University of Chicago
C. Methodist
D. No
E. Professor of Church History, Duke Divinity School
F. 48
G. "Social Responsibility and the Late Medieval Mystics." *CH* 21
   (March 1952): 3–19

1952   *Sanford Fleming*
(2 May 1888, Adelaide, Australia–14 June 1974, Santa Barbara, CA)
A. Fiftieth
B. Ph.D., Yale University
C. Baptist
D. Yes
E. President, Berkeley Baptist Divinity School

F. 64

G. No address because of President's illness and nonattendance

1953　　　　*Sidney Earl Mead*
(2 August 1904, Champlin, MN–)

A. Fifty-first

B. Ph.D., University of Chicago

C. Baptist

D. Yes

E. Professor of American Church History, University of Chicago

F. 49

G. "Abraham Lincoln's 'Last, Best Hope of Earth': The American Dream of Destiny and Democracy," *CH* 23 (March 1954): 3–16

1954　　　　*Carl Edward Schneider*
(23 March 1890, Jefferson City, MO–29 July 1981, St. Louis, MO)

A. Fifty-second

B. Ph.D., University of Chicago

C. Evangelical and Reformed

D. Yes

E. Professor of Church History, Eden Theological Seminary

F. 64

G. "Americanization of Karl August Rauschenbusch, 1816–1899," *CH* 24 (March 1955): 3–14

1955　　　　*Leonard John Trinterud*
(25 September 1904, Aneta, ND–)

A. Fifty-third

B. Th.D., University of Lund

C. Presbyterian

D. Yes

E. Professor of Church History, McCormick Theological Seminary

F. 51

G. "The Task of the American Church Historian," *CH* 25 (March 1956): 3–15

1956　　　　*Quirinus Breen*
(3 March 1896, Orange City, IA–25 March 1975, Eugene, OR)

A. Fifty-fourth

B. Ph.D., University of Chicago
C. Presbyterian
D. No
E. Professor of History, University of Oregon
F. 60
G. "John Calvin and the Rhetorical Tradition," *CH* 26 (March 1957): 3–21

1957   *Hilrie Shelton Smith*
(8 May 1893, near Greensboro, NC–8 January 1987, Durham, NC)
A. Fifty-fifth
B. Ph.D., Yale University
C. United Church of Christ
D. Yes
E. Professor of American Religious Thought, Duke Divinity School
F. 64
G. No paper; though recovering from eye surgery, he presided and led a general discussion on "the nature and prospects of American Church History"

1958   *George Huntston Williams*
(7 April 1914, Huntsburg, OH–)
A. Fifty-sixth
B. Th.D., Union Theological Seminary (NY)
C. Unitarian
D. Yes
E. Professor of Ecclesiastical History, Harvard Divinity School
F. 44
G. "The Wilderness and Paradise in the History of the Church," *CH* 28 (March 1959): 3–24

1959   *Robert Theodore Handy*
(30 June 1918, Rockville, CT–)
A. Fifty-seventh
B. Ph.D., University of Chicago
C. Baptist
D. Yes
E. Professor of Church History, Union Theological Seminary (NY)
F. 41

G. "The American Religious Depression, 1925–1935," *CH* 29 (March 1960): 3–16

1960   *Jerald Carl Brauer*
(16 September 1921, Fond du Lac, WI–)
A. Fifty-eighth
B. Ph.D., University of Chicago
C. Lutheran
D. Yes
E. Professor of the History of Christianity, Chicago Divinity School
F. 39
G. "Images of Religion in America," *CH* 30 (March 1961): 3–18

1961   *Harold John Grimm*
(16 August 1901, Saginaw, MI–10 November 1983, Columbus, OH)
A. Fifty-ninth
B. Ph.D., Ohio State University
C. Lutheran
D. No
E. Professor of History, Ohio State University
F. 60
G. "Social Forces in the German Reformation," *CH* 31 (March 1962): 3–13

1962   *Lefferts Augustine Loetscher*
(24 July 1904, Dubuque, IA–19 November 1981, Princeton, NJ)
A. Sixtieth
B. Ph.D., University of Pennsylvania
C. Presbyterian
D. Yes
E. Professor of American Church History, Princeton Theological Seminary
F. 58
G. "The Problem of Christian Unity in Early Nineteenth-Century America," *CH* 32 (March 1963): 3–16

1963   *Raymond Wolf Albright*
(16 July 1901, Akron, PA–15 July 1965, Cambridge, MA)
A. Sixty-first

B. Th.D., Divinity School of the P.E. Church, Philadelphia
C. Episcopalian
D. Yes
E. Professor of Church History, Episcopal Theological School
F. 62
G. "Conciliarism in Anglicanism," *CH* 33 (March 1964): 3–22

1964   *Albert Cook Outler*
(17 November 1908, Thomasville, GA–)
A. Sixty-second
B. Ph.D., Yale University
C. Methodist
D. Yes
E. Professor of Theology, Perkins School of Theology, Southern Methodist University
F. 56
G. "Theodosius' Horse; Reflections on the Predicament of the Church Historian," *CH* 34 (September 1965): 251–61

1965   *Jaroslav Jan Pelikan*
(17 December 1923, Akron, OH–)
A. Sixty-third
B. Ph.D., University of Chicago
C. Lutheran
D. Yes
E. Professor of Ecclesiastical History, Yale Divinity School
F. 42
G. "An Essay on the Development of Christian Doctrine," *CH* 35 (March 1966): 3–12

1966   *John Robert von Rohr*
(14 March 1916, Roseau, MN–)
A. Sixty-fourth
B. Ph.D., Yale University
C. United Church of Christ
D. Yes
E. Professor of Historical Theology and History of Christianity, Pacific School of Religion

F. 50

G. *"Extra Ecclesiam Nulla Salus*: An Early Congregational Version," *CH* 36 (June 1967): 107–21

1967   *Richard Morgan Cameron*
(28 September 1898, Somerset, PA–2 April 1978, New York, NY)
A. Sixty-fifth
B. Ph.D., Boston University
C. Methodist
D. Yes
E. Professor of Church History, Emeritus, Boston University School of Theology
F. 69
G. "The Attack on the Biblical Work of Lefevre d'Etaples, 1514–1521," *CH* 38 (March 1969): 9–24

1968   *Elwyn Allen Smith*
(17 September 1919, Wilmington, DE–)
A. Sixty-sixth
B. Ph.D., Harvard University
C. Presbyterian
D. Yes
E. Professor of Religion, Temple University
F. 49
G. "The Fundamental Church-State Tradition of the Catholic Church in the United States," *CH* 38 (December 1969): 486–505

1969   *John Tracy Ellis*
(30 July 1905, Seneca, IL–)
A. Sixty-seventh
B. Ph.D., Catholic University of America
C. Roman Catholic
D. Yes
E. Professor of Church History, University of San Francisco
F. 64
G. "John Henry Newman, A Bridge for Men of Good Will," *Catholic Historical Review* 56 (April 1970): 1–14

1970   *Robert McQueen Grant*
(25 November 1917, Evanston, IL–)
A. Sixty-eighth
B. Th.D., Union Theological Seminary (NY)
C. Episcopalian
D. Yes
E. Professor of New Testament and Early Christianity, University of Chicago Divinity School
F. 53
G. "Early Alexandrian Christianity," *CH* 40 (June 1971): 133–44

1971   *Martin Emil Marty*
(5 February 1928, West Point, NB–)
A. Sixty-ninth
B. Ph.D., University of Chicago
C. Lutheran
D. Yes
E. Professor of the History of Christianity, University of Chicago Divinity School
F. 43
G. "Ethnicity: The Skeleton of Religion in America," *CH* 41 (March 1972): 5–21

1972   *Carl Oliver Bangs*
(5 April 1922, Seattle, WA–)
A. Seventieth
B. Ph.D., University of Chicago
C. Methodist
D. Yes
E. Professor of Historical Theology, St. Paul School of Theology (MO)
F. 50
G. "'All the Best Bishoprics and Deaneries:' The Enigma of Arminian Politics," *CH* 42 (March 1973): 5–16

1973   *William Anthony Clebsch*
(27 July 1923, Clarksville, TN–12 June 1984, Palo Alto, CA)
A. Seventy-first
B. Th.D., Union Theological Seminary (NY)

C. Episcopalian

D. No

E. Professor of Religious Studies and Humanities, Stanford University

F. 50

G. "Toward a History of Christianity," *CH* 43 (March 1974): 5–16

1974   *Clyde Leonard Manschreck*

(27 January 1917, Krebs, OK–)

A. Seventy-second

B. Ph.D., Yale University

C. Methodist

D. Yes

E. Professor of the History of Christianity, Chicago Theological Seminary

F. 57

G. "Nihilism in the Twentieth Century: A View from Here," *CH* 45 (March 1976): 85–96

1975   *Sydney Eckman Ahlstrom*

(16 December 1919, Cokato, MN–3 July 1984, New Haven, CT)

A. Seventy-third

B. Ph.D., Harvard University

C. Lutheran

D. No

E. Professor of American History and Modern Religious History, Yale University

F. 56

G. "The Romantic Religious Revolution and the Dilemmas of Religious History." *CH* 46 (June 1977): 149–70

1976   *John Frederick Wilson*

(1 April 1933, Ipswich, MA–)

A. Seventy-fourth

B. Ph.D., Union Theological Seminary (NY)

C. United Church of Christ

D. No

E. Professor of Religion, Princeton University

F. 43

G. "Jonathan Edwards as Historian," *CH* 46 (March 1977): 5–18

1977   *Lewis William Spitz*
(14 December 1922, Bertrand, NB–)
A. Seventy-fifth
B. Ph.D., Harvard University
C. Lutheran
D. No
E. Professor of History, Stanford University
F. 55
G. "History: Sacred and Secular," *CH* 47 (March 1978): 5–22

1978   *Edwin Scott Gaustad*
(14 November 1923, Rowley, IA–)
A. Seventy-sixth
B. Ph.D., Brown University
C. Baptist
D. Yes
E. Professor of History, University of California, Riverside
F. 55
G. "George Berkeley and New World Community," *CH* 48 (March 1979): 5–17

1979   *Brian Albert Gerrish*
(14 August 1931, London, England–)
A. Seventy-seventh
B. Ph.D., Columbia University
C. Presbyterian
D. Yes
E. Professor of Historical Theology, University of Chicago Divinity School
F. 48
G. "Schleiermacher and the Reformation: A Question of Doctrinal Development," *CH* 49 (June 1980): 147–59

1980   *Robert McCune Kingdon*
(29 December 1927, Chicago, IL–)
A. Seventy-eighth
B. Ph.D., Columbia University

C. United Church of Christ
D. No
E. Professor of History, University of Wisconsin
F. 53
G. "The Church: Ideology or Institution," *CH* 50 (March 1981): 81–97

1981   *William Robert Hutchison*
(21 May 1930, San Francisco, CA–)
A. Seventy-ninth
B. Ph.D., Yale University
C. Society of Friends
D. No
E. Professor of the History of Religion in America, Harvard University
F. 51
G. "Innocence Abroad: The 'American Religion' in Europe," *CH* 51 (March 1982): 71–84

1982   *Clarence Curtis Goen*
(4 July 1924, San Marcos, TX–)
A. Eightieth
B. Ph.D., Yale University
C. Baptist
D. Yes
E. Professor of Church History, Wesley Theological Seminary
F. 58
G. "Broken Churches, Broken Nation: Regional Religion and North-South Alienation in Antebellum America," *CH* 52 (March 1983): 21–35

1983   *Jane Dempsey Douglass*
(22 March 1933, Wilmington, DE–)
A. Eighty-first
B. Ph.D., Harvard University
C. Presbyterian
D. No
E. Professor of Church History, Claremont School of Theology
F. 50

G. "Christian Freedom: What Calvin Learned at the School of Women," *CH* 53 (June 1984): 155–73

1984   *Henry Warner Bowden*
(1 April 1939, Memphis, TN–)
A. Eighty-second
B. Ph.D., Princeton University
C. Episcopalian
D. No
E. Professor of Religion, Rutgers University
F. 45
G. "Ends and Means in Church History," *CH* 54 (March 1985): 74–88

1985   *David Curtis Steinmetz*
(12 June 1936, Columbus, OH–)
A. Eighty-third
B. Th.D., Harvard University
C. United Methodist
D. Yes
E. Professor of Church History and Doctrine, Duke Divinity School
F. 49
G. "Luther and the Ascent of Jacob's Ladder," *CH* 55 (June 1986): 179–92

1986   *Winton Udell Solberg*
(11 January 1922, Aberdeen, SD–)
A. Eighty-fourth
B. Ph.D., Harvard University
C. Episcopalian
D. No
E. Professor of History, University of Illinois
F. 64
G. "Science and Religion in Early America: Cotton Mather's *Christian Philosopher*," *CH* 56 (March 1987): 73–92

1987   *Jay Patrick Dolan*
(17 March 1936, Bridgeport, CT–)
A. Eighty-fifth

B. Ph.D., University of Chicago
C. Roman Catholic
D. No
E. Professor of History, University of Notre Dame
F. 51
G. "The Immigrants and Their Gods," *CH* 57 (1988).

Appendix B

Awards

Brewer Prize

1938   Waldo E. L. Smith, "Episcopal Appointments and Patronage in the Reign of Edward II"

1940   Raymond P. Stearns, "Congregationalism in the Dutch Netherlands"

1941   Frederick A. Norwood, "The Economic Life and Influence of the Protestant Refugees During the Sixteenth Century"

1943   Babette May Levy, "Preaching in the First Half Century of New England History"

1945   Maurice W. Armstrong, "The Great Awakening in Nova Scotia, 1776–1809"

1946   Franklin H. Littell, "The Anabaptist View of the Church"

1949   Ira V. Brown, "Lyman Abbott, Christian Evolutionist: A Study in Religious Opinions"

1955   Timothy L. Smith, "Revivalism, Perfectionism, and Social Hope in American Religion, 1840–1865"

1957   William R. Hutchison, "Transcendental Religion: A Study in American Liberalism"

1963   Rollin S. Armour, "The Theology and Institution of Baptism in Sixteen Century Anabaptism"

1965   Alf E. Jacobsen, "The Congregational Ministry in Eighteenth Century New England"

1969   Daniel W. Howe, "The Unitarian Conscience"

1971   Gerald P. Fogarty, "Denis J. O'Connell, Americanist Agent to the Vatican, 1885–1903"

1973   J. William T. Youngs, Jr., "God's Messengers: Religious Leadership in Colonial New England, 1700–1750"

1974   Frederick V. Mills, Sr., "Bishops by Ballot"

1975   James H. Moorhead, "American Apocalypse: Northern Protestant Interpretation of National Purpose, 1860–1869"

1976   Anne Jacobson Schutte, "Pier Paolo Vergerio: The Making of an Italian Reformer"

1977   Richard I. Rabinowitz, "Soul Character and Personality: The Transformation of Personal Religious Experience in New England, 1790–1860"

1978   James David Essig, "Break Every Yoke: American Evangelicals Against Slavery, 1770–1808"

1980   Douglas H. Sweet, "Preserving the Peace: Community Development and Ministerial Ideals in Revolutionary New Hampshire"

1981   Thomas M. Safley, "The Control of Marriage in the German Southwest: A Comparative Study, 1550–1600"

1982   James O. Farmer, Jr., "The Metaphysical Confederacy: James Henly Thornwell and the Synthesis of Southern Values"

1983   David A. Weir, "Foedus Naturale: The Origins of Federal Theology in Sixteenth Century Reformation Thought"

1984   Jon H. Roberts, "Darwinism and Divinity: The Response of the American Protestant Intellectual Community to the Theory of Organic Evolution, 1859–1900"

1985   Bruce W. H. Tolley, "Religious Life in Wüttemberg During the Late Reformation"

1986   Thomas D. Hamm, "The Transformation of American Quakerism: Orthodox Friends, 1800–1907"

Philip Schaff Prize

1979   Thomas N. Tentler, *Sin and Confession on the Eve of the Reformation* (Princeton, 1977)

1981   Steven E. Ozment, *The Age of Reform, 1250–1550* (New Haven, 1980)

1983   Timothy D. Barnes, *Constantine and Eusebius* (Cambridge, MA, 1981)

1985   Ronnie Po-chia Hsia, *Society and Religion in Münster, 1535–1618* (New Haven, 1984)

Sidney E. Mead Prize

C. Arnold Snyder, "Revolution and the Swiss Brethren: The Case of Michael Sattler," *CH* 50 (1981): 276–87

Randall H. Balmer, "The Social Roots of Dutch Pietism in the Middle Colonies," *CH* 53 (1984): 187–99

Contributors

GERALD H. ANDERSON is Editor of the *International Bulletin of Missionary Research* and Director of the Overseas Ministries Study Center in New Haven, Connecticut. Earlier he served as Professor of Church History and Ecumenics at Union Theological Seminary near Manila, Philippines, and President of Scarritt College, Nashville. A graduate of Boston University (M.Div., Ph.D.), he also studied at Marburg, Geneva, and Edinburgh. He edited and co-authored *The Theology of the Christian Mission, Christ and Crisis in Southeast Asia, Studies in Philippine Church History, Asian Voices in Christian Theology,* and co-edited the *Concise Dictionary of the Christian World Mission, Christ's Lordship and Religious Pluralism,* and *Mission Trends.*

HENRY WARNER BOWDEN is Professor of Religion at Rutgers University in New Brunswick, New Jersey. He received degrees from the Universities of Baylor and Princeton and has held various posts at Rutgers since 1964. Among his more notable publications are *Church History in the Age of Science* (1971), *Dictionary of American Religious Biography* (1977), and *American Indians and Christian Missions* (1981). The only honor ever conferred on him was the presidency of the American Society of Church History in 1984.

GLENN F. CHESNUT is Professor of History and Religious Studies at Indiana University, South Bend. He earned his bachelor of divinity degree at Southern Methodist University and his doctorate at Oxford University. He has also taught at the University of Virginia, and as Visiting Professor of History and Theology at Boston University. He won the Prix de Rome in Classics in 1978, and is a Fellow of the American Academy in Rome. His *First Christian Histories,* a study of Eusebius of Caesarea and his successors, received a special award from the American Society of Church History's Philip Schaff Prize Committee in 1979. He has been a member of the society's Committee on Research since 1981.

JAY P. DOLAN is Professor of History at the University of Notre Dame where he directs the Charles and Margaret Hall Cushwa Center for the Study of American Catholicism. He has published extensively on the social history of American Catholicism. His most recent book is *The American Catholic Experience: A History From Colonial Times To The Present*. He is a member of the Immigration History Society and has served on the society's executive council and also on the History Committee of the Statue of Liberty-Ellis Island Centennial Commission. He is active in the American Society of Church History and served as its President in 1987.

JOHN T. FORD is Associate Professor of Theology at the Catholic University of America, Washington, DC, where he has served as Coordinator of Ministerial Studies (1973–77) and Chairman of the Department of Theology (1977–83). A graduate of the University of Notre Dame, he received a master's degree in theology from Holy Cross College in Washington, DC, and earned a licentiate and doctorate in theology at the Gregorian University in Rome. His areas of teaching and research include contemporary ecumenism, theology of ministry, and nineteenth-century theology.

He has served as President of the North American Academy of Ecumenists, a member of the United Methodist-Roman Catholic Dialogue, a participant in the Reformed-Roman Catholic International Dialogue, an observer consultant for the Consultation on Church Union, and a member of the Faith and Order Commission of the National Council of Churches.

AIDAN KAVANAGH is a Benedictine monk and presently Professor of Liturgics at the Divinity School, Yale University. He is author of *The Concept of Eucharistic Memorial in the Canon Revisions of Thomas Cranmer* (1964), *The Shape of Baptism* (1978), *Elements of Rite* (1982), *On Liturgical Theology* (1984), and *Confirmation: Origins and Reform* (1987). For eight years he was Director of the Graduate Program in Liturgical Studies at Notre Dame University and has twice been Acting Director of the Yale Institute of Sacred Music.

ROBERT M. KINGDON is Professor of History and member of the Institute for Research in the Humanities at the University of Wisconsin-Madison. He was educated at Oberlin College (A.B., 1949), Columbia University (M.A., 1950; Ph.D., 1955), and the University of Geneva, Switzerland (*docteur ès lettres, honoris causa*, 1986). Before settling in Madison, he taught at the University of Massachusetts-Amherst (1952–57), at the University of Iowa (1957–65), and, as a visitor, at Amherst College (1953–54) and Stanford University (1964, 1980). He was President of the ASCH in 1980 and serves as Editor of the *Sixteenth Century Journal*. His research specialty is the impact of the Calvinist Reformation on politics and society in Geneva, France, and other countries. He has written or edited many articles, book reviews and ten books, the most recent of which, *Myths About the St. Bartholomew's Day Massacres, 1572–1576,* was published by the Harvard University Press in 1988.

DAVID W. LOTZ is Washburn Professor of Church History at Union Theological Seminary in New York City. He was educated at Concordia Senior College, Fort Wayne (B.A., 1959); Concordia Theological Seminary, St. Louis (M.Div., 1963); Washington University, St. Louis (M.A., 1964); and Union Theological Seminary, New York City (S.T.M., 1965; Th.D., 1971). He also studied at Oxford University, England. He joined the Union faculty as an instructor in 1968, becoming Washburn Professor in 1976. His publications include *Ritschl and Luther* and (as co-author) *A History of the Christian Church,* as well as numerous studies in Reformation history and theology and in nineteenth-century Protestant thought.

BERNARD MCGINN is Professor of Historical Theology and the History of Christianity at the Divinity School of the University of Chicago and a member of the University's Committee on Medieval Studies. He received a licentiate in sacred theology from the Pontifical Gregorian University in 1963 and a Ph.D. degree in history of ideas from Brandeis University in 1970. His books include *The Golden Chain, Visions of the End, The Calabrian Abbot,* and two volumes of translations from Meister Eckhart in the Classics of Western Spirituality series. Recently, he collaborated with John Meyendorff in editing *Christian Spirituality: Origins to the Twelfth Century.*

JOHN F. WILSON, after graduating from Harvard College, studied at Union Theological Seminary, New York City, from which he received the M.Div. and Ph.D. degrees. Since 1960 he has been on the faculty of the Department of Religion, Princeton University, which he chaired from 1973 to 1980. Since 1977 he has held the Collord Chair. He is a specialist in American religious history.

John Wilson's early scholarship concerned Puritanism in seventeenth-century England. Subsequently his work has touched on various aspects of American religion, including the church-state issue in the culture (on which he is currently directing a project) and Jonathan Edwards. Among many publications, he is author of *Public Religion in American Culture* (Temple University Press, 1979), which concerns political and civil religion in American society.

Index

Adams, Henry, 77
Adams, Herbert Baxter, 4–6, 77, 148, 294–95
Aeterni Patris, 48, 79, 82
Ahlstrom, Sydney E., 138
Ambrose, viii, 230
American Historical Association, 4, 79, 148, 294–98
American Historical Review, 90–91, 127, 139–40, 297
American Society for Reformation Research, 102–6
American Society of Church History: constitutional changes, 297–301; founding, 1–2, 294–96; governing council, 300–301; incorporation, 298–99; prizes for scholarship, 307–8, 363–65; statistics: general membership, 301–4, presidents, 304–5
American Society of Missiology, 197–99
Anderson, Rufus, 178
Annales school of historical studies, 81–83, 113
Aristotle, 41–43, 62
Arius, 64
Augustine of Hippo, viii, 19, 56–59

Bacon, Leonard W., 123
Bainton, Roland, 102–5, 111
Baird, Robert, 121
Batiffol, Pierre, 227
Battles, Ford Lewis, 108–9
Baur, Ferdinand C., 3–5, 7–8, 12, 14, 17, 30, 36, 38, 43–44, 54, 74, 76
Beauduin, Lambert, 221–22, 229
Beaver, R. Pierce, 179–80, 197, 199
Bender, Harold S., 111–12

Bernard of Clairvaux, 19
Bethune-Baker, J. F., 53–54, 63
Bilateral conversations on ecumenism, 269, 271–72
Billington, Ray Allen, 129–30, 132
Bismarck, Otto von, 39–40
Blake, Eugene Carson, 275–76
Blegen, Theodore C., 129–30
Bloch, Marc, 81
Boaz, Franz, 135
Boethius, 43
Bollandists, 76
Boxer Rebellion, 176, 182
Braudel, Fernand, 81, 113
Breen, Quirinus, 108–9, 330
Brown, Peter, 45, 57–59, 83
Brown, Robert McAfee, 255
Brown, William Adams, 161
Brownson, Orestes A., 24, 222
Bucer, Martin, 7–8, 19, 100
Burckhardt, Jacob, vii

Calvin, John, viii, 19, 101, 103, 225–26; modern studies of, 107–10
Carey, Lott, 179
Case, Shirley Jackson, 302, 305
Center for Reformation Research, 105
Charlemagne, 75
Christian Century, 184, 187
Church History, viii, ix, 89–91, 296, 302, 306–8
Cicero, 62
Clarke, William Newton, 174–75
Clebsch, William A., 322–24
Clement of Alexandria, 54
Cochrane, Charles N., 60
Columbian Exposition, 172, 178
Congar, Yves, 267, 279